T0265623

Indulging Kleptocracy

Indulging Kleptocracy

British Service Providers, Postcommunist Elites, and the Enabling of Corruption

JOHN HEATHERSHAW, TENA PRELEC, AND TOM MAYNE

OXFORD
UNIVERSITY PRESS

Oxford University Press is a department of the University of Oxford. It furthers
the University's objective of excellence in research, scholarship, and education
by publishing worldwide. Oxford is a registered trade mark of Oxford University
Press in the UK and certain other countries.

Published in the United States of America by Oxford University Press
198 Madison Avenue, New York, NY 10016, United States of America.

CIP data is on file at the Library of Congress

ISBN 978–0–19–768822–9

DOI: 10.1093/oso/9780197688229.001.0001

Printed by Sheridan Books, Inc., United States of America

To our friends and family who indulge us

Contents

Foreword By Oliver Bullough

This is a book about the world's third oldest profession, by which I mean that which followed the prostitute, who is generally accepted to have been first, and her pimp, who came second. The trades in sex and power remain lucrative, but neither of them would have been nearly so profitable or as pervasive had it not been for the sidekick, the minion, the crony, and the enabler who is prepared to hold a victim's arms back while the pimp punches them.

There's little glory in being the crony, but there's a good living to be made if you're good at it. Just like the first wolf who broke the solidarity of the pack to become a human's dog, the first person who traded the friendship of his fellows for a ready source of food from their oppressor will have done very well. That's why it's a certainty that almost as long as there have been criminals, there have been enablers, people willing to live on the crumbs that fall from their bosses' tables, and they don't get nearly enough attention. We talk about mafia dons, but not about their consigliere; we talk about corporate barons, but not about their lawyers; we talk about the grandly corrupt, but not about the people who manage their money. All of these people are crucial to the functioning of the criminal economy, which means we cannot understand why so much of the world has been conquered by the corrupt, and why we struggle to do anything about that, without understanding the role that enablers play.

Once upon a time, enablers were easy to spot. They looked like Sir Guy of Gisborne as he helped the Sheriff of Nottingham hunt Robin Hood; like Igor, who cackled while assisting Dr Frankenstein in his bid to conquer the world; like Grima Wormtongue in *The Lord of the Rings*; like Biff Tannen's friends in *Back to the Future*, who laughed at his jokes as he terrorized Hill Valley's teenagers back in 1955. But modern technology means sidekicks no longer need to stand literally beside their bosses, ready to anticipate their needs, fulfil their orders, or to fetch them drinks. Nowadays, the best enablers can be thousands of miles away, sitting at a screen, moving money, structuring assets, obscuring crimes, and creating the appearance of respectability for themselves and their employers alike.

The first enabler I came across was like that. A US-educated European lawyer living in a micro-state, he had created the British, Caribbean, and other companies behind which the Ukrainian president obscured his ownership of luxury real estate, profitable companies, and other assets that had no legitimate explanation. I'd stumbled into investigating corruption almost by accident, so someone like him was completely new, and he fascinated me. Frustrated by the fact that he never replied to my emails, I would stare at the photograph on his corporate website, trying to work out if this smiling, sleek-haired, brown-eyed man was a villain or not.

Back then, I had not yet become accustomed to how respectable people are prepared to work for appalling people, and such encounters would genuinely surprise me. This naiveté lasted until one oligarch's lawyer invited me to a meeting in Milan, a city neither he nor I had any connection to. I'd seen too many mafia movies to fall for that one, and came away with the strong impression that Tom Hagan, the charming, capable, and utterly amoral family lawyer in *The Godfather*, isn't so far from reality as I might have hoped.

Still, after every encounter with an enabler, I've always found myself asking the same question I asked at the start: Are they a villain or not? They're often prominent members of their countries' business, professional, or political elites; they engage in public acts of philanthropy; they sit on the boards of august organizations, guiding them as they do their important work; and yet they provide the services required for the worst people in the world to get away with terrible crimes.

They're not all glamorous though, of course; in the building next door to one of my favourite takeaways is a service office used as a cut-out by hundreds of companies involved in frauds large and small. It's small and unremarkable and there is no reason to stop and look at it, unless you happen to study financial crime, and are waiting for a curry. The window is grubby and the paint on the frame is flaking, so these enablers aren't making much money out of their trade, but their shop is at least open, unlike many others on this little town's rather sad High Street.

At the other end of the scale are family offices in Mayfair, Zug, or Connecticut, seamlessly combining the services of a financial planner, a bodyguard, a concierge, a butler, and a secretary, all hidden from view behind a glossy front door and a receptionist. No, you can't come in, I'm afraid, not without an appointment; and no, I'm not at liberty to provide any information without express permission; but please do come again.

In between these two extremes of the enabling business are millions upon millions of bright, entrepreneurial people able and willing to make a living by standing beside, rather than in front of, the world's bullies. If they can come up with a new technique which will keep the bullies' assets safe—whether from business rivals, criminals, tax authorities, law enforcement investigations, or other threats—they can earn a percentage of those assets for themselves.

'Our main problem is that these high-ranking officials are all registered abroad, in Monaco, or Cyprus, or Belize, or the British Virgin Islands, and so on', one Ukrainian prosecutor told me when I asked him why his office was failing to bring cases against the most egregiously corrupt officials of the former regime. 'And we write requests to them, we wait for three or four years, or there's no response at all. As a rule, the BVI don't reply, we don't have an agreement with them. And that's that, and it all falls apart. We wait, it has been re-registered five times just while we're waiting for an answer to come. It's all been re-registered, and that's our main problem, checking and receiving these documents.'

One of these officials had a British lawyer, who I'll call Victoria because it's not her name. I managed to extract enough information from various sources to piece together a solid account of what he'd been up to, and he was so keen to prevent me from revealing it that he hired Victoria to threaten me. She wrote to warn me of severe legal consequences if I published the investigation I'd been conducting into her client's affairs. Her letter was successful, and I never found a publisher for that particular piece of work.

As a result, her client's deeds were never revealed. The thousands of people whose lives he had ruined, and whose livelihoods he took away, never received any kind of justice. For a while, I was angry about this. I may never have gone quite as far as Arya Stark in *Game of Thrones* and recited a list of all the people I'd like to have killed before going to sleep at night. But, had I done so, Victoria's name would certainly have been very near the top of the list, perhaps even ahead of her client's.

Funnily enough, Victoria had a biography remarkably similar to mine: we are about the same age, we moved to Russia around the same time, both fascinated with the country, and yet she'd ended up working for the people who had looted it, and destroyed its nascent attempt to build democracy. Was she a villain? Not surely in her own eyes. No one engages in this kind of behaviour because they want to be bad. Everyone is the hero of their own life. So why do they do it? Why has enabling become so deeply embedded in the world's economy that it's become the basis for how an entire class of countries—we call them 'tax havens', although 'everything havens' would be a more accurate description—makes its living?

Partly the answer must lie in the same modern communication systems that make it possible for enablers to work on the opposite side of the world to their clients. In 2016, academics from the University of Leicester looked at the impact of automatic check-out technologies in supermarkets on the level of theft.[1] As soon as people were removed from the process of verifying that supermarket customers had actually paid for the groceries in their baskets, those customers were willing to steal far larger amounts. It's not just important that a crime should be easy to get away with; it also needs to feel victimless. The more victimless a crime feels, the study showed, the more likely people are to engage in it.

This makes intuitive sense. It is much easier to steal from someone and leave them to starve if you don't have to literally prise coins from the desperate hands of children, but can instead just divert electronic deposits from one shell company to another, on behalf of a client you've never met, before going to the gym. And the easier something is, the more people will do it.

This same sense of distance makes it hard to interest politicians or the public in the importance of cracking down on this new breed of crime. Everything seems so complicated, so far-flung and so clean. How many genuinely successful screen portrayals of grand corruption have there ever been? *The Night Manager*, certainly, but other than that? It's very hard to create public interest in crimes that primarily involve people sitting in meeting rooms, writing emails, and talking on the phone. Enablers don't just help with the committing of crimes; they also smooth the edges off, and they make them . . . boring. There is no pale-faced Grima Wormtongue here, whispering his poison into King Theoden's ear while helping the evil wizard Saruman control the Riders of Rohan; just people in suits, sitting around hardwood tables, tapping away at MacBook Airs. When criminality and accountancy look the same, it is hard to convince anyone that these criminals aren't just, well, accountants. And no one is interested in accountants.

Funnily enough, last year Victoria wrote to me again. She wasn't threatening me this time, quite the reverse in fact. Her company was doing some work on financial crime and wondered if I'd be willing to talk on a panel she was organizing. I replied that I would be happy to do so, although I would of course make a point of mentioning her own role in preventing me from exposing financial crime in the past. She clearly had no memory either of me, or of the previous letter I'd received, because she seemed genuinely stunned by the suggestion that I might think of her as anything other than a goodie. I had to send her a copy of the letter she'd sent me before she'd accept that she'd written it at all.

It was too good an opportunity to miss, so I asked her out for a coffee. I wanted to delve into the mind of an enabler, and to find out how she justified to herself the work that she does. Funnily enough, she'd apparently come with the same intention, and was every bit as confused by me as I was by her. For her, I was unjustifiably exposing confidential information. Her client had a right to privacy, and it was her job to ensure that was upheld. She was clearly interested in what I had to say, because she invited me for coffee again a few weeks later, but I never came close to convincing her that she was part of the problem; nor, for that matter, did she convince me that I was.

I came away thinking that perhaps the reason that sidekicks don't recognize their complicity in their bosses' misdeeds is that they don't want to, and society indulges them in their misapprehension. And that, I think, is why this book is so valuable. As the first detailed treatment of the interlocking ways that different enablers assist their employers and each other, it reveals the mechanisms that underpin the worst kinds of acquisitive crime. It is not a definitive account of every technique, as that would be impossible; enablers are restlessly and endlessly inventing new tricks as they adapt to their clients' needs. Instead, it lays out a framework into which we can fit our understanding of the 'corruption services' industry, and which helps us understand the nature of the world's third oldest profession, and what the rest of us can do to stop it.

Preface

Professional Indulgences and Political Transformations

Johann Tetzel is one of early modern Europe's best-known enablers of corruption. Tetzel was a Dominican friar and former inquisitor of Poland who in the early sixteenth century preached that sinners may receive freedom from punishment in the next life in return for their investments, charitable contributions, and devotion to the faith.[1] These 'indulgences' were not new to Christendom and had been routinely used across Europe to finance crusades and other papal projects.[2] But what one historian calls 'the salvation-marketing business'[3] attracted the attention of Albrecht, archbishop of Mainz, who spied a solution to his debt problems by appointing Tetzel as his general commissioner in 1510. Albrecht secured permission from Pope Leo X to split these indulgences with the Vatican and inadvertently sparked the protestant Reformation, a theological and political revolt against the Roman Catholic Church. The Reformation itself precipitated the great transformation of early modern Europe in which wars of religion were waged and modern states were transformed.

The reformation began in part with debate between professionals over the selling of indulgences. Tetzel became notorious because of Martin Luther. When Luther famously hammered his Ninety-Five Theses on the door of the cathedral at Wittenberg on All Hallows Eve of 1517, his primary objection was to the church—especially Tetzel and Archbishop Albrecht—enabling corruption. Indulgences were a professional service dreamed up in a Western world which was far more religious than today; they required true devotion. But for Luther the problem was that they denied God's saving grace. By selling indulgences, Luther argued that Tetzel and Albrecht were enabling the defiling of the gospel, the corruption of the church, and by extension the world. 'When money clinks in the money chest, greed and avarice can be increased', he wrote in the Theses.[4] Many have remarked that the reformation was sparked by a debate about corruption. But this is not quite correct. Luther was quite convinced that the world was utterly corrupt and that there was no temporal solution to this problem. Rather, his specific problem was the professional enablers: 'Those indulgence preachers are in error who say that a man is absolved from every penalty and saved by papal indulgences'.[5]

The sixteenth-century clergy were the paramount professionals of their age. They possessed landholdings and extensive business interests, clear career pathways and managerial hierarchies, and intellectual debates between different schools of thought. Power was held by the clergy over the laity, many of whom, even some of the wealthy, were illiterate. As Luther remarked in his famous list of complaints regarding indulgences, 'most people are necessarily deceived by that indiscriminate and high-sounding promise of release from penalty'.[6] Indulgence letters were, in Luther's understanding, a technique used by Tetzel, Albrecht, and others to exploit the weak and corrupt lay person who already has grace which is 'granted him by God, even without indulgence letters'.[7] He concluded, citing scripture, that the sale of such letters offered 'the false security of peace (Acts 14:22)'.[8]

There are, of course, crucial differences between Luther's sixteenth-century enablers of corruption and those found in Europe today. The reformation was naturally about much more than the selling of indulgences. What was then presided over by the Catholic Church is now governed by the preeminent pastoral powers of our age: the financial and legal services companies of the global economy. The letters of the medieval world that remitted sins have been replaced by legal letters and documents with political and economic import: sanitized due diligence notes, superficial 'know your customer' checks, residencies and second citizenships, naming rights to university buildings, hefty donations to political parties, and an effectively managed and positive reputation for elites from kleptocracies. However, the general function of today's indulgences bears a good deal of resemblance to those of 500 years ago. They enrich the enablers, assuage the corrupt, and muddy the waters between right and wrong, truth and falsehood. In short, indulgences are professional services which provide passage to the next life—not heaven but a new country where residency may be obtained and reputation as well as money-laundered. Indulgences thrived in medieval societies characterized by kleptocratic rule and were challenged by early modern innovators.[9] But, noting their use in the twenty-first century by Pope Benedict XVI, and the parallel to today's secular philanthropy and social investments, one leading historian of them has argued that 'indulgences are very much alive and kicking'.[10]

The crisis of indulgences holds parallels for the present day. Luther's questions of professional conduct quickly became those of morality and politics. The German monk had no intention of bringing down Christendom, the civilization of the day, but his actions were one of the major catalysts which divided the Roman Catholic Church and led to a plural political and religious order. Similarly, the exposure of the professional enabling of corruption in contemporary Western democracies does not seek to bring down capitalism, but it does challenge the legitimacy of governments, expose their lack of capacity to protect the rule of law, and hint at a new age of kleptocratic networks in global politics. Governments are frequently hit by such exposures—think of Malaysia's, which was brought down due to the 1MDB scandal, a corruption and bribery scheme which saw over $4.5 billon embezzled from the country's sovereign wealth fund. Others undergo hypertrophy from corruption and become dangers to the rest of the world—think of Putin's kleptocracy. However, it is the global transformation to which cases such as these allude which is the concern of this book. They suggest that the world is not simply run by states, companies, and organizations, but also by elites, their networks, and their enablers. With a little professional help, post-communist elites can buy assets, residencies, kudos, and political access in the most venerable of democracies. While the medieval world was one of intertwined church and monarchy, the capitalist world is one, in Kristin Surak's words, of 'co-dependence between public and private sectors',[11] often to the detriment of the rule of law.

In this book we outline nine indulgences across nine professional service sectors which are working to transform the world from one dominated by sovereign nation states, as has been the case for the last 200 years in Europe, to one where public-private networks of elites dominate, and which is more like that at the time of Luther. These indulgences each have their own technical and legal rationales, but they must not be seen purely in these terms. When we analyse them as a set of comparable services being offered to wealthy individuals, some of whom are the world's oligarchs and kleptocrats, we can see that they offer much more than the laundering of money or the remission of sins. These indulgences provide a series of economic, social, and political goods which create space for elite networks to flow. It is in these spaces and through these networks that we see a very different form of international relations to that which is characterized as geopolitics or great power politics.

The *nine indulgences* are not exhaustive of the enabling of transnational kleptocracy, but together they indulge the principal 'sins' of kleptocrats, oligarchs, and political exiles: their corrupt acquisition of wealth, status, and power. The first five of these relate to the buying and selling of assets and privileges and include *hiding money* (through limited liability partnerships, trusts, and bank accounts), *listing companies* (and raising capital on the London Stock Exchange), *buying rights* (residences or 'golden visas' such as the UK's tier 1 scheme), *purchasing properties* (principally London real estate), and *explaining wealth* (the legal services offered in response to anti-corruption investigations such as unexplained wealth orders). The next four relate to reputation management and authoritarian influencing and include *selling status* (by gift managers at elite universities), *making friends* (via the receipt of donations to political parties), *tracking enemies* (with the services of private intelligence companies), and *silencing critics* (through what are known as strategic lawsuits against public participation and similar reputational services).

The UK is a world leader in selling many of these indulgences. In over 50 years of combined experience of studying and working on policy with respect to these problems, we have learned that they are as much about what the private sector indulges as what the public sector allows. Understanding this codependence between private and public is key to explaining the problem. We have observed the weakness of our elected authorities regarding the kleptocracy problem with a mixture of fascination and alarm. We are writing this book to convey this problem, its form, and its consequences. We are particularly concerned with the service provision itself: what we call *the enabler effect*. This effect matters not just for what it achieves for a kleptocrat or oligarch in a particular transaction, but for what it tells us about the transformation of global politics by the forces of transnational kleptocracy.

The effects of transnational kleptocracy and its professional indulgences are hitherto unclear. We do not seek to offer false certainty about these. Like Luther's theses, our book and its nine identified indulgences seek to elicit a public debate about the professional enabling of kleptocracy in the UK and beyond. While our theses are perhaps less consequential and certainly fewer in number than Luther's 95, they are sufficient for us to make the kleptocracy problem explicit. From this we may infer something about the global transformation that is being enabled. While we treat our data impartially, we are not neutral on these changes and, as will become clear by the end of this book, simply by publishing prominent research on post-communist kleptocrats we have found ourselves targeted by the very enablers, oligarchs, and kleptocrats that we study.

Only in the final chapter of this book do we sketch a pathway to a world where democracy and the public interest may once again seek to limit, if not eradicate, the professional enabling of the kleptocratic and the corrupt. The first task if one wants to address a problem is to understand it, where it comes from, how big it is, and what forms it takes. Before we address the kleptocracy problem, we need to understand it.

Acknowledgements

This book has benefited from the burden sharing of an enormous number of fellow travellers. Its origins are found in 2019 when we joined together with Alexander Cooley, Casey Michel, David Lewis, Jason Sharman, and Ricardo Soares de Oliveira to begin a project under the Anti-Corruption Evidence program of what was then the Department for International Development and managed by what was then Global Integrity. Several papers and reports with those colleagues and coauthors have been foundational in the research and arguments for this book. Peter Evans from DfID and Ambika Samarthya-Howard, Paul Heywood, and Johannes Tonn from Global Integrity supported our project through its trials, even when its findings came under attack from some of our research subjects and were inconvenient for the government of the day. The work and insights of Elizabeth David-Barrett, Jackie Harvey, Peter Sproat, and Dan Haberly were especially valuable. That both DfID and Global Integrity no longer exist is to the detriment of research on kleptocracy.

A second and decisive point of origin of this book is found at the Royal Institute of International Affairs (Chatham House), where we coauthored *The UK's Kleptocracy Problem* in 2021. Chatham House's Russia and Eurasia Programme and its director James Nixey provided extraordinary support through the forensic editorial process of double-blind peer review, multiple rounds of legal checking, and editing. Many others at Chatham House including Ľubica Polláková, Anna Morgan, and Kate Mallinson were unstinting in their support. The director Sir Robin Niblett asked challenging questions to ensure that the report's findings were robust and understood that the report was as much about the UK as about Russia and Eurasia. The handling of the legal challenges which we faced after publication (see Chapter 13) are the responsibility of the new director and senior managers, not programme staff who continued to support our research. The Economic and Social Research Council, British Academy and Leverhulme Trust supported our research at this time. The Department of Politics and International Relations (DPIR) at the University of Oxford provided precious support for the legal review of our book.

Colleagues and students at our academic institutions were some of the most astute observers of our work. At Exeter, special thanks go to Alex Prichard, Archie Norman, Catarina Thomson, Catherine Owen, David Blagden, David Lewis, Flo Marks, Gregorio Bettiza, Irene Fernandez-Molina, Kevork Oskanian, Martin Thorley, Mick Dumper, Katya Kolpinskaya, Max Cramer, Shaun Ingeldew, Shayakhmet Tokubayev, Stephane Baele, Weeda Mehran, Zhanat Myrzabekov, and colleagues at the Centre for Advanced International Studies. At Oxford, we thank Alexander Morrison, Bob Service, Dariusz Wójcik, Edmund Herzig, Jody La Porte, Marnie Howlett, Michael Rochlitz, Neil MacFarlane, and St Peter's and St Antony's colleges. The LSE European Institute's research unit on South Eastern Europe (LSEE) and the Sussex Centre for the Study of Corruption (CSC) have both provided wonderful intellectual homes, especially in regard to the rule of law in the Balkans. The many excellent authors and editors whom we have worked with include Alexander Dukalskis, Alvin Camba, Anne Pitcher, Claire Elder, Dušan Pavlović, Edward Lemon, Kyle Long, Marlies Glasius, Nate Schenkkan, Rachel Epstein, Ronen Palan, Saipira Furstenberg, Xymena Kurowska, and Yana Gorokhovskaia. Draft chapters of the book were also presented at Exeter, Oxford, the London School of Economics, the Central Bank of the Bahamas, and Queen Mary University of London. Brooke Harrington, Charles Littrell, Dan Nielson, David Szakonyi, Elisabeth Schimpfössl, Kristin Surak, Kimberly Kay Hoang, Madeleine Reeves, Mike Findley, Omar McDoom, Robert Barrington, Sue Hawley, Tom de Waal, Tomila Lankina, and Ronen Palan were insightful contributors at these events.

Kris Lasslett's tireless work exposing kleptocracy in Central Asia makes him one of our closest collaborators and the editor of the report, *Criminality Notwithstanding*, authored by Mayne and Heathershaw, which forms the basis of Chapter 9. The Elite Studies Working Group hosted us for a presentation of Chapter 13; special thanks go to Sarah Kunz and Kate Higgins for continuing the work on academic SLAPPs. In the Academic Freedom and Internationalisation Working Group, we found such colleagues in Andreas Fulda, Andrew Chubb, Chris Hughes, Corinne Lennox, Eva Pils, John Chalcraft, Katarzyna Kaczmarska, Kelli Rudolph, Sophia Woodman, Terrence Karan, and Yesim Yaprak Yildiz. We also benefited from the support of Chelsea Blackburn Cohen, Jesse Levine, and Denise Roche of Scholars at Risk and Stephen Wordsworth of Council for At-Risk Academics. Special thanks go to Nicole Piché of All-Party Parliamentary Human Rights Group for bringing the group together in 2019 and arranging space in parliament for our discussions, as well to Aleksandra Stankova for her excellent support to the group as project manager.

It has been a great joy to work with some outstanding investigative journalists. These include Alexandra Gillies and colleagues at the Organized Crime and Corruption Reporting Project, with whom we are now working on a new phase of research. Several chapters were directly influenced by our partnerships with journalists. Jenna Corduroy and colleagues at OpenDemocracy worked tirelessly on the issue of anonymous donations to universities while Suzanne Antelm at the *Cherwell* was tenacious in her investigation of Oxford's Nizami Ganjavi Centre (Chapter 10). Franz Wild, Ed Siddons, Lucy Nash, and colleagues at the Bureau of Investigative Journalism have shone a light on the holding structures arranged by corporate intelligence professionals to shelter Kazakh assets (Chapter 12) and have exposed SLAPPs in the UK (Chapter 13). Among the many excellent UK-based journalists we have worked with we must especially thank Andy Verity, Catherine Belton, Charlie Parker, George Greenwood, James Oliver, Mark Hollingsworth, Matt Oliver, Matthew Valencia, Patrick Wintour, and Tom Rowley. Special thanks go to Tom Burgis, who features in Chapter 12, and Oliver Bullough, for writing the wonderful foreword.

In civil society there are several organizations, coalitions, and individuals who have made important contributions to the research. Tom Mayne's work with Global Witness colleagues is foundational to Chapters 5 and 6, and his work at Freedom for Eurasia with Leila Nazgül Seiitbek crucial to Chapter 8. Many other wonderful colleagues from the Eurasian region will go unmentioned for their own safety. At Transparency International, Ben Cowdock and Steve Goodrich have plugged away on these UK-Eurasia kleptocracy cases for years. Our work on higher education (Chapter 10) was supported by Melissa Aten at National Endowment for Democracy. At Spotlight on Corruption, Sue Hawley, Helen Taylor, and James Bolton-Jones have an extraordinary grasp of the (mis)governance of economic crime in the UK and the problem of political donations (Chapter 11). At the Royal United Services Institute, Tom Keatinge, Maria Nizzero, and Helena Wood have often led the way in nudging the government to take these issues seriously. At Foreign Policy Centre, Adam Hug, Aijan Sharshenova, Susan Coughtrie, and Poppy Oggier aided our research; Susan and Poppy's recent work on SLAPPs (Chapter 13) has been path-breaking. The Illicit Finance Working Group (IFWG), chaired by Peter Munro, has been crucial in amending the economic crime bills in 2022 and 2023 towards more transparency and accountability while also pushing the government on the crucial issue of enforcement. Their ideas are drawn on in our conclusions (Chapter 14). IFWG and our work has been supported financially by the Joffe Trust. Alex Jacobs at Joffe deserves special thanks. Beyond the UK, we would like to thank the colleagues at the Balkans in Europe Policy Advisory Group (BiEPAG) for keeping the attention high on grand corruption in the region and alerting policymakers in Brussels to the risks of mistaking stability for democracy.

Members of all three main UK-wide parties are found in this book to indulge kleptocratic wealth. On the flip side, we have found allies from all parties who have acted to tackle this problem. These members include Alison Thewliss, Alicia Kearns, Ben Bradshaw, Bob Seely, Liam Byrne, David Davies, Richard Foord, Andrew Mitchell, Tom Tugendhat, Baroness Vivienne Stern, and Lord William Wallace. Special thanks must go to Jesse Norman for his valiant but ultimately unsuccessful attempt to require universities to be transparent about their foreign funding. Most of all, Dame Margaret Hodge, who stepped down at the end of the last parliament, is an extraordinary supporter of anti-corruption research, supporting us on several occasions in recent years. Her departure is a huge loss to the Commons. Among those in Brussels willing to acknowledge the EU's complicity in the kleptocracy problem, as well as the role it has to play in the fight against it, we would like to thank in particular Viola von Cramon MEP.

In financial and legal services, most professionals do not willfully indulge kleptocrats. Some have provided crucial evidence and insights to aid our research. Most will remain unmentioned to protect them. Special mentions should go to several working in corporate intelligence and related fields including Ben Godwin, Kseniya Shvedova, Olivia Allison, and Tim Ash. Special thanks to James Yallop, who drew the figures for the book. Among lawyers, we have spoken to many who understand the problem of legal enablers and that lawyers are for-hire actors in global games of power and money. Special thanks go to Anita Clifford, Andrew Mitchell KC, Ben Keith, and Jonathan Fisher KC. Extra special thanks go to the excellent lawyers David Hirst of 5RB and Erin O'Reilly of OUP, who painstakingly read through the manuscript.

There are others without whom this book would not have been produced. University of Exeter interns and research assistants which did background research and editorial work include Aisha Ahmad, Annabel Ashley, Ben Lewis, and Jody Bispham. Our editors at OUP, Dave McBride and Emily Benitez, have been supportive of the project throughout. Thanks also to the many peer reviewers for their kind and critical comments which helps us develop this book.

Abbreviations

AML	anti-money-laundering
AUB	AsiaUniversalBank
BFSAC	British Foundation for the Study of Azerbaijan and the Caucasus
ENRC	Eurasian Natural Resources Corporation plc
EU	European Union
FATF	Financial Action Task Force
FCDO	Foreign Commonwealth and Development Office (UK)
JTL	Jusan Technologies Limited
LSE	London Stock Exchange
NCA	National Crime Agency (UK)
ONGC	Oxford Nizami Ganjavi Centre
PEP	politically exposed person
PRCA	Public Relations and Communications Association
SAR	suspicious activity report
SFO	Serious Fraud Office (UK)
SLAPP	strategic lawsuit against public participation
UWO	unexplained wealth order

1

Indulging Kleptocracy

There are people in government that will get the job done for you . . .
but you have got to pay for that.
    —John Davy, former CFO of Uzbek telecoms company UCell[1]

Around Christmas 2009, a senior executive from Scandinavian telecoms
firm TeliaSonera emailed Mohamed Amersi, a British businessman and lat-
terly a philanthropist and political donor, asking him to join a conference
call about urgent work in Uzbekistan. Amersi had been advising the company on mergers and acquisitions since 2008,[2] but this was the first time he
was being asked to advise on Uzbekistan. The deal's origins dated further
back to 2007, when TeliaSonera sought to enter the Uzbek telecoms market,
having heard that the country was looking for a European partner. But there
were considerable risks: Uzbekistan was widely considered one of the most
corrupt countries in the world, arguably *the* most corrupt country at that
time where this kind of telecoms deal could be struck.[3] This does not mean
that doing business in the country was impossible, but that extensive due
diligence must be performed by companies, especially on local partners, to
ensure that they are not controlled by regime figures or corrupt officials. The
warning signs were readily apparent. Publicly available media articles by
that time suggested that Gulnara Karimova—the daughter of the then Uzbek
president—was a key figure in Uzbekistan's telecoms sector, with multiple
reports of unlawful enrichment through questionable business practices,
with at least one article from 2008 saying that she controlled this sector.[4]

    Yet this landscape did not deter TeliaSonera's executives in their quest to
obtain a stake in Ucell, an Uzbek telecoms company. Key to the negotiations
was an Uzbek businessman and Karimova associate, Bekzod Akhmedov.
To outsiders, Akhmedov's involvement in talks with TeliaSonera would
have appeared strange, as he was also the director of Uzdonrobita, an apparent rival to Ucell. However, such conflicts of interest were commonplace

in Uzbekistan. Akhmedov's involvement would have made sense to certain TeliaSonera executives as they knew from early on that Karimova was to be their local partner in Ucell, and they were negotiating directly with both her and her associates.[5] For example, in May 2007, one of TeliaSonera's senior managers sent a memorandum to the management and board of a Kazakh telecoms company that TeliaSonera owned shares in. It said that a provisional agreement had been struck regarding 'the starting points for a potential partnership with Gulnara Karimova's investment team'.[6] Karimova also met with TeliaSonera managers during a trip to Tashkent.[7] Karimova's involvement in the deal, and Akhmedov's link to her, appeared to be common knowledge within Tashkent business circles. A March 2007 email from the president of a company part-owned by TeliaSonera referred to Akhmedov as 'the telecom representative of Gulnara Karimova'.[8] In February 2008, a Swedish newspaper even ran an article in Swedish that reported the rumour that Karimova controlled the local partner that owned shares in Ucell, a Gibraltar registered company called Takilant Ltd.[9] What was a fact to some people within the company and widely known in Uzbekistan was even beginning to be publicized internationally. The involvement of Karimova—a 'politically exposed person' by definition—had become public knowledge, with information readily accessible even to those not intimately involved in this deal.

How did Mohamed Amersi become involved in this story? Amersi had studied law and worked as a barrister and solicitor at a variety of London law firms until 2001, before specializing in financial deals involving the issuing or selling of shares, becoming an expert advisor in the telecoms industry mainly working in the former Soviet Union.[10] His CV and his knowledge of telecoms in the region was impressive. For instance, in 2005, Amersi reportedly made £4 million helping a Luxembourg company secretly owned by a top crony of Vladimir Putin, Leonid Reiman, to buy a Russian telecoms business.[11] His advice in Uzbekistan was required for something slightly different: a share buy-back deal.[12] Over six weeks across the new year of 2010, Amersi worked as one of the advisors on the Uzbek deal, which included personally drafting a key message to Akhmedov that formally introduced propositions from the Scandinavian firm about how to structure its next stage. When informed that following further restructuring of the deal, Akhmedov was broadly happy with TeliaSonera's offer, Amersi replied: 'This is great!'[13] By the definitions of business studies and corruption research, Amersi was an intermediary.[14]

Ultimately, TeliaSonera paid $220 million for Takilant's shares in Ucell, almost 10 times what Takilant had bought them for.[15] This was later judged by the US authorities to be a bribe to Karimova, which indicted her and Akhmedov on various financial crime charges related to the scheme.[16] In September 2023, the Swiss authorities indicted Karimova and an unnamed Uzbek businessman likely to be Akhmedov on fraud and organized crime charges.[17] Akhmedov denies any wrongdoing but Karimova remains in jail in Uzbekistan, having been found guilty of other financial crimes.[18]

Amersi was paid a $500,000 success fee for his work on the transaction,[19] although in total he received $65 million for his work with TeliaSonera from 2008 to 2013 advising on various deals in countries where grand corruption is rife including Kazakhstan and Nepal.[20] Beyond the Uzbek deals, many of the company's other dealings were placed under scrutiny. Indeed, in 2014, Telia's chairwoman Marie Ehrling said that following a review conducted by law firm Norton Rose Fulbright on Telia's behalf, 'the board can unfortunately say that several transactions and practices have not been handled in accordance with good business practice . . . It cannot be excluded that certain actions have been criminal'. The probe focused on Kazakhstan, Nepal, Azerbaijan, Tajikistan, and Georgia.[21] No known criminal investigations have been launched regarding the company's work in any of these countries. Amersi's lawyers told the *Guardian* that after details of the Norton Rose Fulbright report emerged in 2014, he had no reason to believe its allegations referred to him.[22]

A Story of Indulgence

Cases like that of TeliaSonera are often presented by anti-corruption activists as straightforward examples of kleptocracy—and how foreign companies and professionals enable it. However, Mohamed Amersi's role in the story reveals a more complex picture where enabling is dispersed across multiple entities and many years with different enablers involved at different stages. There is no doubt that key executives at TeliaSonera (since renamed the Telia Company) knew of Gulnara's business interests in Uzbek telecoms. The company was later found by the US government to have paid bribes to her. But outside of Karimova and Akhmedov, no individuals have ever been held accountable for what happened. Many of them, like Amersi, claim to be unwitting of the beneficiaries of the payments they were advising upon.

Kleptocracy was enabled—indulged, we might say—but legal responsibility and criminal conviction for its enablers is conspicuous by its absence.

In Amersi's case, the question remains what he knew about Bekzod Akhmedov, Takilant Ltd, and its beneficiaries at the time of the deal in 2010. Amersi claims that he did not know that Akhmedov was the director of Uzdonrobita, nor of media reports that Karimova had been a shareholder in Uzdonrobita, as this was not part of his remit, nor was he even aware of media reports that indicated that she had interests in the Uzbek telecoms sector. In response to the authors regarding this deal, Amersi commented that Uzbekistan was 'far from the worst' country in terms of corruption.[23] He further stated that: 'Detailed KYC [know your customer], UBO [ultimate beneficial ownership] and due diligence was conducted by an army of lawyers on ownership questions and source of funds. At that point in time, despite wide but unsubstantiated media reporting no evidence was found of any wrongdoing'. He added that he had no responsibility for doing checks on the beneficial owner.[24]

So was Amersi a wilful enabler of kleptocracy or a highly paid professional who was unwittingly caught up in one of the most notorious cases of grand corruption in recent years? This question is difficult to answer, but a fair opinion may be offered. Amersi was an intermediary who expressed approval of the deal—which resulted in a payment of $220 million to a shell company in Gibraltar. His claim that Telia did not know who Takilant's owners were is contradicted by information provided by the US authorities and even Akhmedov himself.[25] Irrespective of what Amersi knew, it is clear that he played a key role in one of TeliaSonera's transactions in Uzbekistan, which later, in a settlement between the company and the United States government, was found to be one of a series of systematically corrupt payments.[26] Even if his enabling was unwitting, it was surely reckless. But this story of indulgence does not end there. Following the money, we see that the professional enabling of kleptocracy goes from upstream places like Uzbekistan (the source of wealth) to downstream locations such as London (its destination).

Having been successful in business, Amersi decided to give generously to some of the UK's most famous institutions. In 2015, he became a trustee of the Prince's Trust International (the charity of then Prince of Wales, now King Charles III), and was made an honorary fellow of Brasenose College, Oxford. He funded the refurbishment of the college's lecture theatre, which was subsequently named after his charitable foundation. The opening ceremony in 2019 featured a keynote speech from former UK Prime Minister Theresa May.[27] Amersi was also invited as a guest speaker at many conferences and summits where he sometimes spoke out against corruption. In 2017 he spoke at the One Young World Summit, saying that 'corruption is a very, very heinous crime' highlighting that 2% of the world's GDP is lost via corruption, 'every stolen dollar robs the poor of an equal opportunity in life'.[28]

Amersi is also a major political donor. Since 2017, he and his wife Nadezhda Rodicheva have donated more than £750,000 to the Conservative Party.[29] At a fundraising dinner in London in late 2019 he successfully bid £100,000 for breakfast with the then Prime Minister, Boris Johnson. Amersi said that he had retired from the business world and donated to help the party and the country. However, Amersi also began to question the kind of donations that give the wealthy access to politicians. In an interview from 2022 Amersi opined: 'As a Tory donor, I can tell you the system is undemocratic', calling it 'access capitalism' for the 'privileged few'. He went on: 'Our society, I feel, has made the colossal error of allowing wealth to purchase the chance to make quasi-governmental decisions as a private citizen . . . The rot at the very top has to stop'.[30] To get such access, he claimed, 'one needs to cough up £250,000 per annum or be a friend of Ben'—a reference to Ben Elliot, who at the time served as co-chairman of the Conservative Party while also running Quintessentially, a concierge service for wealthy people. Amersi was now a campaigner against corruption. But rather than seeing this as a break from his business dealings of the past, he presented it as in keeping with his self-image as a responsible and reputable businessman. In an interview with the *Financial Times*, Amersi said, 'I have not made a dishonest deal in my life, in Russia or elsewhere'.[31]

Maintaining his innocence, Amersi has threatened to sue or has sued various journalists and researchers for reporting on his Uzbek advisory role—widely alleged to be acts of 'lawfare' designed to stifle public interest reporting, although Amersi states his legal actions are a genuine defence of his reputation.[32] These include the BBC, King's College London, and Chatham House (for a report cowritten by the authors of this book). Amersi's lawyers Carter-Ruck were able to force concessions out of King's College and Chatham House (see Chapter 13). However, he has not always been accommodated—or 'indulged'. The former Conservative MP Charlotte Leslie vetted Amersi when he attempted to become chair of the Conservative Middle East Council, an influential foreign affairs group of the party. She commissioned a private due diligence note and sent this to several figures in the party as well as 'a handful of political and intelligence sources'.[33] Amersi's friends hit back with Carl Hunter OBE, another party figure in February 2020, advising her to 'consider your position, as in being able to walk the dog at night, being able to sleep well at night'.[34] Amersi sued Leslie but his libel action was dismissed in June 2023 by Mr Justice Nicklin, who also questioned Amersi's motives and 'exorbitant way' he approached the legal action.[35] A few weeks later, in the House of Commons, David Davis MP argued that the case was 'an attempt to bully, intimidate and financially ruin Ms Leslie in order to suppress the truth'.[36]

Two Narratives

Amersi's is a fascinating story whose telling is a matter of considerable public interest. Two narratives are woven through his case, and each must be heard if we are to understand it fully. The first of these is that of anti-corruption activists—a narrative of *indictment* or culpability in which Amersi is accused of responsibility for the outcome of transactions from which he himself made a great deal of money. But this story is refuted by a second narrative: that of the accused and their indulgers. Both moral and legal responsibility are flatly denied by Amersi. In response to the letter which one of the authors (Heathershaw) wrote to offer him an opportunity to comment on the evidence we are presenting in this book, he wrote that our research was 'manifestly inaccurate, incomplete and misleading'[37] and accused Heathershaw of having 'a biased agenda' against him. Furthermore, he copied the University of Exeter's vice chancellor to strongly recommend that they terminate Heathershaw's professorship on grounds of professional misconduct.[38] In the accounts of Mohamed Amersi and others[39] it is not just that the narrative of indictment is rebutted in defence of themselves and their clients. Rather, a whole new narrative justifying indulgence emerges. It arises from legal-professional discourse where service provision in kleptocratic contexts is normalized, and the wider political economy is ignored.

According to Amersi, the very fact that many other major Western companies had been involved in Uzbekistan, and the fact that Telia was operating to the same rules, means that the only difference between himself and the others is that he has been unfairly targeted. He wrote to the authors:

The logical extension of your argument is that endemic institutional corruption was so notorious in Uzbekistan that *no legitimate company businessman or adviser who wish to conduct legitimate business would have contemplated conducting business.* This is obviously wrong and unsupportable.[40]

According to this reasoning, bribes are rare and unfortunate. Corruption may only be written about by journalists and researchers with respect to a particular person if that person has *already been convicted* in a criminal court. Such reasoning makes most public interest journalism in this area impossible.[41] And yet it would be foolish to dismiss Amersi's account out of hand. He is correct that the narrative of anti-corruption would suggest that it was impossible to do business in Islam Karimov's Uzbekistan without indulging kleptocracy. But rather than this being wrong and unsupportable, we will present evidence that Western professional enabling of corruption is rife not just in Uzbekistan but across much of the post-communist world.

This book is about professionals like Amersi whose work has indulged kleptocrats (unwittingly or otherwise) and who have themselves been indulged by major public institutions and regulators. It is a book about kleptocracy, but it is not primarily about kleptocrats or oligarchs. Rather, it is about the enablers: those professionals who are integral to kleptocratic enterprise or sustaining it. While Amersi's lawfare and the publicity surrounding his case are extreme, in other ways he is typical of enablers. They are intelligent and highly qualified professionals who have engaged in transnational business which connects corruption hotspots to the UK. Although they have been subject to criticism, they, like medieval clerics, see themselves as the good guys. They exist in a moral and political universe where what might be identified as the enabling of kleptocracy is constituted as legitimate conduct. According to this view, money makes the world go around, rich people earn their success through hard work, only a tiny minority of their wealth is genuinely troublesome (Nazi gold, for example), and those that suggest otherwise are 'left-wing' critics who are envious of the rich. But for the anti-corruption activists—including Conservatives like Davis and Leslie—these arguments are self-serving and indicate a world on the brink of losing its moral compass.

We sympathize with the narrative of indictment and have engaged in anti-corruption activism ourselves on the grounds of public interest. But to make sense of the kleptocracy problem, we cannot simply indict the enablers and kleptocrats. We must seek to understand their world—not just their incentives but their values and networks. What is clear from the two narratives above is that the indicters and indulgers are not simply two sides in a struggle. They are not just different accounts of what happened but have entirely different universes. On the very day that Davis made his claims about Amersi in parliament, the Foreign Policy Research Institute in the United States announced Amersi's appointment as a new member of their board.[42] Amersi remains a person of influence in the UK too, serving on the committee of the Conservative Foreign and Commonwealth Council in 2023 under the chairmanship of former UK intelligence chief Baroness Pauline Neville Jones.[43] As this book went to press in 2024, the publication of Tom Burgis's *Cuckooland* made new accusations of his involvement as an intermediary in crooked deals in Kazakhstan and Nepal as well as a donation to the Conservative Party which may be investigated for whether it complied with electoral donations laws.[44] For those who indulge him, Amersi is given the benefit of the doubt and remains a credible anti-corruption campaigner. For the most anti-corruption activists, there is enough evidence to consider him an enabler of corruption.[45] Neither narrative can yet declare victory but, with few convictions, it is the professional indulgers which still hold sway. It is a world on the brink which we explore in this book. It is a world where kleptocracy is political, global, *and* professional.

Kleptocracy Is Political

In December 2021, we coauthored a Chatham House paper entitled 'The UK's Kleptocracy Problem', which highlighted the role the UK played in hosting suspicious wealth and accepting political influence from elites hailing from post-Soviet kleptocratic states. When then Foreign Secretary Liz Truss was asked at Chatham House—on the very same day our report was launched—whether the UK government was doing enough to counter Russian money laundering in the City of London, she responded that 'we have very tough anti-money-laundering rules and anti-corruption rules'.[46] Two months after Truss's speech, Russia invaded Ukraine. The House of Commons' Foreign Affairs Committee said in June 2022 that UK government complacency had contributed to the war being financed by Russian money laundered through the UK. 'The government's unwillingness to bring forward legislation to stem the flow of dirty money', it argued, 'is likely to have contributed to the belief in Russia that the UK is a safe haven for corrupt wealth'.[47] With the UK scrambling to impose later-than-last-minute legislation sanctioning Russian oligarchs who had found a convenient environment to prosper in London, the facts spectacularly contradicted Truss's statement. Already in 2020, the National Crime Agency had estimated that money-laundering causes at least £100 billion of economic damage to the UK every year.[48]

Kleptocracy is political in the vernacular sense that it generates controversy among politicians. But it is also political in that it refers to a form of rule. Classically understood as 'rule of thieves', kleptocracy has found a new generation of analysts in the last decade. The term has been popularized in Oliver Bullough's *Moneyland*,[49] Tom Burgis's *Kleptopia*,[50] and Sarah Chayes's *Thieves of State*,[51] while it has also been widely deployed by civil society organizations.[52] In the months since our report's launch, events dictated that kleptocracy briefly rose to the very top of the political agenda in Western states. More than half of all mentions of 'kleptocrat' and 'kleptocracy' in Westminster from 1800 until June 2022 occurred in those first six months of 2022. Many of these were with respect to the 'bloody January' crisis in Kazakhstan and Russia's attack on Ukraine. The British government rushed through a long-delayed Economic Crime Act (2022) in the weeks after the war and passed a second in the autumn of 2023. The update to the government's foreign policy statement in March 2023 included the first-ever mention of 'kleptocrat' in such a high-level government document.[53] Government had finally decided that the rulers and oligarchs of (some) kleptocratic states were a problem that needed urgent attention. It took an international security crisis to arrive at this point.

Most definitions of kleptocracy identify it as a national system where business and politics merge. The UK's Financial Conduct Authority (FCA) indirectly provides a definition of kleptocracy in its guidelines on countries with a high risk of corruption: 'a political economy dominated by a small number of people/entities with close links to the state'.[54] A similar term is 'grand corruption', defined by Transparency International as 'the abuse of high-level power that benefits the few at the expense of the many, and causes serious and widespread harm to individuals and society'.[55] Grand corruption may be used interchangeably with kleptocracy, as both indicate the subversion of political office for personal enrichment and advantage. According to a recent definition employed in the *Journal of Democracy* to explain 'the rise of kleptocracy':

> Kleptocracy is a system in which public institutions are used to enable a
> network of ruling elites to steal public funds for their own private gain.[56]

However, kleptocratic systems employ many methods of self-enrichment
other than traditional 'theft': the awarding of a lucrative contract to a family
member of a senior political figure, or a private company owned by a crony
receiving state loans, for example. Due to the kleptocratic character of the
state, the majority of 'illicit financial flows' will not necessarily be illegal.[57]
As Tuesday Reitano, an expert from Global Initiative on Transnational and
Organised Crime, comments: 'Policies and laws determine what is illegal—if
they are warped under the influence of dirty money to permit and protect
those who do wrong, they may no longer be illegal, but they remain illicit: in-
herently wrong by the norms of democratic governance'.[58]

This point about the warping of laws to make legal that which is illicit is
crucial for us to understand kleptocracy. Kleptocracies are, in Jody La Porte's
definition, 'autocracies in which the ruler and his inner circle of advisers—
collectively referred to . . . as "ruling elites"—exploit public office to illegally
enrich themselves and their families'.[59] This presentation of kleptocracy as
a type of autocracy has become a way of explaining the global authoritarian
resurgence that has taken place over the last 20 years.[60] According to the 2022
edition of the academic index V-Dem, the number of closed autocracies is up
from 25 to 30, covering 26% of the global population, while 'electoral autocracy' remains the most common regime type with 44% of the world's population, or 3.4 billion people.[61] Most autocracies, covering a total of 70% of the
global population, have features of kleptocracy, but so do some states which
are widely considered to be democracies.[62]

Kleptocracy Is Global

The geographic focus of studies of kleptocracy is often the post-Soviet states,
with the works mentioned above covering Azerbaijan, Kazakhstan, Russia,
Ukraine, and Uzbekistan, among others. Groundbreaking books by the academic Karen Dawisha and journalist Catherine Belton have both deployed
kleptocracy as the prism through which to understand Russia and its network
of politically connected oligarchs.[63] However, kleptocracy is in fact global in
the sense that it is found in every region of the world. It has certainly spread
to governments in Europe, with Hungary and Serbia identified in Freedom

House's 2022 report as having 'kleptocratic tendencies'.[64] In Latin America, states generally considered to be democracies such as Mexico and Ecuador have strong kleptocratic tendencies due to the role of illicit finance in their political economies. A 2023 National Endowment for Democracy report singled out the UK and Luxembourg for enabling kleptocracy and Turkey and the United Arab Emirates as 'two of the most prominent bridging jurisdictions' which allow access to the global financial system.[65] Angola, the Republic of the Congo, Equatorial Guinea, Gabon, Nigeria, Afghanistan, Malaysia, and Pakistan are some of the states in Africa and Asia most-often regarded as kleptocracies. Even the world's two most-populated states— China and India—have strong kleptocratic features in their recent past or present, despite the fact that they possess two very different political systems.

The evidence that kleptocracy is global and found across very different states and types of government demands a conceptual rethink. Our approach emerges from the study of political economy where oligarchy and kleptoc- racy have long puzzled academics. In 2003, the economist Daron Acemoglu and colleagues noted that the paradox of kleptocracies 'is their longevity, despite the disastrous policies pursued by the rulers'. Kleptocratic regimes exist, they argue, in a definition which captures the character of most of the world's governments, 'where the state is controlled and run for the benefit of an individual, or a small group, who use their power to *transfer* a large frac- tion of society's resources to themselves'.[66] What is crucial to understand the global nature of kleptocracy is that transfer is almost never contained within the borders of the society in question but goes to overseas accounts and as- sets. Therefore, kleptocracy itself is never entirely national but transnational. In this book we do not study cases of, for example, Kazakh kleptocracy but Kazakh-UK kleptocracy or in some cases Kazakh-UK-US-Swiss kleptocracy.

Acemoglu and colleagues' puzzle regarding kleptocratic regimes' longevity can thus only be addressed by recognizing them as extended not merely over time but over space. Not only do kleptocracies endure, but they have been globalized to the extent that their elites are no longer content to capture and command their own states. When corruption has mainly a foreign rather than domestic source it may be more likely to fuel an authoritarian regime as more power is placed in the hands of a sovereign elite.[67] These elites are transnational: buying assets, laundering reputations, and gaining influence in democracies. In turn, their divide-and-rule strategies which Acemoglu et al. observed are not merely national but global.[68] From this perspective, the ideas of a national kleptocracy or a post-Soviet region of kleptocracy are, strictly speaking, misnomers. All kleptocracies are transnational, rather than confined to a particular region, and as they merge with one another are potentially global—an idea implied by the monikers *Moneyland* and *Kleptopia*.

These ideas indicate the need for a second definition of kleptocracy to complement the first. It is not merely the character or properties of a regime. It is not just a cabal of corrupt individuals or sum of corrupt acts in a given territory. *Transnational kleptocracy* in this alternative definition is

> the transactions, relationships, and networks operating across borders for a person or entity whose wealth is fully or partially a product of kleptocratic rule, to hide and protect assets, acquire status, and achieve influence in a third country or countries.

In brief, transnational kleptocracy is a cross-border enterprise to indulge elites who have used their political access to enrich themselves and maintain power. A critical aspect of any such enterprise is how global actors and institutions establish networks to transform these resources into globally available assets. This involves the comingling of illicit funds with legal ones, concealing beneficial ownership and questionable sources of wealth, and establishing 'legitimate' global reputations. As the ultimate 'private gain' is an asset, status, or influence, not simply the source of wealth, such transnational enabling is not external to kleptocracy but is intrinsic.

From this understanding of transnational or global kleptocracy, this book discusses cases of wealthy persons and their entities with sources of wealth of Russian and Eurasian origin—countries recognized as possessing kleptocratic systems—who we refer to as 'post-Soviet elites' or simply 'elites'.[69] These persons are sometimes recognized and presented as kleptocrats, oligarchs, 'minigarchs'[70] or more positively businesspersons and exiles. They are not the 'apolitical rich', as Mark Galeotti has proposed, as it is not possible to be truly apolitical when your wealth originates in a kleptocratic context, but neither are they straightforward clients of their home regimes.[71] We outline our categories in Chapter 3.

To establish whether elites are within the scope of this book we make two judgements. First, when we speak of systems being recognized as kleptocratic we refer to an assessment widely made about the country or countries of origin and the sources of wealth. The notion of a widely made assessment requires us to exercise our judgements as area experts on the post-Soviet region. But as the kleptocratic systems cross borders we are also making assessments about which transnational relationships with the UK are 'klep-tocratic'—our second judgement. For instance, UK-Kazakhstan appears to be a kleptocratic relationship to a far greater extent than UK-Georgia, and Georgian oligarchs do not appear in our book. Nevertheless, this may change; there is plenty of state theft in Georgia. We recognize that diagnosing kleptocracy is based on scarce data and expert opinion. These are our own professional judgements.[72]

Wealthy exiles may oppose their inclusion alongside kleptocrats and oligarchs whom they legitimately accuse of persecuting and unfairly prosecuting them. However, it is their wealth's widely perceived klepto-cratic origins and its transfer to the UK that places them within the remit of this book.[73] By such a definition, wealthy exiles are within the scope of this book: even those figures who claim to have made money independent of a kleptocratic state have nonetheless flourished, even if only for a limited pe-riod, within the system by playing by the rules. We do *not* include political exiles who are not high-net worth individuals and/or who are not making major purchases and donations. It is those who made serious money in a kleptocratic context and seek to extend and defend their assets, status, and influence in the place of destination that are included within our analysis.

Kleptocracy Is Professional

To build kleptocratic enterprises beyond borders, these elites need help from legal and financial professionals. This professional service provision is known as *enabling*. The term captures a variety of behaviours—some licit and some illicit; some willingly complicit and some reflecting negligence rather than deliberate corruption—which act on and within the structure of transnational kleptocracy as defined above. While the word 'enabling' is seen as pejorative by those offering such services, it is a term which grasps the phenomenon in practice. Adapting the definition of 'middlemen' by Jennifer Bussell, we define *professional enablers* as individuals or organizations that facilitate transactions between two or more parties, at least one of whom has a source of wealth which is illicit.[74]

This political economy definition differs from the legal one which was introduced by the UK's National Economic Crime Centre, working with private sector professionals including the Law Society, in 2023. They define a 'professional enabler' as 'an individual or organisation that is providing

professional services that enable *criminality* via behaviour which 'is deliberate, reckless, improper, dishonest and/or negligent' to the point that they
are guilty of misconduct.[75] By such a definition, only criminal enablers are
enablers. This only includes the very thickest end of the wedge of witting and
noncompliant professional enabling and seems very close to the definition
of a criminal accessory. At the thinner end of the wedge, we find compliant
and/or unwitting enabling. Both have the effect of enabling kleptocracy so
both must be studied. Our research suggests that noncriminal enabling is far
more common than criminal enabling given the very few convictions despite
the widely acknowledged extent of the activity. In our definition, enabling is
defined by the illicit source of the wealth of the person or entity, not whether
the action or transaction on their behalf is itself illicit or illegal. Professionals
enable kleptocracy by providing services—or what we call *professional
indulgences*—such as the explaining of kleptocratic sources of wealth, the
concealing of a kleptocrat's beneficial ownership, or the laundering of a reputation which is tainted by ties to kleptocracy.

There is therefore an important relationship between illicit (all that which
is criminal, unethical, and noncompliant) and the licit (all that which is
lawful, ethical, and compliant according to professional standards). The
whole point of enabling is to provide services to get a client, entity, or asset
from the illicit to the licit. It is the process of crossing this frontier that
matters and that process includes all sorts of activities which are not themselves illegal in any way. It is at this boundary of il/licit that the bulk of work
is done. As the sociologist Kimberly Kay Hoang was told by an asset manager
in Vietnam, 'to make money anywhere in Asia, you need to master the art of
"playing in the grey"'.[76] As Hoang herself puts it, the task of the researcher is
'to reveal how elites finesse the grey space between legal and illegal practices
to establish significant social and political connections that allow them to exploit *new frontiers*'.[77] It is these new frontiers made by elites and their enablers
which interest us in this book too. To play in the grey in the indulging of
kleptocracy is to make that which could be illegal legal and, just as importantly, that which may appear illicit licit. The key enablers are largely witting,
but others may be unwitting or, perhaps more accurately, wilfully unwitting.
They operate not merely when the wealth is made (*upstream*, as we call it)
but when it is spent and donated (*downstream*).

The enablers we concentrate on are largely downstream in the flows of
transnational kleptocracy. Some—estate agents, lawyers, accountants,
and trust and company service providers—are referred to as Designated

Non-Financial Businesses and Professions (DNFBPs) by the Financial Action Task Force (FATF), an intergovernmental body created to promote global standards on preventing money laundering and terrorist financing. They are 'nonfinancial' but are regulated in a similar fashion to financial services because these groups that have been found to be at high risk of exploitation for money laundering by, for example, the UK's National Crime Agency (NCA), due to the services they provide and in part due to a lack of proper supervision in the past, and arguably still to this day.[78] In addition, we consider the unregulated professionals, such as public relations (PR) agents, wealth managers, citizenship-by-investment advisors, and corporate intelligence companies. At the far end of this professional ecosystem, we consider the gift managers of universities, charities, and political parties who are enablers but not intermediaries. These professionals work for institutions in receipt of gifts and donations from origins deemed kleptocratic, rather than merely being the go-between for these transfers. Gift officers at universities which indulge wealth linked to kleptocracy, for example, are not buying status for their clients but selling status on behalf of their institutions. They may also be attracting much-needed support for underresourced areas of research. When we begin to consider how deeply kleptocratic wealth has penetrated the UK, the moral dilemmas of its acceptance or refusal become acute.

Why Londongrad?

Over the last decade or two, much of the groundbreaking work on kleptocracy has been done by investigative journalists and civil society groups such as the National Endowment for Democracy, the Hudson Institute, Global Witness, and Transparency International. We know many of these people and organizations well and have often followed in their wake as they have broken a new story or successfully pressed government to bring in a new law. One of the three authors used to work at Global Witness and conducted many of their leading investigations into London and the post-Soviet world—we return to some of these investigations in the following chapters. However, this book is written from an academic perspective with the larger aim of understanding how kleptocracy and its enabling matter in global politics through the focus on a series of case studies all of which originate in or flow through 'Londongrad'.

Recent investigative works provide brilliant narratives and vivid descriptions of a world in which kleptocracy is on the rise. These particular histories tell us a great deal of how we got here from the emergence of the eurobond and eurodollar markets in the 1950s and 1960s, the creation of the offshore system and US- and UK-led financial deregulation in the 1970s and 1980s, and the creation and/or economic transformation of the post-communist states in the 1990s. *Unaccountable* (2014) by the anthropologist Janine Wedel, *American Kleptocracy* by the journalist Casey Michel (2021), and *What's the Matter with Delaware* (2022) by Hal Weitzman offer analyses of how globalization and self-regulation combine to erode earlier systems of accountability for professions and institutions in the United States.[79] Oliver Bullough's *Butler to the World* (2022) and Tom Burgis's *Cuckooland* (2024) are revealing and erudite stories of how Britain's service sectors cater for kleptocrats.[80] But none of these books explains how and why professional enablers make a difference and how and why they do not. Are they merely doing what governments allow and encourage? Or do they have the power themselves, making new global spaces, regardless of the interests of states? Is the kleptocracy problem mainly about demand or mainly about supply?

Londongrad is an exemplary place to study in this regard not because the UK is the dominant global financial centre nor because the former Soviet world is the most kleptocratic region of the world. The term arose colloquially in the 1990s to describe the presence of new Russian money in London. It was captured for posterity in a subsequent book and has since entered the academic lexicon too.[81] Since 2022, in the wake of Russia's second invasion of Ukraine and with the introduction of a new public register on the beneficial ownership of property, there has been an attempt to dismantle Londongrad.[82] But Londongrad was always more about core features of British capitalism that made it vulnerable to illicit finance than the external threat of Russia. The UK has perhaps seen the greatest shift of power from public to private service sectors of any G7 economy and the greatest ability to export its model to the rest of the world through English common law and the British Overseas Territories. Londongrad is not just a story about finance and corruption; it tells us about relative decline after the loss of its empire where the UK has become an entrepôt for the corrupt and a market for short-term capital. In short, the case study of British enabling of post-communist kleptocracy tells us not merely about the dark shadow of globalization and capitalism but about the everyday concentration and mobility of capital.

Our problem is therefore an intellectual puzzle, but it is also a policy and political conundrum. This book arises out of a worry that many diplomats, geopolitical thinkers, and intelligent readers may have read or heard about the problem of kleptocracy and its enablers but continue to underestimate its significance or even regard it as irrelevant. Many diplomats carry on as if only states and national interests matter in decisions about going to war, making foreign policy, negotiating trade agreements, and forming alliances. The UK's Integrated Review of foreign policy in 2021 made no mention of kleptocracy,[83] with only one mention in the 2023 version of the need 'to make it harder for organised criminals, kleptocrats and terrorists to use opaque entities to abuse the UK's financial system'.[84]

However, power also flows through money and is found in who owns capital. As such, it stands to reason that many decisions are shaped by the rise of kleptocracy. Did Russia really attack Ukraine from 2014 onwards simply because of the unlikely prospect of it joining NATO,[85] or more generally because its whole political-economic model—founded in Russian imperialism and fuelled by its transnational kleptocracy—risked being fatally undermined, not least by Ukraine's membership action plan with the EU? Many geopolitical thinkers continue to assume that military balances are the main determinant of processes and outcomes in foreign affairs and by far the most important actors are states. Even intelligent critics of kleptocracy often see it as derivative of geopolitics—a sharp power against the soft power of democracies.[86] There is some value to these geopolitical accounts of kleptocracy, but they risk overemphasizing the differences between the state and business, and between kleptocratic regimes and their networks across the global economy.

It is the task of this book to explain what is at stake in the emergence of these blurred boundaries and network ties. We are part of the small group of academics that not only take this problem seriously but are seeking to outline its grander implications. We work on post-communist Europe and Eurasia and their ties to London. We have found that transnational kleptocracy has also been instrumental in the ending of civil wars, the emergence of privatized regime security, and the rise of highly unequal economies across the world.[87] While we generalize from a relatively small number of comparative cases studies, our findings are consistent with those of global field experiments which demonstrate that the formation of companies and opening of bank accounts universally take place without effective checks on kleptocratic sources of wealth.[88] Colleagues have demonstrated that the 'globalized individual' is a new actor on the world stage and a product of the transnational professionals and networks enabling illicit finance by sovereign elites.[89] Together with them, we have shown that such globalized individuals form uncivil society networks to take on the activists and engage in reputation laundering as a companion practice to what we define as their money laundering.[90]

Plan of the Book

These arguments will be developed in a dialogue between two narratives. The first of these is the collective voice of ourselves and our colleagues in civil society, academia, and journalism who study kleptocracy. Many of these colleagues have developed powerful explanations for the kleptocracy problem which we draw upon as we develop our approach to the issue in the coming chapters. Is the problem confined to professional indulgences offered to allies of the government of the place of destination? Is it that incumbent elites—those that remain in favour in their countries of origin—are the main beneficiaries of indulgences? We incorporate the *enabler effect* as a third explanation which may sometimes challenge and sometimes supplement the first two. This explanation—that of transnational kleptocracy—is required to make sense of the extension of kleptocracy. As academics, we approach the evidence with impartiality. But insofar as we also work with civil society and journalists, our narrative is often interpreted by the persons we study as a *narrative of indictment*. It is more commonly described as critique.

The second set of voices is a contrary one: it is that of the professionals working for those we study. Theirs is a narrative of professional practice and reasonable defence which we label, harking back to medieval Europe, a *narrative of indulgence*. Each of our nine chapters profiles an individual case study of corruption and kleptocracy, and each of these contains a variety of professional service providers. Where we have found an indulgence, we approach the major elites and enablers included in the case study—and other persons who feature heavily in the story—to provide them an opportunity to comment, sometimes known as the right to reply. Where this is not possible, or we have not received a response, we quote their responses to similar allegations made by other researchers or journalists. This opportunity to comment is a significant factor in the English legal jurisprudence on protection of investigations on matters of public interest. Some of the persons included in our study have a litigious track record and some of them have accused us of unfairly defaming them in the past. However, such comment is also of value methodologically. When subjects respond, they provide new data—*both* facts regarding how the enabling of kleptocracy works *and* fascinating moral justifications for their actions. It also allows us to introduce an ethnographic richness, an insider perspective in our analysis, and reflect on our own positionalities with respect to those we study. By including these new data in our research, we begin to see inside the moral universe of an emergent and elitist political order.

Over Chapters 2 and 3 we outline the historical and contemporary political context of the UK's kleptocracy problem in which *demand* for its enabling services has emerged. While Londongrad has garnered huge public attention, especially since the invasion of Ukraine, we consider whether it is exceptional or a harbinger of an emerging new global politics. On the one hand, history tells us that former European imperial centres develop networked relations with elites from their former colonies. Britain's relations with Gulf states, France's with L'Afrique Francophone, and Portugal's with their Lusophone ex-colonies are all good examples. On the other hand, new financial centres such as Dubai and Singapore are famously open to all on the basis of market demand, having few long-standing networks and a weaker regulatory framework—but deploying English common law in financial rules and courts. London's relations with Eurasia demonstrate both the post-imperial decline of the UK and its ongoing significance as an entrepôt for postcolonial elites and an exporter of professional services.

Our approach to the kleptocracy problem is outlined in Chapter 4 of this book. Our theory contends that the *supply* of indulgences enables kleptocracy both at home and abroad. This is what we call the *enabler effect*. We outline it alongside two alternative mechanisms: the *incumbency advantage* and *alliance effect*. We argue that these mechanisms may be observed across a diverse array of most-different professional sectors and practices from real estate purchasing to defamation law to philanthropy. The enabling effect necessarily differs from one indulgence to another. However, between and among them we find family resemblances. This allows us to evaluate whether similar enabling effects are causal across diverse professional sectors, how the problem can be attenuated, and what this means for how we understand global politics. Explaining when, how, and why the enabler effect works is the key task of the book.

Across Chapters 5 to 13, we assess the nine indulgences. These nine are not an exhaustive list of the services provided by professional enablers. As we have seen with Mohamed Amersi, services also include those in the kleptocratic context itself. These services are 'upstream' in the flow of transnational kleptocracy while our focus here is on 'downstream' services. In each of them, we have purposively chosen a single case or a small number of comparative cases of professional indulgence. We select cases partly due to the availability of data, but we do so according to clear scope conditions concerning the source of wealth of the person in the kleptocratic post-Soviet region and the purchasing of services and/or assets in the UK. Almost all cases are drawn from our published database which contains 99 cases of property purchases worth more than £2 billion and made over the period from 1998 to 2020 on behalf of the elites of Russian and Eurasian states.[91] All cases hold important conditions of similarity. All have completed residential real estate transactions in the UK (London and southeast England), many using complex offshore structures to conceal either uncertain beneficial ownership or dubious sources of wealth. In all cases, we can see some variation in outcome: kleptocratic or corrupt wealth, status, or power was fully indulged for some persons or periods, but for others or at other times it was only partially indulged or refused.

This variation in outcome allows us to assess which of our three mechanisms of transnational kleptocracy—incumbency, alliance, and enabling—matter most (see Table 1.1). The cases differ firstly in terms of the political status of the client (incumbent or exiled) at the time of the service taking place, the political relationship of their country of origin to the UK (partner or nonpartner), and the professional service provided (the degree and kind of the enabling effect). A wide array of enablers across financial, legal, educational, political, and other services are covered. With investigations and prosecutions occurring over an extended period there are also differences of regulation, particularly regarding the changes in the UK's anti-money-laundering regulations, and the introduction of unexplained wealth orders (UWOs) in 2018. We attend to these differences in our case studies. In each of the chapters, we assess which of our three mechanisms—the enabler effect, the incumbency advantage, or the alliance effect—makes the most difference across the set of nine cases. In essence, we ask which of these mechanisms is present and making a difference across most or all the transactions in question.

Table 1.1 Nine professional indulgences

Chapter	Indulgence	Service Sector	Client(s)	Source of Wealth (1)	Incumbent? (2)	Ally? (3)	Enablers? (4)
5	hiding money	banking	Maxim Bakiyev	Kyrgyz Republic	No	No	APCO Worldwide Kroll
6	listing companies	stock market	Kazakhmys ENRC	Kazakhstan	Yes	Yes	JP Morgan Deutsche Bank
7	selling rights	residency and citizenship	Various	Various	Yes / No	Yes / No	Henley & Partners
8	purchasing properties	real estate (purchase)	Gulnara Karimova	Uzbekistan	Yes / No	No	SH Landes LLP Quastels
9	explaining wealth	real estate (law)	Dariga Nazarbayeva and Nurali Aliyev	Kazakhstan	Yes	Yes	Mishcon de Reya
10	selling status	philanthropy	Nargiz Pashayeva	Azerbaijan	Yes	Yes	University of Oxford (5)
11	making friends	political donations	Dmitry Leus (6); Liubov Chernukhina	Russia Russia	No	No	Conservative Party (5) Quintessentially
12	tracking enemies	corporate intelligence	Nazarbayev regime	Kazakhstan	Yes / No	Yes	Arcanum Global
13	silencing critics	reputation management	Dmitry Leus (6); Mohamed Amersi (6); Nazarbayeva and Aliyev	Russia Uzbekistan Kazakhstan	No No Yes	No No Yes	Vardags Carter-Ruck Mishcon de Reya

Notes

(1) 'Source of Wealth' denotes the kleptocratic context in which all or a part of the person's wealth was earned and/or where their business was established.

(2) 'Incumbent' refers to any person of the political elite, their relatives, or businesspersons who retains political position or business interests in the country of the source of wealth. In some of our cases, the client was exiled or lost their incumbency during the case. In other cases, there are multiple clients: some are incumbents, some are not. These cases are denoted 'Yes / No'.

(3) 'Ally' is denoted where the country of the source of wealth is a formal partner of the UK defined as states with an EU association agreement, or EU Enhanced Partnership and Cooperation agreement signed or 'in negotiation'. Most of our cases predate the UK's departure from the EU. Even after Brexit, these agreements remain a good proxy for the UK's relationships with former Soviet states.

(4) 'Enabler' is individuals or organizations that professionally facilitate transactions between two or more parties, at least one of whom has a source of wealth which is illicit. Usually, the enabler is a third party.

(5) For the Conservative Party and the University of Oxford, 'enablers' are internal: those responsible for due diligence within the recipient organizations rather than a third party.

(6) Neither Dmitry Leus nor Mohamed Amersi is a kleptocrat or oligarch and their inclusion in this table does not suggest otherwise. They are included due to their source of wealth originating primarily from a post-communist kleptocratic context and their subsequent contracting of services comparable to those found in other cases.

We end our book in Chapter 14 with an answer to this question of the difference that enablers make and the role they play in constituting kleptocracy on a global scale. Enriched with examples from case studies of servicing of Eurasian kleptocrats by British professionals, we demonstrate if and how the supply of services makes the difference. Where a difference is found, there is an enabler effect, and the client has been indulged. We draw our evidence together to make two claims. The first is descriptive: the enabler effect is present for both incumbents and exiles, for both allies and enemies. The second is explanatory: while incumbency and alliance both matter for certain indulgences such as explaining away suspicious wealth and avoiding the threat of individual sanctions, these are less powerful than the enabler effect. These two findings suggest a new form of global politics where regime types and balances of power are less important than networks of elites mediated by private professional practice. Such politics has huge consequences for development in the global South, for the rule of law and democracy globally, and security and power relations internationally. It is for the reader to decide whether our logic and evidence bear the weight of these conclusions.

We agree that sensible people can come to different views on the importance of and damage done by professional indulgences. However, we think it is irrefutable that our world is being transformed by the global power of mobile capital which is opening new spaces for elites in a world in which nation states were, for a late-modern moment in the twentieth century, territorially distinct and empowered by decolonization and democratization. Perhaps this resurgence of elite networks of wealth and power is a return to the normal pattern of modern history. But such a broad-brush dismissal is unwarranted. The professionals of our book are individuals who exercise moral and intellectual agency in their choices of whom to work for and how to indulge them. The UK's private sector has many thousands of them in the service of oligarchs and kleptocrats and it should be no surprise that they have their own moral and professional justifications for their actions. So far, those that have resisted or blown the whistle appear to have lost ground to those who have indulged kleptocracy. However, there are also many individuals and organizations with the agency to expose and fatally undermine these indulgences. There is not a definitive winner or loser in the fight for and against kleptocracy.

2

The Ends of Two Empires

The real power is not corporate; it is private.
—Chris Hedges, American journalist[1]

How did kleptocracy go global? And how was Londongrad built? After the Second World War, the West was pitted against the Soviet Union. The classic story of international relations is of a bipolar world of the balance of power between the two geopolitical blocs. But there is another story to be told: how from the ashes of the European empires and, during the Cold War, the West opened its doors to all comers—including Soviet capital—and created a new empire of finance. While abandoning its role as the dominant global power, the UK's pre-established networks made it one of the preeminent financial centres of the world. From as early as the 1950s, this went hand in hand with rampant deregulation and, from the 1970s, self-regulation by international finance.

As one commentator describes, Britain, aiming to attract cash into an economy that could no longer rely on industrial production, 'deregulat[ed] itself, again and again, until it was cheaper to do business here than abroad, usually because the cost and consequences were foisted onto another (generally poorer) country'.[2] But the new transnational financial order was no British Empire 2.0, because most of its agents bore no allegiance to the UK and London never controlled it.[3] This is not merely the argument of recent popular works, but is the consensus of academic and nonacademic authors alike—most recently Bullough,[4] Sharman,[5] Shaxson,[6] Palan et al.,[7] Harvey,[8] and Haberly and Wójcik,[9] amongst others—over the past two decades.

These studies all emphasize the widespread deregulation that occurred in the latter half of the twentieth century. This deregulatory wave did not occur in a vacuum; it was the result of a gradual process that relied on seeds sown during the British Empire. The early manifestations of this process can be categorized into three broad factors. The first is economic and structural: the expansion of Britain's bank networks in the second half of the nineteenth century, and their increasing integration with the City, facilitated the large waves of capital to and from Britain. Private companies were only legally recognized in 1907, where previously the market had been dominated by large, publicly listed corporations.[10] Crucially, these banks and companies formed the basis for the sprawling offshore system centred on the City of London that emerged with deregulation in the late twentieth century.

The second development is societal, relating to the manoeuvring of elites who were threatened by the rise of labour movements. Financial sector elites were able to exert a huge influence on Britain's institutions before the demise of its empire. For example, in the late nineteenth century, the Rothschilds were both the most powerful *financiers*, as well as the *regulators* of the finances of the British Empire—a similar role to that played by the 'old nobles' who dominated the Genoese network at the end of the nineteenth century.[11] Such elites were so influential that they managed to weaken the regulatory capacity of Britain's post–World War II institutions shortly after they were established in that social democratic moment.[12]

The third is financial. Even before the end of the British Empire, the collapse of the gold-exchange standard of the pound sterling in 1931 marked the terminal crisis of Britain's dominance over the world monetary system—and thus the final end of its role as the world's hegemon. As stated by Polanyi,[13] 'the rupture of the golden thread was the sign of a world revolution'. While the 'great divergence' in which the UK and Europe saw a huge relative gain in economic growth over the rest of the world in the modern era was more broadly economic,[14] since the late nineteenth century the crucial developments have been specifically in the financial sector.

These three developments provide the backdrop against which post-imperial Britain's economic trouble, and phoenix-like reinvention, was set. All was ready for the emergence of one of the most consequential deregulatory creations of our times: the eurodollar. It is a tale closely linked to the global financial story of the Soviet Union. When the Soviet empire collapsed, the fate of its remnants and survivors was deeply tied to the aftermath of Britain's empire. This chapter tells that story of two empires unravelling one after the other. In both cases, dramatically weakened states created the conditions for thriving private sectors. By the late twentieth century, reductions in inequality which had been achieved in earlier decades had begun to be reversed by new mobilities and secrecies in finance capital which favoured a return to the conditions where wealth was concentred in the hands of relatively few persons.[15] It was only natural that these few would do more and more business with each other across and beyond national borders.

1950s–1960s: The Advent of the Eurodollar Market

Financial innovation is considered crucial for the efficiency of the economy and as a spur for growth. But how, and for whom? In its broader sense, financial innovation is supposed to 'promote broader financial development that spirals into economic growth through its positive impact on saving, investment, and output . . . [thus being] a critical deriving factor of growth'.[16] In modern finance, innovating often involves identifying a mismatch between two systems that have different rules. By placing one part of the activity in one system and another slice in another, bankers and their clients can pick and choose the set of rules they like best in each place—dodging the obstacles faced by mere mortals. For example, a mismatch between the United Kingdom and the United States ended up radically redefining global finance.

This is how the eurobond and the eurodollar, tools that were instrumental in the rise of British financial services, were born. Unlike other bonds, eurobonds did not incur a tax at the source, and they were issued in bearer (rather than registered) form, making them virtually anonymous.[17] These two features made them an attractive option for tax evaders, criminals, and others seeking to conceal illicit funds starting from the 1960s, as several popular authors have highlighted.[18] Eurodollars, although discussed less frequently, were also critical. By enabling banks to secure funding without limitations, they became a crucial tool in facilitating financial transactions. Their inception dates to developments that accompanied the transformation of Britain's imperial structures into a high-powered financial centre with subsidiaries throughout the world, poised to grant indulgences.

Eurodollars originated when the Midland Bank and the Moscow Narodny Bank discovered a mutually beneficial way to make profits in the face of regulatory limitations. In the mid-1950s, Midland—a small UK clearing bank— was unable to attract clients in the face of strong competition. This hindered its ability to loan money, grow, and expand its customer base, locking it in a vicious circle. But Midland's luck changed when its interests serendipitously coincided with another bank of a very different kind. During the Cold War, the USSR was eager to keep its dollar reserves safe in case of an unforeseen crisis, leading them to store their funds outside the United States through financial institutions such as the Soviet-owned Moscow Narodny Bank, which had been founded in 1919 but had remained a minor entity until the late 1950s.[19] Due to a US rule called Regulation Q, the interests Narodny were making on these deposits were capped at 1%. However, Narodny possessed the much-needed dollars that Midland required to purchase pounds and revitalize its loan-making operations. Midland, in turn, was willing to pay a lucrative sum to Narodny for the transaction, well beyond the standard 1%. However, the post–World War II rules on the limitation of capital transfers enshrined in the Bretton Woods agreement prevented Midland from directly acquiring those dollar reserves. This hurdle sparked a stroke of financial innovation: If the dollars cannot be bought, why not opt for *borrowing* them instead?

This tactic simultaneously allowed Midland to dodge the limits placed on its activities in Britain, and Narodny to make a much bigger profit. As Bullough remarks, 'financial surgeons in the City of London had operated on the heart of the sterling system, and installed a bypass around an obstruction that was stopping capital from flowing freely into the British economy and stopping the Midland from making profits'.[20] This represented a significant departure from the established legal framework and warranted the attention of regulatory authorities. The Bank of England, however, turned a blind eye: Midland may have been violating the spirit of the law, but not its specific provisions. Making banks abide by voluntary restrictions was a horrific thought for the mentality that dominated the Bank of England at the time (and largely continues today). By borrowing the dollars instead of buying them outright, Midland was able to enjoy the benefits of their use without the liability and limitations that come with ownership. Finance innovated, and the eurodollars were born.

A year later, an international crisis became the game-changer that propelled this regional financial tool to planetary proportions. Key among the vestiges of the British Empire and gateway to the trade wonders of Asia, the Suez strait remained under the strong influence of the Crown after World War II. The Suez Canal Company, which administered it, had British and French shareholders. In 1956, a prolonged stand-off over Egypt's nationalization of the canal, pushed through by Nasser's government, came to a head with an ill-conceived and ill-executed coup by Britain, France, and Israel. Unbeknownst to the Americans, the coup-plotters agreed for Israeli forces to move into Egypt, followed by a joint military action by Britain and France. Upon learning of the scheme, US President Dwight Eisenhower threatened to sell the US government's bonds in pound sterling, which would inflict serious harm to the UK economy. London's attempt to salvage and revive Britain's financial might had thus spectacularly backfired. The British caved in and withdrew. In return, the US threw a lifeline to the British economy, lending as much money as was needed to salvage the pound, if only for a short while. The episode ended as badly as it could for London and Paris, which saw their power greatly diminished, while potentially emboldening the USSR to invade Hungary. Britain's international lustre was thus irremediably harmed. It was the end of Britain's role of a major world power.

Despite the United States' last-minute injection of funds, from this moment on Britain's monetary policy seemed to be on an unstoppable downward curve. Both the Bank of England and the Treasury intervened to try to salvage the pound's role as the world's dominant currency by keeping its $2.8 peg to the dollar. The Bank of England raised the interest rate from 5% to 7%. More consequentially, the Treasury imposed limitations on the use of the pound to finance international trade. This restrictive move signified deep trouble for the merchant banks of the City, which relied on their pound reserves to finance their business and thus had to urgently find another way to fund their transactions—the alternative, for many, was outright closure. This is how Midland's and Narodny's innovation went mainstream: the City of London adopted the eurodollar as a standard modus operandi, but with a twist. Whereas Midland borrowed dollars to buy pounds and finance domestic business, the merchant banks dodged the second part. They used the borrowed dollars to conduct business directly.[21]

This innovation emboldened the Bank of England to change tactics. It realized that it did not need to save the pound to save British finance; it could simply change the way in which money flowed from country to country. In Bullough's words: 'It wasn't the blood (sterling) that mattered, but the tubes it passed along. If they transfused dollars into those old sclerotic arteries, the blockages fell away, and life-giving capital poured through once more into the global economy'.[22] And indeed, while the pound crashed, British finance did not. Instead, it went from strength to strength. While the $2.8 peg to the dollar is now a long-forgotten fantasy, the City of London became and remained one of the pre-eminent financial centres of the world.

This transformation was underpinned by the leadership of a tight-knit group of people who led the Bank of England in this period. Among this group of people, the innovation was greeted with open arms, and it fed an appetite for more. The flaunting of the rules started to take up a recurrent excuse: if we do not do it, someone else will. In a 1963 letter, a Bank of England official wrote: 'It is par excellence an example of the kind of business which London ought to do both well and profitably. . . . If we were to stop business here, it would move to other centres with a consequent loss of earning for London.'[23] Another argument used related to the advantages of the free market and international financial flows to ease geopolitical tensions. In a 1961 speech, Bank of England official Bolton claimed that expanding financial flows would help address Cold War issues with the Soviet Union.[24] Looking back at this statement from 2022, we can appreciate all its irony and mistakenness; but this argument dominated policymakers' beliefs for a long time.

At the eve of the Suez crisis, Midland held half of the world market in eurodollars. By 1962, that share had fallen to just 3% as other British, American, and Japanese banks quickly followed suit. The eurodollar thus became an extremely practical arrangement for Britain, and one moulded around the shape of the empire, a moribund global entity London had fought hard to save; until it understood, rather fortuitously, that its old imperial structure might serve a more modern, though not less powerful, purpose. The broader consequence was a widespread erosion of controls on money moving between countries and the internationalization of this philosophy of deregulation.

1970s–1980s: The Offshore Empire and Financial Deregulation

Eurodollars and eurobonds were only the beginning of post–World War II financial innovation. The success of these new financial tools inspired the bankers of the City to explore more profitable practices, underpinning the emergence and growth of the offshore system and its associated tax havens. This trend was soon mirrored by their colleagues in the United States, as both British and American financiers sought ever more creative ways to maximize profits, often exploiting legal loopholes to do so. Bankers and lawyers from around the globe eagerly embraced these new practices, making them a hallmark of modern finance. A new British capitalism emerged. Whereas in the past Britain had managed a trade surplus, the shift to finance and services gave it, in David Edgerton's analysis, a 'new internationalist political economy', where inward flows into its capital account allowed it to run a perpetual deficit.[25]

Britain was special because of its empire. The size of it—the largest empire that ever was—was only one of the reasons. Also important were the institutions and practices it dispersed globally. The British Empire and many of its outposts could rely on commercial and financial elites, which were necessary human resources to integrate and sustain such hotspots within the new financial network. Furthermore, much of the world economy until World War II was handled within the British Empire, making use of its vastness as well as of Britain's advantage as home of the first and the second industrial revolutions. And from a legal standpoint, the adoption of English common law proved to be useful for the creation of loopholes—or mismatches—that were used to pursue further financial innovations.

The combination of these factors, Palan, Murphy, and Chavagneux write, 'proved a heady cocktail',[26] generating a unique political economy that centred on the City of London and relied on a network of UK-dependent jurisdictions. With time, other important centres emerged that joined this nucleus. Tax havens were not only profitable for the City; they were a good deal for the Crown, too. Far-away imperial outposts whose economy was ailing had become a burden for London: Britain was happy to allow tax haven status if that meant—as it did—making them financially independent and relieving the need to foot their bill. That is precisely what happened in the case of the British Virgin Islands (BVI).

Once an agricultural economy, in the 1970s the BVI's finances had hit rock bottom. The economy of these four islands in the middle of the Atlantic Ocean relied on little more than sugar cane plantations and a not-so-developed tourism industry. While the BVI had obtained autonomy from the British Empire in the 1967 and would go on to receive increased powers in 1977, they had no money to support this expanded decision-making capacity. The BVI's economic salvation came with it setting itself up as a tax haven, which offered an efficient and secret home to capital. While the overseas territory was British, the capital in question was US-centric: the eurodollar market had served American business well and it was hungry for more.

It was two international developments that brought the BVI to centre stage. The first one concerns Panama. Not unlike Gibraltar for the UK, Panama was considered the place where America's shady businesses went to hide. Increasingly tense relations between the US and Panama in the 1980s, however, meant that Panamanian lawyers—including the very Ramon Fonseca who would later become famous as one half of the Mossack Fonseca firm from whence the Panama papers came—counselled their clients to use the BVI as an alternative. The second event took place on the other side of the Pacific: in the mid-1980s, Britain agreed to leave Hong Kong, which was returned to China. The episode prompted a huge capital flight from the former British protectorate. Businesspeople from Hong Kong sought to conceal their assets from China's communist government, unleashing 'a wave of funk money as large as anything the world had yet seen'.[27] Importantly, Hong Kong's richest man, Li Ka-Shing, decided to transfer his shipping assets to a BVI-registered company. This high-profile client boosted the BVI's prestige, and soon enough many of his compatriots followed suit.

The end result was the emergence of the BVI as the main global centre for shell companies. By 1997, they were registering more than 50,000 companies a year: almost half of the world's offshore company market.[28] By 2017, BVI registered companies had assets of more than US$1.5 trillion—more than half of the value of the UK economy.[29] As shown in the examples above, intentions of the clients choosing to incorporate a company in the BVI were mixed, and sometimes—but not always—nefarious or illegal. While the substance of the business was often grey, the legal protection offered was always squeaky clean. The efficiency of the BVI-based enablers' service, and the reliance on British courts, were factors that played a big role in the popularity of these companies: investors could be satisfied that their money was protected from the whims of an unstable government. Through these financial innovations, British jurisprudence increased its presence in global finance, penetrating economies throughout the world.

On the back of such developments, the UK built—whether serendipitously, or by design—what is most likely the world's largest network of offshore centres. Britain and its overseas territories, of course, are not the only countries to blame in what is now a truly global market. The other early players were Western, including New York and a variety of American offshore jurisdictions from Delaware to Nevada. European countries such as the Netherlands, France, Austria, and others, and their former colonial dominions—as well as, of course, the banking centres of Switzerland and Luxembourg—were in the game too. By the late twentieth century, the connections between these nodes had been made easier by the EU services market with its various opt-outs for London. More recent entrants—reflecting the shift of power in global finance—are from the East: new financial centres in 'emerging' economies such as Dubai, Hong Kong, and Singapore.[30] But by the beginning of the twenty-first century, London's three-layered grouping of offshore structures—termed, by Nicholas Shaxson, its 'spiderweb'—accounts for over a third of all international bank assets worldwide; and with the City of London, this brought the total to nearly a half.[31]

The size of the network around London means that it is very difficult to distinguish it from other networks and centres. However, Shaxson's spiderweb remains a useful sketch. The web's inner ring revolves around the three remaining Crown Dependencies: Guernsey, Jersey, and the Isle of Man. These three jurisdictions are conveniently located at a very short plane ride from London and used to specialize in specific financial instruments. By 2007, these three havens hosted about $1 trillion of potentially tax-evading assets. An intermediate ring is made of 14 overseas territories, including the Cayman Islands, Bermuda, the BVI, Turks and Caicos, and Gibraltar. They are partially independent from Britain but still linked to it: many of them still have a governor appointed by the monarch, with varying degrees of authority.[32] Their final appeal court is the Privy Council in London. Finally, the outer ring comprises a more diverse array of havens, which are outside of the UK's direct control, while keeping strong links with the City of London due to their historical ties to the empire. These include Hong Kong and the Bahamas, but also places such as Dubai, Singapore, and even Astana in Kazakhstan, whose new financial centres have adopted English law according to their colonial histories or postcolonial interests.

In practice, London's large spiderweb of finance overlaps with other smaller ones. Such a set-up gives London-based service providers a global reach. This is apparent in the way they have been able to expand into new geographies via the offers of capital freedoms and common law. It also lets it be involved in business that might be forbidden in Britain, distancing the London-based financial industry from the places where the real dirty work takes place. Business that might raise too many red flags in the first or second ring is often conducted in the outer outposts of the network. In the words of a Jersey professional quoted by Nick Shaxson: 'We in Jersey regarded Gibraltar as totally subprime. This was where you put the real monkey business'.[33] By the late twentieth century there was a new wave of emerging markets, constituting a fourth ring of the global financial system.

1990s–2000s: Post-Communism and
the Rise of Londongrad

While the collapsing British Empire was providing ways for people to move through the globalizing economy with little trace, another empire was to enter its final stages, too—the Soviet one. After the fall of the Soviet Union in 1991, things moved fast in a chaotic policy of voucher privatizations recommended by neoclassical economists. By 1994, Russia had 40 million shareholders: more than half the number of the much bigger market of the 'stock-crazy United States' at the time.[34] In only five years, a wholly state-owned economy of a 9,000 km-wide landmass rich with natural resources transformed, to the point that in 1996, 80% of it was in private hands, much of it held by a small circle of new Russian oligarchs. That was a far greater proportion of private ownership than found in the EU's single market.

Russia was thrown into capitalism but lacked almost every institution to make capitalism work as is imagined by its enthusiasts. Instead, it had oligarch-owned banks, politically dependent courts, and an absence of almost all features of a well-regulated market economy. For financiers looking for mismatches between regulation and opportunity, this was a time to make serious money. The first decade threw the bulk of the Soviet citizenry into abject penury, while providing a crooked casino for those who already knew or could pay off the manager. This illusion came to a head with the economic crisis of 1998, after which its economy shrunk to half the size it was a decade earlier.

The only people who prospered in the new Russia were a tiny layer of the super-rich and a slightly larger group of skilled and educated professionals who had the ingenuity and skills to thrive. By 1999, the top 10% of the population owned half of the nation's wealth. Crucially, their prosperity was not achieved with new business and new technologies, but by capturing pieces of the old state. Key among these were the country's sprawling natural resources: oil fields and nickel mines, but also export permits and even government bank accounts. Once conquered, this loot was whisked out of the country. In the period from 1991 to 1999, between $100 and $150 billon in estimated capital flight left Russia.[35] Chrystia Freeland, the FT's Moscow correspondent in the 1990s (who went on to become Canada's Minister of Foreign Affairs), recounts a Russian friend telling her: 'Everything Marx told us about communism was false. But it turns out that everything he told us about capitalism was true'.[36]

The pact President Boris Yeltsin sealed with the oligarchs in 1996 power-charged the rise of this small caste of Russia's super-rich and super-powerful. In exchange for propping up Yeltsin's ailing rule, the oligarchs took de facto control of significant portions of government. But Vladimir Putin had different plans. After his surprising rise to power in 2000, Putin took a different route: he made it very clear that the control stayed with him and him alone. From then onward, Russia became essentially an 'adhocracy', in which 'the true elite is defined by service to the needs of the Kremlin rather than any specific institutional or social identity',[37] which naturally tended towards kleptocracy.[38] Power in Russia became diffuse, with an army of officials and acolytes trying to anticipate what Putin wants, without necessarily getting a direct order, in exchange for ample benefits.[39] The stealing could and did continue, but only for those who accepted the regime's unwritten conditions. For those who didn't, there was the door, or rather the penal colony—former oligarch Mikhail Khodorkovsky's tale being the showcase of this new policy.

To make full use of offshore possibilities, Russian lawmakers created offshore territories that would act as springboard for such flows. Starting from the mid-1990s, special federal regulations allowed several regions of the Russian Federation to obtain preferential tax status: these included Kalmykia, Ingushetia, Altai, Buryatia, Evenkia, Mordovia, and Chuvashiya, and the cities of Uglich, Kursk, and Smolensk.[40] Such spots were used as transshipment points for capital to be sent abroad. A conservative estimate puts funds shipped from there at $2 billion per year. A variant of the shell company emerged: branches of large companies mushroomed in close proximity or even at the same address. In Elista, Kalmykia, 249 Lenin Street housed 145 companies, including outposts of the oil giants Lukoil and Sibneft.[41] In the following decades, capital flight intensified further. According to the Central Bank of Russia, from 1994 until the first quarter of 2019 a total of $784 billion in net private capital left Russia, while some economists put the figure as high as $1.3 trillion.[42] This is equivalent to about half the size of the economy in this period.

Russia wasn't the only country that was changing according to global expectations. All post-communist states underwent a 'triple transition', as famously formulated by Offe and Adler:[43] politically, from monopartitism to a pluralist democracy; economically, from a planned to a market economy; and socially, from a state-controlled to an independent civil society. That was the liberal dream, underpinned by the belief in the ultimate success of the Washington Consensus and emboldened by the Zeitgeist of the End of

History.[44] And yet as exemplified by Russia's striking case, things often ended up unfolding quite differently.

In Central Asia, too, the forces of globalization did not work as hoped. Instead of allowing competitive political parties, during the 1990s Central Asia's rulers, all of them former Soviet officials, consolidated power, increasingly marginalized opposition movements and structured their economies in such a way as to loot state assets through insider privatization.[45] The 2000s brought a further deterioration of governance: as geopolitical competition intensified, Vladimir Putin made Central Asia a strategic priority for his regime. China, too, increased its engagement with the region. These regimes found it easy to establish a common language with the tight-fisted rulers of Central Asian states. As a consequence, the authoritarian model solidified and prospered.[46]

In parallel, these countries were also opening up to the West. Astana, Baku, and Moscow became embedded in transnational networks, with both the light and dark sides of globalization prominently on display. While whisking away funds stolen from their publics, ruling elites and oligarchs learned to use the might of the legal protection offered in the West to list their companies and settle disputes in an environment where law can be trusted, as well as their ample reputation management opportunities, to shield themselves from criticism. These elites, too, started using offshore-registered companies to conceal stolen funds and use them to buy real estate, goods, and lifestyle in the most prestigious addresses in the world.

At the other end of post-communist Eurasia, the transition countries are generally assumed to have avoided the excesses of hydrocarbon-rich former Soviet states. But Balkan elites underwent a specific transition which enabled klepotocracy. Former Yugoslavia occupied a geopolitically important place during the Cold War: due to its function as a cushion zone between the West and the area under Soviet control, it was most often able to maintain good relations with both blocs. Thanks to the relatively open character of their country, high-placed managers and traders had the opportunity to live and work abroad, acquiring networks that they were able to use during the grey transition years. In this sense, Yugoslav republics possessed a category of people who could be seen as 'pre-capitalism capitalists',[47] unlike other communist countries that did not possess this openness.[48] The economy had a mixed character: neither a pure command economy, nor fully market-oriented, it placed focus on workers' self-management and it introduced a third type of ownership in law that was neither private, nor public—but 'social'. This interesting albeit often confusing legal category (social owner-ship was referred to as 'of everyone and of no one') gave privatization an added layer of complexity.

Before oligarchs could 'prey on the state', as had happened in many other post-communist countries including South East European nations such as Albania and Bulgaria,[49] in successor Yugoslav countries it was the state that had to consolidate ownership first, while later proceeding to distribute it to politically connected actors.[50] The violent disintegration of Yugoslavia worsened the situation by drawing attention away from undue enrichment and allowing for many practices to go almost unnoticed in real time. As a result, while the sums of money involved were relatively smaller than those embezzled by post-Soviet elites due to the sheer differences in the economies' size and structure, the detrimental effects on the population remained similar—with a distinct rise in economic inequality across Central and Eastern Europe[51] and a particularly stark perception of it in the Balkans.[52] In the meantime, the weak pull of a painfully slow and often inconsistent EU accession process may have encouraged as much as it deterred corruption among the new elite.[53]

The Growth of the Enabling Industries

The services that these new elites desired and accessed in the marketplace of global finance were identical. Such services included, but were by no means limited to, the financial sphere: bank accounts, trusts, limited liability partnerships, and special purpose vehicles. The financial sector was not the only industry to experience a revolution in the second half of the twentieth century. In parallel, enabling services sprung up in a range of other areas. With the globalization of business and finance often come exemptions for investors from the rules and laws of the territory in which their money is invested; this in turn creates markets in all sorts of ancillary services. The vast majority of around 2,500 bilateral investment treaties between states have been signed from the 1980s onwards.[54] Almost all of these come with carve-outs and special privileges for companies and corporate officers of the foreign investors. But it is not just states and companies that gain specific rights through investment. It is wealthy individuals.

The classic example of these new enabling services to the global elite is the global passport. Being able to choose the destination for money went hand in hand with being able to pick your residency—or passport—of choice. The practice of purchasing citizenship through financial means dates back to ancient times. As early as two millennia ago, individuals of wealth and means could acquire Roman citizenship through monetary transactions: the New Testament book of Acts even includes a conversation between Paul the Apostle and a Roman centurion who claimed to have secured his citizenship through a significant financial investment.[55] Roman citizenship conferred several privileges, including unrestricted travel across the Empire (reminiscent of the modern-day Schengen Area), the right to vote, and immunity against torture and capital punishment, except in cases of treason. But in more recent times, economic citizenship through investment programs dates back to the twentieth century, with the emergence of the first modern-day citizenship by investment (CBI) program launched in St Kitts and Nevis in 1984. The Citizenship by Investment Act of St Kitts and Nevis allowed for citizenship to be obtained through a financial investment of $250,000. The Commonwealth of Dominica followed suit and launched its own CBI program in 1993, while several Pacific countries offered passports in exchange for investments.

However, the most enduring and influential schemes were offered in Europe and the British overseas territories. Countries such as Cyprus, Malta, Montenegro, and the UK itself soon followed St Kitts and Nevis to offer extremely successful golden visa (Residency by Investment, RBI) and golden passport (CBI) schemes for investors in the 2000s–2010s. Scholars have argued that this practice challenges traditional notions of citizenship, as it allows wealthy individuals to bypass the usual processes of naturalization and instead purchase citizenship rights.[56] These RBI and CBI schemes are products of the structural changes wrought by the ends of empires. It is hardly a coincidence that some of the first movers were former British colonies whose industries served the elites of postcolonies that benefited from independence. But as Kristin Surak points out, golden passports have a broader economic logic of the 'double layering of inequality'—it is the rich within a poor country (intrastate inequality) that seek the rights of citizens of rich countries (interstate inequality). The naïve view that golden passports are a legitimate innovation against inequalities in citizenship is belied by the fact that those that can afford to buy a second citizenship or residency were able to do so because of the success of their first.[57] This market serves victors, not victims.

Serving the world's winners is a lucrative market. London-headquartered Henley & Partners, founded in 1997 and present today in 40 countries worldwide, proudly markets itself as the 'global leader in residence and citizenship by investment'.[58] Aside from advising private clients on how to make use of these opportunities, service providers also started to counsel governments on how to create—and even run—them. Henley's website states that the firm has raised over $10 billion in foreign direct investment by being involved in the 'design, set-up, and operation of the world's most successful residence and citizenship programs'.[59] This is another instance in which service providers did not only respond to a demand, but helped generate it, too.

Shaping and defending reputations soon became another cornerstone service sought after by these elites as they looked to internationalize their capital and become global citizens themselves. Many PR companies— epitomized by Bell Pottinger—hurried to help clients shape hearts and minds to suit their preferred image of themselves. A former advisor to Prime Minister Margaret Thatcher, Lord Tim Bell used his experience and connections to found the prominent PR firm in 1987. 'Morality is a job for priests', he stated in a 2018 *New York Times* article, 'Not PR men'.[60] The firm quickly rose to fame for its high-profile clients, including dictators, multinational corporations, and controversial political figures. One of the defining moments in its history was its work for the Gupta family, which had ties to South African President Jacob Zuma: Bell Pottinger became embroiled in a scandal after it was accused of promoting a racially divisive narrative to deflect attention from the Gupta family's corruption, which led to the PR firm's collapse in 2017.

Lord Bell is not the only political figure to engage in political counselling and narrative shaping on behalf of clients in authoritarian or semiauthoritarian regimes, Tony Blair being another prominent example, advising the corrupt president of Kazakhstan.[61] As a whole, the PR industry keeps going from strength to strength, being worth over £15 billion in the UK alone, with a jump of almost 8% between 2018 and 2019[62] and a swift recovery after a short pandemic blip.[63] As knowledge is power, business intelligence and private security firms provided another avenue to acquire information on one's adversaries and to keep them in check (see Chapter 12). When the power of narrative shaping was not enough, the legal industry was there to help by intimidating and suing critics into silence (more about this in Chapter 13).

From Ashes to Cashiers

Professional services have today become the sacred cow of the UK's economy. In summer 2022, with inflation and skyrocketing prices affecting industry and consumers, economic hardship of scale unseen since the 1980s swept through much of Britain. But the services sector did not only hold; it prospered. Between May and June that year, its overall turnover increased by 5.7%, to £240 billion; and within professional services, the legal sector had it best, with a 10% jump in revenues in the same period. The place it occupies in the country's economy is hard to overstate. According to the same Office of National Statistics (ONS) data, professional services now account for a huge 78% of the UK's total economic output and provide an even more gargantuan share of UK jobs, at 82%.[64] This is the largest among the world's leading economies of the G7.

While a move from the primary and secondary to the tertiary sector is common throughout the developed world, in the UK this has happened in a particularly brash and consequential way. This chapter has argued that the seeds of the dominance of the financial and related services were sown during the British Empire and its aftermath. The connection between financial regulators and financial powers was already blurred during the imperial period and helps explain why it was relatively easy to meld British financial institutions to the will of the professionals during the moment of transformation itself. The elites of the finance sector have pushed for deregulation and obtained it. Today, therefore, the state's capacity to establish limits is very weak relative to the private sector's capacity to evade them. A series of ideologically driven and tactical compromises in favour of free movement of capital have led to a new strategic environment where regulators are always on the back foot. Unfettered globalization of the international financial architecture did the rest. Capital flows 'towards the place that will do the least to impede them':[65] jurisdictions with the greatest opportunities and the lowest standards. The UK has thus become a nation of cashiers—or, to use Bullough's word, financial 'butlers'—cashing in on the wealth acquired (and administered) anywhere else in the world, while rising from the ashes of the British Empire.

Londongrad emerged in an era in which two empires—British and Soviet—declined. In the wake of decolonization, a new era of 'statist globalization' emerged with state-owned companies and sovereign wealth funds from former colonies managing global investments and portfolios. Some political economists allege that their interests are not national but those of a 'transnational capitalist class'.[66] The relationship between British enablers and post-communist elites appears to demonstrate the illicit aspects of the emergence of this new class. At least £1.5 billion (comprising 150 land titles) was purchased by Russians who are either accused of corruption or have close ties to the Kremlin. At least £830 million of UK property is owned by Russians through shell companies based in Crown Dependencies. Transparency International UK calculated these figures, identifying at least 81 law firms, 86 UK banks, and 177 UK education institutions involved in these transactions.[67]

Londongrad's indulgences are not exceptional but have emerged in this much wider context of the developments of global capitalism. The net social impact of the transnationalization of finance is huge. Worldwide, the 2020 State of Tax Justice report by the Tax Justice Network estimates that $427 billion is lost to tax abuse—*yearly*.[68] Of this sum, almost $245 billion is down to multinational corporations' 'tax optimization' efforts (which involves shifting money into tax havens to underreport their profits). The remaining $182 billion are what wealthy individuals hide beyond the reach of the law offshore every year. On its own, this latter figure corresponds to approximately 26 times the annual GDP of Somalia.

The next two chapters will introduce, respectively, the demand and supply that compose this market of post-communist elites and UK service providers. Some services were specifically tailored to Londongrad residents, but others would be attracted to the wider population of the wealthy. Known as, depending on their fortune, high-net-worth or ultra-high-net-worth individuals (HNWIs/UHNWIs), these customers were, and still are, courted by entire, often ready-made, industries. Lawyers, bankers, accountants, and PR specialists scrambled to provide better and shinier services to clients. In so doing they were not merely meeting demand but *generating* it. They offered new products to the market that kleptocrats and oligarchs may not have otherwise imagined. The supply of services and the demands of Londongrad are codependent.

3

Demand

Who Wants What

London is to the billionaire as the jungles of Sumatra are to the orang-
utan . . . We're proud of that . . . I mean, we're quite proud of it . . .
and let's be clear we're . . . we have mixed feelings.
                                        —Boris Johnson, Mayor of London[1]

'I have often amused myself with thinking how different a place London is
to different people', wrote James Boswell, the biographer of Samuel Johnson,
at the end of the eighteenth century.[2] This thought continues to capture the
many facets of one of the world's most exciting urban centres. Depending on
your inclinations, passions, and interests, it is possible to experience London
from an endless variety of angles. In a place where diversity is encouraged
and celebrated, being a Londoner is a great equalizer.

At the same time, Boswell's observation is almost prescient in pointing
to the increasing wealth inequality that characterizes its dwellers. The UK's
wondrous capital has become a magnet for elites around the world, including those who have earned their money through corrupt or dubious
business practices. The city offers no shortage of tailor-made services for the
moneyed elites—helping to shore up demand for a diverse array of enablers.
Consequently, central London real estate has opened itself to the best offer,
pushing the middle classes further and further into the outskirts while
gutting some central districts of social life and making the profits for ab-
sentee owners and landlords as their assets continue to appreciate in value.[3]

Officials of some conservative authoritarian states rail against the 'de-
pravity' of the liberal West, while their children, spouses, extended families,
and even themselves lead exuberant lives in cities such as London. Lavish
townhouses, luxury apartments in the best postal codes, access to the most
exclusive shopping, world-class education, and of course no shortage of arts,

culture, and entertainment—many of these elements that make London a world capital are also those that attract the wealth of kleptocrats. But London's world capital status is not a given. It is achieved by meeting the demands of communities of wannabe 'global citizens'.

Post-communist elites are one such community. Their Londongrad is not merely a means to an end but a home from home. This chapter gives an overview of the main steps followed by kleptocrats intent on making the most of what the UK in general, and London in particular, have to offer—from how to hide it to how to spend it, how to legitimize it and how to leverage it—demonstrating how each of these areas has been met with the service provided by a set of enablers. However, not all post-Soviet elites are equal and not all receive equal treatment on arrival. Assessing the various elites from kleptocracies in terms of their relation with their home country's regime, three primary types emerge: we will call them here the *loyalists*, the *fencesitters*, and the *opponents*, analyzing them in the second part of the chapter.

The Kleptocrat's Demands

The demand side of the transnational kleptocracy problem is in one sense astonishingly simple. Rents accrued from control of national assets must go through several stages. Money laundering is a part but not the whole of this process. But the primary object is not money; it is the person themselves, their family, and their key allies in business. These persons require four things from the UK. These are to be hidden, protected, legitimized, and global. Each of the nine professional indulgences explored in Chapters 5–13 service at least one of these four demands. While each demand may appear in any of the indulgences, there is progression from hiding and protecting in the earlier indulgences to legitimizing and becoming globally influential in the latter ones. In this section we draw from a variety of examples from post-communist elites and beyond to outline these demands.

Being Hidden

The first thing a kleptocrat, oligarch, or exile must do is hide or obscure certain parts of their past, and their sources of wealth especially. Whether they are from the former Soviet Union or another world region, this demand is the same. In order to hide the origins of their wealth and status they must create complex webs of shell companies and bank accounts in a variety of jurisdictions. Through these structures, monies of various origins flow, both legitimate and illegitimate, masking the original source. These monies can then be utilized in the purchasing of shares of legitimate companies (often in banking, extractives, and telecoms) and placed into structures in more 'reputable' places. To achieve the height of secrecy, the UK offers a series of wealth management products including trusts which avoid many of the checks of bank accounts (see Chapter 5). In addition to moving money to a UK bank account, a kleptocrat or oligarch may attempt to form a company in Britain.

Various kleptocrats have used the UK in a similar way to post-Soviet elites. A striking case is that of James Ibori, the former state governor of the oil-rich Delta State in Nigeria between 1999 and 2007. Ibori was already a convicted small-time criminal in the UK when he embarked on his political career in Nigeria. His closeness to dictator Sani Abacha made him climb the ranks fast. Engaging in 'financial criminality on an eye-watering scale', Ibori set out to make the most of his position, in a textbook example of abuse of entrusted power for private gain. Misappropriation included funds from state telecoms and oil companies. All the while, his ability to create a constituency of people who are close to him is what allowed him to strengthen and keep a certain standing in his state, even after his conviction on 10 counts of money laundering and conspiracy to defraud in 2012.

Due to the depth of the five-year-long investigation and the considerable court battle that ensued, the Ibori case provides us one of the clearest cases of what it takes to be a fully fledged enabler, in the form of his lawyer Bhadresh Gohil.[4] The boutique lawyer embraced the illicitness of the source of wealth, helping Ibori create 'unnecessary and fictitious consulting services through corporate shell[s]'.[5] With Gohil's help, Ibori funnelled the ill-gained proceeds into real estate in the UK—six houses in London including in Hampstead, Regent's Park, St John's Wood, and a mansion in Shaftesbury, Dorset—as well as other luxury goods, including the attempt to purchase a Canadian Bombardier Challenger Jet worth £20 million.

In a clear-cut example of wilful enabling, Gohil described Ibori as a 'significant tribal leader with family connections in the oil industry going back to the 1950s, of substantial wealth, who is occasionally called upon to participate in political events' on a due diligence form for a Barclays bank account. According to Jonathan Benton, a former Metropolitan Police officer who investigated the case, the incongruence with reality could not have been bigger: at the time when Gohil was writing those words, Ibori was 'a convicted shoplifter in the UK, using a false identity, with a Governor's salary below £20,000 a year, who was found to have been laundering money for dictator Sani Abacha through a Credit Suisse account'.[6]

While being Ibori's key fixer, Gohil was far from the only UK-based enabler that assisted the Nigerian politician. Banker Elias Nimoh Preko[7] left his position at Goldman Sachs when the bank refused to take Ibori as a client, likewise entering into a work relationship with him with his eyes wide open. Other enablers in the Ibori case included fiduciary agent Daniel Benedict McCann and corporate financier Lambertus de Boer. They are among the few enablers who have been conclusively convicted by the British courts.

Being Protected

A second demand of the kleptocrat which London serves is protection— the protection afforded by the rule of law. It might be intuitive to think that those who hide illicit wealth look for loopholes in the rule of law, but this is true only to a certain extent. Part of the kleptocrats' way of navigating the obstacles that may hinder them in making use of their wealth relies, in fact, on the *strong* rule of law offered by the UK court system and the rules and regulations that govern its financial markets.

Their wealth, having been legalized by the offshore world, must be made further safe from predatory hands. Having established themselves in the UK, a kleptocrat, oligarch, or exile may attempt to list their companies on major world stock markets such as the LSE (see Chapter 6), with enablers working to clean up the history of the individual and the company in a glossy listing prospectus, explaining away or hiding any allegations of historic impropriety. There is no safer place from which to do this than as a resident or citizen of a country governed by the rule of law (Chapter 7). Security (their own, their families', and their wealth's) is a big concern for elites from authoritarian countries. The integration of monies into sectors such as the property market (Chapters 8 and 9), as exemplified above, is another step towards protection.

Creating a bank account or listing a company also protects a person's assets from the type of corporate 'raiding' often seen in the post-Soviet space. Conflicts over company ownership and other business matters can also be fought and settled in the UK where an industry of legally explaining questionable wealth thrives (see Chapter 9). 'The courts are arguably the only part of the British system that is not corrupt. You cannot corrupt a British judge, it just does not work. Oligarchs know it and take advantage of it',[8] says Mark Hollingsworth, a journalist and coauthor of *Londongrad*[9] who has long studied Russian oligarchs' methods and tactics in the UK. A typical example is extradition: British judges will refuse to extradite defendants if they are unconvinced that they will receive fair trial in their country of origin. Oligarchs can be very litigious: they often sue their business partners and, feeling well protected by the British legal system, they like to do so in England. 'For them, *litigation is better than sex*,' Hollingsworth says, quoting a sentence he heard from one of them. 'They like this feeling of being able to control, dominate'.

A further reason for oligarchs and elites to choose London as their jurisdiction is the illiberal nature of its libel law, which increases the possibility of SLAPP suits and 'cease and desist' letters often addressed to journalists and researchers—as will be treated in Chapter 13. These clients often bring with them multi-million dollar cases, with suitably high fees (often £1000 per hour or more) for the lawyers that would serve them. The London legal scene responded eagerly to this demand, offering no shortage of specialized professionals with the right linguistic, as well as legal and commercial skills—and marketing them openly. For instance, even a barristers' chambers was happy to promote the work for their wealthy Russian-speaking clients almost as a badge of honour or sign of success.[10] This illustrates again how, before Russia's full-scale invasion of Ukraine in 2022, it was commonplace for lawyers to market their services by indicating that they are ready to serve such clients.

The most jarring examples perhaps concern the offspring and relatives of those politicians who continuously rail against the West. The lavish London lifestyle of Polina Kovaleva—the stepdaughter of Russia's foreign minister Sergey Lavrov—came under scrutiny only after it was posted on social media (to much retweeting and media attention) by Russian anticorruption activist Maria Pevchikh after the start of the Ukraine war. A student at Imperial College London, Kovaleva bought a £4.4 million apartment with cash when she was just 21. Kovaleva's social media feeds revealed a constant array of dreamy vacations and appearances in stylish London haunts. In this context, her cash purchase of real estate in London looks like 'a textbook example of unexplained wealth', wrote Pevchikh.[11] Having geopolitical circumstances changed, UK authorities finally listened, and put Kovaleva on the ad hoc Russian sanctions list issued in late March 2022.[12]

Nowadays, law firms need to exercise more caution. The start of Russia's full-scale attack on Ukraine in February 2022 has been a game changer, and the narrative espoused by the British establishment has changed accordingly. In 2012, then-mayor of London Boris Johnson casually commented that 'if one oligarch feels defamed by another oligarch—it is London's lawyers who apply the necessary balm to the ego'.[13] This stands in stark contrast with his March 2022 statement as prime minister, after the start of Russia's full-scale invasion of Ukraine: 'For the oligarchs and the super-rich who can afford these sky-high costs, the threat of legal action has become a new kind of lawfare . . . we must put a stop to its chilling effect'.[14]

Indeed, Russian and Eurasian clients have been top buyers of legal services in the UK. According to 2018 data[15] about foreign litigants in commercial cases, Kazakhstan and Russia were in second and third place, with 36 litigants from Kazakhstan and 29 from Russia, while first-placed USA had only one litigant more than Kazakhstan, despite having a population 17 times larger. Ukraine ended in sixth place with 25 litigants. Moreover, a significant number of the 28 Cypriot litigants are likely to be companies owned by citizens of former Soviet states (or 'naturalized' Cypriots using their newly bought Cypriot passports). Why is the UK legal system so popular? The probity of the British judges and the skills of English lawyers are not the only reason why London's courts have proven to be a receptacle of clients from the post-Soviet space. The sociologist Elizabeth Schimpfössl has argued that the first generation of oligarchs to come to Britain sought not merely property rights but respectability.[16] Their desire for a battle in the courts may be more about the appearance of legitimacy it offers than any specific gains of the legal process, which often end in messy out-of-court settlements or large costs for both sides.

Being Legitimate

A third demand generated in London follows from the first two. This is for kleptocrats, oligarchs, and exiles to legitimize themselves. These demands include those for legal defence (Chapter 9) and offence (Chapter 13). However, to social scientists, legitimacy is about more than the law but extends to beliefs, norms, and forms of consent that a person or entity is legitimate.[17] In this context, wealth is much more easily hidden if the beliefs about a purported businessman are broadly positive, if his reputation is habitually affirmed in public, and if respected persons and entities consent to receive his patronage. In the UK, there is formally no greater endorsement than that from a member of the British Royal Family. While for decades the British public has looked upon the royals with a mixture of affection and amusement, for elites from kleptocracy who have seek the accoutrements of absolute power, their cache is unrivalled.

The links between Kazakh oil and gas official Timur Kulibayev and Prince Andrew show how characters from dubious corruption hotspots seek out relationships with members of the Western elite, to then establish suspicious money flows into Europe and the United States. In June 2007, Prince Andrew sold his 12-bedroom mansion in Ascot, named Sunninghill Park, to Kulibayev, whose net worth runs into billions of dollars. How Kulibayev had acquired that fortune has been subject to much scrutiny, but his marriage to Dinara, the daughter of the first president of Kazakhstan, Nursultan Nazarbayev, certainly aided his path to the top. Kulibayev purchased Sunninghill using a complex web of offshore companies, designed to hide the house's ultimate owner and make it difficult for would-be investigators. The purchase was controversial because the £15 million Kulibayev had paid Andrew for the mansion was £3 million more than the asking price.[18] The building was in such a state of disrepair that it later transpired that the mansion was worth about only £8 million on the open market and possibly as little as £6.4 million at auction, a striking £8.6 million less than what Kulibayev paid.[19] There is no denying that Andrew was overpaid.

A spokesman for Kulibayev said in 2010 that the high price was justified because 'at the time of purchase we were told that there were several interested parties and therefore we simply paid the price that was requested.'[20] This, in itself, is difficult to believe as the dilapidated house had already been on the market for five years. As for Andrew, who was the UK's Special Representative for International Trade and Investment at the time, with an extensive portfolio of work in Kazakhstan, his reaction was one that can be (generously) classified as wilful blindness: 'It's not my business the second the price is paid', the Duke said. 'If that is the offer, I'm not going to look a gift horse in the mouth and suggest they have overpaid me.'[21]

Guidance issued some years later suggests that transactions that do not make clear business sense are a red flag for money laundering.[22] While the business sense of the sale is disputed here, the reputational kudos for an oligarch winning favour with a British member of the Royal Family are quite clear. In this context, the additional £8 million that Kulibayev paid for the house begins to look like a 'quid pro quo': shifting from Andrew simply selling his house to an unquestioning buyer to one where he was helping to give respectability to a controversial oligarch.[23] But Kulibayev's efforts do not seem to have been in vain: in 2011, it was reported that Andrew tried to help the Kazakh businessman become a client of Coutts, the bank used by the British Royal Family. His request left the bank in an awkward position. In the words of a senior source at the bank: 'Kazakh oligarchs are the sort of people we generally don't touch with a bargepole',[24] although Coutts's record regarding money-laundering controls suggest otherwise.[25] Buckingham Palace responded by saying that Andrew, who 'works to encourage economic growth in the United Kingdom', was simply trying to help Coutts make contact with overseas markets.[26]

This case thus exemplifies the links between the enablers servicing the real estate market, the companies providing offshore services, the banking system, and the power of high-ranking members of the Western elite to bring them all together. For Andrew, his controversial business deals involving Kazakhstan did not end there. It has emerged, for instance, that he helped a Greek sewage company and a Swiss finance house pursue a £385 million contract in Kazakhstan, using his relationship with Kazakh oligarch Kenges Rakishev—a Kulibayev associate who brokered the sale of Andrew's house[27]—to act as a 'fixer'.[28] (At the time Buckingham Palace said that claims that the Duke acted as a so-called fixer were untrue.[29]) Andrew's appointment as the UK's Special Representative for International Trade may be understood in terms of the perceived opportunities and challenges of doing business with kleptocracies. Before he fell from grace due to the adverse publicity surrounding his relationship with the convicted paedophile Jeffrey Epstein, Andrew held 230 patronages. The quid pro quo of royal patronage for a member of a kleptocratic elite is clear: investment in the UK for legitimacy from the British establishment.

Being Influential

A fourth key demand of elites of kleptocratic origin is exclusive access to pathways which allow themselves or their children to become globally influential. The British establishment offers such opportunities and is a means to the end of passing as a bona fide member of the global elite. Philanthropy and political donations are often cited as mechanism of influence. However, besides these political goods (which we will look at in Chapters 10 and 11) and related security goods (such as the use of private intelligence which we will consider in Chapter 12), there are basic social goods which serve as entry criteria to join the global elite. Language and educational credentials are therefore key commodities.

Educational institutions in Britain are among the most sought-after in the world. Private boarding schools start at £35,000 per year, per child, which is hardly affordable for politicians from developing countries, whose yearly salaries sometimes fail to match this fee. And yet many still do send their progeny to school and university in the UK. A 2021 Carnegie report[30] revealed that illicit financial flows are utilized by anglophone African elites to pay fees. It is estimated that from Nigeria and Ghana alone, they amount to £30 million annually. For these elites, this is also a 'means of reinforcing their family's preeminent social, political, and economic status from one generation to the next',[31] thus further hardening social mobility in their countries of origin. Sometimes, enablers have more than one function: the aforementioned Bhadresh Gohil sent tuition fees for James Ibori's children from an offshore account controlled by him.

Like education, healthcare for the few is also the norm in kleptocratic countries. Here, too, private service provision in the UK comes in handy. During the COVID-19 crisis, many elites were thrown into disarray, not being able to get access to basic healthcare, because their doctors were all in London (or Paris, or other world capitals).[32] For years, the Nigerian elite could ignore the crumbling state of the health system in their country by seeking treatment abroad. The lack of investment in health resulted in 0.5 hospital beds per 1,000 people (for a population of roughly 200 million), far below the World Health Organization's threshold.[33] Sitting President Muhammad Buhari spent five months getting treated in London for an undisclosed ailment. In 2019, Gabon's President Ali Bongo recovered in Morocco from a stroke, while Robert Mugabe, Zimbabwe's former leader, died in a hospital in Singapore. But when crisis hit in spring 2020, these elites were grounded, and the first victim of the pandemic was a former state oil company executive, Suleiman Achimugu.

Being hidden, protected, legitimate, and influential are the demands of the clients which we study in this book. Figure 3.1 relates these demands to how they are met by enablers.

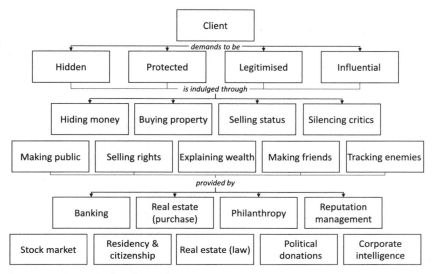

Figure 3.1 Demand and supply

Three Kinds of Client

From privacy and property rights to establishing relationships and global identities, it is not hard to see what makes London in high demand for the world's kleptocrats, oligarchs, and exiles. While these three types appear static and have some basis in law, the political relationship they have with those in power is more dynamic. The alternative set of categories adopted below allows us to understand how the elites which are indulged by British professionals are situated with respect to the politics of their home countries. Here, it matters less whether you are a member of a ruling family, a wealthy oligarch, or an exile who has gained asylum or is now a UK citizen. What matters is whether you are in or out of the influential networks which shape who has access to power and wealth. Are you a naturalized British citizen and nominal exile who continues to do business in your country of origin and retains fealty to its elite or the lonely young man from a family kleptocracy who speaks out against his grandfather, the president? Are you willing to be a Trojan horse within your new-found home, are you organising against the kleptocratic government of your home country, or are you just trying to keep your head down? Three pathways are apparent: we call them the *loyalists*, the *opponents*, and the *fence-sitters*. They are each quite different clients for UK professional services, each with their own problems.

The Loyalists

The loyalists are those close to the elite in power in their country of origin. They are not necessarily kleptocrats themselves but offer important, perhaps necessary, auxiliary services, for the survival and enrichment of the kleptocratic system. They act as 'bridges' between their country and the West, pursuing goals of self-enrichment, while sometimes also acting as 'extended arms' of their country, conducting influencing operations. Quintessential examples of this type are members of the Aliyev and Pashayev families of Azerbaijan (those of the country's president and his wife) who, having made fortunes from state control of the economy, directly or through associates spent over £400 million on UK property between 2006 and 2017. Meanwhile—as will be explored in Chapter 10—they make major investments into UK universities and charities. The 'caviar diplomacy' scandal that shook the Council of Europe in 2016 (see Chapter 11) shows beyond a doubt that the intention of influencing the political elites of the West is there, alongside the investments in real estate and philanthropic donations.

But loyalists can also be oligarchic allies who have long presented themselves as exiles. While an exile may typically be an opponent or fence-sitter, they may become a loyalist in certain conditions. Roman Abramovich went to huge lengths to argue that he did not possess close ties to Vladimir Putin and the Russian government and did not receive instructions from the Russian president. In so doing, he issued a lawsuit against Catherine Belton's book *Putin's People* and her publisher, Harper Collins. Once the war in Ukraine started, however, Abramovich quickly changed gear, styling himself as a mediator between Russia and the West. In so doing, he almost had to convince people of the opposite—that he had enough good standing with the Kremlin to be up for the job. 'Had this situation occurred earlier, we would have not had to go through all this pain', said Arabella Pike of Harper Collins. The lawsuit could not have been pursued by a sanctioned person, as Abramovich became.[34]

The Fence-Sitters

Not all elites want to play politics with their money: some just want to spend it well. Still, shifting money offshore and burnishing their profile, thus becoming part of the Western crème de la crème, is a prerequisite to enjoy this wealth in full. Elites pertaining to this category sit on a spectrum: from 'insider agnostics'—such as mid-ranking business figures, or those family members who do not hold significant state roles, such as Gulnara Karimova[35](Chapter 8)—to 'nonpolitical', sometimes former or quasi-opponents, who want to enjoy their newly acquired British assets in relative peace, like Liubov Chernukhin (Chapter 11), a British citizen, yet one married to a former deputy finance minister of Russia who retained ties to Russian business after leaving office.

Some present themselves as critics of the regime, or even as victims. Yet the business they forged in kleptocratic states raise question marks over their sources of wealth and potential ties to their country of origin. Some, such as Alexander Temerko, another British citizen, operated at a high political level: Temerko worked in the Russian defence industry in the 1990s and had long-standing ties with Russian security agencies, which had made him, in his own words, essentially untouchable.[36] Others lower down the food chain, like banker Dmitry Leus (Chapter 11) have tried to position themselves as victims of the regime since relocation to London. Although Leus denies all ties to Putin and has never made any political pronouncements in the press (making him apparently a nonpolitical figure) he made millions of dollars in business in Russia by selling his banks' shares and land he had acquired in Sochi,[37] leading to a suggestion by an MP speaking under Parliamentary privilege that ties to the Russia security services must exist.[38] As these claims cannot be verified, we categorize Leus as a fence-sitter.[39]

The Opponents

The opponents of the regime are previous kleptocratic figures who decide to use their wealth and assets to agitate from abroad. They sometimes find themselves targeted by Western investigators and pressured from the regime from which they emerged. A typical example is Kazakh businessman

Mukhtar Ablyazov (Chapter 12). A former Kazakh government minister, Ablyazov was jailed in 2002 for abuse of office in a case believed to have been brought as punishment for his oppositional activities.[40] Ablyazov continued to fund opposition activities after his release but fled to the UK in 2009, accused of embezzling up to $5 billion from a Kazakh bank he chaired.[41] He was initially given asylum in the UK, but was stripped of it after he was found in contempt of the UK High Court for failing to reveal his assets and fleeing to France.[42] British judges found that Ablyazov had defrauded the bank,[43] though Ablyazov maintains the case was pursued by the Kazakh government due to political motivations.

Many such opponents are those who were once on the very inside and have all the secrets to betray. Such a person is Boris Berezovsky: having supported Vladimir Putin at the beginning of his rule and having been a very close ally of Boris Yeltsin beforehand, Berezovsky fell out with Putin, started funding opposition outlets, went into self-imposed exile, and lost much of his fortune. The bitter legal stand-off with Roman Abramovich, which he lost, left him further impoverished—by oligarch standards, at least. 'A constant presence in the courtroom was a man who wasn't there: Russia's President, Vladimir Putin', wrote author Masha Gessen of the lawsuit between the two Russian political and economic heavyweights that played out in central London.[44] Berezovsky's death in his English country villa in 2013 was never conclusively proven as a suicide and recorded as an open verdict.[45] A previously foiled plot to murder him—in 2007, British police arrested a contract killer minutes from his office[46]—throws a further shade on the matter, as does his closeness to ex-KGB spy Alexander Litvinenko, who was famously assassinated in London with a weapons-grade toxin in 2006. Several of Berezovsky's close associates have also lost their lives in the UK in circumstances which suggest Russian involvement.[47]

Generating Demand

If it was just a matter of the tapping of demand, the taps could be turned off. But what is apparent from any study of the demand side of the problem is that it is intrinsically related to and at times led by supply. In short, the UK is so much in demand because the UK has many innovative services to offer politically exposed and high-risk clients. What it offers—from centuries-old private schools in need of cash injections to a readiness to entertain libel tourism—are often not available, and not as prestigious, elsewhere. UK professional services have long shown themselves to combine elitism and nondiscrimination, being open to all those of high- or ultra-high-net worth.

One reason why this is so might be the prevailing cultural attitude that has taken shape. The underlying ethos in large swathes of the services industry is the assertion of the supremacy of capital. In a presentation from a representative of one such boutique company—now no longer accessible on the internet—we learned that foreign political figures and their families are subject to 'distinct negative bias'[48] and that going from business into politics or vice versa is not a sign of a possibly corrupted public sphere, but 'a facet of culture or also somehow aspirational'.[49]

Thus, reputation managers will help elites who move to the UK craft a 'coherent narrative' for who they are,[50] and will advise against them making 'out of place' investments that will draw attention to themselves.[51] As remarked above, such companies will often work with law firms who will be able to help the client purchase property, fend off negative attention by issuing 'cease and desist letters' to journalists and NGOs, and suggest wealth managers who can place the client's funds in safe projects that can generate even more capital. This integrated service-providing to shady elites across sectors—and its cultural normalization over the course of decades—is what has made of London a kleptocrat's heaven to enjoy, and a secure haven in which to hide.

4

Supply

The Enabler Effect

[Discreet Law has] at all times complied fully with their legal and professional obligations.

—Discreet Law's Roger Gherson on representing
Russian warlord Vladimir Prigozhin[1]

Our previous chapter focused on the demand from kleptocrats, oligarchs, and other high-risk persons from kleptocracies for British professional services. The sheer scale of the kleptocratic wealth and kleptocracy-linked elites that have entered the UK from post-communist states, most of which are not key allies of the UK, has also led increasing numbers of journalists, activists, think tankers, and academics to consider the supply side of the problem. This is not merely a matter of opportunity—the absence of effective regulation and enforcement—but of creating demand by the provision of services that allow elites to achieve forms of secrecy, protection, legitimacy, and globality that they would not otherwise attain. In this chapter we unpack these arguments and offer an account of transnational kleptocracy in terms of the supply side of the problem.

If kleptocracy were purely a matter of the internal structure of regimes, their corrupt economic systems, and what these systems require—that is, if it is exclusively a demand-side problem—we would primarily need to understand these regimes to explain the nature of this problem. Furthermore, states with large financial centres that may be targeted by elites from such regimes would merely need to place such states on a 'grey list' and then properly enforce rules which make it very difficult for money and reputations from such states to be laundered. However, many of the world's states are characterized by political economies controlled by a few, across their whole economy or a section of it, and aspects of kleptocracy are generously dispersed across all regions of the world, continuing to adapt to changing circumstances.[2]

The prevalence of kleptocratic demand is surely part of the reason why the high-risk third country list from the EU and 'grey' and 'black' lists of the FATF are so lacking. But there is also an enormous collective action problem and regulatory failure on the part of the suppliers. The FATF and EU are dominated by states with big financial services sectors and complex relationships with both allies and geopolitical competitors. This makes it impossible to recognize the sheer volume of members, would-be members, and friends which may be designated kleptocracies in whole or in part. Moreover, if EU members like Bulgaria and Malta retain vulnerability to grand corruption, then kleptocracy is a majority problem. In short, much like with drugs or alcohol, the demand side of the problem is a constant, an enduring feature of social life. Equally, far from achieving a liberal international order, democracies have always had kleptocrats in their midst and as allies. Although the emergence of postcolonial states may have increased their volume, the world has always had and will always have predatory elites.

The supply side is much more of a problem which has been created by human ingenuity. The emergence and deregulation of global financial centres—two processes which are inextricably entwined—have essentially given rise to the problem of transnational kleptocracy. As we saw in Chapter 2, London has emerged as a global financial centre via a half-century process of creating more and more opportunities for the hiding and spending of wealth. Regulation has been outsourced to the private sector while the oversight of a largely self-regulatory system is undertaken by a bewildering number of supervisory bodies. This multiplicity of supervisors is not indicative of a strong system, but one which has inconsistently reacted to crises of integrity as they have arisen. Still, many service providers face multiple regulators, fall between two, or lack any regulator at all. As the state has receded from financial services, it has lost the capacity to understand the problem, much less supervise its regulation.

From this morass of nonregulation, self-regulation, and market competition, the supply of services to meet kleptocratic demand has mushroomed. These services indulge or enable kleptocracy to the extent that they meet the four demands—secrecy, protection, legitimacy, and influence—outlined in the previous chapter. But truly effective supply not only meets demand but also creates it. To understand the nature of enabling we need to first answer some basic questions. In this chapter, we first establish the basis of the supply-side problem in the failure of the British state to effectively regulate the suppliers. We then consider the *when* and *where* of supply by looking at the difference between upstream and downstream enabling. In the third part of the chapter, we unpack the crucial *how* and *why* questions about transnational kleptocracy, looking at its mechanisms of the incumbency advantage, the alliance effect, and the enabler effect. By way of a conclusion, we say a few things about the method we apply to trace these mechanisms through our case studies.

Creating a Supply-Side Problem

Perhaps the clearest evidence of the supply side of the problem is found in the outcomes experienced by kleptocratic clients. The three kinds of clients we surveyed in Chapter 3 get differing treatments in the UK, but not in the way that regulators and rights activists would hope. Loyalists who retain ties to an incumbent political figure in a kleptocracy rarely lose their property, legal cases, or financial standing, yet opponents often do. Examples are numerous: Ablyazov's properties were seized, Berezovsky lost his claim against Abramovich, the assets of former Putin insider turned enemy Sergei Pugachev were frozen.[3] One trait is common: as long as elites keep a low profile and pose no threat to the regimes overseeing their countries of origin, they rarely need to be concerned with their futures in Britain—even if they are laundering money and reputations. It is this permissive environment for high-risk clients which demonstrates that a large part of the problem of transnational kleptocracy is found on the supply side.

Professionals in regulated industries can absolve themselves of much legal liability by filing a suspicious activity report (SAR), but unless the UK authorities step in, the system allows the deal to be completed. Services could easily be withdrawn at any point of the transaction by the professional, yet with money to be made and commissions to be earned, this seems to be the path least travelled. Those who do file suspicions in the form of a SAR encounter another problem (or an advantage, if they are an enabler): the National Crime Agency simply do not have enough time or resources to investigate the reports they receive. Between 2021 and 2022 the agency received over 900,000 SARs, the vast majority (70.77%) from banks and other financial institutions.[4] This reflects an industry which has a tendency to file 'defensive' reports: where there is any doubt over a transaction, a report gets filed. But crucially, unless the NCA steps in, the money continues to flow, the accounts remain open, and banking fees continue to accrue. Meanwhile, bank officials are absolved of any legal liability emanating from failing to report suspicion if it is subsequently discovered that money is being laundered.

Outside of the banking sector, the numbers of SARs filed are extremely low. From 2021 to 2022, only 2,859 SARs (0.32% of the total) were received from lawyers and just 780 (0.09%) from real estate agents, despite these both being big industries for kleptocratic clients.[5] The SAR reports published by the NCA also indicate that the information that is received is best used at detecting and disrupting low-value criminality. Of the cases where, following a property transaction SAR, immediate asset denial action was taken by UK law enforcement in 2020–2021, 1,202 instances relate to properties worth under £500,000, with only two instances concerning properties worth over £5 million, those most likely to be owned by kleptocrats and high-level criminals. The situation improved a little the following year, with asset denial actions taken over 13 properties worth over £5 million each.[6]

All of the industries that are regulated for money-laundering purposes have a system of supervision. However, the system is not only bewilderingly complex but seemingly ineffective. For example, according to research by UK NGO Spotlight on Corruption, almost a quarter of legal firms visited by the nine legal sector supervisors in 2019–2020 were assessed as non-compliant with anti-money-laundering rules. Seventy-one percent of firms visited by the biggest legal sector supervisor—the Solicitors Regulation Authority (SRA)—in 2020–2021 had not put in place an independent audit function to gauge the effectiveness of their anti-money-laundering policies, controls, and procedures. Fifty out of 241 (21%) of firms subject to a full on-site visit in 2020–2021 by the SRA displayed a continued failure to do proper checks on their customers.[7]

On top of the pyramid, a state body, the Office for Professional Body Anti-Money Laundering Supervision (OPBAS), formed in 2018, oversees the supervisors. Reports from OPBAS have highlighted major structural flaws in the oversight regime: gaps remaining in most enforcement frameworks, with most professional bodies not implementing an effective risk-based approach in tackling money laundering. Most professional body supervisors were also found not to have maintained an effective supervisory approach to ensure members took adequate and timely corrective actions. Enforcement actions do happen, but at a low level. In the accountancy sector, from April 2019 to April 2020, 31 memberships were cancelled, 9 were suspended, and 259 fines were issued. There are over 43,000 accountancy firms in the UK, with the largest professional accountancy body supervising 11,000 of these.[8]

Regulation in the UK hasn't been enough to address the stream of clients and cut off the demand for enablers. The examples above suggest that there are few limits to what may be sold and to whom it may be offered. We may imagine that it ought to be a straightforward task of regulation to require transparency in property ownership, to prevent aggressive litigation against major UK news outlets and researchers, and to insist that UK private schools do proper money-laundering checks. Similarly, we may assume that it is a simple question of making foreign influence transparent through a registration scheme so that light may be shone on the regime loyalists of the world's kleptocracies. But it turns out that the supply side is more complicated and raises questions of how services economies like the UK can be open for business without enabling kleptocrats. These questions are not unanswerable, but they require us to understand when, where, and how enabling occurs.

When and Where? Upstream and Downstream Enabling

Not all enabling is equal. Enablers' activities vary. Given the range of the activities that service professionals engage in to support kleptocratic behaviour—and given variations in and under-enforcement of the law—it is inevitable that most of them are legal, in the sense of not having been found to be illegal.[9] Indeed, achieving nominal compliance with the law and regulations is a key function of enabling. Far from being criminal or an 'exception to the rule', enabling is a systematic part of a global economy which flow from the highlands of wealth creation to the lowlands of spending and enjoying. Drawing on a recent article by Prelec and Soares de Oliveira,[10] we suggest that it is more useful to think of enablers in terms of mutually reinforcing layers and that the environment of enabling professionals can be more helpfully divided into upstream and downstream roles (Figure 4.1).

Upstream enablers typically enter into deals with politically exposed clients in full knowledge of their sources of their wealth and the connections which have made it possible. While offering the right skills and possessing useful contacts (often on the basis of earlier employment with a top legal firm, bank, management consultancy, or commodity trader), they mostly work alone or for boutique 'family offices' without a household name.

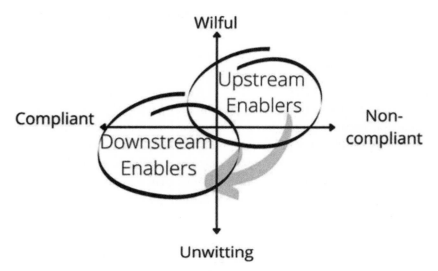

Figure 4.1 Upstream and downstream enablers
Source: Prelec and Soares de Oliveira (2023).

They often become 'fixers' at the earlier stages of the laundering process, arranging tailor-made solutions for the kleptocrat or oligarch they service. 'Upstream' does not mean exclusively in the country of the sources of wealth; it includes company formation and registration which often requires off-shore actors confirming deals made at the mine or on the veranda. Although overrepresented in media coverage, in the few legal judgements that concern enabling, and in policy discourse, they are arguably a minority.

Generally, and more subtly, but also potentially much more numerous and problematic, are downstream enablers. These enablers are usually executives in reputable banks, large financial services, and law firms which typically do not participate in the early stages of the laundering process.[11] Here, major services firms headquartered in global financial centres like London enter the fray. They enter the value chain at a later stage, allowing them to evade legal scrutiny by taking advantage of the respectability established by others. This plausible deniability means that their actions often fall within the realm of legality, even though they are integral to the process of laundering illicit funds. Despite the appearance of legitimacy, their actions remain problematic due to their contribution to the systemic nature of the problem. Moreover, these individuals and firms often justify their role as necessary for the sake of business,[12] making it difficult to identify and address their enabling activities.

The degree of involvement of an enabler also varies. Transparency International UK (TI-UK) has categorized practices that allow for active compliance, unwitting participation, wilful blindness, corruption, and complicity.[13] However, this framework assumes that the level of involvement is linear, which does not take into account the fact that compliant behaviour is not always carried out in accordance with the spirit of laws and regulations, while noncompliant behaviour may be carried out more or less consciously depending on the situation. Building on TI-UK's work, Prelec and Soares de Oliveira propose to structure the enabling of behaviour along two axes. The procedural axis ranges from behaviour that is compliant (i.e. trying to be or presents itself as lawful), to noncompliant (i.e. contradicting laws or regulations outright). The axis of (in)voluntariness refers to the degree of participation, which can be unwitting or wilful. This results in four broad groups of practices: Compliant/Unwitting, Compliant/Wilful, Noncompliant/Unwitting, and Noncompliant/Wilful (see Table 4.1).

Enabling behaviour that falls into the Compliant/Unwitting category attempts to follow the law and identify potential red flags, but efforts fall short due to a lack of awareness or negligence. Service professionals may not realize that they are facilitating corrupt sources of wealth or clients, but their lack of diligence allows the activities to proceed, nonetheless. Those who fall into the Compliant/Wilful category formally comply with the law but deliberately ignore red flags or use loopholes to facilitate corrupt activities. They may exploit ambiguities in the law or regulations to enable corrupt behaviour, while still being law-abiding professionals; the term 'legal enabler' is used to

Table 4.1 Categorization of enabling practices

Compliant / Unwitting	Enablers attempt to follow the law and identify red flags, but their efforts fall short due to a lack of awareness or negligence.
Compliant / Wilful	Enablers knowingly comply with the law but deliberately ignore red flags or use loopholes to facilitate corrupt activities.
Noncompliant / Unwitting	Enablers unintentionally disregard the law or regulations, either due to lack of knowledge or misunderstanding.
Noncompliant / Wilful	Enablers knowingly engage in behaviour that violates the law or regulations, often in exchange for financial gain or other benefits.

Source: Prelec and Soares de Oliveira (2023).

refer to lawyers who create new wealth and reputation management services for kleptocrats to operate within the law.[14] Professionals who are compliant, whether unwitting or wilful with respect to the kleptocratic origins of wealth, typically oppose the use of 'enabler', which they see as a pejorative term used by activists. We adopt the term for all professionals—including compliant ones—servicing kleptocrats as it is now in common usage and is an accurate description of what these professional services do for persons or wealth with kleptocratic origins. Compliant enabling is likely to constitute a very large majority of the professional activity on behalf of a kleptocratic source of wealth or client. It is important to remember that kleptocracy itself, though illicit, is not generally illegal both because of impunity in the country of origin and the failure of law in the countries of destination to categorize it as a form of organized crime.

Noncompliant enabling is far less common but offers necessary assistance to such persons and wealth at critical junctures in transaction chains. Enablers who fall into the Noncompliant/Unwitting category unintentionally disregard the law or regulations, either due to lack of knowledge or misunderstanding. They may not realize that their actions are in violation of the law or regulations, but their ignorance or inexperience allows corrupt activities to continue. Finally, those who fall into the Noncompliant/ Wilful category knowingly engage in behaviour that violates the law or regulations, often in exchange for financial gain or other benefits. They may actively seek out opportunities to enable corruption, and their actions are a key part of the corrupt process. More than merely being enablers, they are accessories. Given the illicit or occasionally illegal nature of this enabling activity, examples which can be properly evidenced are rare. From the examples which are explored below and elsewhere, it appears the noncompliant are only truly unwitting if they are incompetent. However, across all these categories, there are grey areas. We use the term 'wilfully unwitting' to capture those professionals who should have known better but chose not to find out. Why do they do this? This raises questions of how far geopolitics, law, and business shape the transnational kleptocratic enterprise.

How and Why? Alliance, Incumbency, and Enabling

To shift from micro questions of 'what, when, and where' enablers act to macro questions of 'if, how, and why' enabling makes a difference is to put these enablers in the wider contexts of the kleptocratic enterprises which they have wilfully or unwittingly joined. Heathershaw, Cooley, and Soares de Oliveira have tried to achieve something like this through the meta-concept of 'transnational uncivil society'.[15] This concept gives us a clue to how kleptocratic networks form. Transnational kleptocratic enterprises may begin as contractual, in the limited sense of purchasing professional services in the marketplace where the professional services companies are the patrons and the kleptocratic elites are the clients. However, in the conditions of transnational kleptocracy, this relationship may reverse where the patronal leaders of post-Soviet states lock the enablers into clientelistic relations as each party gains greater knowledge of compromised behaviours of the other.[16] Such patron–client relations or *clientelism* are 'a form of direct, contingent exchange which requires specific contractual performance'.[17]

While clientelism is typically understood at a national level between political patrons and their clients in business or the bureaucracy, it can also be extended to the transnational scale where the laundering of monies and reputations by uncivil elites takes place. Such *transnational clientelism* pertains to the 'discharging of order-making to brokers and intermediaries via an asymmetric distribution of benefits and co-optation' across borders.[18] Jana Hönke further identifies transnational clientelism as a form of 'veranda politics' in African mining ventures, which she contrasts to the 'air-conditioned' politics of transnational activism and corporate social responsibility projects. Transnational kleptocratic enterprises, however, extend from the veranda to air-conditioned spaces where they may co-opt actors in settings supposedly characterized by the rule of law.[19]

The presence of enabler practices and the formation of clientelistic networks say something important about how kleptocratic wealth is indulged. But it does not in itself explain why it is indulged. This is the primary question we seek to answer in this book. To do so we make three hypotheses from the existing literature. For the purposes of illustration, in each case we give examples of how this might work with respect to court cases and legal services.

First, we hypothesize an *alliance effect*. We postulate that indulgence is more likely to occur where the kleptocratic wealth originates in a state which is an ally or partner of the UK. One current of the academic literature suggests that 'as the politics of different national systems become more intertwined, we may expect that collective actors in one state will increasingly have strong incentives to work together with actors in others'.[20] For example, the English court is more likely to accept the evidence submitted by, and judgements of the courts and regulators of, an established partner than those of a nonpartner. Given the politicized nature of legal judgements in kleptocracies, this suggests that cooperation between states makes legal accountability for corrupt friends less likely.

How might this occur in an environment where the rule of law is supposedly pre-eminent and where judges cannot be paid off? Great powers with large markets and high regulatory capacity deploy a mixture of coercion and concession to achieve regulatory compliance and exchanges of financial information from their allies.[21] The UK, as a middle power, has lower capacity than the much larger United States or European Union. Indeed, an alliance effect with respect to anti-corruption is more likely to work in the opposite direction as an 'inside-out' effect.[22] For example, following the al-Yammah deal, British Prime Minister Tony Blair intervened in 2006 to stop a UK Serious Fraud Office investigation into bribery at the request of the Saudi government, who were threatening to withdraw security cooperation. More commonplace than this extreme case may be the tendency to accept and retain clients from states which are allied to the UK. Our hypothesis is that whether by hook or by crook, elites from UK partners are more likely to retain their property and position than those from nonpartners.

Our second hypothesis is that there is an *incumbency advantage* where elites who remain on the inside of kleptocratic states might leverage public power for private gain. The alliance effect is focused on international politics but the 'inside-out' aspect illustrated in the rare public example of Blair's intervention on the al-Yammah investigation suggests that there is a strong domestic aspect. While Saudi Arabia is certainly a UK ally, could it be that all 'incumbent' elites (loyalists and well-connected fence-sitters), even from nonpartners and adversaries, are more likely to be indulged than exiles? While in the first case security and diplomacy trump due process and the regulatory framework, in the second it is the power relations within a kleptocratic state which overcome the rule of law in a place such as the UK. In kleptocracies, the rule of law and even foreign policy is subject to the private and business interests of the kleptocrats themselves. This much is well-established in the literature on post-Soviet states.[23] But for this to be transposed to the UK would be especially worrying. How might this occur?

Although small states may not be able to shape the international money-laundering regime, their elites can resist new global standards by techniques ranging from foot-dragging to rejection.[24] Just as multinational firms have 'networked liabilities' when their affiliates are subject to legalized theft or extra-legal influence by kleptocrats,[25] statutory rules and ethical safeguards against professional enabling may be vulnerable to noncooperation or selective cooperation by kleptocracies. Ironically, the legal principle that the evidence of foreign courts may prima facie be accepted itself might undermine the legal system's ability to tackle kleptocracy. In the courts, we expect to see noncooperation or selective cooperation in favour of the defendant in the case of loyalists, and cooperation or selective cooperation against opponents. The mechanism at work here is the evidence from the home country which is made available to the investigators and the court. Where this evidence helps establish the legitimate sources of wealth and business practices of an incumbent elite defendant, or is deployed by the incumbent against an exile, we see an incumbency advantage.

Third, we hypothesize that there is an *enabler effect*. Such an effect is thoroughly transnational, relating to networks which cross borders, rather than being a matter of politics inside or outside the country. According to the enabler effect, professionals outside of a kleptocratic state work to sustain rather than challenge all-comers—loyalists, opponents, and fence-sitters.[26] They operate both upstream and downstream in transnational kleptocratic enterprises. They may be unwitting or wilful or a combination of the two. Regardless, some may assume they are merely service providers, just doing what they are asked. We posit two reasons why the enabler effect may be potent.

The first of these is their professional knowledge of the destination country. While kleptocrats, oligarchs, and businesspeople working in kleptocracies may know how to 'play in the grey' there, they often need help to understand how to do so overseas.[27] For example, money laundering entails 'the process of creating a veil of legal cleanliness' while its techniques are 'minor variations on methods used routinely by legitimate businesses'.[28] A legal defence against money laundering is partly that of defending a legitimate set of business methods and thereby keeping the sources of wealth hidden or at least uncertain. Therefore, professional intermediaries, specifically lawyers, are potentially a key factor explaining successful money laundering. Although legal professionals are all regulated and are therefore required to support investigations against their clients, they clearly have other primary goals which they see as conflicting with their regulatory duties.[29] They are market actors who offer new legal products to their clients; they generate the demand for their services.

The second reason for the enabler effect is the relative advantage of the private over the public sector in a largely self-regulated environment. Enablers have an advantage over regulators as they play a big role in working with them to set and reset the rules of the game. As private authorities and big international law firms play an increasing role in setting regulatory standards, they possess insider knowledge on how those standards may be evaded by their clients.[30] With respect to wealth managers, Brooke Harrington uses the term 'inside outsiders'.[31] Transnational professionals, including those in law and high-value real estate, have arguably 'transcended both public- and private-sector bureaucracies'.[32] Previous studies of anti-money-laundering efforts in the UK have found that regulation encouraged a box-ticking exercise where lawyers 'resorted to their own professional competence and knowledge of clients and their businesses'.[33] This achieves the worst of both worlds where lawyers face a conflict of interest in exercising judgement while providing information which is of little use to the authorities and finding 'ways to keep clients informed'.[34] Professionals, especially legal professionals, are crucial in both the detection and avoidance of money-laundering charges. The observable mechanism of the enabler effect is the use of specific professional techniques at critical junctures in the indulgence of kleptocratic wealth.

How Do We Know If the Enabler Makes the Difference?

The purpose of this chapter has been to develop a 'theory' of transnational kleptocracy with which we can investigate our nine professional indulgences over the remaining chapters. We embark from the proposition that the enabler effect has particular value in explaining how and why indulgence occurs. Our aim is to achieve a convincing general explanation of how and why professional enabling makes transnational kleptocracy possible—in doing so we will also say something about the prior questions of the what, where, and when of enabling. Our overall proposition if that *the enabler effect is the primary mechanism of transnational kleptocracy, which may interact with the secondary mechanisms of the incumbency advantage and the alliance effect.*

However, a risk that arises from such an exercise in theory-building based on experience and practice is that our explanation becomes a tautology where the evidence on which the theory is tested is essentially indistinguishable from that on which theory is built. Such circular reasoning is often convincing to the audience and is a feature of many popular books. But it does not count as a viable explanation as to how and why kleptocracy happens. In trying to avoid that problem over the remainder of this book, we will attempt to carefully assess how the incumbency advantage, the alliance effect, and the enabler effect are independent of or dependent upon each other and how these relationships affect outcomes. Each is considered as a process or *mechanism* which is present across several steps from 'sin' or problem (e.g. legal charges concerning the source of wealth) to the indulgence or solution (e.g. explanation of wealth accepted by the judge).

Assessing how these effects might combine to explain transnational kleptocracy is a question of method. In each of the three mechanisms, we would expect to see certain steps of a process which we can trace from start to finish. In the case of the incumbency advantage, we would expect that the loss/retention of power in the home state is causal in explaining the loss/retention of secrecy, protection, legitimacy, and influence in the UK; this means that those who become exiles or take the stance of the opponent are strongly disadvantaged. In the case of the alliance effect the process may be similar, but the content of each step may be different as we suppose that incumbency itself may not be enough. The presence and significance of partnership between the UK and the home state has a strong effect on outcomes; out-of-favour exiles from partner states would be expected to lose some of their gains in the UK, while exiles from enemy states might retain theirs. In the case of the enabler effect, we would expect to see that professional expertise and innovation—a new product or technique offered by the professional—will be shown to make the difference in the loss/retention of property, reputation, or influence.

We chart the three mechanisms across nine professional indulgences in Chapters 5–13. We, furthermore, offer three tests for each of the three mechanisms (see Table 4.2). First, we identify the presence or absence of each of these mechanisms in each case. The cases and the service sectors in which they sit differ considerably in terms of the conditions of the market and regulatory environment. While correlation is not causation, the persistent presence of a given mechanism across a diverse range of cases is itself significant. In short, we can assess which of the three mechanisms is present across the most cases and services. If successful indulgence correlates with improving geopolitical relations with a kleptocrat's state, this suggests an alliance effect. If a client ceases to be indulged after they have lost power at home and become an exile, this suggests that there was an incumbency advantage. If fee-paying clients with kleptocratic sources of wealth are indulged regardless of

Table 4.2 Summary of the three hypotheses

Hypothesis	Observable outcomes
Alliance effect	Loyalists of allies and opponents of enemies are *indulged*; loyalists of enemies and opponents of allies are *not indulged*.
Incumbency advantage	Loyalists and well-connected fence-sitters are *indulged*; opponents are *not indulged*.
Enabler effect	Loyalists, elites, and fence-sitters are *all indulged* when represented by elite professional services; pro bono and unrepresented elites are *not indulged*.

their incumbency at home or relationship to the UK, this suggests an enabler effect.

Second, we compare the significance of each of the three rival mechanisms—alliance, incumbency, and enabling. Which of these mechanisms makes a difference even in the absence of the other two? Which presents the strongest evidence? Which ones are present within a case from beginning to end and across all critical junctures? All three mechanisms may potentially be present in each case but to varying degrees. Such findings are to be expected, as complex social phenomena are always explained by multiple and sometimes contradictory causes. We are aware of this problem and consider what counts as strong or weak evidence of an effect in each case. For example, we can be more confident about the enabler effect where it can be seen to be critical in hiding, protecting, legitimizing or generating influence for the person in the absence of the two rival mechanisms; in such cases, the enabler effect is strong.

Third, and finally, we test each of the three mechanisms against what is said by the enablers and the kleptocratic elites themselves about the process and outcome of their case. We offer an 'opportunity to comment' to the elite and their legal enabler in each of our nine cases either by approaching them directly or drawing on their comments to others. Our letters to enablers provide detail on our claims which may be confirmed or denied by the respondents. Often these respondents will deny any wrongdoing while confirming the techniques used legally and willfully to avoid disclosure, burnish reputations, or evade accountability. In some of our cases, elites from kleptocratic states and their UK-based enablers appear to believe that they are battling against racism, misogyny, and other immoral values—even accusing us of being motivated by such values in our research or the authorities of being driven by such values in their anti-corruption investigations. However, their answers sometimes reveal hitherto unknown actions they have taken in support of their client. Do the enablers and kleptocrats invoke incumbency or alliance in their replies? Or do they reveal special professional methods which were instrumental at key moments in a transaction?

Our three mechanisms offer contending explanations for how and why kleptocrats are indulged. In a sense, they offer different theories of the creation of Londongrad. So indulged, some clients of British professional enablers will make reckless moves to launch legal actions with little chance of success or move tainted money from one place to another, apparently believing it is in their interests to do so. As we will explore in the coming chapters, it is network relations that make such perverse value judgements and calculations of interest possible. Being from a friendly state or being in power may help. But if you are without these advantages, we postulate that it is the enablers which often make the difference.

5

Hiding the Money

Britain is saying: 'We want to help with democratic development in Kyrgyzstan'. That's a lie. You're hosting a guy who robbed us.
—Almazbek Atambayev, president of Kyrgyzstan[1]

The website of APCO Worldwide, a public relations firm headquartered in Washington, DC, which helps organizations navigate 'through a changing, complex global environment', speaks of progressive values when detailing some of its former clients and their causes: urban forestry projects in Chicago, stopping the poaching of African elephants, helping the Pope on his first visit to the Arabian Peninsula.[2] Missing from their website is the work the firm did for AsiaUniversalBank (AUB), formerly the largest bank in the Kyrgyz Republic, a less than wholesome story.

A feature of the system if you are a member of the ruling family in a kleptocracy is to grab for yourself the lucrative companies, contracts, and assets. But you also need to be able to bank the proceeds and get that money out of the country. AUB is central to the story of the Kyrgyz Republic under its second president Kurmanbek Bakiyev, who ran the country as a family kleptocracy with his son, Maxim, and brothers in control of the lion's share of the economy. AUB was a key institution in relation to their kleptocratic power, allowing them to capture the state and take a cut on private and foreign capital.

This incredible tale demonstrates how Western institution after Western institution bolstered AUB's credibility. Yet an audit—conducted by a top accountancy firm after Bakiyev's removal from the presidency—concluded that it was probable that the bank was a money-laundering vehicle designed to funnel funds out of the Kyrgyz Republic.[3] As with many of the indulgences outlined in this book, banking is a transnational process indulged by financial and legal professionals. It was the supplying of these professional services to AUB that made the difference.

In this chapter we explore the indulgence of *hiding money* for post-communist elite clients, the first of nine professional indulgences which will be explored in this book. Each indulgence is a professional service offered to an individual or company for remission of 'sins' related to their source of wealth. Indulgences never take place fully upstream as this is the point of origin of that wealth itself.

The first stage of this process straddles the upstream and downstream: the hiding and protecting of private assets through the creation of shell companies—entities that are created for no economic purpose other than the moving of money from and into a variety of bank accounts. Yet money laundering itself is rarely about making everything public or keeping everything hidden. Rather, it is the strategic combination of both the public and the hidden that is effective in making the illicit licit.

We focus on the case of Maxim Bakiyev, a kleptocrat who became an exile and a fence-sitter in the UK. During his father's presidency, a coterie of white-collar firms around the world formed shell companies and opened bank accounts for the Bakiyev family and their associates. Beyond Bakiyev, we show that there are many other cases which follow this pattern and ask whether the alliance, incumbency, or the enabler effect provides the mechanism for hiding the money.

The Missing Billions and the Dead Shareholder

In the first two decades of this century, the Kyrgyz Republic became one of the most politically volatile places in the world. Within the space of 15 years, three presidents were forcibly removed or resigned amidst popular protests. The second of these was Kurmanbek Bakiyev, who served from 2005 to 2010, having come to power on a wave of populism after the long-serving first president following independence, Askar Akaev, was forced out in what was dubbed the Tulip Revolution. In 2005, protestors railed against Akaev's corruption and authoritarianism, yet once in office Bakiyev turbocharged the system, placing all power into the hands of his friends, relatives, and cronies before he too was ousted in 2010. One financial advisor characterized his rule as an attempted takeover by the Bakiyevs of 100% of the republic's GDP in record time.[4]

The most prominent of President Bakiyev's relatives was his youngest son, Maxim, who in 2009 became the head of the Kyrgyz Central Agency for Development, Investment, and Innovation whose acronym in Russian, rather tellingly, was TSARII. This was a state body which would control all foreign financial inflows, including aid and credits, and would also oversee the country's major national hydroelectric and gold companies. Having Maxim Bakiyev in charge of a state body responsible for business was already a clear conflict of interest, as he owned a variety of private businesses in the country.

According to Eugene Gourevitch, a former ally of the Bakiyevs, himself accused in the Kyrgyz Republic of financial crime: 'Maxim Bakiyev controlled everything, especially that related to the country's economy. He absolutely consolidated power'.[5] Being put in charge of a variety of state funds, such as the country's Development Fund, also raised eyebrows. The UK's Department for International Development commissioned a 'criminal investigation audit' of the fund's operations which voiced concerns that money laundering or other illegal activity may have happened under Maxim. The findings also highlighted potential conflicts of interest: Maxim was the head of TSARII at the same time as being the chairman of the Development Fund, meaning that the fund had no independent oversight as it was reporting to TSARII.[6]

Along with part of the Development Fund, other state funds, including the State Property Fund and the Social Fund, which held state pensions, had been moved to the Kyrgyz Republic's largest bank, AUB. The bank's origins dated back to 1999, when a Russian businessman, Mikhail Nadel, bought a Kyrgyz subsidiary of a Western Samoan bank, named International Business Bank, for $150,000. He renamed it AsiaUniversalBank in 2000. The bank originally focused on corporate banking, but moved into retail banking, and continued to grow under Bakiyev, likely helped by the fact that Nadel was close friends with Maxim. Nadel later denied that Bakiyev played a role in the development of AUB or held accounts there, but the two men were very close: when Maxim opened a new hotel on a Kyrgyz lake in June 2009, an American diplomat reported that Nadel acted like the second host of the party, loudly proposing toasts.[7]

AUB had a good reputation and had even won awards from such media outlets as *The Banker*, *Global Finance*, and *Euromoney*. But after another popular uprising removed President Bakiyev from power, the new Kyrgyz authorities discovered something shocking—in the days leading up to the removal of Bakiyev, it appeared that billions of dollars had been withdrawn from AUB, the bank's market value was nil, and that its liabilities outweighed its assets. Further inspection—which included an independent audit by multinational accountancy firm BDO, funded by the European Bank for Reconstruction and Development (EBRD)—indicated that the money had not been there in the first place, that the funds had already been siphoned out. The BDO audit was damning for AUB: it concluded that it was probable that the bank was predominantly being used for criminal purposes, and that AUB's managers knowingly facilitated money laundering. The audit indicated that the bank's Russian IT system was likely manipulated to disguise payments: more than 80% of transactions that took place in the final weeks before the revolution were not corroborated by SWIFT, the international payment system. In short, the money had already gone, and the books were cooked to try and account for the missing funds.[8]

AUB's management disputed these findings, claiming that they were being scapegoated by the new authorities due to political motivations, and that any money moved from the bank in the days before the revolution was due to concerned customers removing their funds in a time of instability. However, an in-depth report by Global Witness entitled *Grave Secrecy*, published in 2012, presented evidence as to how the AUB laundering scheme appeared to work. Dozens of shell companies had been set up through which suspicious transfers were made. Many of these companies had been registered not offshore, but in the United Kingdom. In a period of 30 months, $1.2 billion passed through accounts held at AUB by just three UK-registered companies. Yet these companies never filed any account information to the UK's registry, Companies House.[9]

Instrumental in this abusive behaviour was the use of nominee directors and shareholders to conceal the ultimate beneficial owner. The directors of these companies were proxies, working in a variety of company service providers around the world, many in the Seychelles. The given shareholders were a host of nondescript Russians, further proxies. In the most eye-opening example, the Russian shareholder of one UK company used to transfer $700 million from AUB was not even alive: his identity had been fraudulently used after his death to hide the real owner of a company. The state money that was held at AUB in the three state funds—up to $64 million, according to Global Witness—had also disappeared, and Bakiyev stood accused by the new authorities of stealing it.[10] Following the revolution, Maxim Bakiyev (who was out of the country at the time) flew to the UK on a private jet and claimed asylum, which was granted.

According to Gourevitch, in total the Bakiyev family withdrew $200–$300 million from the Kyrgyz Republic, beginning the moment they came to power, although he did not say through which banks the money was taken, and Gourevitch doubted that the money came from the state social and development funds.[11] Key to the success of the AUB scheme was the system of correspondent banking, relationships which allow a smaller bank's transactions to be routed through other banks. These were not minor institutions: the largest amounts of money from AUB went through Citibank in New York, the UK's Standard Chartered, and Austria's Raiffeisen Bank.

How could such major institutions with huge compliance departments allow such malfeasance to take place under their watch? The answer to this question points to the limits of anti–money laundering in the banking sector. Although the local bank is scrutinized by the correspondent partner before a relationship is established, individual transactions are not. These are the responsibility of the original bank—in this case AUB, which was itself acting as a money-laundering vehicle. This is why correspondent banking has been identified as a high risk for financial crime.[12] By 2003, AUB already had correspondent banking relationships with over 120 banks across the globe. In 2006, the Russian Central Bank issued a warning to its regional banks about 'dubious transactions' passing through AUB's correspondent accounts at Russian banks. Soon after this, Swiss bank UBS closed its correspondent account with AUB, but others kept theirs open. As research on company formation and banking shows, it only takes one weak link in the system for the dodgy shopper to access the benefits of global banking.[13]

Banks, Shell Companies, and Other Tools of the Kleptocrat's Trade

Transporting bags of cash around is high risk, and not practical for kleptocrats whose assets can run into the billions. Banks not only provide a way of holding unlimited amounts but transporting corrupted funds at a push of button to other jurisdictions. For the kleptocrat, the easiest way to facilitate this is just to own the bank yourself, or in the case of AUB, a bank owned by a loyalist. In neighbouring Kazakhstan, a similar picture is apparent. Timur Kulibayev and his wife Dinara (the daughter of former President Nazarbayev) own Halyk, Kazakhstan's largest bank, and before his enforced exile and subsequent death, a second Kazakh presidential son-in-law, Rakhat Aliyev, owned another Kazakh bank, Nurbank, with Dinara's elder sister, Dariga.[14]

To launder money and reputation and buy property abroad, money will at some point have to be moved into a bank that the kleptocrat does not control, and in a jurisdiction that will be subject to stricter anti-money-laundering controls. The penalties for not adhering to these regulations can be tough: in 2004, Riggs Bank, a venerable American institution which had banked for Abraham Lincoln, was sold and the Riggs name deactivated after it was found to have failed to conduct due diligence on politically exposed persons and was holding accounts for President Obiang of Equatorial Guinea and his family, as well as for former Chilean dictator Augusto Pinochet.[15] The possibility of having funds seized in such circumstances is a major no-no for the kleptocrat, who therefore needs to hide his or her assets through trusts, offshore entities or shell companies, whose ownership can be easily obscured via the use of nominees.

What was impressive (from a kleptocratic viewpoint) about AUB is that the bank did not just have money moving through several shell companies for the political elite, but that the bank's whole operation was seemingly constructed through a myriad of shell companies, designed for a variety of corrupt purposes. The majority of the dubious shell companies at AUB had been set up by just four trust and company service providers around the world. One in particular, the GT Group, highlighted the lack of accountability that accompanies some of these businesses. It was registered in the South Pacific island of Vanuatu by a British citizen, Geoffrey Taylor, who emigrated to New Zealand in the 1960s. Taylor claimed to be both a Lord and a knight, having supposedly been given the honorific title by the unrecognized Hutt River Principality in Australia. Taylor's son, Ian, continued to run GT Group after his retirement. The GT Group said it was not responsible for the actions of the companies that it registered.[16]

The picture in London was not much better. It was reports such as Global Witness's *Grave Secrecy* that indicated how UK registered companies were being used as vehicles for financial crime, and how out of control the situation had become.[17] Between 1979 and 2014, the number of UK companies incorporated every year increased from 66,500 to 533,000,[18] no doubt helped by cheap cost of doing so—as little as £50, until May 2024. At the time of the Global Witness's report there were literally no checks on who was registering the companies, no verification on the submitted information, and even no requirement that the actual owner of the company be recorded anywhere;

it was perfectly legal to employ proxies to act as company shareholders and directors.

When one of the researchers went to one address where various AUB companies had been registered, he found a corporate service provider called Apollo International. The office was staffed by several women with Slavic accents, who sat at tables surrounded by large stacks of paper. When the researcher inquired about the verification of the ownership of specific companies involved in the AUB scandal, one of the women said that they were not Apollo's clients but were set up by a man in Moscow, an agent helping the Russian shareholders register companies in the UK via Apollo. It was therefore his responsibility to 'make sure they are real'.[19]

After so many horror stories in the press about the misuse of UK companies and much campaigning from NGOs, the UK became one of the first countries in the world to require that the real owners of companies—the beneficial owners—be placed on record, thus meaning that those registering a company could no longer hide behind proxy directors and shareholders, in theory at least. The register, dubbed the Persons of Significant Control (PSC) register, was introduced in 2016. However, the new register did little to clean up the UK's dirty company problem, in large part because there was still no verification of the information, and few penalties for those submitting false information. There was no better indication of this than the fact that the first person in the UK to be charged with submitting false information to Companies House was Kevin Brewer, a 65-year-old whistle-blower who had registered UK companies in the name of various British politicians in order to show, with no verification, how easy it was to perpetrate something potentially fraudulent. He was fined £12,000. The then-business minister Andrew Griffiths boasted of the prosecution in 2018 as 'the first of its kind in the UK', without irony and utterly failing to acknowledge the farcical nature of the case.[20]

However, with the PSC register and an ongoing reform process at Companies House, the UK now appears to be ahead of the game. Businesses that help people register companies—referred to as trust and company service providers (TCSPs)—are regulated for money-laundering purposes and a new register of the beneficial ownership of UK residential property has been introduced. Many other countries in the Western world have none of these. Registrations of UK companies have continued unabated despite the introduction of a public register that was opposed by most in the industry on grounds of competitiveness. In 2020–2021 there were 810,316 new company incorporations, the highest number of incorporations on record.[21] Numbers were a little down in 2021–2022, but this was still the second highest number of incorporations on record.[22] As of September 2022, there were just under five million companies on the total register.[23]

In 2022, the UK government introduced plans for verification measures for all new and existing registered company directors and persons of significant control, and to give Companies House more effective investigation and enforcement powers. It is the enforcement which will be key: a large part of the issue is that there has been no accountability. In the AUB case, some of the shell companies claimed to Companies House that they were dormant yet were transferring millions of dollars out of the Kyrgyz Republic—a violation of the UK Companies Act.[24] But with the directors and shareholders resident in Seychelles and Russia there seemed to be little point in pursuing an investigation. Barring such people from being involved in company registration in the future would be a good first step, although with proxies there would likely be a seemingly endless supply of people willing to sign their name for a few dollars.

There is no question that the incorporation of abusive shell companies will have to cease for cases like AUB to be made more difficult. The argument against proper regulation and enforcement is typically that this would encumber the UK's 'dynamic' market economy. The evidence highlighted above suggests that that the public register of owners has not reduced company formation. However, this may be due to the lack of enforcement, verification, and the continued low cost (now £50) of formation. Yet there are two powerful arguments to suggest that eradicating the ability to form abusive shell companies will not harm the UK economy. First, we know that only a small proportion of registered companies are economically active in the UK. Eliminating these companies reduces the regulatory burden without reducing British GDP. Second, we know that comparable economies with stronger growth rates have few or no shell companies. Indeed, the UK is in a rather unique position when it comes to the registration of such companies. There is no such thing as a German shell company, for example, because the creation of a company in Germany requires at least €10,000 to be placed into a bank account.

However, Britain's model of capitalism is driven more by ideology and vested interests than evidence and national interests. In the United States, similar arguments are heard. Certain factions have fought for years against collecting any information on company owners, arguing that more transparency would be somehow bad for business. Yet to have a system where more ID is needed to get a library card than create a company is ridiculous in the face of national security threats such as terrorist financing and Russian kleptocracy. Finally, after years of unsuccessful lobbying and bills that went nowhere, in 2022 the US Financial Crimes Enforcement Network agreed that it would start collecting information on beneficial owners, although the information would not be publicly available and would only be available to US law enforcement. More progress was made with the proposed ENABLERS act, which would require a new set of middlemen to do basic due diligence on money flowing through their businesses to determine if the funds are the proceeds of crime. Unlike the UK, which regulates a whole host of businesses for money-laundering purposes, up until now only the banking industry in the US has been subject to extra checks. The bill was rejected by one vote in 2022 but could be introduced in a future session.

The contrast between the US and UK is that between a system of narrow regulation but relatively effective enforcement in the former case and broad regulation but extremely ineffective enforcement in the latter. Which is better? The fear of asset seizure and high-profile US Department of Justice cases against several kleptocrats has meant that many others have generally stayed away from parking their money in the United States, either in banks (post the Riggs bank scandal) or real estate (although there are some exceptions). These criminal cases—against former Ukrainian Prime Minister Pavlo Lazarenko, Uzbekistan's 'robber baron' Gulnara Karimova (as described in Chapter 8), and Nazarbayev associate James Giffen—have not only had a deterrent effect but have also provided NGOs and investigators with a wealth of information about how kleptocracy works in practice. This stands in contrast to the UK, whose law enforcement authorities, such as the Serious Fraud Office, release very little information, and whose court system does not allow easy access to documents, as happens in the US through the Public Access to Court Electronic Records (PACER) system.

Enabling All the Way Downstream

The fact that Kyrgyz Republic's largest bank was in effect a money-laundering vehicle did not cause many ripples in the world of finance. Few outlets outside of the Kyrgyz Republic reported on Global Witness's findings. The BDO audit was kept under lock and key, and a full version has never been made public. The EBRD, which funded the audit, also kept quiet about the Bakiyev regime's crimes. It seemed that nobody wanted to admit that the global financial system had aided and abetted a kleptocratic administration. But how did AUB pass so seamlessly into the world's banking system, with its 120 correspondent banking relationships? Here is where the enablers enter the story. Again, this is not a demand-side issue. None of these individuals or companies had to provide services to AUB. The testimony of financial enabler turned whistle blower Eugene Gourevitch is profuse on the actions of the enablers he worked alongside.

A variety of professional services were contracted to give AUB a veneer of legitimacy and propriety. In response to the warning issued by the Russian Central Bank in 2006, AUB hired APCO Worldwide to act as strategic consultant and help it meet international standards of compliance. APCO secured an agreement with AUB that it would put in place an independent board of directors. Thus, it came to pass that former US Senators J. Bennett Johnston and Bob Dole—a former presidential candidate, no less—were hired to AUB's board in June 2007. Dole resigned from AUB's board due to travel obligations in early 2010 to be replaced by another former US Senator, Donald W. Riegle Jr.

The willingness of credible Western figures to lend their names to this unknown bank was remarkable. According to Gourevitch, speaking to US kleptocracy researcher Casey Michel, when APCO recommended hiring someone to the bank's board they were seeking:

> a heavyweight and who will sort of stand up and say that the bank is a squeaky clean institution and that it's doing absolutely nothing wrong, etc., etc. . . . My feeling was that there was absolutely no way any of these reputable people would ever get involved with a bank in a small country, and I certainly wouldn't expect a former presidential candidate to even consider it. But I didn't know how Washington worked, and that people are basically willing to sell their reputation to the highest bidder, which we now keep seeing again and again and again. What really surprised me, jumping ahead a bit, was how little understanding the senators and the professionals at APCO had about anything having to do with the banking business. . . . there was this lack of even the most basic curiosity about what we do, even just as simple as asking, 'How is this Central Asian bank able to generate the money to pay me what they pay me?'[25]

APCO went further in cleaning up the reputation of AUB by hiring Kroll, arguably the most famous investigations company in the world. As Gourevitch tells it:

> we didn't say that they needed to confirm that we're kosher and legitimate. It was understood that we weren't going to be paying them these outrageous fees just to say we weren't running a world-class, compliant operation. They came over and gave us a clean bill but said that we really need to get a regular maintenance plan with them. It was a classic deal with the devil—they could give us a clean bill, and they would also keep getting paid.

While Gourevitch was a wilful and noncompliant enabler, AUB's money laundering was also enabled by passivity and nominal compliance: due diligence companies and regulated professionals failing to ask the necessary questions. By 2006, there were already some red flags, not only the warning issued by the Russian Central Bank in 2006, but Deloitte & Touche, who had audited AUB in 2003 and 2004, suspended its audit in 2005 and was replaced by another firm.[26]

While conceding that if AUB was manipulating its banking transaction system, it may have been difficult for Kroll to spot fraud, Global Witness cast doubt on the thoroughness of Kroll's reporting, especially regarding political risk. The Kroll report dealt with the key subject of Maxim Bakiyev's influence—the man, who in Gourevitch's words 'controlled everything' in Kyrgyz business—in a mere footnote, dismissing it as a rumour without much further investigation: 'This tells us no more than if people want to see Maxim Bakiyev behind business and banking in [Kyrgyz Republic], then that is what they will see. Kroll has found no evidence to suggest that [AUB chairman] Mikhail Nadel and Maxim Bakiyev have any commercial ties'. Such statements claim an unwitting enabling. But they also indicate a wilful ignorance with respect to political reality in kleptocratic environments on behalf of one of the world's leading investigations firms. Bakiyev and Nadel may well have had no commercial ties, but what about the ability of the former to influence the latter, or exert control over the bank in other ways? Kroll did not respond to Global Witness's requests for comment.[27]

By contrast, wilful enablers are those who explicitly acknowledge the way finance works in kleptocracies and act accordingly. Gourevitch, as a wilful enabler, describes how unwitting enabling worked in the AUB case:

I feel like it's a microcosm of the way world works: everyone pretends things are okay. You have kind of this round-robin system, where APCO says everything is cool because Kroll says everything is cool, and Kroll says everything is cool because they hear no evil, see no evil. And [Bob] Dole says that if APCO says it's okay and Kroll says it's okay, relying on these sort of white-shoe institutions to say they're okay, they're okay! And basically as soon as the senators joined the board, the amazing thing about it is it worked. As soon as we revealed that Dole and Johnston were on the board, all of these Western companies agreed to continue doing business with AUB.[28]

This quote is telling for the relationship it posits between active, upstream enablers (Gourevitch and AUB directors) and the apparently passive, downstream enablers (APCO and Kroll). In response to its investigation, APCO told Global Witness that it was 'factually inaccurate and offensive' to say that it inadvertently lent credibility to a potentially criminal enterprise. It added that it heard rumours in Bishkek about Bakiyev's influence, but that when contacted these officials said they did not have supporting evidence. There is no evidence to suggest that the former senators and APCO had any knowledge when working with AUB that the bank may have been used as a money-laundering vehicle.[29]

The story of AUB demonstrates that there was a lack of accountability all along the transactional stream by people and organizations supplying the services. Each individual entity upstream may have been nominally compliant, but they were all checking their own homework. This is a finding which is echoed elsewhere in this book by the enablers and was found in the Amersi/Telia explanation for their conduct in Uzbekistan with which we began in Chapter 1. It further suggests that upstream and downstream enabling services are intimately connected. The company service providers passed the buck to other providers organizing the registration of the companies, or to the shell companies themselves. The correspondent banks relied on AUB, which in turn was given a clean bill of health by Kroll and from a board comprised of several former US senators, whose services were garnered by APCO, a top PR company based in Washington, DC.

Perhaps APCO genuinely believed that its services could make a difference to the Kyrgyz Republic, often considered the most 'democratic' country in post-Soviet Central Asia, by promoting good 'Western' standards of responsible business. But their services had the opposite effect, cleaning the reputation of AUB with the help of former senators and Kroll. As one former Kyrgyz official said about Bob Dole: 'I remember being disgusted by how cheap US politicians [were] on sale.'[30] As AUB board members, the US senators were willing to wade a long way upstream—all the way to Bishkek—to indulge kleptocrats.

Neither Realism Nor Idealism

The complete lack of accountability for Maxim Bakiyev after his flight from the Kyrgyz Republic and eventual appearance in the UK in 2010 shows that exiles can overcome their disadvantage and continue to hide their money in the UK if they are professionally enabled. Given that the UK had a formal partnership with the Kyrgyz Republic through its EU membership, and that the post-2010 government in Bishkek pursued Bakiyev, it also suggests that the alliance effect may be superseded by the enabler effect. However much the UK government may have wished to assist the Kyrgyz Republic, British law firms were able to provide him with privacy, protection, and legitimacy. Understandably, this did not go down well with the then-president of the Kyrgyz Republic, Almazbek Atambayev:

> Why are there double standards against Kyrgyzstan? Britain is saying: 'We want to help with democratic development in Kyrgyzstan'. That's a lie. You're hosting a guy [Maxim Bakiyev] who robbed us . . . I spent 20 years in opposition and have always fought for democracy but I didn't know that behind the beautiful words of democracy are very dirty lies. That's terrible. Britain is one of the founders of democracy and it's impossible to understand its actions against us. I am ashamed for Great Britain and didn't expect politics to be this cynical and corrupt.[31]

Indeed, it was left to the US authorities to attempt to bring some kind of justice to Bakiyev. The Department of Justice tried to extradite him to face charges of insider trading—a rather lesser charge than state theft, but seemingly the only thing the US authorities could pin on him. However, the case collapsed when Eugene Gourevitch, who apparently was utilized by the US authorities in a scheme that would implicate Bakiyev, sabotaged the investigation in 2013 and found himself in jail in the US as a result.[32] Gourevitch said he did this out of loyalty as Bakiyev had helped him escape to Belarus, after having been apparently smuggled out of Kyrgyz Republic to Kazakhstan in the boot of a car of a Chechen gang.[33]

The United States did try to repair some of the damage with their ally: along with the extradition attempt it helped to repatriate $6 million in funds that they considered stolen by the Bakiyevs.[34] But it appeared more than willing to work with him when he was in power and was described in a leaked cable issued by the US embassy in Bishkek as 'smart, corrupt and a good ally to have'.[35] There were also persistent rumours that Maxim had a hidden interest in the fuel supply contract to a US airbase stationed in the Kyrgyz Republic. Gourevitch, speaking in 2021, said he 'knew for sure' that Maxim had a direct hidden interest in the two companies, Mina and Red Star, involved in the supply.[36] However, a US Congress report which concluded a committee investigation 'uncovered no credible evidence to link them financially' to the Bakiyev regime, although it conceded that the contracting arm of the Department of Defense 'conducted only superficial due diligence on Mina and Red Star, and turned a blind eye to allegations of corruption'.[37]

The UK government, by contrast, proved unable or unwilling to repair any damage, and British professionals continued to support Maxim to fend off the charges from the US. This pattern is a common one which will recur in this book. It suggests that the balance of power favours the enablers in the UK, whereas the prosecutors are a relatively more powerful force in the US. While the US government's record during the Bakiyev regime suggests that liberal values were not predominant, it is at least explicable from the perspective of realpolitik and immediate security priorities. By contrast, for the UK neither global norms nor national interests appear to have affected Britain's role with respect to Maxim Bakiyev, arguably the most important issue in its relations with the Kyrgyz Republic, a supposed partner in Central Asia, for many years after 2010. There is no evidence to suggest that the UK government actively opposed the aims of the Kyrgyz government to repatriate Maxim's wealth and some have suggested it tried to help, for example, with the offer of mutual legal assistance in 2014.[38] But it stood by while UK registered companies enabled AUB's money laundering, allowed Maxim to settle, claim asylum, and buy a property in the UK.

UK weakness, US realpolitik, and the professional enablers of both combined to have tremendous consequences and implications for the development of the Kyrgyz Republic. Not only had the country backslid under Bakiyev into greater corruption, crony capitalism, and human rights abuses, the revolution which removed him from power saw 118 dead and a further

400 injured. Thousands more were caught up in violence between Uzbek and Kyrgyz communities that broke out at the time of the revolution: the clashes killed nearly over 400 people and displaced 80,000. Maxim Bakiyev was accused at fomenting this violence by the new authorities, something he denied. But regardless of whether he was directly involved, the corrupt system created by the Bakiyevs played a significant role in the instability that led to the violence.

In the final analysis, the enabler effect is apparent. Gourevitch subsequently admitted to being AUB's wilful enabler while drawing the veil from those who were merely wilfully unwitting. Undoubtedly the services provided by these professionals facilitated corruption. And this corruption caused untold damage to the Kyrgyz Republic, and ultimately led to the death of hundreds of people, increased instability, and enhanced security risks in Central Asia. In recent years, asylum seekers have come to the UK only to face obstruction, vacillation, and even humiliation from the UK authorities. And yet Maxim Bakiyev, despite clear evidence of criminal behaviour, continues to live out his days in extreme luxury in the UK, having never faced any kind of justice and no known criminal investigation. His story takes us further downstream to the acquisition of residency rights and real estate—the topics of Chapters 7 and 8. Yet as his family was only in power for five years, Maxim Bakiyev never achieved the kind of legitimacy in the UK afforded to more stable—and asset rich—regimes. As we will see in the next chapter, loyalists of those regimes were welcomed with open arms by London's business elite.

6

Listing Companies

> What we [ENRC plc] can't be is a hybrid where we present a FTSE
> 100 façade behind which stands a private company, run by its former
> owners.
>
> —Ken Olisa, ENRC director[1]

There is much money to be made in so-called emerging markets, yet many of these countries are kleptocracies. How do professionals preparing a company for a public offering of shares on London's prestigious stock exchange mitigate the risks of dealing with such companies and their possible links to corrupt autocrats? One way is to pretend these risks do not exist in the first place.[2]

In October 2005, one of Kazakhstan's largest companies, Kazakhmys, was listed on the London Stock Exchange. Kazakhstan, the ninth largest country in the world, was no doubt attractive to London's money men because of its plentiful reserves of oil, gas, and minerals. By becoming a public limited company, Kazakhmys was legally a British entity, and its annual meetings were held in a very English location, a cosy building just on Lincoln Inn Fields, London's largest public square and home to many barristers' chambers. But it was essentially still a Kazakh company, and in 2012, the messy reality of Kazakh business (and politics, as the two are inextricably linked in kleptocracies, as we have established) made a rather rude intrusion into the rather English proceedings. Halfway through the meeting, a man stood up and announced he was issuing legal papers to Vladimir Kim, Kazakhmys's chairman. Kim looked flustered and mumbled that he did not know anything about the issue at hand. But he would have known exactly what this intervention was about, even though it happened back in Kazakhstan over 10 years prior.[3]

The intervener said he was acting on behalf of someone well known to Kim and to others in the Kazakh elite. A former prime minister and now political opponent of the current regime, Akezhan Kazhegeldin, had been forced into exile in 1998 after announcing his intention to stand in the next election against the country's autocratic president, Nursultan Nazarbayev. Kim was a loyalist of the Kazakh regime,[4] and back in 2001 Kim had testified in a Kazakh court that he was forced to give bribes to Kazhegeldin, including two cars.[5] Kazhegeldin says such claims were false, and were provided by Kim at Nazarbayev's bidding as a justification to convict him in absentia of abuse of office. The issuing of legal papers was Kazhegeldin's attempt to win compensation in international courts.[6]

Kazakhmys plc, a mining company, was the first corporation from the former Soviet Union to be granted a listing on the main market of the London Stock Exchange—to be *made public* by London's professional services. It was soon followed by the listing of another Kazakh mining group, Eurasian Natural Resources Corporation plc, or ENRC, in 2007. However, the ownership of both companies remained in large part in the private hands of Central Asian businessmen, all of which owed their position, and hence were loyalists, to the Kazakh president: Kazakhmys chairman Vladimir Kim was also the company's largest shareholder,[7] an asset which made him Kazakhstan's richest man.[8] ENRC was owned by the so-called trio: Patokh Chodiev, Aleksandr Mashkevich, and Alijan Ibragimov, three Central Asian billionaires who made their fortune from assets acquired in Kazakhstan's mid-1990s privatizations. ENRC only floated around 18% of its shares in 2007, with the trio retaining around 44% and the Kazakh government 19%.[9] Kazakhmys's debut raised over US$491 million in capital,[10] while ENRC's raised £1.4 billion.[11]

Unlike the annual general meetings of the largest companies on the FTSE 100—household names like HSBC, GlaxoSmithKline, and Tesco—which draw hundreds of shareholders to large venues, the annual meetings of those further down the share index, like that of Kazakhmys in 2012, drew just a couple of dozen people, only a few of whom will be members of the public, even though these companies are still worth billions. Millions of people in the UK rely on these companies to generate capital via pension funds and other investments, yet few know much about them and their operations. This is especially an issue when it comes to companies whose main operations are in kleptocracies, companies which—in increasing numbers over the last 20 years—have made London their financial home. The biggest companies stream their meetings live on the internet, in contrast to Kazakhmys, which one year banned all recording devices after Kim's words about the company supplying lead dust to a noxious smelter were leaked to the press.[12]

With companies operating in kleptocracies, a parallel set of realities can be observed. One version is on display to the public, presented in glossy prospectuses and annual reports by besuited executives who demonstrate their companies' rising profits through impressive-looking charts and graphs. A lot of emphasis will be placed on corporate responsibility, 'going green', and caring for local communities. Yet from time to time, like when Kazhegeldin's representative appeared at the Kazakhmys meeting, a second reality can be spied through the curtain—the genuine reality of having companies in the FTSE 100 whose bottom line depends on striking deals in corrupt neighbourhoods. Often this alternate reality is only revealed through the work of investigative media and NGOs. Shell plc, for example, is unlikely to dwell for too long in public over the fact that in 2011, along with Italian energy colossus Eni S.p.A, it paid $1.1 billion to the Nigerian government, knowing full well that that the money would almost immediately be transferred to Dan Etete, a man convicted of money laundering in France. Etete is a former petroleum minister of Nigeria, who back in 1998 had awarded himself one of the country's most lucrative oil blocks, the same block Shell and Eni were now buying the rights to.[13]

How do these realities—the upstream and downstream—combine in the minds of the professionals and regulators of the City? The belief was that by allowing entry to the London Stock Exchange to companies from Kazakhstan, a UK partner, we would not only be bringing profitable businesses to these shores, but would be introducing British standards of good governance, transparency, and accountability. But what happened is the reverse—the Central Asian shareholders retained the power and influence and much of these companies' operations were cloaked from public view—the hidden reality spoken of above.

Our second indulgence is a natural counterpart of the first. After shares in lucrative companies have been grabbed in flawed privatizations and money has begun to be stashed away outside of the country, elites need to legitimize their wealth by making public a certain image of their business. This chapter thus concerns the service of *listing companies*. This is arguably a midstream indulgence, one of two key steps which enablers take for kleptocrats, oligarchs, and other elites. The two indulgences which are covered in Chapters 5 and 6 are the fulcrum on which the scales swing to separate licit wealth from its illicit origins. By performing the service of creating a public limited company, the enablers make the company from a kleptocracy like any other legitimate corporate giant on the London Stock Exchange.

Mysteries of Kazakhmys

With Kazakhmys plc, the reality of the company was hidden from the very beginning of its London journey with the publishing of the company's listing prospectus. This is the document which aims to give prospective investors the whole truth about the company's prospects, opportunities, and risks. Presenting the full facts is crucial; not accurately presenting risks and liabilities could open the company up to potential lawsuits and could even be seen as fraud. Such documents thus become an opportunity for companies about to list to air their dirty laundry in public. Indeed, the prospectus of Novolipetsk, a Russian steel company that listed its global depository receipts in 2005, contained, according to the *Financial Times*, 'more drama than a Dostoevsky plot.'[14]

Yet knowledgeable observers from Kazakhstan and elsewhere spotted some rather startling omissions from the Kazakhmys plc prospectus. One of the board directors, Vladimir Ni, was described as 'a mining engineer by profession.'[15] There was no mention of the actual career that Ni was best known in Kazakhstan: he was the former chief-of-staff of President Nazarbayev. Ni had indeed trained as a mining engineer but had spent the next 28 years as a government official, including a 13-year period[16] working in Nazarbayev's office. Despite the power imbalance, the two men were very close friends. In Jonathan Aitken's official (thus fawning) biography of Nazarbayev published in 2009, Ni warmly recalls making his boss sausages and eggs in Soviet times.[17] There were other omissions from the prospectus that showed clear links to President Nazarbayev: the president's brother, Bolat, was a shareholder in Kazakhmys in 2004 before it listed, and company chairman Vladimir Kim was a former member of the council of Nazarbayev's political party.[18] In short, all the ties to Nazarbayev loyalists were omitted. These ties were so strong that anti-corruption NGO Global Witness alleged, based on numerous interviews with knowledgeable sources, that Kazakhmys plc de facto belonged to President Nazarbayev, that Kim was likely to be holding the shares in proxy for him, and that the company was being managed by the more senior Vladimir Ni, the president's man on the inside.[19] There was strong evidence to suggest this was the case,[20] including the fact that in 2006,

Vladimir Kim granted *gratis* 2.5% of Kazakhmys from shares he owned to Vladimir Ni. These were valued at around £125 million, making it likely the largest loyalty bonus in history.[21]

Kim's wealth was almost entirely built on Kazakhmys, but the prospectus did little to explain how he and two other company officials had come to earn practically all of the company at the time of listing, something that came as a surprise to the general public in Kazakhstan who had been led to believe that South Korea's Samsung was a major shareholder.[22] There was no discussion at all in the prospectus of the kleptocratic underpinnings of Kazakhstan's political economy—and of course no mention of Kim's involvement in the legal case against Kazhegeldin that came back to haunt him in London some years later. One would think that with such close ties to Nazarbayev, a change in Kazakhstan's leadership could severely impact Kazakhmys plc. Yet all the prospectus said was that 'should a new president be elected, the pro-business atmosphere in Kazakhstan could change'.[23]

Time and again, the parallel reality of having what was essentially a Kazakh company on the London Stock Exchange became apparent, but only through investigations by NGOs and journalists. When President Nazarbayev made a three-day state visit to the UK in 2006, meeting with then Prime Minister Blair and Queen Elizabeth II, Kazakhmys plc paid for Nazarbayev's £29,000 hotel bill.[24] Such a payment would likely have fallen foul of the UK Bribery Act had it occurred after this law came into force in 2011. Yet in 2020, the *Financial Times* reported that on the day the UK Bribery Act did come into force, Kazakhmys appeared to be arranging a luxury holiday to Disneyland Paris for Karim Massimov, Kazakhstan's then prime minister.[25] The loyalist-run company was simply doing what most large companies do in klepto-cratic states: paying for whatever the patron wants.[26]

In July 2010, Global Witness produced a report, *Risky Business*, highlighting all the omissions from the Kazakhmys's prospectus and documenting other allegations, such as that Ni and Kim appeared to ar-range the purchase of a new presidential jet for Nazarbayev in 2007.[27] One might imagine that such a report would lead to, at the very least, an inves-tigation by the London Stock Exchange or the body that regulated it, the Financial Conduct Authority (FCA). Yet when the NGO wrote to the FCA to document its findings, it responded that not only could it not comment on any findings in the Global Witness report, but even on whether it was launching an investigation.[28] Kazakhmys faced no known investigation and no penalty for producing a potentially misleading prospectus, and no known investigation into any of the other allegations, such as appearing to arrange a holiday for the Kazakh prime minister, a potential bribe.[29]

Kim stepped down as Kazakhmys chairman in 2013 but remained a non-executive director and the company's largest shareholder. On leaving the role, Kim said the new chairman should be independent and understand the City.[30] Nonexecutive British director Simon Heale took the job. But this was not to last: Heale stepped down in 2017 to be replaced by Kim's associate and company CEO Oleg Novachuk, one of the original shareholders when the company listed in 2005—another Nazarbayev loyalist.[31]

Triumphs of the Trio

ENRC's journey in London was rockier. The trio came to London with an already chequered history. There were the usual accusations of the businessmen having financed the presidential campaign of Nazarbayev in exchange for the smooth privatization of state assets in the 1990s.[32] But the allegations ran deeper. Controversy had surrounded the trio since the 1990s, when a Belgian power company called Tractebel sought to gain entry to Kazakh markets and paid €55 million in consulting fees to the trio which allegedly was used to bribe members of the Kazakh political elite.[33] The Belgian authorities investigated the trio in 2001 for forgery and money laundering,[34] yet the investigation was dropped 10 years later, with the trio avoiding trial and a potential criminal record.[35] The trio were beneficiaries of a recent change in Belgian law which meant that the men could pay a settlement (over €520,000 each) with no admission of guilt, rather than face trial. A French judicial investigation examined whether former French President Nicolas Sarkozy pulled strings in Belgium to get the law changed in exchange for a lucrative deal between France's Airbus and Kazakhstan.[36] Although a Belgian parliamentary enquiry found that neither France nor Kazakhstan had influenced the legislative process, Armand de Decker, a lawyer acting on behalf of trio member Patokh Chodiev, was indicted in 2018 for abuse of power, with the prosecutor's office believing that he had abused his position as a former president of the Belgian Senate to stop the potential prosecution of Chodiev and push for the change in the law back in 2011.[37] (De Decker died before a trial could commence.) The Central Asian oligarchs, all Nazarbayev loyalists, thus relied on their patron's incumbency to retain their assets at home, and relied on enablers abroad, and allegedly the alliance effect, to make issues disappear.

Then in 2009, ENRC acquired an entity called Camec for an estimated $955 million, a company which held the rights to lucrative projects in the Democratic Republic of the Congo, Zimbabwe, and elsewhere.[38] One of its shareholders who thus profited from the deal was Billy Rautenbach, a Zimbabwean businessman who was at that time facing fraud charges in South Africa and had been placed under EU and US sanctions for a deal he had brokered for Camec with Robert Mugabe's regime.[39]

This granted him a platinum prospect in exchange for a payment of $100 million to Mugabe's regime in the runup to the 2008 elections, which saw Mugabe triumph in an election characterized by political violence.[40] The purchase of Camec by ENRC was eventually licensed by the UK Treasury on the condition that ENRC had no further dealings with Rautenbach.[41] The platinum mine in Zimbabwe was left undeveloped for over a decade, and no raw material appears to have ever been mined.[42]

This and other governance matters caused ructions on ENRC's board. In June 2011, two of its British directors, Sir Richard Sykes and Ken Olisa, were voted off the board by the trio, with Olisa saying that the way the Central Asian oligarchs had acted was 'more Soviet than City'.[43] Prior to this decision, Olisa had spelt out to his colleagues the risk of allowing the trio to dictate terms to ENRC's management: 'Are we a proper FTSE company or are we a private company with a public listing . . . What we can't be is a hybrid where we present a FTSE 100 façade behind which stands a private company, run by its former owners'.[44]

ENRC lurched from one crisis to the next. In April 2013, the UK's Serious Fraud Office (SFO) launched a criminal investigation into what was now ENRC Ltd which 'focused on allegations of fraud, bribery and corruption around the acquisition of substantial mineral assets'.[45] For example, in 2010, ENRC agreed to pay an astonishing $300 million for a smelter in Zambia, 46 times what the previous owner had paid for it just seven years earlier, in a transaction which appeared to be a suspicious vehicle for graft. From 2010 to 2012, the trio acquired mining concessions in the Democratic Republic of the Congo through opaque dealings with the assistance of Dan Gertler, a controversial Israeli businessman later sanctioned in the United States under the Global Magnitsky Act.[46]

ENRC denied any wrongdoing and launched several legal challenges against the SFO over its investigation, including a £70 million lawsuit against the SFO in 2019, accusing them of acting illegally.[47] ENRC's spending on legal fees dwarfed the SFO's annual budget—money apparently well spent, as the SFO investigation was eventually closed after 10 years in August 2023 with 'insufficient admissible evidence to prosecute' cited as the reason.[48]

However, the investigation marked the beginning of the end of ENRC's London journey. It delisted in November 2013, has since been renamed ERG, and is now headquartered in Luxembourg. In October 2014, Kazakhmys plc was divided into the private Kazakhmys Corporation LLP and the public KAZ Minerals plc: Vladimir Kim continued to own the private company and retained a large shareholding in the plc. Finally, in October 2020, Nova Resources, a consortium of businesses led by company chairman Oleg Novachuk, took KAZ Minerals private, delisting the company from the London Stock Exchange.

Licentious Listings

The Kazakh companies are a great example of the enabling of kleptocracy at the highest levels of British business. Both companies had primary listings on the main market of the LSE, both for a time entering the prestigious FTSE 100 share index by virtue of their size. While Kazakhmys was the first it was not the last. Moreover, the record suggests that such listings are not a form of access afforded just to ally nations. At the time of Russia's invasion of Ukraine, by which time UK-Russian relations had been in terminal decline for at least two decades, 31 companies from Russia were listed on the LSE, with a combined market value of £468 billion. Most of these were secondary listings (with the primary being on the Moscow Exchange), with the listing of depositary receipts in London. Many other Russian companies were listed on the smaller Alternative Investment Market exchange. At their peak in 2007, Russian companies raised $19.7 billion on London's equity markets, according to the data company Dealogic.[49] This was one year after the assassination in London with chemical weapons of Alexander Litvinenko and the first year of Vladimir Putin's State Rearmament Plan which would be funded by the proceeds of these major Russian companies.

Eleven years later it seemed that little had changed. Three days after the poisoning of defector Sergei Skripal by the Russian security services in Salisbury in 2018, which led to the death of a member of the public, Dawn Sturgess, the Russian Embassy in London asked if it was 'business as usual?'

from its official Twitter account as the listed Russian company EN + had a very successful bond issuance raising €750 million on the LSE.[50]

The alliance effect appears not to be the primary mechanism when it comes to stock market listings. Trading in Russian companies was suspended following the 2022 full-scale invasion of Ukraine, but until that point, many were companies with large state shareholdings: Gazprom, Lukoil, Rosneft Oil, Sberbank. Others were owned by oligarchs who were later sanctioned: Evraz plc, part of the FTSE 100, was 29% owned by Roman Abramovich. EN + Group, which raised $1.5 billion in that 2018[51] listing in London, is part-owned by Oleg Deripaska, who was sanctioned by the US in 2018 and by the UK in March 2022, along with Abramovich. As the UK's Intelligence and Security Committee's Russia report stated: 'Successive Governments have welcomed the oligarchs and their money with open arms, providing them with a means of recycling illicit finance through the London 'laundromat', and connections at the highest levels with access to UK companies and political figures'.[52]

Yet it is the lesser-known examples from Kazakhstan that stress the 'no questions asked' policy of subjugating everything to the City of London in the hope that 'the market' will win out. It is notable that these companies did not list in New York, but preferred London, with its lighter touch approach to regulation. This lighter touch means few questions asked about sources of wealth, regulators who appear to be asleep at the wheel, and an inactive law enforcement, especially when compared to the US Department of Justice. Another key reason why such companies have generally avoided US markets is personal criminal liability. Under US legislation, criminal charges can be brought against company managers for fraud and illegal or unethical conduct that harms the public.

The listing of Kazakh and Russian companies on the LSE is a clear example of a supply-side problem. There is no reason why Russian or Kazakh companies with ties to their respective regimes should be allowed to list in London, given the concerns about corruption and kleptocracy, and—now— the funding of Russia's war effort and propaganda campaign. It is the supply of services that has made the difference. Two of our mechanisms are apparent in the above cases. First, there is the incumbency advantage: both Kazakhmys and ENRC were the companies of loyalists and insiders, inextricably tied to Kazakhstan's family kleptocracy. Second, we have the enabler effect: the law firms, accountants, and investment banks that made the unpalatable palatable by presenting a rather different story to the British public and regulators than what is the reality. The enabling quickly proceeded from midstream to downstream: by the time Kazakhmys listed, considerable work had already been done to square the accounts, house Kim's shares in legal offshore structures, remove Nazarbayev's brother from the shareholding, and so on.

This downstream enabler effect was understated in the relaying of these examples above. The Kazakh companies were brought to the market by some of the world's biggest international players. When Kazakhymys listed, it was helped by its sponsor and financial advisor, JPMorgan Cazenove, which also acted as its global coordinator, along with Credit Suisse First Boston. Deutsche Bank, HSBC, and JPMorgan acted as its co-lead managers. When ENRC listed, Deutsche Bank acted as its global coordinator and sponsor, and worked with Credit Suisse, Morgan Stanley, and ABN AMRO Rothschild as joint bookrunners. Behind the scenes, scores of legal firms, accountants, and due diligence companies worked on preparing the books, the prospectus, and the reports that created a respectable face for these shadowy companies. Some of these enablers may have been wilful in their disregard of kleptocratic origins; others may have been wilfully unwitting in the failure to ask the obvious questions regarding parts of the two Kazakh companies' businesses. It is not suggested that the advisors were noncompliant but rather that they wilfully or unwittingly gave these post-communist enterprises credibility and respectability by association.

Elite Networks

These two examples from Kazakhstan also illustrate the power of networks. These companies' boards were comprised of senior figures from British business. Kazakhmys plc's board included Baron Renwick of Clifton, a former British Ambassador to the United States, and at the time of Kazakhmys's listing, the vice chairman of investment banking for JPMorgan Europe. He was also a member of the House of Lords, first as a Labour peer, before moving to the crossbenches in 2007. ENRC's Sir Richard Sykes was then the rector of Imperial College and a director of Rio Tinto plc, while Ken Olisa was a director of Thomson Reuters plc. All of these firms, companies, and individuals were happy to lend their name in support of Kazakhstan's kleptocracy, albeit downstream and indirectly. Even Ken Olisa, speaking just three months before leaving ENRC with his 'more Soviet than City' remark, was towing the company—and the City's—line, when facing criticism:

> Attracting companies such as ENRC to London is good for the company because it provides capital and liquidity but it is very, very good for London where companies such as ours make a major contribution to the City fee pool. Snide remarks may make for good propaganda, but they are bad for national productivity.[53]

Olisa's suggestion that there is a public good for Britain is debatable. However, the evidence that UK-Kazakh business relations are lucrative for already-wealthy and powerful individuals on both sides is indisputable.

Several British businesses have done well in Kazakhstan. In 2001, the UK's BAE Systems plc invested in a 49% stake in Air Astana, Kazakhstan's leading air carrier, forming a joint venture with Kazakhstan's sovereign wealth fund, Samruk. The inauguration was attended by President Nazarbayev and Sir Richard 'Dick' Evans, BAE Systems chairman. Evans had close ties to the Labour Party, described by one industry insider as 'one of the few businessmen who can see Blair on request'.[54] After Evans left BAE Systems in 2004, he became chairman of the board of Samruk. In a conversation reported in a leaked diplomatic cable from 2008, Evans told the US Ambassador that Nazarbayev's son-in-law, Timur Kulibayev, was the one real businessman he had met in the entire Samruk structure.[55] In October 2010, former UK First Secretary of State Peter Mandelson addressed a conference organized by Samruk in which he said that the fund was 'a saviour of the world economy' for its apparent help in the banking crisis.[56] Sir Richard Evans was elected as an independent director of the board of Samruk, now called Samruk Kazyna, again in January 2014, stepping down in 2019.

After he left politics, Tony Blair helped Kazakhstan burnish its image. The approach was made by Blair's former chief-of-staff, Jonathan Powell, who contacted one of Nazarbayev's aides in 2008, saying that Blair 'would be happy to provide private strategic advice to President Nazarbayev'.[57] Blair's consultancy firm, Tony Blair Associates, eventually signed a deal to advise Kazakhstan's government in 2011, and is believed to have been paid up to $16 million for its services.[58] In December of that year, at least 14 oil workers protesting against working conditions were shot dead in the Kazakh town of Zhanaozen. Blair advised Nazarbayev on how to deal with the media before the Kazakh president's appearance at Cambridge University in 2012. In this letter, Blair commented: 'These events, tragic though they were, should not obscure the enormous progress that Kazakhstan has made'. Many of Blair's other associates also made money from Kazakhstan. When members of the Kazakh government visited the United States in September 2011, its lobbying efforts were carried out 'through Windrush Ventures Limited, through Portland PR Limited'. Windrush was the largest of Blair's management companies, while Portland is a public relations firm in which Blair's former spokesperson Alastair Campbell acted as an adviser at the time.[59]

Why Listing Matters

These examples illustrate how transnational kleptocracy networks function in the shadows of the public face of shareholder meetings in the UK and listing documents (see Figure 6.1). The indulgence of 'making public' is to make certain things visible while concealing less-convenient facts. But what impact did these listings have on Kazakhstan? Firstly, they consolidate kleptocracy in Kazakhstan, making the rich owners of these companies even richer. Vladimir Kim's net wealth now stands at $4.6 billion, as of December 2023.[60] They also legitimize what is essentially the theft of formerly state

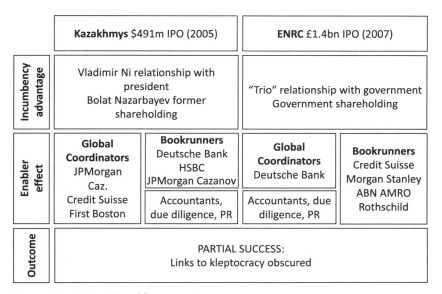

Figure 6.1 Listing Kazakh companies

assets through shadowy privatizations. As documented in the Global Witness report, many employees and minor shareholders of Kazakhmys were in effect deceived out of their shares prior to listing.[61] It also conferred on a kleptocracy a sense of legitimacy: the white-collar firms that brought these companies to market were saying that ENRC and Kazakhmys were worthy of investment, suitable for a listing in London, and were viable options of wealth creation for millions of UK citizens—none of which, arguably, was true. Whatever wealth was generated by ENRC has surely been undone by the millions of pounds spent by the SFO's ultimately unsuccessful probe.

Secondly, the incumbency advantage and enabler effect don't just make kleptocrats richer, they also have huge costs for the poor. ENRC's actions in Africa show us that corruption is not a victimless crime. ENRC's purchasing of Camec rewarded Billy Rautenbach, a longtime friend of the Mugabe regime, whose original acquisition of the mine may have saved Mugabe's political career. The UK-based charity Rights and Accountability for Development (RAID) identified 32,000 Congolese residents and 700 former workers of one of the mines as possible victims of corruption in the transfer of the project to ENRC. According to RAID, people living in communities on or near to the mining concessions suffered direct harm because they were deprived of their livelihoods, denied access to health and social care, and forced to live in a polluted environment without access even to clean water. Separately, 16 residents came forward as potential victims in the SFO's investigation, seeking compensation for the harm caused by a failure to prevent corruption.[62]

Finally, the absence of an alliance effect, as demonstrated by the Russian listings, refutes the notion that listing companies is simply a matter of realpolitik between friends. In fact, the LSE and the UK-based professionals which enable its listings and bond issuances appear to be working at times in direct opposition to British foreign policy. This is not merely an observation on the undermining of UK diplomatic response to the Salisbury poisonings by the EN + bond issuance a few days later. More broadly, rather than providing accountability for the sources of wealth, the London listers have allowed kleptocracies to become essentially transnational. In the first instance, this enriches key elites. But, when a kleptocracy like Russia is also a global and revisionist power it undermines the ability of the Western alliance to deter Russian aggression. Why would you take the threats of NATO leaders seriously if their country's businesses are supporting your own and thereby indirectly funding your own rearmament?

7

Selling Rights

No passport case is clean and clear ... None of them ... They all have
their issues. That's why they want a passport.
—Andreas Pittadjis, Cypriot lawyer[1]

In February 2012, one of the authors (Heathershaw) was contacted by
Gherson LLP, lawyers acting on behalf of a 'high-profile Kyrgyzstani
client' seeking expert witness testimony to support their client's application for asylum in the UK. Heathershaw took a conference call with the
firm's principal Roger Gherson and colleagues. He was told that the expert
would be 'very-well compensated' and that 'anonymity' could be offered.
The client turned out to be Maxim Bakiyev, whom we first met in Chapter
5. Heathershaw and two of his PhD students from the Kyrgyz Republic sat
and listened to a long monologue by Gherson regarding the role of Russia
in backing the 'coup' against the Bakiyev regime in April 2010. No mention
was made of the allegations that Maxim Bakiyev had ordered the murder of
a British businessman or of the violence and rampant corruption of the government in which he was a part. Heathershaw declined this no doubt lucrative offer, and he never heard from Gherson LLP again. However, one month
later Heathershaw was contacted by Diligence, a firm conducting 'commercial intelligence' on behalf of an unnamed client to carry out 'an assessment
of recent political events in Kyrgyzstan' with a list of questions remarkably
similar to the line of argument followed by Gherson several weeks before.

Logic suggests that any asylum seeker who arrives in the UK amidst
accusations that he stole money from his home state and ordered the murder
of a British citizen may face difficulties in garnering residency. These were
the accusations facing Bakiyev when he arrived in the UK in 2010 following
his father's ousting. Furthermore, there was evidence that he had spent some
time in Latvia and possibly Germany, and therefore may have been in con-
travention of the Dublin Agreement which states that an asylum seeker must

make the claim in their first point of entry into the EU. Bakiyev was briefly detained on his arrival, but subsequently released.[2]

Yet supported by his downstream professional enablers, Bakiyev managed to gain asylum in the UK. The British citizen who believed Maxim Bakiyev had ordered a hit on him in 2006 in the Kyrgyz Republic (a bullet severely damaged the man's internal organs but he survived) brought a civil claim in 2014, seeking damages in respect of the injuries he sustained, yet the claim was dismissed, with the judge saying that the claim was not credible.[3] As described in Chapter 5, a US case against Bakiyev for insider trading was dropped, though the US authorities did recover $6 million that they considered stolen from the Kyrgyz state by Bakiyev and his associates,[4] a fraction of what went missing, yet Bakiyev has faced no known investigation, let alone prosecution, for any crime in the UK.

For most applicants, asylum is extremely difficult to acquire without the kind of elite legal support contracted by Bakiyev. As Global Witness summed up: 'It is fair to question whether such generous treatment would be afforded to anyone other than a multimillionaire princeling of Baki[y]ev Jr.'s standing'. Bakiyev would have been eligible for UK citizenship around 2016, though it is unknown whether he has acquired it.

Bakiyev's route into the UK was unusual, but for most kleptocrats there are alternative and far easier routes. The UK, and many other countries in the Global North, have long provided special paths for the wealthy who wish to acquire residency. These are investment visa schemes where an individual can obtain the right to live in a particular country, either temporarily or permanently, if they invest enough money and fulfil certain requirements. Some countries have taken it even further, with citizenship gained after a sizeable financial contribution. These programmes have become known as golden visas and golden passports schemes. By contrast, what the UK government calls 'safe legal routes' have only been opened in recent years to those fleeing Ukraine, Hong Kong, and (a small number from) Afghanistan, countries to whom the UK has made political commitments. Elsewhere, the private sector is the predominant actor.

This chapter explores the indulgence of *selling rights*—the global business of providing visas, residency rights, and citizenship to investors. This business is generally denoted as Citizenship by Investment (CBI), a term we use here as shorthand for a basket of schemes which include citizenship (selling passports) and residency by investment (RBI), like the UK state's 'Tier 1' programme. Most CBI/RBI clients are not kleptocrats, and there are a variety of legitimate and semilegitimate reasons why someone may apply for such schemes: from wealthy Americans looking to reduce their taxes by moving to the Caribbean to rich middle-class residents of unstable regimes looking for a bolt hole. But clearly such schemes are likely to attract the corrupt; according to the US government's landmark Strategy for Countering Corruption: 'Corrupt actors use CBI benefits to achieve enhanced access to the international financial system and visa-free mobility'. Furthermore, 'ineffective legal and regulatory oversight has led to the abuse of CBI programmes by criminal actors, sanction evaders, and corrupt officials'.[5]

Unlike other chapters where we focus on a small number of in-depth cases of enabling, in this chapter we survey the industry as a whole and give many examples of how elites from post-communist kleptocracies have been indulged by its regulated and unregulated professionals. We begin by focusing on the industry leader, Henley & Partners, a firm that began in a UK Crown Dependency before going global. We then undertake a comparative analysis of some of the leading CBI/RBI schemes, many of them in former British colonies in the Caribbean and Mediterranean. Finally, we explore the scandal surrounding the UK's own Tier 1 scheme, the regulation of which was at least partially outsourced to the private companies that submitted the applications for their clients. The indulgence of selling rights turns out to be a postimperial phenomenon where the enablers are kings.

The 'Global Leader' in Selling Citizenship

The UK's private sector leads the way in CBI around the world. Founded in the Crown Dependency of Jersey, Henley & Partners (hereafter Henley) describes itself as the 'global leader in residence and citizenship by investment' and now has operations in over 40 countries.[6] This British firm stands head and shoulders above all others when it comes to involvement in a variety of CBI schemes around the world. It largely operates beyond the UK, demonstrating once again the transnational nature of the problem and the role of British companies and professionals in dubious schemes which are typically associated with small island states including former colonies of the British Empire.

St Kitts and Nevis, the island state which is the smallest country in the Western hemisphere, was the first to launch a CBI programme following its independence from the UK in 1983.[7] However, it attracted few applicants until 2006, when Henley signed a contract to run the scheme,[8] which it did until August 2013. The government agreed to pay Henley a $20,000 fee for every successful applicant. When family members of applicants were taken into account, up to 50,000 passports were likely issued through the program from 2006 to 2021, according to one of the country's ministers—a number in excess of the country's recorded population.[9] 'It was as if we had discovered an oil well. We changed the country completely', said Henley chairman Christian Kälin, who was appointed St Kitts and Nevis's Special Envoy for Bilateral Agreements (as well as its honorary consul to Switzerland) and spearheaded the Caribbean country's negotiations with the EU to make their citizens exempt from Schengen visa requirements.[10]

Henley told the St Kitts and Nevis government to create a charitable fund, the Sugar Industry Diversification Foundation (SIDF), that would receive the monies paid by passport applicants. Until 2011, Henley was the only firm allowed to submit applications under the SIDF route, so the firm made money twice, in application fees and commissions. Research by OCCRP showed that the SIDF made unsuccessful investments in a company owned by an associate of Henley's chairman, and a debt-ridden luxury resort project with links to the same associate, a potential conflict of interest.[11] In 2014, the US authorities stated that 'certain foreign individuals' were abusing the St Kitts CBI programme 'to obtain SKN [St Kitts and Nevis] passports for the purpose of engaging in illicit financial activity'.[12] Canada also removed visa-free travel for St Kitts and Nevis's citizens in 2014.[13] The St Kitts and Nevis government commissioned its own review into the foundation receiving the investments but this was never published.[14]

Another former British colony in which Henley operated was Malta. Under a public services concession, Henley was also involved with Malta's scheme from 2013 to 2020, designing, implementing, and promoting it.[15] In the programme's early days, as it was in St Kitts and Nevis, Henley not only found applicants on commission, but also conducted their due diligence, a clear conflict of interest.[16] In total, Henley helped 851 Russians seeking Maltese citizenship. Henley insists that 'Chinese walls' protected business functions from conflict[17] and denied that there was a systemic problem with its scheme or that its programmes are used for nefarious purposes. It is believed that between 20% and 50% of Malta applicants are rejected. Henley added: 'Ultimately it is the responsibility of the countries involved to investigate and vet applicants. As a private company, we are neither required by law to do so, nor do we have access to the same level of background information, contacts and resources that government authorities have'.[18] In November 2020, Malta introduced a new law to apparently increase due diligence and insist on a modest charitable gift alongside investment in real estate.[19]

Henley has also been active in Cyprus, another former British colony. One of the world's most wanted fugitives, Low Taek Jho, better known as Jho Low, the alleged mastermind behind the 1MDB $700 million fraud in Malaysia,[20] applied for a Maltese passport in 2015, to add to the St Kitts and Nevis one he acquired in 2011.[21] He was not successful, so applied for a Cypriot one instead. As Transparency International (TI) pointed out, Jho Low did not get his Cypriot citizenship through a rogue trader, but with help from Henley. Although Henley's Malta operations had identified that 'entering into a business relationship [with Jho Low] would pose undue reputational risk and/ or disrepute to Henley & Partners',[22] and identified him as a high-risk person with political exposure, Henley went ahead with issuing Low's Cypriot application, earning a total of €710,000 for services directly or indirectly provided to him. As TI commented, Henley's role 'debunks the common myth that the rogue players in the golden visa industry are only a minority of small local businesses that engage in sketchy practices and tarnish the reputation of the wider sector',[23] something that could be said of every other indulgence covered in this book.

Tier One Residents

However, it is not simply British companies and ex-colonies that are active in the CBI/RBI industry. Even large countries, such as Russia and Turkey, are now getting involved in CBI. And the British state offered an attractive RBI programme for more than a quarter of a century. The UK's version of the golden visa scheme ran from 1994 to 2022 and was rebranded as the Tier 1 (Investor) Visa in 2008. Although the prize on offer was temporary residency, not full citizenship, after five years living in the UK the individual could apply for permanent residency, and finally citizenship after a year of permanent residency.[24] This time period was reduced if more money was invested via two fast track routes introduced in 2011: a £5 million investment allowed for a permanent residency application within three years if certain residency conditions were met, or just two years if the individual had £10 million to spare.[25] As with other nations, the UK government completely failed to realize—or simply ignored—the money-laundering and security risks that the scheme presented.

The UK made a distinction between two types of business-oriented visas under 'Tier 1': investor and entrepreneur.[26] The latter was for those foreign businesspersons who wanted to come to the UK to start a new business or invest funds in an existing one. The rationale was to give residency to skilled individuals with a proven track record of making money and creating jobs. Even this entrepreneur scheme, which seems a reasonable way of attracting talent, was criticized by the UK's migration advisory committee in 2016, which said that the 'entrepreneur route was not working as intended, with a substantial proportion of low-quality businesses being established under the route'.[27] The rationale for Tier 1 investment visas was simpler: show me the money. Although some applicants may remain in the UK and engage in business activity to the benefit of the state, there is no residency requirement and, unlike the entrepreneur visa, no requirement for the applicant to be proficient in English.

Among those individuals known to have acquired a Tier 1 visa in the UK are Russian oligarch and former owner of Chelsea FC Roman Abramovich; Zamira Hajiyeva, the wife of a former chair of Azerbaijan's state bank, the recipient of the UK's first-ever unexplained wealth order (UWO), who infamously spent over £16 million in Harrods over a 10-year period (see Chapter 9); Izzat Javadova, a cousin of the Azerbaijani president who was forced in 2021 to hand £4 million of unlawfully acquired money to the National Crime Agency (NCA); Nirav Modi, who as of the time of writing is fighting extradition to India from the UK for a £1.5 billion alleged fraud; and Madiyar Ablyazov, son of Mukhtar Ablyazov, a former government official from Kazakhstan accused of siphoning up to $5 billion from a bank he chaired (see Chapter 12), who used as his investment a £1 million gift from his father.[28]

The system that was in place in the UK from 2008 to early 2015 was particularly egregious as the checks that were carried out on the applicants were the sole responsibility of the private sector law firms and wealth managers representing them who were to benefit financially from applicants' success.[29] Weaknesses in the system abounded: there was no requirement to provide evidence of the source of wealth held for more than two years or for gifted investments, and investors were usually only assessed for their compliance with the rules of their visa three years after entering the UK. From 2004 to 2014, the money could even be borrowed from a bank if the applicant could 'prove' a certain net worth. This provision was added after lobbying from a major bank.[30] Of course, such a financing provision would generate revenue for the banks providing the loans, yet arguably wouldn't lead to any new money entering the UK.

Between 2008 and 2015, only 8% of Tier 1 investment applications were refused, compared to 42% of asylum applications. The typical turnaround for a visa application was three weeks, compared to six months for asylum applications.[31] The largest number of UK investment visas granted by nationality between 2008 and end of 2014 were to Chinese citizens—1,117 visas issued, 34.3% of the total. The second largest group were Russian citizens, totalling 734 people (22.5%). Kazakh citizens also featured in the top 10, with 58 successful applicants.[32] As Kazakhstan is a country where, as of 2019, just 162 people own 55% of the country's wealth,[33] this suggests that the UK may have granted residency to a significant proportion of that country's kleptocratic elite.

As such facts about the scheme began to emerge, the UK government scrambled. In April 2015 the Home Office tightened requirements so that investors needed to have a UK bank account before making a Tier 1 application—in effect, passing the burden of due diligence to the banks. This in itself was ironic, as prior to this, British banks had actually used the fact that individuals were granted an investor visa as a sign of good standing when assessing the individual's suitability as a banking client.[34] In other words, before 2015, not only were potentially corrupt applicants gaining such visas with few if any checks, but their newly acquired status may have helped reduce a bank's due diligence checks.

From September 2015, Tier 1 applicants also had to prove that they had no criminal record before being granted a visa, and that the money had not been acquired illegally or through conduct that would be illegal in the UK. The Home Office was also granted powers to refuse a visa if the person's presence was deemed to be detrimental to the public good.[35] Applications for the scheme surged before the 2014–2015 revisions and declined dramatically thereafter, likely because people wanted to avoid the additional cost and/or requirements. For example, 126 applications were made from Russia in 2013 and 241 in 2014, but just 30 in the first nine months of 2015.[36] However, no data were collected by the Home Office on the number of politically exposed persons (PEPs) who were granted a visa, despite the fact that the identification of PEPs is a requirement of the UK's anti-money-laundering regulations in certain sectors, such as banking and real estate, as they pose a higher risk for financial crime.

The extraordinary risks to the integrity of the UK economy from the Tier 1 scheme were justified on mercantile grounds. However, even the supposed gains to the UK economy were routinely called into question. Until 2015 the investment could be in the form of a loan, usually via investing in gilts (UK government bonds). As Professor Sir David Metcalf, the then chair of the UK's migration advisory committee, stated: 'The investor gets the rule of law, property rights, access to efficient capital markets and an excellent education system for their children. What do UK residents get?'[37] In a 2014 assessment of the investment visa, Metcalf concluded: 'We express some healthy scepticism concerning the benefits normally asserted.'[38] Metcalf pointed out that UK taxpayers would even be paying applicants' interest if they invested in gilts.[39]

Government bonds were the most popular investment option, but were removed as a qualifying investment in March 2019, because such investments had limited benefit to the UK economy. Yet loopholes remained. In April 2021, a UK court concluded that it was even legal for a Russian couple to route investments in a circular fashion, with money borrowed from overseas companies to make investments through British shell companies that ultimately went to businesses or assets overseas.[40] Clearly, such circular investments would be of zero benefit to the UK economy. One hundred applicants are known to have used such a scheme to acquire a visa, most of them Chinese nationals.[41] One such visa decision was overruled by the UK's supreme court in June 2023, but it is unclear whether the other investors who used this scheme have had their visas revoked and have been required to leave the UK.[42]

Concerns about the scheme eventually became those of national security. These were voiced by the UK parliament's intelligence and security committee's investigation on Russia, published in July 2020, which said that 'it is widely recognised that the key to London's appeal [for Russian oligarchs and their money] was the exploitation of the UK's investor visa scheme'. From 2008 to the end of March 2020, the UK government issued 2,581 residency visas to Russian citizens.[43] As Transparency International UK commented, it was 'highly likely that substantial amounts of corrupt wealth from China and Russia have been laundered into the UK' through the Tier 1 scheme, citing the fact that since April 2015, £82 billion of suspected corrupt wealth had been laundered out of China and placed under criminal investigation by Chinese authorities. The Central Bank of Russia also estimated that £31 billion of illegal outflows had left Russia in 2012. This would not include the

Table 7.1 UK Tier 1 investor visas applications by country of origin, 2008–2014 (50+ applicants)

Country of nationality	Total	Proportion of total applicants in period (%)
China	1,117	34.3%
Russia	734	22.5%
United States	151	4.6%
Hong Kong	77	2.4%
Pakistan	76	2.3%
Iran	73	2.2%
Egypt	68	2.1%
India	68	2.1%
Kazakhstan	58	1.8%
Canada	56	1.7%
Australia	50	1.5%
Ukraine	50	1.5%
Total	3,261	

Source: 'Details of Tier 1 Investor Visa Applications, Approvals, Refusals and Cost', WhatDoTheyKnow.com, 12 January 2016, https://www.whatdotheyk now.com/request/details_of_tier_1_investor_visa#incoming-753828; 'FOI 37851 Tier 1 Investors Apps Final 23 dec2015.Xlsx', WhatDoTheyKnow.com, 2015, https://www.whatdotheyknow.com/request/307071/response/753 828/attach/html/6/FoI%2037851%20Tier%201%201%20Investors%20apps%20fi nal%2023%20Dec2015.xlsx.html.

billions of dollars accrued in illicit—but nearly always not illegal according to Russian law—circumstances by the oligarchs and Putin's inner circle.

According to UK NGO Spotlight on Corruption, 6,312 golden visas—one-half of all such visas ever issued—were being reviewed for possible national security risks by the Home Office in 2022.[44] Only around half of these were issued during the 'blind faith' period, suggesting that due diligence issues remained after the scheme's requirements were supposedly tightened in 2015. In response to Russia's invasion of Ukraine, the UK government abolished the Tier 1 investment scheme in February 2022, a clear case of closing the barn door after the horse has bolted. The Home Office originally said it would publish a report on the scheme, including the findings of an investigation into security concerns,[45] although after a five-year wait, the government announced the report was not going to be made public and a statement was issued instead.[46] In this statement, UK Home Secretary Suella

Braverman said that there was 'a small minority of individuals connected to the Tier 1 (Investor) visa route that were potentially at high risk of having obtained wealth through corruption or other illicit financial activity, and/or being engaged in serious and organised crime'.[47] There were also 10 Russians awarded visas who were later placed under UK sanctions, although these individuals were not named.

'Absolutely Immoral and Perverse'

With the Home Office's report unpublished and those who received visas unnamed, it is harder to ascertain the extent to which kleptocratic networks extended their reach into the UK via the Tier 1 programme. However, the dangers of visa and CBI/RBI schemes are clear: they open doors to criminals, kleptocrats, and the corrupt, who may use tainted or illicit proceeds for the investment.

Such schemes are not new. After St Kitts and Nevis started the ball rolling in 1984, others followed with variations of the scheme. The United States established its immigrant investor programme, named EB-5, back in 1990, and the UK with its version in 1994. Many of Europe's CBI/RBI schemes started to appear in or after 2008 as a way for countries hit hard by the financial crisis to create easy capital. Even so, questions have also been raised about whether some of the world's richest countries should be seeking at all to gain financially by channelling wealth from countries that are either poorer or mired in corruption.[48]

By 2018, four EU Member States had golden passport schemes (Austria, Bulgaria, Cyprus, and Malta) and 12, including the UK, offered some form of investment visa.[49] The vast majority of countries in the world—190 in total—have similar provisions that are not clearly codified in law.[50] With so many countries vying for investors' cash, this inevitably created a 'race to the bottom' with prices lowered, residency and language requirements dropped, and special offers introduced. The only requirement for Cyprus's CBI scheme, the Cyprus Investment Programme, when it launched in 2013 was that the applicant had to visit the country just once every seven years. Many of the schemes allow for investments to be made into real estate, or in the case of Antigua and Barbuda, the country's movie industry.[51]

Such schemes are perhaps the clearest illustration of transnational kleptocracy in action as they vividly illustrate the divide between haves and the have-nots. Sarah Kunz, an expert in investment programmes at the University of Bristol, also highlighted the irony of a situation where hundreds of people with dubious capital were being granted residency in the UK at the same time that the government was wrongly detaining and deporting British citizens originally from Caribbean countries who arrived prior to 1973— the Windrush scandal, referencing the ship which brought one of the first large groups of people to the UK from the Caribbean in 1948. 'The Investor visa', she commented, 'thus works alongside other immigration legislation introduced by successive UK governments to further entrench wealth-based and racialised inequality not only within the UK immigration system but within British society more generally'.[52]

Yet what is truly remarkable is how virtually every country that adopted such a programme disregarded the dangers of dirty money that had already been well-documented through the experience of, for example, Ireland and the United States, whose investor scheme was tightened over the years to address due diligence issues and fraudulent investments. Other major changes from the early 1990s to the late 2000s were the fall of the Soviet Union and dissolution of Yugoslavia, which had created many new countries where corruption, both petty and grand, was rife, fuelling the rise of a new class of oligarchs and an often corrupt business elite. It was already well-established by the time the UK created its investor scheme that many of these individuals were looking to create second homes in the EU.

In Portugal, visa recipients included several figures involved in a Brazilian scandal known as Operation Car Wash, a vast bribery and corruption network that was subject to a judicial investigation in Brazil. Members of kleptocratic dynasties were also applicants (see Table 7.2).[53] In 2014, Portugal's interior minister Miguel Macedo resigned when it was revealed he was a partner in a company that has been identified in an investigation by Portuguese authorities that examined allegations of corruption, influence peddling, and money laundering in the issuing of visas. Macedo said he had no administrative involvement in the attribution of visas, but 11 people were arrested including the head of the country's immigration and border service and the former head of the registries and notaries service,[54] who were accused of accepting gifts in exchange for expediting residence permits. Portugal's visa scheme was dubbed 'absolutely immoral and perverse'[55] and 'insane'[56] by one Portuguese politician.[57]

However, it is another EU state which offers the most obvious comparison to the UK and some insights into the way such programmes work. As a

Table 7.2 Comparison of some leading CBI and RBI schemes

Country	Years of operation (CBI/RBI)	Volume of high-risk applicants	Legal and security concerns raised	Examples of successful applicants
UK	2008–2022 (RBI; revised in 2015; ended in 2022 after Home Office report)	57% (1,851) applicants from Russia and China between 2008 and 2014, a period with an overall 92% success rate	'About half' reported as being reviewed for security concerns; 10 Russian recipients were later subject to sanctions	Roman Abramovich, the Russian former owner of Chelsea FC; Zamira Hajiyeva, the wife of a former chair of Azerbaijan's state bank, the recipient of the UK's first ever unexplained wealth order; Nirav Modi, awaiting extradition to India from the UK for a £1.5 billion fraud
Cyprus	2007–2020 (CBI; abruptly ended after Al Jazeera investigation)	39% (992) passports issued to Russians between Nov 2017 and Sept 2019	53% (3,592) deemed unlawful	Oleg Deripaska, later placed under US sanctions in 2018 and UK sanctions in 2022; exiled Russian oligarchs Ali Beglov and Nikolai Gornovsky; Jho Low, alleged Malaysian fraudster of the 1MDB scandal; Allies and relatives of Cambodia's dictator Hun Sen
Malta	2013– (CBI; ran by Henley, 2013–2020; revised in 2020)	55% (1,3000) from Chinese, Russian, or Saudi Arabian citizens	The European Commission refers Malta to court for the new scheme being incompatible with EU treaties	Unknown. Jho Low and several suspected criminals were turned down by Henley & Partners
Portugal	2012– (RBI; revised in 2015)	66% of visas issued were to Chinese applicants (2012–2016)	In 2014, Operation Labyrinth, led to 11 arrests on allegations that bribes had been received in exchange for visas.	Otávio Azevedo, a Brazilian business who was jailed for 18 years on corruption charges in 2016; João Manuel Inglês, an Angolan colonel and aide to the head of the Angolan military; Mir Jamal Pashayev, the director of Pasha Holding and leading member of Azerbaijan's ruling Aliyev-Pashayev families.
St Kitts and Nevis	1984– (CBI; ran by Henley, 2006–2013; revised in 2014)	Unknown. 15,000 passports recalled as place of birth not denoted in the document.	In 2015, the prime minister stated that the scheme allowed 'illicit actors to be able to move about with disguise'	Iranian businessman Alizera Moghadam; Russian investor Ruben Vardanyan; Jho Low (passport was later deactivated); Firuza Kerimova, wife of Russian billionaire and politician Suleyman Kerimov, who was placed under US sanctions in 2018.

member of the Commonwealth and the European Union, Cyprus affords its new citizens certain voting and residency rights in the UK even after the UK left the EU. In Cyprus, investigative journalists discovered that many Russian and Ukrainian oligarchs had been granted citizenship.[58] But the corruption in the Cypriot scheme went much further than a lack of due diligence over the applicants. An undercover investigation by Al Jazeera implicated several Cypriot politicians in the issuing of passports. The investigations, dubbed collectively as 'the Cyprus Papers', involved undercover reporters acting as fixers trying to get Cypriot citizenship for a Chinese individual who, the story ran, had been convicted in absentia in China for bribery and money laundering.[59]

This depressing story of thousands of passports or visas issued with little oversight played out in other countries that had similar schemes. Malta was forced by the EU Commission in 2014 to require applicants to spend at least a year in the country to qualify,[60] yet a loophole was easily found—applicants could just rent a cheap apartment without even being physically present. And despite further legal pressure from the Commission, Malta is the one EU member that has yet to abandon its investment for citizenship programme: it scrapped one version of the investor citizenship scheme only to establish a new one at the end of 2020. The European Commission charged that this new scheme was 'not compatible' with EU treaties.[61] In Cyprus, 53.2% of the 6,779 citizenships granted between 2007 and 2020 were found unlawful (and only 30.4% could be conclusively proven to have been obtained lawfully).[62] These included at least 1,100 family members of applicants who bought Cypriot citizenship, despite the fact that the country's attorney general had said that this could be in breach of the law. This practice continued for at least four years.[63] At least 30 people of those issued with passports faced accusations of criminal activity, while 40 of them were politically exposed persons.[64] As of September 2022, 52 Cypriot passports have been revoked. Eight of these were reportedly allies and relatives of Hun Sen, Cambodia's authoritarian and kleptocratic prime minister. Attempts are also being made to strip alleged Malaysian fraudster Jho Low of his Cypriot citizenship.[65]

Enabling 'Global Citizens'

While the CBI/RBI industry has exploded, Henley remains a leader. An internet search for a combination of golden visas, 'citizenship by investment', and a host of other related terms invariably finds one particular provider—Henley & Partners—displayed prominently as the first search result, in the form of a Google ad. The ad headline reads 'Golden Visa—free consultation—henleyglobal.com' and goes on to explain:

> Each year, hundreds of wealthy clients rely on our expertise in this area. Benefits include the right to live, do business, and many more. Get a free consultation. Safety and Security. Global Mobility. Access Global Markets. Become a Global Citizen.

This highlights the significance of the enabler effect in CBI schemes. Service providers such as Henley are not merely responding to a 'need' that is out there, however shady it might or might not be: they are creating new demand in a market dominated by wealthy individuals from kleptocratic states. For example, it was Henley who recommended that St Kitts and Nevis remove the place of birth from its passports. According to the country's prime minister at the time, they were advised by Henley that this was, 'an important convenience for our citizenship applicants'.[66] In doing so, they created a more attractive product where the country of origin was wholly concealed. In essence, immigration and nationality has essentially been outsourced to the private sector for the wealthy, while poorer immigrants are still dealt with by the state.

What is known about Henley's operations largely stems from investigative journalism including one report by OCCRP published in 2022 which uncovered documents and witness testimonies about schemes which were previously shrouded in secrecy. A local political fixer seems to be crucial to the design and operation of any CBI scheme in a small island state. In St Kitts and Nevis this was Wendell Lawrence, a former politician and long-term finance secretary. As OCCRP reported, when the programme was relaunched in 2006, 'Lawrence was employed as Henley's local representative, collecting a $5,000 fee for each citizenship application and an extra fee for any client using the fast-track service', making millions of dollars per annum by 2011–2012 in line with market rates. Lawrence would also collect fees from real estate purchases. However, Henley made much more: from $35,000 to $70,000 per application, according to internal documents.[67]

This pattern of professional indulgence—the confluence of political and private enablers across citizenship, financial investment, and real estate—is evident in other CBI providers. The Al Jazeera exposé of Cyprus highlighted how crucial the enablers are in facilitating these deals. The undercover journalists, posing as fixers for a Chinese criminal, were put in contact by a former London police officer turned enabler with a Cypriot real estate firm run by a British couple. They boast of a 100% success rate in getting clients citizenship through property investments, and attribute this to knowing Christakis Giovanis, a member of the Cypriot parliament—and also owner of one of the country's largest property developers, Giovani Group. Giovanis, the British couple said to the undercover reporters, had the 'connectivity to break all the rules'.[68] The fixers met not only with Giovanis, but also with the speaker of the Cypriot parliament, Demetris Syllouris, a former employee of Giovanis before entering politics.[69] Both men were told that the Chinese client had a criminal conviction in China. Despite this, Syllouris was caught by a hidden camera saying, 'He has to send money here to be sure that we do something and he doesn't change his mind',[70] and later that he 'will have full support from Cyprus at any level—political, economic, social, everything'.[71]

The supply of indulgences is stark in this example and contains a level of wilfulness, alleged noncompliance, and even direct political involvement which is usually hidden from view. However, the specific mechanisms of such indulgences are more complex than in the sixteenth century, although some of the words heard in the Al Jazeera documentary have the ring of what a friar might have said when receiving a payment: 'When you know the angels, you don't need God',[72] a reference to Giovanis being key to getting the Cypriot interior ministry to issue passports. These words are spoken by a Cypriot lawyer, Andreas Pittadjis, a registered service provider for the Cyprus Investment Programme. Having been told about the Chinese applicant's criminal convictions, he remarks:

> I had a guy who was in custody for two years. He was in prison for two years for corruption and money laundering. We had ways to justify everything and he went through. We submitted his passport application. He now has his visa waiting for him and passport. No problems whatsoever.[73]

Pittadjis was covertly filmed suggesting that the investment is made through a family member of the Chinese criminal in order to avoid the bank's checks.[74] Most disturbingly of all, Pittadjis also says that the name of the individual can be changed when they receive their Cypriot passport, and that this can be done within five minutes, with the client signing only one document. When asked if he had done such a thing before, Pittadjis jokes: 'Of course! This is

Cyprus!'[75] This is an easy win for individuals who are sanctioned or on visa blacklists, makes due diligence harder to perform by other professionals, and clearly undermines international law enforcement attempts to bring people to justice.[76] It is the difference that enabling can make. Thus, wilful and potentially complicit enablers are employed to find, in Pittadjis's words, 'ways to overcome the problem'.[77]

Giovanis, Syllouris, Pittadjis and a fourth man faced trial in Cyprus on corruption charges in connection with the investigation into the passport scheme. In October 2023 the prosecution dropped all charges against Pittadjis, who claimed in a Facebook post that the Al Jazeera documentary had been 'obscenely edited'. The trial of the other three men was about to take place at time of writing.[78]

But surely the ways deployed in the small island state of Cyprus would not work in the major financial centre and G7 country of the UK? One would hope so. However, the investigations of Channel 4's *Dispatches* programme which aired in July 2019 suggest otherwise. Tanya Laidlaw, an immigration solicitor and partner at Quastel Midgen (since renamed Quastels, whom we will meet again in Chapter 9) is told by an undercover reporter posing as a prospective client that they have an uncle who 'has helped members of Putin's inner circle with overseas managing of funds, getting them out overseas'. The reporter asks, 'Is that also a worrisome part of . . . are we ok with his application?' Laidlaw replies: 'I don't think it should be a problem . . . Many people who applied in the past didn't have such a clean past, I must say. Not necessarily with me, but with everyone . . . So, I personally think that it is worth trying to open a bank account. Once a bank account is open, that's more or less you in . . . You'll try with one bank, the bank is saying no. You try it with another, maybe the other one will say yes'.[79]

Such quotations from these investigations are valuable to researchers such as ourselves, as they reveal fragments of the narrative of indulgence. However, such quotes contrast dramatically with the public representation of professionals. In response to Channel 4, Tanya Laidlaw said that they were 'extremely confident that the firm's vigorous due diligence processes would have identified any investment funds that did not meet the required standard of the Home Office's visa application process and would have refused to act for the potential investor'.[80] The key to understanding the indulgence of selling rights is surely that of identifying the independent power of both hidden and public narratives. The hidden narrative explains how CBI/RBI has become so popular for kleptocrats, oligarchs, and others with high-risk backgrounds. The public narrative explains how the enablers convince the regulators that they are compliant with the rule of law and pre-empting national security risks.

The enabler effect almost always entails one version of reality in public and another in private. It is about both generating demand and removing bureaucratic or regulatory obstacles to supply. Due diligence by UK banks was introduced as a requirement for the Tier 1 visa only in 2015, some seven years after the scheme had been rebranded, and 21 years after it began. Yet the due diligence performed by banks is not viewed as an impediment by the enablers themselves, as they have the ability to shop around on behalf of the client and thereby find those institutions with the least stringent checks. The definition of a banking institution also included wealth management organizations which use an underlying custodian bank to make investments.[81] One advisor for a firm of immigration lawyers was caught by undercover reporters saying: 'Some of the bigger banks, to be honest with you, can be quite difficult to deal with . . . er, very rigid, If I use a diplomatic term'. He recommends using 'our guys', a small investment fund, Shard Capital, specializing in golden visas, adding,

> If you get past these guys, then getting past the government is, is easy peasy . . . Because, the Home Office, you have to understand the context. There's not a financial team at the Home Office, right . . . They probably don't have an idea of what complex financial products are or source of wealth.[82]

A representative from Shard Capital says to the undercover reporter that none of the reforms introduced over the last five years have radically changed the system: 'It's still easy, frankly'.[83] Indeed, it was repeatedly stressed to the undercover reporters that the Home Office only needed to know about the origins of the specific £2 million they were investing, not the person's overall wealth.[84]

Although the Cyprus case seems more extreme, there appear in essence few differences between the Cyprus and UK schemes in terms of the type of client who was using these services and the lack of due diligence performed on these clients. The Cypriot version led to criminal charges and government resignations, while the British one was quietly covered up with minimal data released and no investigation of accountability. The UK rules were so poorly drafted that a political connection likely wasn't needed, just a good lawyer, which indicates the difference that enablers make even for elites who are now exiles (from China, in the fictional Cypriot application addressed to the lawyer Pittadjis) or are from states which are hostile to the country granting CBI (from Russia, in the putative UK application considered by Laidlaw).

In the UK Tier 1 case, there are examples of successful applications from nonincumbents—many of the cases mentioned above related to exiles and opponents—and persons from nonpartner states. The enabler effect appears to be a constant of the processes while the incumbency advantage and the alliance effect are not apparent at all. This finding suggests that Britain's RBI industry was driven far more by the supply and demand of the market than the priorities of the governments which ultimately issue the visas and passports. The private sector triumphed over the public interest. The imbalance between weak public officials and strong private professionals is especially pronounced in the UK Tier 1 scheme, perhaps more than any of the other cases of professional indulgence we consider in this book. From 2008 to 2015, successive UK governments, Labour and Conservative, essentially outsourced the scheme entirely to the private sector. Long after this period, legal professionals might have been correct in asserting that officials at the Home Office 'probably don't have an idea of what complex financial products are.'[85]

Worth the Risk?

Beyond the individual enablers, and even beyond the individual countries, the trouble with special mobility allowances for the rich—as with most of the other indulgences we treat in this book—is their widespread acceptance by the most upstanding members of the international community. The selling of residences is an indulgence which appears to routinely be offered to all-comers if they have the money. While key aspects of making public and hiding money appear to arise during a period of incumbency, for RBI and CBI schemes that advantage appears to be unnecessary. Many of the clients listed in Table 7.2 are exiles. In the UK, some of these, like Zamira Hajiyeva and Nirav Modi, are the exiles of British partner states. Others, like Roman Abramovich, are loyalists to states which threaten the UK.

The impact of such schemes on the countries in which the money has been corruptly acquired is clear—further money is taken out of the country and the individual gains legal protections by becoming a resident or citizen of another country. But there are also effects on the places of newly found citizenship. Firstly, RBI/CBI schemes provide yet another means through which money can be taken out of the country, and—if the money has been illicitly acquired—laundered into whatever asset the government scheme allows, be it real estate or government bonds. It also confers legitimacy on the kleptocrat and allows them to travel more freely around the world, potentially helping them to evade capture if warrants are issued in certain countries. A person who has acquired EU citizenship in Cyprus or Malta is allowed to travel visa free throughout the entire Schengen zone. As well as EU nationals, all citizens of members of the Commonwealth (including Caribbean island nations like St Kitts and Nevis) who are resident in the UK are allowed to vote. Once they are on the electoral register, they are also allowed to donate to political parties. Chapter 11 highlights an individual who, having acquired Cypriot citizenship, moved to the UK and did just that. For the British government, its investor visa scheme was eventually identified as a threat to the rule of law, national security, and thus the national interest.

Is the risk of providing haven to some of the world's most corrupt individuals worth it? Between 2008 and 2018, these schemes have seen an estimated 6,000 new citizens and almost 100,000 new residents in the EU.[86] Not only have the schemes opened the doors to potential kleptocrats and criminals, importing organized crime into the EU and UK, the presumed economic benefits have also been called into question. On the one hand, some countries—notably the ones with the most corrupt schemes—appear to have benefited: since 2013, Cyprus raised €4.8 billion through the sale of citizenship,[87] though it is debatable whether the country benefits as a whole, or just specific industries and sectors in the country (i.e. landlords, construction companies, and professionals catering to wealthy clients). On the other hand, Hungary's disastrous 2013–2017 scheme (in which applicants invested indirectly in special Hungarian government bonds) may have actually cost the country €192 million, with the profits going to offshore companies.[88]

Research has shown that golden visa programmes may plug short-term economic gaps but have negligible national-level economic impact for larger economies.[89] While we are still waiting for proof of any demonstrable economic benefits for the British economy, we know that companies like the UK's Henley & Partners have profited from this lucrative business and have exported their model to the world. They are the winners in this deal, along with their clients, who, having acquired a new citizenship, can start looking for a place to live in their adopted country, as described in the next chapter.

8

Purchasing Property

Don't talk to me about how [the money] comes here. I don't need to know . . . We have certain regulations within our industry where I don't need to know where things come from.

—Benson Beard, London real estate agent[1]

Plane spotters can be an invaluable source of information for kleptocracy watchers. In October 2010, an enthusiast snapped a smart new arrival at Geneva airport: a Bombardier Global Express.[2] The photographer would not have known that the plane's owner on paper was a former Uzbek pop star called Rustam Madumarov, or the fact that the jet, which cost around $48 million, was bought with the proceeds of crime.

When London-based accountancy firm SH Landes LLP helped Madumarov acquire the jet in 2010 it approached a company service provider with the aim of sourcing an offshore company which could formally make the purchase. Yet SH Landes seemed rather reluctant to discuss his sources of wealth: 'Please note that Mr R Madumarov is not going to finance the purchase of an aircraft out of his own funds and we believe that the question regarding his personal wealth is not relevant in this situation.'[3] However, on being told that such checks were necessary, SH Landes provided a statement of wealth which referenced Madumarov, amongst other business activities, as being involved with an Uzbek mobile phone company, Uzdonrobita.

A quick search of this company by any professional required to perform money-laundering checks, such as accountants, would have discovered two articles from 2004. One, published by in the UK's *Independent*, was an interview with Gulnara Karimova, the daughter of the then-president of Uzbekistan, in which she said she held a major share in Uzdonrobita.[4] The second, published in English by the *Moscow Times*, documented some more lurid details about Karimova's involvement with this company, as we discussed in Chapter 1: allegations that she had received her stake in

Uzdonrobita for nothing and was now selling some of its shares for around $159 million, and that she had milked the company for as much as $20 million in ill-defined consulting services.[5]

Clearly, had SH Landes seen these articles, it would have been a major red flag, prompting them to ask further questions about Madumarov's involvement with Uzdonrobita, and whether he had any connection to Karimova. Maybe the accountancy firm had missed these articles, or perhaps Madumarov simply denied all involvement with Karimova and her allegedly criminal activity? Missing red flags about Karimova's potential involvement in companies was nothing new. In the same year, 2010, the board of Swedish-Finnish company TeliaSonera and their British advisor Mohamed Amersi failed to ask questions about the ultimate controllers and beneficiaries of Uzdonrobita's apparent rival, Ucell, when proceeding with a $220 million share buyback deal (see Chapter 1). Amersi continues to argue that this was not within his remit.

In December 2012, further revelations were published about the growing scandal surrounding Karimova. One report highlighted assets held by 'Gulnara Karimova's alleged boyfriend, Uzbek pop star Rustam Madumarov', including a historic castle and 67 acres of land just outside of Paris.[6] The same article described another of Karimova's associates, a young woman called Gayane Avakyan. Under the heading 'paying off a dictator', OCCRP wrote that TeliaSonera had paid close to $320 million in total for a 3G license, not from the Uzbek state as defined by law, but from an offshore company, Takilant Ltd, registered in Gibraltar and controlled—on paper at least—by Gayane Avakyan.[7] Avakyan and Madumarov were thus outed not only as PEPs—business associates of a government official (Karimova)—but also as potential money-laundering risks.[8]

In September 2013, some 10 months after international media had started reporting on Karimova, Avakyan, Madumarov, and their involvement in the telecoms scandal, a UK registered company that was directed by Avakyan submitted their yearly accounts. The accounts declared that the company's ultimate legal owner was a Gibraltar entity called Takilant Ltd—the very same company involved in the telecoms scandal. The accounts were submitted by SH Landes LLP.[9] Was SH Landes a witting or unwitting enabler? In response to enquiries made by the BBC, it said that relevant regulatory authorities were notified, but it is not clear at what point.

This chapter addresses the indulgence of *buying properties*, perhaps the most obvious way in which professional services indulge kleptocrats and others with questionable sources of wealth. This indulgence crosses multiple sectors including luxury goods, the arts and antiquities markets, the infamous super yachts and private jets, and residential real estate in world cities such as London. Our focus is on the latter. What all these purchases have in common is that they are high-value and regulated financial transactions in which both buyer and vendor, and their respective agents, have legal responsibilities to check the sources of wealth and beneficial ownership in the UK. It is probable that if these checks were completed properly and the authorities notified, many of these acquisitions would not proceed. As it is, the question remains: Why are so many kleptocrats able to buy properties in the UK and/or via UK agents?

The Robber Baron of Uzbekistan

Islam Karimov was Uzbekistan's autocratic president from 1992 until his death in 2016. For the last 15 years of his life, however, it was his elder daughter Gulnara who made most of the headlines, culminating in the TeliaSonera scandal. Yet her greed and insatiable spending were well-known long before the Scandinavian company made payments which were later shown by the US authorities to constitute bribes to her.

From the early 2000s, media articles about Karimova concentrated on her lavish lifestyle: she owned a jewellery business, hosted fashion shows, and embarked on a singing career under the stage name GooGoosha, duetting with figures like Enrique Iglesias and Gerard Depardieu. She became notorious for her conspicuous consumption and self-promotion. By 2013, the BBC TV series *The Ambassadors*, a satire of British diplomacy in Central Asia based loosely on UK diplomats' direct experiences, centred on the embassy in fictional Tazbekistan and starring comedians David Mitchell and Robert Webb, provided a thinly veiled portrait of Karimova under the name of Fergana Karzak. Yet periodically, articles from reputable outlets highlighted a darker side, including the *Moscow Times* article from 2004, as mentioned above. A pattern emerged of Karimova abusing her position as the president's daughter to become what was described in a leaked US diplomatic cable as a 'robber baron' who expropriated countless businesses in Uzbekistan,[10] and solicited bribes from various others looking to do business in her country.

Her downfall in Uzbekistan, caused by an apparent rift with her father, was surprising, as kleptocrats usually enjoy the fruits of their spoils for as long as their relative is in power. Subsequent developments have seen an international investigation into Karimova involving over a dozen countries, leading to Karimova being indicted in the United States for money laundering[11] and a combined $2.6 billion in fines and disgorgements against three telecoms companies which bribed her, including TeliaSonera (since renamed the Telia Company), whose financial penalties were the largest ever to resolve a US Foreign Corrupt Practices Act investigation.[12] The investigation was also described by the US Department of Justice as one of the largest forfeiture actions ever brought to recover bribe proceeds from a corrupt government official (Karimova moonlighted as a diplomat), estimated at around $1 billion.[13] Karimova is unlikely to spend any time in an American jail—she is currently in prison in Uzbekistan, having been found guilty of a variety of crimes in trials that did not meet international legal standards.[14]

Multinational investigations have since shown just how rapacious Karimova was: not only had she acquired properties in France (including the castle mentioned above, built in 1815 for the daughter of the governess of Louis XVI and Marie Antoinette), Switzerland, Dubai, and elsewhere worth over $240 million in total,[15] she had stuffed these properties full of stolen loot. When activists broke into her home in Geneva, they found hundreds of luxury items, antiques, and artworks, including rare paintings by celebrated Uzbek artists that had been illegally removed from museums and galleries and smuggled out of Uzbekistan by Karimova. Uzbek authorities claimed that in total nearly a thousand historical, cultural, and artistic objects worth a combined $33.5 million were seized from Karimova's homes.[16]

Karimova bought at least five separate properties in the United Kingdom: three flats in the exclusive Belgravia area of London, purchased for a combined £14.67 million; a small house in Mayfair bought for £3.68 million for her son; and, grandest of all, a palatial manor house in Virginia Water, Surrey, bought for £18.1 million in August 2011, but likely worth £30 million in 2022. All of the properties were bought using British Virgin Island companies to hide the ownership.[17] In October 2017, the Serious Fraud Office (SFO) issued freezing orders on three UK properties still held by Karimova: one of the Belgrave apartments, the house in Mayfair, and the Virginia Water mansion.[18]

While Britain was only one of many states where Karimova had bought properties, it was distinct for the feebleness of its response to the money laundering by her and facilitated by her enablers. The UK authorities lagged behind their counterparts in other countries in investigating Karimova.

By the time the SFO issued a press release about the case in 2018, the US authorities had issued nearly $1 billion in penalties against Telia for its role in the bribery scandal,[19] issued orders to seize Karimova's assets held in foreign accounts,[20] had sanctioned her for corruption, and was building a criminal case against her, leading to her indictment the following year.[21] Sweden seized around US$30 million held by one of her companies in 2012.[22] Swiss authorities searched Karimova's villa in Geneva to gather evidence in August 2013, with Karimova identified as a suspect several months later.[23]

Properties in Europe had also been frozen. In July 2013, working in cooperation with Swiss police French authorities raided Karimova's three properties, having established that Karimova's partner and former husband Rustam Madumarov—they were briefly married in an apparent scam to transfer assets more easily—was acting as the beneficial owner. Thus, Karimova lost access to her castle, which she had bought in 2011 for €28 million.[24] In September 2014 French authorities froze these properties, and have since returned $20 million to Uzbekistan, albeit in a repatriation that lacked transparency.[25] Karimova's global property empire is depicted in Figure 8.1.

In the United Kingdom, the SFO announced it had finally seized the three properties in August 2023,[26] six years after it froze them and 11 years since the start of international investigations into Karimova. Making a move against her should have been easy: Karimova had lost power at home and therefore lost the incumbency advantage and her diplomatic passport. Any reluctance of foreign regulators to prosecute her as a privileged elite within a sovereign state had now gone. But Britain still failed to act, despite public reports of Karimova's UK properties dating back to 2012 and the fact that her associates were on record as being involved in UK registered companies. Is it because Uzbekistan is not a close ally? Or is the explanation found in the

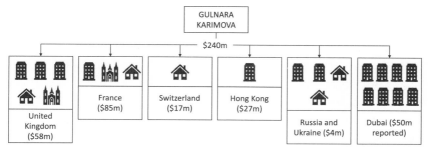

Figure 8.1 Gulnara Karimova's property empire

UK's private sector? We will return to the question of why before the end of this chapter, but in order to answer that question, we must first establish the attractiveness of UK property to post-communist elites and the key British professionals whose services are required to indulge these clients.

Partners in Property

It is not just those with the incumbency advantage that are enabled to acquire assets in Britain and beyond—although it is incumbents who appear to dominate the market.[27] Nor is it exclusively those from allied or partner countries that have access to the market. The Karimova story is just one of countless examples of elites linked to kleptocratic states investing in real estate in the UK. Since Russia's full-scale invasion of Ukraine, much attention has been focused on Russian-owned properties, including a BBC investigation from April 2022 which highlighted how a dozen newly sanctioned Russians were linked to an estimated £800 million worth of property in the United Kingdom.[28]

Yet Russian-owned properties form the tip of a very large iceberg. Knight Frank, founded in 1896 with its headquarters in London, is one of the world's leading real estate agents specializing in high-value property and high-net-wealth individual (HNWI) clients. They market themselves as 'partners in property'. In their annual survey of wealth managers, they ask about the assets and intentions of their HNWI buyers both at home and abroad. Overseas real estate properties and future purchases are a reportedly popular option for most HNWIs (see Table 8.1). Yet one group stands out for its preference for foreign over domestic assets. Russia and eight other former Soviet republics Commonwealth of Independent States[29] constitute the only regional group where HNWIs are more likely to own investment property overseas than at home, with a staggering 71% of them having a real estate asset abroad. This group was also almost twice as likely to invest overseas as to buy at home.

Examples of politically connected individuals from kleptocracies buying property in the UK are numerous. Chapter 3 described how Timur Kulibayev, the son-in-law of the first president of Kazakhstan, bought Prince Andrew's former residence using several different BVI companies for up to £8.6 million more than what the house would likely sell for at auction. Yet Kulibayev bought at least five other properties in London, including one

Table 8.1 HNWIs, by region, on real estate investments and residences

Survey Question	Africa	Asia	Austral-Asia	Europe	Latin America	Middle East	North America	Russia and CIS	Global Average
Investment Property, Home Country (%)	61	57	75	62	68	61	56	57	62
Investment Property Abroad (%)	27	30	16	37	42	55	27	71	38
No. of Current Residential Properties	2.1	2.9	2.3	2.7	2.9	4.0	2.7	3.5	2.9
Plans to purchase (next year) in home country (%)	16	27	13	21	24	33	20	22	22
Plans to Purchase Residence Abroad (next 12 mos) (%)	17	23	10	22	28	36	10	39	23

Source: Knight Frank, *The Wealth Report 2018*, London, 2018, 82–83.

purchased for £4.3 million more than the owner had purchased it—earlier on the same day. The businessman who made the quick profit had previously agreed to sell an oil terminal in Georgia to the Kazakh state oil and gas company, KazMunaiGas, although he denied there was a connection between the two deals.[30] In 2007 alone, Kulibayev bought properties in the UK worth over £88 million, including Andrew's mansion and the birthplace of James Bond writer Ian Fleming.[31]

After creating chaos and corruption in the Kyrgyz Republic when his father was president, Maxim Bakiyev arrived by private jet in the UK in 2010 and soon after purchased a £3.5 million mansion in Surrey. It had been purchased—without a mortgage—using a company registered in Belize called Limium Partners Limited. It was a rather startling coincidence that a number of the companies involved in the suspicious transfers from AsiaUniversalBank (see Chapter 5), including one that allegedly transferred $30 million out of the country through AUB around the time President Bakiyev was deposed, were also registered in Belize—at the same address and by the same company service provider as Limium Partners. The London law firm, Goodman Derrick LLP, that represented Limium in the purchase of the property told Global Witness, which issued a report about the property, that it could not respond to these 'allegations' as it would be breach of their code of conduct.[32] In 2018, the UK introduced unexplained wealth orders (UWOs), an investigative tool which requires politically exposed people or those linked to serious crime to reveal the sources with which they purchased a property, else risk having it confiscated. To date, Maxim Bakiyev's property has not been issued with such an order, despite the Belize connection indicating that an investigation into possible unexplained wealth would be legitimate. In early 2022, the title was sold or transferred, and the property is now in the name of two British lawyers.[33]

In 2018, OCCRP reported how family members and associates of President Aliyev of Azerbaijan had amassed a staggering $694 million in London property.[34] None of these properties have been subject to any known investigation, freezing order, or UWO, yet two other properties owned by Jahangir Hajiyev, an Azerbaijani banker, have been. Hajiyev had fallen foul of the regime and was jailed in 2016 in Baku on financial crime charges. His properties were a townhouse in the exclusive area of Knightsbridge, bought in December 2009 through a BVI company for £11.5 million, and the Mill Ride Golf Club in Ascot, purchased in September 2013 by a company registered in Guernsey for £10.52 million.[35] Hajiyev's properties were frozen by the UK's National Crime Agency in the first unexplained wealth orders issued in 2018, in a rare case of successful action (see Chapter 9), although as of January 2024, the properties remained only frozen, not confiscated, as legal proceedings dragged on, as they so often appear to do in the UK.

All of these examples—Karimova, Kulibayev, Bakiyev, the Aliyev family, Hajiyev—feature properties owned through offshore companies with a coterie of wealth managers, accountants, real estate agents, and solicitors constructing the deals to ensure maximum secrecy. But what of the UK's supposedly strong anti-money-laundering legislation, and the responsibilities it confers on regulated professionals? After all, real estate has been identified by the UK authorities as posing a high risk for money laundering.[36]

Time and again we see red flags seemingly missed, ignored, or at the least not investigated by the responsible authorities, with certain professionals continuing to act for their clients even when the circumstances should have caused them to consider the position carefully. In 2015, a television documentary *From Russia with Cash* used hidden cameras to highlight how real estate agents reacted when a 'Russian minister' (actually an undercover anti-corruption campaigner) told them he was planning on using funds that he had stolen from the health ministry. Most of the agents said they did not need to know about the source of funds, and several went so far as to put the 'minister' in touch with a solicitor.[37] One of those captured by hidden cameras (whose words introduce this chapter) was expelled from the Royal Institution of Chartered Surveyors for failing to notify his nominated money-laundering reporting officer about the incident.[38]

When Karimova, via Madumarov, purchased the three Belgravia apartments, she used a BVI company, Oregon Group Limited, which was administered by a London law firm called Quastel Midgen LLP, now Quastels,[39] whom we first met in the previous chapter. At the time of the purchase of the properties, there were no links in the public domain about Madumarov's relationship with Karimova, but he should have been assessed as a high-risk client regardless, given his residence in corruption hotspot Uzbekistan, the cost of the properties (a combined £14 million), and the fact that the company buying the property was registered offshore.

In March 2012, with the tide starting to turn against Karimova in Uzbekistan, the largest of the Belgravia apartments (a penthouse suite) was put up for sale. One month later, internet posts in English started to appear which indicated that Madumarov was Karimova's partner, both personally and in business.[40] Then came the articles from more reputable sources in late 2012 highlighting Madumarov's relationship with Karimova and her involvement in the telecoms scandal.[41] Yet despite this, the apartment was sold for £13.25 million in April 2013—at which point articles linking the two had been in the public domain for 12 months. A second smaller apartment was sold five months later for £1.85 million, making Karimova a combined profit of £1.54 million over the two sales based on their purchase price.[42]

Professionals in the property sector extend widely from real estate agents to chartered surveyors. But it is solicitors like Quastels and wealth managers and accountants like SH Landes that are the key enablers as they oversee the legal and financial dimensions of the purchase. The UK's anti-money-laundering regulations state that firms who provide ongoing services should continue to monitor their client, conduct further due diligence, and update their risk assessments accordingly. A simple internet search at any point in 2013 would have revealed the purported links between Madumarov—the given owner of the offshore companies that owned the properties and the private jet mentioned at the beginning of this chapter—to Gulnara Karimova. If these articles had been seen by any of professionals involved in the transactions it should have alerted them to potentially criminal financial activity, and a suspicious activity report should have been filed to the National Crime Agency, as a precaution if nothing else, especially if Madumarov had not disclosed to the solicitor his links to Karimova, a politically exposed person. As the filing of such reports is confidential, we do not know if one was filed: the fact that two properties were sold suggests either that a report was not filed, or the UK authorities failed to step in based on the information they had. Indeed, no investigative body appears to have looked at these transactions until years later. This may therefore be a case of the enabler effect, or one of regulatory failure and the authorities' inaction.

Enabling the Baronial Manor

Could the UK professionals have done more? SH Landes did not reply to Austrian NGO Freedom for Eurasia after it requested comment regarding its work for Madumarov. It told the BBC in 2023: 'SH Landes LLP was never engaged by Gulnara Karimova. SH Landes LLP did act on behalf of Rustam Madumarov. SH Landes LLP obtained due diligence on all its clients and relevant regulatory authorities were notified and kept appraised.'[43]

When Freedom for Eurasia wrote to Quastels to get their comment on the above matters, the law firm said it complied with its professional obligations and had not done anything wrong, but were bound by professional obligations, including that of confidentiality, and so were unable to respond to the NGO's enquiries.[44] Quastels were of course under no obligation to respond, but according to the Solicitors Regulation Authority the duty of confidence falls away if a solicitor was used by a client to perpetrate a crime, as seems to have occurred here, based on the evidence presented by the SFO that led to Karimova's properties being seized.[45] Quastels also threatened Freedom for Eurasia with a defamation lawsuit should the firm be mentioned in any article—not just in relation to the Karimova case, but in relation to any controversial area 'even if coverage may not mean to criticise or stigmatise this firm and/or its personnel'.[46] Such tactics aimed at stifling public interest reporting, referred to as SLAPPs—more commonly employed by kleptocrats rather than the enablers themselves—are discussed more in Chapter 13.

A common feature is found between the Karimova case and its most obvious comparator, convicted Azerbaijani kleptocrat Jahangir Hajiyev. The fact that the properties have been frozen by the UK authorities (and confiscated in Karimova's case) may be evidence that the enablers' activities were noncompliant but unwitting. However, the way the UK's anti-money-laundering legislation is set up (which absolves professionals of legal liability for continuing transactions where there are suspicions of money laundering as long as they report such suspicions[47]) means that even when enablers' actions allow criminal funds to enter the UK, they may be compliant. This demonstrates how ineffective the legislation is, as it allows significant wiggle room for enablers to either claim ignorance or, if suspicions are too great to ignore, escape liability by reporting it to an underfunded National Crime Agency, which is likely to concentrate on easy wins rather than go after politically linked and well-heeled individuals from overseas.

Hajiyev's wealth was managed by Werner Capital, a London-based boutique firm providing wealth management services for rich clients, including Hajiyev. The Guernsey company that owned Hajiyev's golf club was in turn owned by a UK company. Its company officials were Daniel and Tomas Werner of Werner Capital. Yet even when Hajiyev was found guilty in Baku in October 2016, Werner Capital continued to help him manage his money, and placed on the market another property that Hajiyev's company had built. The listing appeared on a website 10 days after Hajiyev's conviction. Werner Capital has faced no known legal action or investigation regarding its relationship with Hajiyev.[48] (When approached by Transparency International, Tomas Werner declined to comment on the business relationship with the Hajiyevs citing client confidentiality. Werner Capital stated they have never been involved in money laundering.[49])

However, this behaviour, whether wilful or unwitting, compliant or non-compliant, typically goes unpunished by both regulators and law enforcement. One other property transaction featuring the family of the president of Azerbaijan provides us with a rare example of where a professional enabler was sanctioned, albeit not prosecuted. However, as with the Karimova case (which snowballed after information about her dealings were leaked from Uzbekistan), it was not discovered because of diligent work by the UK's National Crime Agency or regulatory authorities but because information had been leaked—in this case, as part of the Panama Papers.

In 2015, President Aliyev's daughters, Leyla and Arzu, attempted to buy two luxury Knightsbridge flats for £59.5 million using a BVI company. Leyla and Arzu were represented in this deal by Khalid Sharif of Child & Child, a solicitors' firm. However, Sharif failed to identify the two women as politically exposed persons, a requirement of the relevant UK money-laundering legislation. Sharif was referred to the solicitors' disciplinary tribunal for not detecting 'a significant risk of money-laundering'.[50] A second deal Sharif acted in involved Mirjalal Pashayev, cousin of both the Azerbaijan president's wife and Nargiz Pashayeva, whom we will meet in Chapter 10. This transaction, in which Pashayev received as a gift from a business associate a $6 million apartment in London, was also scrutinized as it posed 'warning signs' because the property was a high-value gift that was transferred between foreign-owned entities in an offshore jurisdiction.[51] Sharif admitted that he failed to conduct ongoing monitoring of his business relationship with an associate of the Azerbaijani president who was involved in the deal, circumstances which again 'disclosed a significant risk that money laundering was taking place'. He was fined £45,000 and charged a further £40,000 in costs.[52]

Sharif argued that he was unwitting. He had simply failed to conduct research on his clients, but this seems unlikely seeing the amount of information freely available about the Aliyev daughters, and the fact that his contact was an associate of the Azerbaijani president. Sharif was not prosecuted either for a failure to implement the money-laundering regulations or for a failure to report a suspicion of money laundering. However, despite the fact that a competent professional should have ascertained this risk, and the fact that the disciplinary tribunal had identified that both transactions posed a significant risk for money laundering (although the Knightsbridge flats' transactions was never completed), Sharif does not appear to have been investigated by the police and was not prosecuted. Indeed, in none of the above cases have we seen any known criminal investigation into possible breaches of the law on behalf of any regulated professional in the UK.

A Specific Type of Client

These case studies demonstrate the professional indulgence of purchasing assets, with certain professionals apparently marketing themselves to a specific type of wealthy and politically exposed client. The accountancy firm at the heart of the Karimova case, SH Landes LLP, also features in an unrelated case, but one that also figures a daughter of a kleptocratic president. This story revolved around Landes Ltd (a UK company owned by Steven Landes,[53] the managing partner of SH Landes LLP) acting as the company secretary to several companies linked to Dariga Nazarbayeva, the daughter of the first president of Kazakhstan.[54] One of the companies, Beatrice Alliance, featured in the unexplained wealth order case discussed in our next chapter.[55]

But the disclosures to the court inadvertently revealed a potential criminal offence: when she sold the shares of a Kazakh sugar company to Beatrice Alliance Ltd, the company filed dormant accounts for that year, indicating that the company had conducted no financial or business activity. This is a violation of the Companies Act, an imprisonable offence.[56] Perhaps Landes was misled concerning the accuracy of the accounts, or Beatrice Alliance Ltd did not buy the sugar company shares (which would throw doubt on Nazarbayeva's explanation of the source of funds, as explained in the next chapter). When asked about this seeming discrepancy by investigative group SourceMaterial, Steven Landes did not reply.[57] Nazarbayeva's lawyers, Mishcon de Reya, said that Nazarbayeva was not involved with the company at the point these accounts were filed, and therefore was not responsible for them.

The fact that Landes was working for several high-net-worth individuals from kleptocracies stresses the 'clientelist' aspect of enabling networks—that professional enablers are not randomly selected on a transactional basis, but rather sell their services to a particular kind of client or clients from particular countries, who may recommend them to others on a similar basis. In such circumstances, how can they claim to be unwitting of their potential kleptocratic origins of wealth?

Quastels—the solicitor involved in the Karimova/Madumarov UK property purchases—marketed itself prior to the Russian invasion of Ukraine as 'offering bespoke legal consultations and advice for Russian-speaking clients wishing to relocate to the United Kingdom or purchase UK assets',[58] although Quastels took this page down in 2022. The firm, however, still features specialized lawyers in both immigration ('from HNW business relocations to visitor visas')[59] as well as residential property and UK inheritance (for 'high net worth individuals domiciled in the UK and abroad').[60] These are the same lawyers who were featured on Quastels' now-defunct 'Russia and CIS' page, indicating the interconnectedness of the two areas in London lawyers' dealings with high-net-worth individuals from this region.

Quastels can surely not claim to be ignorant of the sources of wealth in Russia and Eurasia. As described in Chapter 7, it was Quastels' Head of Immigration, Tanya Laidlaw, who said it would not necessarily be a problem when approached by someone (actually an undercover journalist) in 2019 trying to get an investment visa in the UK for a fund manager who was described as helping members of Putin's inner circle. But in 2022, as the Kremlin's reputation in Britain descended to a new low, a different message was being posted by Laidlaw. Following Russia's invasion of Ukraine, Laidlaw reposted on LinkedIn a 'Stand with Ukraine' plea asking for a visa ban on all Russian citizens.[61]

In this chapter, we have found that Karimova's network of proxies and companies had substantial ties to the UK and its overseas territories. These proxies were indulged by British professional services, as they were in many other countries, yet the UK did comparatively little to investigate the illicit funds and bring enforcement actions. The predominant explanation for how Karimova managed to buy and sell property, despite a growing scandal around her, appears to be the enabler effect. Even when she lost her incumbent status and details started to emerge about her links between certain proxies and herself, enablers continued to act for those proxies. Similarly, despite Uzbekistan's weak relations with the UK in this period, SH Landes and Quastels were more than happy to offer their services to a rich Uzbek national, Rustam Madumarov, who was looking to buy a private jet and several high value properties. The other cases touched upon in this chapter suggest the UK property is open to all buyers—those of allies and those of enemies, incumbents, and exiles—despite question marks over their sources of wealth. In all cases, enablers are the enduring feature. The enablers here will likely claim their actions were unwitting, but the information available in the public domain from 2012 may suggest otherwise. This presents strong evidence of the enabler effect in action.

The actions of kleptocrats like Karimova—and their enablers on their behalf—have very real-world consequences. Information from one international company operating in Uzbekistan suggests that the government agents she directed 'utilised torture, and threats of torture, to coerce false statements from witnesses' to support the charges against the company's manager.[62] The money that Karimova claimed for herself drained resources from the Uzbek budget: 'She single-handedly created a budget deficit', said one Uzbek official.[63] Her criminal activities were later said to have cost her home country more than $2.3 billion.[64] Her main residence in Uzbekistan consisted of 94 acres of land which were festooned with dozens of blue fir trees that cost $5,000 each.[65] This in a country where the average salary in 2013—the year Karimova was stripped from her diplomatic posts—was around US$575 per month.

This highlights the clear link between kleptocracy and human rights abuse: not only the individuals repressed by Karimova because they stood in her way, but the Uzbek people as a whole, many who remained impoverished and unable to change their government due to the repressive infrastructure needed to maintain the kleptocratic system. In the Karimov family era in Uzbekistan, no dissent was tolerated, and even moderate economic opportunities are closed off in favour of the elite. The professionals involved with Karimova and her cronies lend support to such a system, unwittingly or otherwise, directly or indirectly.

Meanwhile, Karimova continues to employ a coterie of enablers while in prison, who have managed to sell some of her properties. What is remarkable about her case is that despite overwhelming evidence of not just corrupt, but criminal conduct, there is still the possibility that hundreds of millions of dollars will be returned to her,[66] although a new indictment issued by the Swiss authorities in September 2023 on fraud and organized crime charges appears to be an attempt to stop this.[67]

And it is striking that while various companies have been fined for their involvement with Karimova's bribery scheme, no figure outside of Karimova's inner circle has been successfully prosecuted for bribery or facilitating illicit financial flows. Three executives from telecoms firm Telia were charged in 2018 with bribery offences. However, all were found not guilty on a legal technicality, as Karimova was not a government official in charge of telecoms at the time of the bribes, a requirement of Swedish bribery law.[68] The UK amended their bribery law in 2010 to cover payments to any individual to seek improper advantage, though high-profile enforcement cases are few and far between—a common theme throughout this book.

As for Karimova's jet, plane spotters photographed it in Malta in October 2014 where it acquired a new tail number.[69] It acquired another number in September 2017.[70] Such moves indicate either an attempt by Karimova to further hide its ownership, or a possible sale. The Uzbek authorities are looking to seize it as they believe it was bought with the proceeds of crime.[71] Luckily, the airplane is not registered in the UK or an overseas territory. If it had been, their chances of asset recovery would be very low indeed.

9

Explaining Wealth

There is a woman [Dariga Nazarbayeva] . . . who might just have
conceivably earned her own money through her own wits in support of the family rather than simply sitting back and taking what
might be produced by her husband or son.
—Claire Montgomery KC, March 2020[1]

In March 2020, members of Kazakhstan's ruling family were in court in
London. Yet it was a common Western narrative of equality which was
deployed against the British state and in defence of Dariga Nazarbayeva,
the chair of the Kazakh senate and the daughter of long-time kleptocrat
Nursultan Nazarbayev. Nazarbayeva's barrister Claire Montgomery KC
even accused the National Crime Agency (NCA) of 'an absurdly patriarchal
view of the world' in failing to recognize that Nazarbayeva was a woman of
independent means who 'earned her own money through her own wits'.[2]
Montgomery's narrative of Nazarbayeva as a self-made woman was auda-
cious, and, according to those who sat in court, the brio of its delivery compelling. It was an act of a wilful yet entirely compliant legal enabler. The
spectacle of a gender equality trope being instrumentally deployed in support of a leading figure in one of the world's most corrupt regimes felt like a
scene from a cinematic satire of Western hubris. In fact, this was one claim of
a real and ultimately successful legal narrative deployed by Montgomery—
an experienced and acclaimed barrister described by a colleague as 'one
down from God'.[3]

Notwithstanding its success, the political and economic evidence
suggested that this was a false narrative, as was much that was heard during
these proceedings. Montgomery was instructed by Nazarbayeva's law firm
Mishcon de Reya. Together, they claimed that Dariga's wealth was completely separate from her criminal ex-husband, Rakhat Aliyev.[4] This included the claim that Dariga's shareholding in one of Kazakhstan's largest

banks, Nurbank, the sale of which funded one of the properties issued with an unexplained wealth order (UWO), was also separate from her husband.

However, a close analysis of Nurbank documents suggests that this could not be. Dariga had simply acquired most of his shares from Rakhat after they divorced. The tale of the 'independent woman' was also not the story Dariga was telling a Russian newspaper in 2008 about when she married Rakhat in the 1980s: 'The last time my dad [Nursultan Nazarbayev] gave me money was when I was in university. As soon as I got married, he said: "Your family is Rakhat, so let him feed you." Rakhat started, like many others—he took goods for sale, guarded the cargo, carried it through customs, earned start-up capital with his own hands'.[5] Dariga was—to paraphrase her own words— happy to sit back while her husband did the dirty work, which was shown to be very dirty indeed.

In this chapter we move further downstream from how a property is purchased with suspicious wealth to how this wealth is explained away by legal enablers. We begin with a summary of the organized crime which in-disputably lies behind Rakhat's wealth before going on to outline the UWO system, which was designed to challenge property purchases linked to such wealth. By comparing to the relatively successful cases against Zamira Hajiyeva, we see how the incumbency of Dariga and her son Nurali, and the innovation of Mishcon de Reya combined to explain the wealth. We con-clude by showing that this is a general pattern found across our dataset of £2 billion worth of property in London and the southeast of England purchased by post-communist elites.

Murder in Kazakhstan

Kazakhstan's short history of sovereign statehood is full of political intrigue, corruption, and violence. In January 2007, a series of events combining all three was to have seismic repercussions on the country's ruling family. The incident featured Abilmazhen Gilimov, the chairman of Nurbank. According to Gilimov, after a board meeting the bank's main shareholder, Rakhat Aliyev—having apparently discovered that the bank had issued some suspect loans—threatened Gilimov with a gun when he refused to sign over to Rakhat the ownership of the building in which Nurbank's main office was located. A few days later two other senior bank officials were reported missing.[6]

By this point Rakhat had been married to Dariga Nazarbayeva, the eldest daughter of the president, for almost 20 years. But Gilimov also had friends in high places: he was the cousin of the then mayor of Almaty,[7] Kazakhstan's largest city, so this could not be just swept under the carpet like Rakhat's previous crimes. In February, Rakhat was sent to Vienna to act as Kazakhstan's Ambassador to Austria—a demotion of sorts and a way to try to keep him out of trouble. Yet in May, Rakhat was quickly removed from all positions of power and a criminal case opened against him. It was also announced that he had divorced Dariga.[8]

An international arrest warrant was issued by Kazakhstan for criminal association, economic crimes, and the kidnapping of the two bank officials.[9] Over the next few years, money-laundering investigations regarding Rakhat were launched in Austria, Malta, Liechtenstein, and Germany.[10] Rakhat claimed that all the charges were politically motivated, as he had told Nazarbayev that he was going to run against him for the Kazakh presidency. He hired an impressive legal team, including Wolfgang Brandstetter—who later became Austria's minister of justice—who worked for Rakhat from 2007 to 2011, providing legal advice and helping him fight extradition.[11]

But in 2011, the bodies of the two Nurbank officials were found in Kazakhstan. They had been tortured prior to their death, their bodies placed into a metal drum filled with chalk and then buried in a waste dump.[12] Rakhat was charged in Kazakhstan with their murder. For several years, Rakhat evaded justice by moving to Malta, but in June 2014, he gave himself up to Austrian law enforcement in connection with the murder probe, although he denied the allegations.

Two months before the trial commenced, Rakhat Aliyev was found hanged in prison. Rakhat's supporters claimed he had been killed, but the Austrian authorities found no evidence of foul play.[13] The trial of two of Rakhat's alleged accomplices went ahead in 2015, with lead prosecutor Bettina Wallner saying that the case sounded 'like the plot of a Hollywood film'.[14] The two men were found not guilty, something supporters of Rakhat have pointed to in an attempt to exonerate him posthumously. However, the not guilty verdict likely came because of the problem of relying on evidence from a kleptocracy where political motivations play heavily, and there was much discussion during the trial about whether the Austrian legal system was in danger of being manipulated by the Kazakh authorities.[15]

In fact, multiple sources attest to the fact that while in power in Kazakhstan, Rakhat was a key part of Kazakhstan's kleptocracy. He abused positions of power in the tax police and secret police in a criminal fashion to extort companies from rival businessmen. One such individual was forced to give up his media company and flee abroad, fearing 'physical elimination'.[16] Was it plausible that his then wife, Dariga Nazarbayeva, knew nothing about these crimes? Regardless, she appeared happy, then at least, to sit back and enjoy the proceeds of Rakhat's criminal actions.

Unexplained Wealth

Wealth garnered in the manner that it was acquired by Rakhat needs explaining. When such cases go public, they invite two conflicting narratives. The first is that of indictment produced by anti-corruption researchers such as us: that such wealth is, by virtue of its provenance in a kleptocratic state, illicit, even if it is not always technically illegal—although it the case of Rakhat, it appears that much of his wealth was based on the proceeds of crime. In 2015, anti-corruption NGO Global Witness published a report that identified links between a London property empire worth £145 million and Rakhat.[17] The key building was a block of luxury flats located at 215–237 Baker Street, leading to various Sherlock Holmes references in the many press articles that followed. The report documented clear denials from the properties' managers that Rakhat had ever been involved in the buildings' ownership, but they refused to say who the owners actually were, citing 'confidentiality', leaving this 'Mystery on Baker Street'—as the Global Witness report was called—unsolved at that time.[18]

The report came at a time when Transparency International and other organizations were highlighting not only the problem of anonymous property ownership but also the difficulty of investigating corrupt officials who owned such property if they came from countries unwilling to cooperate with UK law enforcement. Such investigations only had the possibility of success if the person was no longer in power (the removal of the 'incumbency advantage') and had been convicted in their home country of financial crime. As an anti-money-laundering action plan released by the Home Office and Treasury in 2016 stated: 'In many cases the country in which the offences took place lacks either the will, the capability, or the human rights record that would allow effective cooperation to take place'.[19]

To address this problem, a new type of investigative tool—the UWO—was introduced in the UK as part of the Criminal Finances Act 2017. The legislation was potentially game-changing as it in essence reversed the burden of proof: when a property is issued with an order, its owners must explain the sources of wealth behind the purchase. Failure to do so creates a legal presumption that the property has been acquired through the proceeds of crime and can thus be confiscated via subsequent civil recovery proceedings under the provisions of the UK's Proceeds of Crime Act, passed in 2002. Despite the rather narrow circumstances in which a UWO can be issued, including the need to have 'reasonable grounds' to issue one, the legal presumption of corrupt wealth led the legal press to question whether the new instrument was based on the principle of 'guilty until proven innocent'.[20]

However, UWOs can only be issued on any property where the court has evidence that it has been acquired with the proceeds of crime, is owned by someone suspected as being involved in crime, or is owned by an overseas state official or politician (a PEP) whose known income would be insufficient to afford the property. Thus, UWOs were framed as a means to tackle both organized crime and grand corruption emanating from kleptocracies. In messaging from government officials, the latter was often stressed over the former. Then Security Minister Ben Wallace said in an interview in 2018 that 'if they are an MP in a country where they don't receive a big salary but suddenly they have a nice Knightsbridge townhouse worth millions and they can't prove how they paid for it, we will seize that asset, we will dispose of it and we will use the proceeds to fund our law enforcement'.[21] He referred to a scandal that saw over $20 billion funnelled out of Russia, saying that 'we are not going to let it happen anymore'.[22] The kleptocracy problem was one that British criminal justice had hitherto failed to tackle. UWOs were a new way to try to crack the nut.

This fighting talk from government ministers put considerable expectation on UK law enforcement. It was therefore important that bodies such as the National Crime Agency that could issue UWOs selected the initial cases carefully, as the Director General of the UK National Economic Crime Centre (NECC), Graeme Biggar, commented after one UWO High Court hearing: 'These hearings will establish the case law on which future judgements will be based, so it's absolutely vital that we get this right'.[23] As Matthew Cowie, a former prosecutor at the UK's Serious Fraud Office, commented: 'It would be bad political PR and bad for [UWOs as an instrument] if they fail'.[24]

In February 2018, UWOs were issued on two properties owned by an individual from Azerbaijan, Jahangir Hajiyev, and his wife, Zamira Hajiyeva.[25]

The NCA's case was that Hajiyev's 'known employment history and income' was 'very difficult to reconcile with a property purchase of over £10 million' as his highest salary, including bonuses, was only around $70,600 with modest share dividends of just under $89,000 in 2008.[26] The investigation into the Hajiyevs received a lot of media attention, especially regarding Zamira Hajiyeva's lifestyle. She had reportedly spent over £16 million in Harrods over a 10-year period, including extravagant purchases such as £30,000 of luxury chocolates in a single day.[27]

In response to the UWO, the legal defence narrative kicked in. Hajiyeva's lawyer argued that Jahangir could not give adequate answer to the order, as he was in prison in Baku as a result of an unfair and politically motivated trial.[28] This was a defence based on the distinction between exile and incumbent. But in this case these arguments were rejected, the UWOs upheld, and Hajiyeva's application to appeal to the UK's supreme court was dismissed in December 2020. This now forced her to reveal the sources used in the properties' purchase, else risk having them confiscated.

The anti-corruption narrative had apparently triumphed. However, it turned out that Hajiyeva's failure to explain her wealth was a direct product of her husband's fall from power, proving the rule that the incumbency advantage and enabling effect are a potent combination. A second UWO case against a foreign political figure was launched in May 2019, with three orders issued on properties in London worth £80 million. This time it was against a very senior incumbent. There was much speculation in anti-corruption circles about the identity of the properties' owner or owners, which was finally revealed in March 2020: the houses were owned by Dariga and Nurali Aliyev, one of the two sons she had with Rakhat. At the time of the issuance of the orders, Dariga Nazarbayeva was the chair of the Kazakh Senate. Nurali Aliyev was an entrepreneur, but had been the deputy mayor of Astana, Kazakhstan's capital city, from November 2014 to March 2016.[29]

Inspired by the anti-corruption narrative, the NCA was attempting to seize the properties on the belief that they had been bought with wealth criminally acquired by Rakhat—now deceased—and that both he and members of their family may thus have laundered proceeds derived from these crimes into the three properties. The NCA drew a lot from the Global Witness report, but surprisingly the block of offices and luxury flats on Baker Street was not issued with an order. This was supposedly because the investigators could not unravel its ownership structure, though clearly this is what such orders were designed to shed light on. Indeed, orders can be issued against offshore companies and company officials when the beneficial ownership cannot be clearly established. And so it was in this case with the three properties: the orders had been issued against a nominee, a classic technique used to hide suspiciously acquired wealth (see Chapter 5), and four legal entities—three private foundations and a company—all of which were involved in the legal ownership of the three properties. The nominee was a legal enabler: a man named Andrew Baker, a British solicitor based in Liechtenstein, who was the president of two of the foundations.[30]

'It's Business. But It's Personal'

In response to the orders, Dariga and Nurali hired a top London law firm, Mishcon de Reya (hereafter Mischon) to craft their legal defence. Mishcon's strapline is 'It's business. But it's personal'. In *NCA v Baker*, as the case is known, they appear to follow this mantra in their professional practice. They argued that there were no links between the properties and Rakhat's criminally acquired capital, and that the orders should be dismissed as a result. Mishcon backed up their argument by submitting 268 pages of documentation about the property purchases.[31] Such defence narratives work best if kept outside of the public view. Mishcon originally sought confirmation that any material it supplied would be held in confidence; however, no such confirmation was given and much of this material was published in court documents, providing an illuminating window into the world of kleptocratic enabling.

The key task of the defence was to effectively deny that Rakhat's criminal wealth was the source of funds for the property purchases. Mishcon made a great deal of the fact that Rakhat had divorced from Dariga soon after falling from grace in 2007. However, Rakhat claimed this was performed without consent, and that his signature had been forged. Indeed, the divorce may have been a pretext to transfer Rakhat's business holdings to Dariga. She then sold the shares in two companies that had previously been owned by Rakhat—the Kazakh bank Nurbank and a sugar company called JSC Kant— and invested most of the proceeds into property in the United Kingdom, two of which were subsequently issued with UWOs.[32] The link between the criminal wealth and the purchase was arguably strong. A great deal of explaining was needed.

Court documents reveal remarkable similarities between the two UWO cases, *NCA v Hajiyeva* and *NCA v. Baker*. Both feature a bank chairman, Jahangir Hajiyev and Nurali Aliyev, respectively, using shell companies to acquire suspect loans from their own bank. One could even argue that *NCA v Baker* contained more evidence of suspicious transactions—given the revelations of the information revealed by Mishcon—in contrast to the lack of information revealed concerning the property purchases by Hajiyev. The key difference was that Hajiyev's family were not incumbents—quite on the contrary. Jahangir Hajiyev had already been jailed in his home country by the time the UWO proceedings started. The British judiciary later de facto confirmed this by denying Zamira Hajiyeva's extradition to Azerbaijan, stating that there was 'a real risk' that she could suffer 'a flagrant denial of justice'.[33] The Hajiyevs thus no longer held any kind of political sway in Azerbaijan, in contrast to the Nazarbayevs in Kazakhstan at the time the orders were issued. Likely as a result of this, the owners of Nurbank when the orders were issued—associates of Dariga, no less—said that the loan to Nurali was legitimate. Nurali used the loan to buy a house on The Bishops Avenue, the so-called Billionaires' Row, for £39.5 million.[34]

Alongside the incumbency advantage, a second mechanism appears to matter: the enabler effect. Mishcon had also represented Hajiyeva (although not in the UWO case, but in relation to her acquiring a Tier 1 investment visa, as mentioned in Chapter 7) and had apparently learnt a good deal from the first UWO case. Just as in the Hajiyeva case, the links between these properties and the origins of the family wealth—the criminal Rakhat—were clear from the evidence submitted to the court.

The evidence showed that Rakhat had abused the position of a state official to create the capital upon which he created businesses which he and then wife Dariga both ran. Following their supposed divorce, most of the assets and companies that Rakhat owned or co-owned were quietly shuffled into the hands of Dariga and Nurali. The latter even became the owner of a property in Kazakhstan that his father had acquired from one of the murdered bank officials prior to his exile.[35] These companies included both JSC Kant and Nurbank—the firms which Dariga said she sold to fund the purchase of the London properties.

However, despite the Hajiyeva precedent, Mishcon won the case for Dariga and Nurali. The UWOs against the property were dismissed by the High Court in 2020 by Ms Justice Lang who ruled that the NCA had not demonstrated the link between the properties and Rakhat. Lang commented that the NCA's underlying assumptions and reasoning were 'unreliable' and 'flawed'.[36]

As the NCA had lost the case—and no cost cap had been placed in the UWO legislation—the investigative body had to pay the £1.5 million of legal fees accrued by Dariga and Nurali. This blew a hole in the NCA's finances: the agency's entire budget has been just over £4 million annually since 2015, and the costs were particularly galling when a 2017 Home Office impact assessment predicted that the legal costs per UWO case would be between £5,000 and £10,000.[37] Yet the NCA decided to fight on. The NECC's Graeme Biggar commented that he disagreed with the High Court's decision to discharge the UWOs: 'The NCA is tenacious. We have been very clear that we will use all the legislation at our disposal to pursue suspected illicit finance'.[38] However, the fight was short lived, as the appeals court refused to give the NCA permission to appeal.

How were Mishcon able to win the case? *NCA v Baker* failed for several reasons which highlight the added value of legal enabling to transnational kleptocracy. Firstly, the relative weakness of the public authorities versus the private sector was acute in this case. *NCA v Baker* was a particularly flawed investigation, with the NCA not establishing the proper context of Kazakhstan's political economy, which allowed the president's family, including Dariga, to accrue billions of dollars in opaque and questionable circumstances.

Secondly, the judge, Ms Justice Lang, favoured the legal defence narrative of Mishcon de Reya over the anti-corruption narrative of the NCA. She dismissed Rakhat as an unreliable witness but did not seem to have considered that Dariga's account may also have been self-justifying or considered how her ex-husband's dramatic fallout with the then Kazakh president, Dariga's father, could have affected legal proceedings in Kazakhstan, including the divorce. Lang appeared to have little understanding of the criminal nature of Kazakhstan or its kleptocratic business environment. In Lang's judgement, Dariga's father, President Nursultan Nazarbayev, is only mentioned once, his name spelt incorrectly.[39] And in one particularly memorable sentence, Lang commented: 'Notwithstanding his criminality, [Rakhat Aliyev] had been a successful businessman'.[40] This highlights how judges in English courts—a system which lacks a specialist economic crime court—are often called upon to make judgements on complex cases in countries where they lack contextual knowledge or expert witness testimony, which the NCA chose not to seek.

Thirdly, the UWO legislation appears to be intrinsically flawed when it comes to tackling grand corruption in that it states that, when assessing a respondent's income, it is judged to be 'lawfully obtained' if it is generated legally under the laws of the country from where the income arises. Dariga received shares in sugar company JSC Kant that were previously held by Rakhat, as part of the supposed divorce settlement. The Kazakh general prosecutor—hardly an impartial body with respect to the president's daughter—had confirmed that Rakhat had not illegally acquired JSC Kant, something cited by Ms Justice Lang in her judgement. Clearly, reliance on such an authority is problematic, given the lack of independence of the Kazakh judiciary and the ability of the country's political elite to interfere in the judicial process.

The Legal Explainers

These two UWO cases illustrate a general pattern of the ineffectiveness of the anti-money-laundering system with respect to the UK real estate market which we began to explore in the last chapter. However, it wasn't supposed to be this way. UWOs were presented as a potentially game-changing piece of legislation in regard to kleptocracy. In 2016, then UK Home Secretary Amber Rudd, said that '[UWOs] send a powerful message that the UK is serious about rooting out the proceeds of overseas grand corruption.'[41] Quoting from Transparency International, she added that it may be 'the most important anti-corruption legislation to be passed in the UK in the past 30 years', legislation that will 'make sure that the UK is no longer seen as a safe haven for corrupt wealth.'[42]

A 2017 impact assessment from the Home Office forecasted that there would be 20 UWOs per year. In April 2018, Donald Toon, Director for Economic Crime at the NCA, told the media that the agency's officers were working on around 100 cases and that he expected about five more UWOs to be secured in the next three months.[43] However, only four UWO investigations were been reported from 2018 (a total of 15 orders were issued across the four cases)[44] to the end of 2021, with no UWO issued in this time frame after July 2019. None of these were issued against Russian nationals, and, as described above, only two have been issued against foreign political figures, with just one upheld. Even though the orders issued against Hajiyeva were kept in place, the properties are yet to be recovered and legal proceedings are still ongoing, at the time of writing, demonstrating the drawn-out process of civil recovery. A freedom of information request submitted by Spotlight on Corruption in late 2022 indicated that a further UWO investigation was ongoing as of July 2022 though it is unclear whether the recipient is suspected of organized crime or is an overseas political figure.

So, despite the government's signalling that UWOs would be a key and oft-used tool in the fight against kleptocracy, the investigations so far suggest that the orders may be more effective against organized criminal figures, where the property can be more clearly linked to illegal activity. UWOs may also be effective when targeted against corrupt political figures from overseas who have lost power and have been exiled or jailed. It is noteworthy that the NCA brought the case on the belief that the properties could be tied to Rakhat Aliyev—not only an exiled opponent of the Kazakh regime, but someone who was dead. When the properties were revealed to be owned by a loyalist, an incumbent political figure—in this case, Dariga Nazarbayeva—the case started to fall apart. Yet as discussed above, UWOs were brought in to specifically address the problem of corrupt officials who are still in power.

The reasons why the suspicious origins of wealth were 'explained' in *NCA v Baker* appear to have relatively little to do with the facts of the case, which in some respects are remarkably similar to that of the Hajiyevs where the wealth was deemed to be 'unexplained'. What made the difference in *NCA v Hajiyeva* is that the enablers were unable to construct a narrative around the funds being used to purchase the house (see Figure 9.1). With new management at his former bank, and Hajiyev no longer protected by Azerbaijan's security services or prosecutor's office, such information—key to the defence against a UWO—was not available to them. The judge in *NCA v Hajiyeva* ruled that it was the income disparity that led him to uphold the orders, rather than the allegations of serious crime (which were tainted by possible political motivations of a kleptocratic state) that resulted in Hajiyev's jailing.[45] Yet without this fall from grace from the Azerbaijani business and political elite, the evidence from Azerbaijan to 'explain' Hajiyev's wealth may have been available to the enablers.

This pattern, which we have named 'the incumbency advantage'—where those in power are largely unaccountable—can be established more widely when we look at properties that have been frozen or seized by the UK authorities. We undertook a study of post-Soviet real estate purchases in London and the southeast of England, and created a database containing 88 properties worth around £2 billion, all purchased between 1998 and 2020.

		Zamira Hajiyeva	Dariga Nazarbayeva
	Source of Wealth	Allegedly husband, bank chairman, criminal Jahangir Hajiyev	Allegedly husband, bank chairman, criminal Rakhat Aliyev
	UWO	Issued against £22m London property (February 2018)	Issued against £80m of London property (May 2019)
	Incumbency advantage	No (does not present evidence of source of wealth)	Yes (presents evidence of source of wealth)
	Enabler effect	Yes (weak UK enforcement, strong defence lawyers)	Yes (weak UK enforcement, strong defence lawyers, learned from previous case)
	Outcome	FAILURE: UWO upheld	FULL SUCCESS: UWO dismissed, NCA liable for £1.5m costs

Figure 9.1 Explaining family fortunes

Table 9.1 Loss/retention of property by incumbents and exiles

Incumbents	100% (72/72) retain property	0% (0/72) lose property
Exiles	81% (13/16) lose property	19% (3/16) retain property
Overall	97% (85/88)	3% (3/88)

To be included in this list, the owner of the property must be either: 1) a government official, head of a state company, or a close relative (classed as 'incumbents'), or 2) a former political figure or businessperson (including close relatives) now out of favour, either in exile or in jail (classed as 'exiles'). All made their money in a high-risk environment, as defined by the UK's anti-money-laundering legislation. A very clear pattern emerges where 85 of 88 cases exhibit the expected outcome of the incumbency advantage where kleptocrats and in-favour oligarchs retain property and exiles lose it (see Table 9.1). In fact, no incumbents (0/72) lose their property. Just three of the cases are exceptions to the logic of the incumbency. They are all of exiles retaining property (3/16); in each of these cases the enabler effect appeared to make the difference. Overall, these results suggest that incumbency is sufficient to retain property and that exiles only have a chance to explain their wealth with very effective legal enabling.

Of the three cases of where there was no exile disadvantage other factors also matter. Two of these cases relate to Dmitry Leus, an exile who has retained property in the UK, and his wife, Zhanna Leus. Dmitry Leus (see Chapter 11) has used the law effectively to suppress reporting about his historic conviction for a money-laundering offence in Russia (which under Russian law he was entitled to have struck out from the record).[46] He has also made philanthropic and political donations and placed paid-for content in UK newspapers.[47] In the other case, Maxim Bakiyev, as we saw in Chapter 5, there was also enabling with respect to both the property and finances. In none of these cases was a UWO or similar civil recovery procedure begun so we lack the evidence of causation found in the Hajiyev and Nazarbayeva cases. But what evidence is available suggests that all three are cases of exiles who have protected their property and status against the odds and through the enabling effect.

For Dariga, the enabler effect is also apparent and works in conjunction with the incumbency advantage. Major law firms representing wealthy figures with political connections from overseas have far more resources to expend on cases than the poorly funded NCA and the UK's other investigative bodies. The importance of enablers in defending these cases appears to be acknowledged by law enforcement authorities themselves. *The Mail on Sunday* reported that NCA financial investigators had told it in private that, in regard to UWOs: 'They believe targeting corrupt businessmen with access to "expensive QCs and claims of private wealth" is a "waste of time"' and that one investigator suggested that more success would result from targeting '"mid to high level organised criminals" with assets but no legitimate income'.[48]

This article came a few months after the NCA's disastrous loss in *NCA v Baker*. It appears to indicate that there was a deterrent effect on law enforcement. The state appeared to have been deterred again from tackling complex cases featuring oligarchs and overseas political figures, given the power of the law firms behind them. But for all its weaknesses, the NCA was quite right for suggesting that the material supplied via Mishcon de Reya was arguably inaccurate, incomplete, and misleading. The NCA said that it filed a detailed witness statement setting out why the voluntary disclosure strengthened rather than undermined its suspicions regarding the sources of income used to obtain the properties. It argued before Ms Justice Lang that the material in the form of a letter with enclosures was inadmissible or that no weight should be attached to it, highlighting that it was not supported by witness evidence or verified by a statement of truth, its provenance was unclear, and there were grounds to believe that documents were forged. This was not accepted by the judge, who accepted the truth of the documents.[49]

After *NCA v Baker* had concluded, investigative group SourceMaterial presented evidence that backed up the NCA's case that the information submitted by Mishcon on behalf of Dariga Nazarbayeva may have been misleading. Its investigation indicated that company documents suggested she may have sold the sugar company JSC Kant not to a third party, but to another company she controlled (whose control was not disclosed to the court), which would therefore not represent a genuine sale, and not explain the wealth used to buy one of the properties.[50] The fact that the NCA—who have much greater powers than investigative journalists—did not pick up on this possibility concerning JSC Kant reaffirms the inadequacies of its investigation, which ultimately led to Mishcon's material being accepted at face value by the judge. (Mishcon de Reya categorically denies that Dariga Nazarbayeva attempted to mislead the court, and there is no suggestion that Mishcon knew that any information submitted on behalf of Nazarbayeva may have been misleading or inaccurate.[51])

Wither the Rule of Law?

The rather disturbing conclusion from all this is that anti-money-laundering legislation, and tools such as UWOs—though designed to weaken kleptocracy by bringing to account incumbent officials—may actually strengthen kleptocracy, as exiled political opponents lose assets and power, with those same assets often returned to the kleptocratic system. If efforts to seize property are most effective only when an individual has been removed from power this means that UK courts are reproducing the power imbalances found in kleptocracies. The danger is that kleptocratic regimes may even seek to initiate and/or manipulate overseas investigations to remove assets from political rivals and people no longer in favour.

Certainly, exiles like Hajiyeva are either targeted by their home governments or at least not helped by them. When exiles fall out of favour, they lose the protections offered by a kleptocratic state to its elites. The Karimova case—described in Chapter 8—may have come about through leaks from Uzbekistan's security service, who were looking to remove from the political scene a powerful rival and potential successor to President Karimov. It is this incumbency advantage which is effectively exploited by law firms like Mishcon, who learnt from the failure of their exile clients and apparently apply these lessons to their cases on behalf of incumbent kleptocratic elites.

Unfortunately, the UWO legislation appears at the time of writing to be another false dawn in the fight against kleptocracy. In March 2022, the UK rushed through the Economic Crime Act which corrected some of the perceived inadequacies of the UWO legislation.[52] These included capping the costs accrued by the NCA and allowing UWOs to be issued against 'responsible officers' of the respondent in cases where the respondent is not an individual, thus widening the scope of who can receive such orders.[53] However, the incumbency advantage has not been addressed and it is this which poses a threat to the future use of UWOs against corrupt incumbent officials. The addition of an alternative test for the issuance of an UWO (where there are 'reasonable grounds for suspecting that the property has been obtained through unlawful conduct'[54]) repeats the mistake of the original legislation, as it is likely to fail in cases where the original sources of wealth were gained wholly or partly due to membership of and/or connection to a kleptocratic regime that remains in power. The problem of kleptocracy thus remains a tough nut to crack from a legislative point of view—trying to reconcile illicit wealth earned in a place that lacks the rule of law while respecting property rights in a place where the rule of law is upheld.

The evidence of the preceding chapters suggests that with a little help from the UK's legal and financial services, wealth made public in company listings and hidden via shell companies and trusts can be used to acquire citizenship and real estate. It can then also be explained both in applications for residency and in defences against anti-corruption laws. The examples of this chapter reveal how money laundering and reputation laundering are related. Ensconced with their laundered money, kleptocrats, oligarchs, and the occasional fortunate exile can move on to wider social and political tasks. In the next four chapters we look at how British professional enablers help them purchase status, make friends, track their enemies, and silence their critics.

10

Selling Status

The signing ceremony that took place at the University of Oxford is comparable to the Contract of the Century in the field of science, education, and culture for Azerbaijan.

—Nargiz Pashayeva, May 2018[1]

On 23 July 2023, Gubad Ibadoghlu and his wife, Irada Bayramova—briefly in Azerbaijan to aid Ibadoghlu's ailing mother—were boxed in by two cars on the outskirts of Baku. About 20 masked men exited the vehicles. Bayramova was punched in the face after attempting to resist arrest but released later that day, while her husband was detained on charges of 'religious extremism' and, at the time of writing (October 2023) remains in prison and denied medicines despite his ill health.[2] Ibadoghlu, an economist who was a senior visiting fellow at the international relations department of the London School Economics at the time of his arrest, is also the chairman of the Azerbaijani opposition Party of Democracy and Prosperity. 'He has always had a critical position', human rights activist Anar Mamedli said, 'he was a staunch advocate for transparency in government activities. For many years, he worked within the coalition for transparency in the oil extraction industry.'[3]

Less than 10 days before his arrest (on 14 July 2023), Ibadoghlu had created a philanthropic project focused on education, the Foundation for Azerbaijani Youth Education. Its founders, alongside him, were Jamil Hasanli, the head of the National Council of Democratic Forces and a university professor, and the former Azerbaijani ambassador to the EU and to the Council of Europe Arif Mammadov, who lives in exile in Brussels after falling out with the Azerbaijani ruling elite in 2015. Ibadoghlu stated that assets confiscated from wealthy Azerbaijanis convicted of money laundering in the UK could be one of the sources used to finance it in the future. The *Washington Post* hypothesized that this may have been the cause for the Aliyev regime to move against Ibadoghlu.[4] Mammadov, the former diplomat and current opponent, agrees: 'Gubad's activities have angered [the ruling elite] in the past. We wanted the main funding to come from the stolen money in the UK . . . this might have been the last drop. You know, their laundered money is like sacred'.[5]

But while the Foundation for Azerbaijani Youth Education might never see the light of day, another philanthropic activity with links to Azerbaijan did. In May 2018, the University of Oxford's Vice Chancellor, Louise Richardson, and Nargiz Pashayeva, one of the board members of the British Foundation for the Study of Azerbaijan and the Caucasus (BFSAC), ceremonially signed an agreement. BFSAC agreed to provide a £10 million endowment for the establishment of the Oxford Nizami Ganjavi Centre (ONGC) dedicated to the study of Azerbaijan, the Caucasus, and Central Asia.[6] Its activities are ongoing. However, BFSAC, originally claimed by the university to be the source of the gift,[7] is not in fact the donor. A clause signed with an anonymous donor, the university claims, prohibits it from divulging their name. And yet the reason for the need for added scrutiny[8] is self-evident to anyone who would so much as type Professor Nargiz Pashayeva's name into a search engine. Aside from her academic titles, Pashayeva can count on another useful qualification—as the sister-in-law of Azerbaijan's current President Ilham Aliyev, the son of Heydar who succeeded him in a dynastic tradition after his father's death.

In announcing BFSAC's agreement with Oxford as the 'Contract of the Century in the field of science, education and culture for Azerbaijan',[9] Pashayeva made clear reference to the original 'Contract of the Century' in 1994, a vast production sharing agreement that the new Azerbaijani President Heydar Aliyev concluded with most of the world's oil majors, including BP, to exploit the Caspian Sea fields.[10] This earlier 'contract of the century' was also the beginning of the state's global campaign to brand Azerbaijan as a part of the modern and democratic world through sporting, educational, and other cultural events[11]—and distract from its authoritarianism and corruption. This has included more direct forms of influencing and reputation laundering via the European Azerbaijan Society and what became known as 'caviar diplomacy'.[12]

This chapter explores the professional indulgence of selling status. According to the leading scholar of indulgences in medieval England, they were 'integral to the social welfare provision of the period, as stimuli and rewards for charitable activity and social donations both institutional and individual'.[13] For the remission of sins, donors may give in their own name or that of an institution, clerical or lay, whose interests they wished to advance. Critics of philanthropy today argue that it is another way in which the wealthy seek to impose their view of the world on others.[14] Donors may cluster around fashionable causes, impose pet projects, or pursue ideological agendas. Defenders argue that a world without philanthropy would be poorer and that the excesses of egoism are deterred by the desire of donors to be seen to be altruistic.[15]

Starting from the case of the Oxford Nizami Ganjavi Centre, we explore high-value gifts to UK higher education by persons—sometimes known, sometimes unknown—who are or who are likely to be allies of kleptocrats. Universities perform checks on these donors to assess the reputational risk to themselves of selling their status. However, they rarely consider the reputational laundering effect of selling their status: where the donor may seek to launder the reputation of a person, company, or country through their donation. In a sector with relatively few intermediaries, universities are potentially enablers of kleptocracy themselves.

The Pashayevs, the Aliyevs, and the Status of Azerbaijan

The central figure in the creation of BFSAC, the above-mentioned academic Nargiz Pashayeva, had been involved in Anglo-Azerbaijani academic cooperation from at least the early 2010s and was also the head of the Baku branch of the Moscow State University. Nargiz Pashayeva's sister, Mehriban Aliyeva (née Pashayeva), is the country's first, and so far only, vice president—a post created by the president (her husband) in 2017 and immediately bestowed upon her. Mehriban and Nargiz are part of Azerbaijan's 'intellighenzia': their official biographies highlight the role played by their family members in fostering higher education in the country. But the Pashayevs are no longer a family of mere intellectuals. A 2010 cable from the American embassy in Baku[16] characterized them as 'the single most powerful family in Azerbaijan', highlighting the control they exerted over a series of business sectors, including construction, telecommunications, and banking.

In the decade that followed, the Pashayevs' power grew even further. At the end of 2021, their conglomerate Pasha Holding declared AZN15.5 billion (more than £8 billion) in total assets, a 34% market share of Azerbaijan's banking sector, and over 16,500 employees.[17] The group includes Pasha Investments, Pasha Insurance, Pasha Construction, and Pasha Travel, as well as a sprawling network of subsidiaries through which it controls companies and investments in Azerbaijan and abroad. The telecommunications company 'Nar' and the cosmetics producer 'Nargiz'—also part of the Pashayev business empire—are indications that the academic heading the BFSAC might be no stranger to business interests herself.

'Everything that is the Pashayevs' is in fact the Aliyevs', Arif Mammadov, the former Azerbaijani diplomat, claims.[18] A manifestation of this connection is an oft-used scheme: Nargiz's and Mehriban's elderly father, Arif Pashayev, frequently figures as the officially designated owner of assets that he later donates to his grandchildren. Examples include flats in Moscow donated to his grandson Heydar Aliyev (named after the former president)[19] and foreign investments such as Montenegro's luxury resort Portonovi, beneficially owned by Pashayev senior and his two granddaughters Leyla and Arzu Aliyeva through Pasha Bank.[20] Much of the $700 million in London real estate, which was identified by OCCRP as belonging to Azerbaijan's ruling family, were held through offshore companies whose formal owner was, once again, Ilham Aliyev's father-in-law. The property has since been moved into a trust, managed by another Pashayev—Mirjalal, Nargiz's cousin.[21]

Philanthropic gifts to education, culture, and the arts are an apt corollary to this economic power. The activities of the Pashayevs are heavily geared towards shaping and presenting a modern and glowing image of Azerbaijan. This includes the production of noncritical research about their own activities.[22] The synthesis of this combination of cultural promotion and rent-seeking business interests is embodied by the Heydar Aliyev Foundation (HAF), headed by Mehriban Aliyeva. Housed in the sinuous Zaha Hadid building that came to symbolize modern-day Baku, the HAF is the premier vehicle through which the First Lady carries out her image promotion work. The HAF is also said by Azerbaijani oppositionists to function as a 'get out of jail free card'[23] for Azerbaijani politicians. For instance, if lower-ranked officials can show that they pay regularly into it, they will be allowed to carry on with their business interests. The person who manages these relationships is said to be Anar Alakbarov[24]—the executive director of the HAF, assistant to President Aliyev,[25] and author of hagiographic books on the First Lady (including *Mehriban Aliyeva: Personification of Good and Hope*)—who has been characterized as Mehriban's personal 'concierge'.[26]

In Azerbaijan it is said that the HAF 'builds more schools than Azerbaijan's Ministry of Education, more hospitals than the Ministry of Health, and conducts more cultural events than the Ministry of Culture'.[27] Abroad, the foundation sponsors high-profile projects including renovating the Louvre Museum, the Versailles Palace, and Strasbourg's Notre Dame Cathedral. The connection with Strasbourg—home to the Council of Europe (CoE)—is perhaps not coincidental. It is a direct reminder of the best-evidenced instance of political influencing in the history of this institution: Azerbaijan's 'caviar diplomacy'[28] scandal, for which politicians from Italy and Germany were jailed and many more were implicated, as we will see in the next chapter. While muzzling their critics at home,[29] Azerbaijani leaders were buying CoE officials into subservience, showing how, in the words of an exposé of the scandal, even international politics can be 'fundamentally reshaped by the personal greed of politicians.'[30]

One of the main instruments for status seeking and influencing operations overseas are think tanks. Founded in 2012 in Azerbaijan, the Nizami Ganjavi International Centre (NGIC) proposes to promote the 'values of peace, justice and human rights'. The centre boasts association with politicians and prominent figures from various corners of the world. Laureates of the NGIC's prizes include former US president Bill Clinton and former US secretary of state Henry Kissinger. Members of the Board of Trustees have included statesmen and stateswomen from EU member states, the Balkans and the Middle East, officials linked to the Arab League and to UNESCO, as well as Robert Kennedy's daughter Kerry Kennedy.[31] The Azerbaijani government has set aside considerable funding that was directed to this centre: between 2016 and 2018 alone, the NGIC received at least US$3.2 million from the Azerbaijani state coffers, mainly through tenders awarded by the state's Diaspora Commission.[32]

This government-funded namesake of the Oxford Nizami Ganjavi Centre should have prompted extensive background checks into the sources of wealth and interests lying behind donations. In 2014, Oxford had already received £1 million for a Nizami Ganjavi programme,[33] but we may expect the size of the gift and the evidence that 'Nizami Ganjavi' was an intellectual brand linked to the Azerbaijani state to be one of a number of factors which would prompt checks. Moreover, the indications that Nargiz Pashayeva is a politically exposed person from a country where state-sanctioned and state-led corruption flourishes could not be much clearer. Given the ruling family has a track record of reputation laundering and of openly funding centres whose activities are aimed at enhancing the image of the Azerbaijani state, there is a strong case for Oxford to be transparent about the origins of the donation and the stipulations of the academic 'contract of the century'. We do not know what specific due diligence steps were undertaken by gift officers within Oxford or why the institution agreed to accept the donation anonymously. Were the enablers within the university, within BFSAC, or a third party? In the medieval church—a world without a modern regulatory state—the enablers of indulgences were also the recipients. But the case of university donations draws our attention back to the failure of the state to require transparency and accountability in its public institutions.

This is the first of two chapters where third-party enablers are either absent or unknown. They are chapters where state weakness—the absence of both regulation of university funding and proper public funding of humanities research—is readily apparent as the corollary of private sector strength. University donations have hitherto been almost entirely unregulated in the UK, unlike in the United States where a reporting requirement has existed since the 1980s. The gift from BFSAC is almost certainly the largest single gift—private or public—to Central Asian Studies in the UK ever. It is also likely to be one of the largest anonymous gifts ever to UK higher education. As autonomous and minimally regulated public institutions, the assessment of the academic independence of ONGC and the risk of reputation laundering by the Azerbaijani ruling elite was a matter for Oxford alone.

Nontransparency and Internal Enablers

The mere fact that Pashayeva is both a member of the ruling family and the key figure in the establishment of ONGC does not make the University of Oxford or its academics automatically party to reputation laundering. University gift managers put safeguards in place to protect their own reputations which ought to provide some defence against reputation laundering by donors. However, in the UK, the focus on universities as 'businesses' has brought reliance on private donations to unprecedented levels. In dynamics worsened by an increasingly privatized business model, universities and charities have often lowered the bar of what is considered acceptable. There is an evident risk that prestigious institutions will take gifts whose sources of wealth come from a kleptocratic context not despite but because 'safeguards' are put in place to protect academic freedom and the university's reputation.

Over the past decade, funding to the humanities and social sciences in the UK has been inconsistent at best, while further impaired by the uncertainties caused by Brexit and cuts in international development aid. During the same period, the amount of private donations to universities in the UK and Ireland has nearly tripled.[34] Some disciplines are less advantaged than others. The study of a particular area or region, especially that related to less well-known regions of the world, is a poorly funded academic subsector. Even at prestigious universities, the sustainability of such humanities programmes which offer no lucrative new patents and only very niche 'employability' for students is constantly at risk. One obvious source of much-needed funds are the governments and big businesses of the region of study. Potential conflicts of interest abound.

Authoritarian governments, ruling elites, and their supporters in business are looking for good causes to throw their money at to burnish their own image. Should universities partake, for the sake of financial benefit? Most academics' answer to this question is 'no'. A 2020 survey of UK social scientists found that 75% of respondents think that academics in UK universities should not accept funding from foreign entities or governments that do not respect human rights.[35] However, the situation is not as straightforward on the other side of the fence. Western governments have been increasingly inviting foreign donations to supplant a shrinking role by the state. This applies to higher education as it does to other sectors—including, but not only, culture, the arts, and even health services. To function appropriately, these sectors have been pushed, and in fact often forced, to vamp up their private fundraising efforts. The department of education supports these efforts with its international education champion promoting the UK's 'academic exports', to states such as Saudi Arabia and China which have little or no tradition of protecting civil and political rights.[36]

To compound the problems arising from the market pressures, the process for assessing gifts is often opaque. As we shall see, the University of Oxford has one of the better processes of the elite Russell Group universities. In the example of the ONGC, Oxford maintains that they have followed all the necessary steps in the process and that the donation of the BFSAC was therefore without question. The university administration's answer to a series of questions we sent to probe the source of funds was laconic: 'The Committee [to Review Donations and Research Funding] was made aware of the original source of funds for this gift, which does not come from a government, and this was considered and approved through our usual due diligence process.'[37] No further information was given as per what this purported nongovernmental source actually was. Two outlets—OpenDemocracy and

Oxford University's own student newspaper, the *Cherwell*—asked the same question, receiving fundamentally the same answer when making Freedom of Information and informal requests.[38]

The final route available to journalists and researchers seeking information about donations to a public authority is a complaint to the Information Commissioner's Office. In April 2023, the Commissioner upheld one complaint against Oxford from OpenDemocracy and partially upheld another two; it ordered that the university release new grounds for refusal with the addition of more information about the donation and the due diligence performed with the name of the donor redacted.[39] In this forced disclosure, the university acknowledged: 'We accept that there is also a public interest that the University has an effective process for the ethical vetting of prospective donors and that there is transparency regarding that process'.[40] However, the disclosure of advice provided to Oxford's Committee to Review Donations and Research Funding in 2017 was minimal and focused exclusively on BFSAC as the vehicle for the donation (not the actual donor). It was less than two pages in length and was largely composed of information already in the public domain.[41] As an exercise in transparency and restoring public confidence, this disclosure was extremely limited.

Yet more troublingly, the Commissioner concurred with the university's claim that it had a legal right to refuse to disclose both the donor and the discussions of other potential donors to the centre. The Commissioner's reasoning here is instructive as it addresses the two major concerns arising from donations from persons or entities linked to kleptocratic governments— academic freedom and reputation laundering. However, it does so in such a way which demonstrates a certain naiveté about how both work with respect to kleptocracy. The Information Commissioner sided against the complainant and with the university that the donor, donations, and other offers should not be disclosed with the following reasoning.

> The complainant is evidently concerned about the Oxford Nizami Ganjavi Centre's links to the Azeri government and that government's ability to exert influence. The Commissioner is satisfied that there is sufficient information in the public domain that allows for the quality of the Centre's output and its teaching to be properly scrutinised. As the Donor's identity remains private, it is difficult to see how a donation of any amount could have an effect on their reputation.[42]

Whether the Commissioner's judgement appears to be legally correct will be determined by a tribunal in 2024.

Regardless of this legal outcome, there are two problems from a political economy perspective—and from common sense—with the Information Commissioner's decision. First, it adopts an extremely narrow definition of academic freedom to assess it purely in terms of outputs: freedom of academic speech. As we will explore, wider issues related to inputs, especially funding, matter too. Their subtle influences on output cannot always be 'properly scrutinised' without knowledge of inputs. Second, it makes the classic error of assuming that reputational laundering cannot occur if a donor is anonymous. In fact, the object of reputation laundering is not necessarily the donor themselves. It often takes place on behalf of an entity such as a state. This is often known as 'national branding' or 'authoritarian image management'.[43] As discussed above, Azerbaijan is a world leader in this field. Moreover, anonymity is not about absolute secrecy but about restricting knowledge to the privileged few. The donation may be kept private, but it would be known among a small elite community which works according to an economy of gift and privilege.[44] This is how both medieval and modern indulgences work. They function to enhance the status of a donor within certain circles, not to the public at large.

Anonymous donations are problematic in certain circumstances, but they are also booming. An investigation by OpenDemocracy published in December 2023 found that UK universities had received £281 million in anonymous donations since 2017 with Oxford the largest recipient with £106 million from secret donors.[45] Oxford argues that being forced to disclose a donor and/or the due diligence conducted on them, would demonstrate that the university was unable to 'protect their anonymity and privacy' and 'would be likely to deter them from making donations'. In effect, if it was forced to reveal donors, the university stated that it 'would have to consider withdrawing from that [anonymous donations] part of the "market" and lose the significant funding that we receive'. The Commissioner agreed with this reasoning, noting, it 'has consistently recognised that higher education institutions operate in highly competitive markets—both the market for students and the 'market' for donations'.[46] Anecdotage and the limited available data suggest that UK universities rely far more on foreign donations than they did in the past.[47] But what is remarkable is the Commissioner's apparent unwillingness to distinguish legitimate and illegitimate reasons for anonymity. Surely an anonymous and relatively low-value bequest from an alumnus is different from a large donation which took place via an entity which is clearly linked to a kleptocratic government?

By the time of the Commissioner's judgement, BFSAC had been dissolved, possibly as part of a wider winding down or refocusing of Azerbaijani influencing activities in the UK.[48] However, there are many signs which indicate links between the foundation and Azerbaijan's kleptocratic elite which the Commissioner was either unaware of or disregarded. BFSAC's own registered address was the same as the office of Ravan Maharramov, a British-Azerbaijani lawyer and a board member of the BFSAC.[49] Maharramov's professional profile states he acted as part of the legal team defending a prominent businessman and member of parliament with close links to the Azerbaijani ruling elite.[50] This appears to be the case of Javanshir Feyziyev who had several million pounds confiscated by the UK's National Crime Agency.[51] Feyziyev's confiscated funds were part of the so-called Azerbaijani Laundromat, the money-laundering operation and slush fund that enriched the Azerbaijani elite and was used to pay several European politicians who lobbied on behalf of Baku. These are the same funds that the research fellow and political oppositionist Gubad Ibadoghlu had hoped to repurpose for a scholarship programme in the UK prior to his arrest and abuse in Azerbaijan in the summer of 2023.

If there are enablers of the donation, it appears to be Maharramov and the BFSAC. However, the university apparently and incorrectly treated the foundation as the donor in its 2017 due diligence and its public announcement of the donation (later amended).[52] As for the actual and still-anonymous donor, the only name thanked publicly by Nargiz Pashayeva for 'first financial support' was that of Iskandar Khalilov,[53] an influential Azerbaijani businessman who used to be vice president of the Russian oil company Lukoil, and who is clearly connected to the Azerbaijani ruling elite in a number of ways.[54] But in reality we have no way of knowing the exact nature of enabling and the identity of the donor due to the lack of transparency by Oxford.

The general absence of regulation in this area means that the ONGC is by no means an isolated case of a nontransparent process which raises legitimate questions about links to a kleptocratic government. Despite their general freedom of information obligations, it is also not unusual for universities to be unduly secretive for all sorts of reasons. Since the Freedom of Information Act (2000), 72 of 122 complaints against Oxford have been fully upheld by the Commissioner.[55] However, it is important to acknowledge that neither in this case nor any of the others discussed below is there hard evidence that academic freedom was violated. We will unpack this risk as well as that of the more subtle concern is that of reputation laundering, the selling of status. Comparable examples from other post-communist states are illustrative of how gifts to UK universities may serve as part of a wider reputation laundering strategy.

The Limits of Self-Regulation

Some inroads in regulating philanthropic giving against such abuses were made starting from the early 2010s. In its wake of the London School of Economics' Ghaddafi scandal in 2011, when it emerged that the university had accepted funds from the son of the disgraced Libyan leader, it commissioned the Woolf inquiry which produced a report that outlined the gold standard for vetting gifts.[56] Our research found that UK universities are, by and large, well aware of these standards and claim to have implemented them.[57] And yet we also found that only seven out of 24 Russell Group universities abide by two of the most important requirements: publishing publicly available ethical guidelines and having an independent gifts committee (see Table 10.1). Oxford is one of these seven, suggesting that it is one of the Russell Group universities which should be best protected from reputation laundering.[58]

Our survey of Russell Group universities found that while most work takes place internally, several gift offers reported that their institutions seek advice on cultivating and checking donors from outside the university sector. One company, Wealth-X, offers advice on performing due diligence on ultra-high-net-worth individual (UHNWI) donors. Wealth-X's 'overview guide' for universities quotes Tom Hill, its head of enhanced due diligence, to summarize the challenge of 'due diligence'.

> Though due diligence is evolving, its purpose should never be 'finding a reason to avoid engaging with someone'; rather, the process should be 'an exercise undertaken to provide a satisfactory level of comfort to all stakeholders', Hill describes.[59] While such external advice may be beneficial in terms of donor development and university reputation management, it does not itself provide transparency and accountability to decisions on donations.[60]

Table 10.1 Procedures for assessing large gifts by Russell Group
Universities (2020)

Name of University	Ethical guidelines	Highest level decision-making body
Durham University	Public	Senior management approval system
Imperial College London	Internal Only	Senior management approval system
King's College London	Public	Dedicated independent gifts committee
London School of Economics (LSE)	Public	Dedicated independent gifts committee
Newcastle University	Upon Request	Senior management approval system
University of Birmingham	Public	Senior management approval system
University of Bristol	Public	Dedicated independent gifts committee
University of Cambridge	Public	Dedicated independent gifts committee
University of Edinburgh	Public	Senior management approval system
University of Exeter	Internal Only	Ad hoc senior management approval
University of Liverpool	Upon Request	Dedicated independent gifts committee
University of Nottingham	Public	Senior management approval system
University of Oxford	Upon Request	Dedicated independent gifts committee
University of Sheffield	Public	Dedicated independent gifts committee
University of Southampton	Public	Dedicated independent gifts committee
University of Warwick	Internal Only	Dedicated independent gifts committee
University of York	Public	Dedicated independent gifts committee
Cardiff University	No response	No response
University of Glasgow	No response	No response
University of Leeds	No response	No response
University of Manchester	No response	No response
Queen Mary University of London	No response	No response
Queen's University Belfast	No response	No response
University College London (UCL)	No response	No response

Moreover, this professional service sector—university fundraising—remains, for now, a largely in-house activity in the UK. While there is an enormous global industry of agents channelling international students to universities, in the university philanthropy sector the use of third parties is growing but is much smaller. With or without enablers, the logic of the system is self-regulation. Donations flowing into the UK higher education sector are overseen largely by those with an interest to accept the gift. While the 10 Russell Group universities reported to us that they had independent gifts committees to review large donations, the actual composition of the gift committees and the inclusion of genuinely independent lay members is unknown. University gift officers who undertake due diligence are also working to income targets. Most of the gift officers to which we spoke from the Russell Group universities who responded to our survey and agreed to a follow-up interview reported that the focus of their due diligence is reputational risk to the institution if a donation stirs up controversy on campus or in the press. This is quite different to assessing whether the donation will enhance the reputation of a person or entity with a chequered past or a vested interest in the subject area. When asked in our survey how many donations were formally rejected for failing to comply with the ethical guidelines, UK universities reported a very low number, ranging from no rejections at all to a maximum number of four rejections over the year 2019–2020.[61]

An impartial analysis recognizes that there is a great deal we don't know about how British universities sell their status. These unknowns include whether the market is more open to UK allies and new-found friends like Azerbaijan. Some gift officers reported to us that donors from 'controversial' countries may receive greater scrutiny while any university which accepted a gift from a sanctioned entity would be in breach of the law. We also do not know whether incumbents are more likely to be indulged and whether an enabler effect will emerge as third parties such as Wealth-X or public relations companies enter the market. We know so little partly because in the UK, there is also no requirement to report donations—anonymous or not—to a public register. In the United States, by contrast, there is such a requirement under Higher Education Act that requires that all contracts with foreign donors and gifts over $250,000 in value be reported to the US Department of Education.[62] For many years compliance checks were minimal, but under President Trump's Secretary of Education Betsy De Vos, the government's highly politicized investigations identified approximately $6.5 billion in unreported foreign donations from 'countries of concern'.[63]

In sum, while our knowledge of the professional indulgence of university donations is limited, there is a great deal of circumstantial evidence to suggest that a problem of self-regulation exists. Self-regulation is considered a companion to university self-governance which is in turn considered essential for academic freedom and integrity. University leaders and their gift officers raise legitimate concerns regarding the bureaucratization of the problem and the risks of unintended consequences. However, as universities become more like large commercial entities whose internal academic governance is weakened in favour of corporate officers, such arguments look self-interested. Effective self-regulation requires transparency and accountability to a wider public. Without transparency in donations, it is difficult for students, academics, and the public to hold universities to account for their choices to accept funding from kleptocratic elites and other potentially problematic donors. This general problem of governance is foundational to two sets of concerns that arise with respect to the ONGC gift and which were acknowledged by the Information Commissioner. Next, we consider how far indulgence occurred in our cases and several other comparable ones.

Academic Freedom Risks

The first set of concerns is that of apparent risks to academic freedom. The first and probably rarest of these is that donors seek to shape or restrict a research agenda. Such direct interference is likely to be uncommon, but if it exists, it is largely undocumented and unreported. There is no evidence of direct interference in the ONGC case. However, there are cases which have come to light. For instance, Jesus College Cambridge came under fire for publishing a white paper that was funded by the Chinese company Huawei with multiple coauthors from that company.[64] Critical voices may be silenced: a UK-based scholar who signed the 'Academics for Peace' petition criticizing the military crackdown on Kurdish rebels in Turkey recounted that they were asked not to write about the Kurdish question for a while. This is because, in their words, their UK department 'was afraid about losing their Turkish partnerships after the criminalization of peace activism in Turkey'.[65]

Sometimes, UK funding participates in and exacerbates these dynamics. An academic at a UK university reported that they were compelled by a senior colleague to avoid the use of the word 'authoritarianism' in a research project related to governance in certain post-communist countries.[66]

Furthermore, there were concerns about potential surveillance of the project by authorities in one or more of the states involved. This speaks of the perils of using UK funds to conduct international research in semiauthoritarian or authoritarian contexts, without proper vetting and oversight. Even when permissions have been gained and a good relationship with the authorities has been fostered, colleagues who are nationals of the country of research are at risk from governments which wish to control the knowledge produced about their activities.[67]

Second, donors may also try to influence the appointment of critical governance positions, such as senior faculty chairs or advisory boards. The ONGC has Nargiz Pashayeva among its board members, alongside another appointed by BFSAC. When asked about the independence of the centre, its then-director Edmund Herzig laid out the composition of its management board, its reporting responsibilities, and wrote that 'at all levels, any suggestion of political interference in the work of the Centre would meet with a robust response'.[68] There is no reason to believe that the institutional structure of ONGC is compromised by the fact that the sister-in-law of the president of the country which is its focus sits on its board. Herzig also pointed to the nature of the centre's funding—by endowment—as one which protects it from interference in its activities by funders.

Third, and related, the effect of kleptocratic elite funding on academic freedom may be reflected in what is considered within scope by funded projects and centres. It is common for universities to recognize questions such as those above and therefore limit the scope of regional studies centres like ONGC to cultural and business matters, avoiding the most sensitive issues. Where war, corruption, or human rights abuses are addressed, these events are hosted by another part of the university. However, certain problems arise from this approach. Research which either addresses politics indirectly or addresses culture and business matters in a de-politicized fashion may become a more significant part of the field of study. As such, individual academics may self-censor if they feel their own research is constrained as job opportunities are more likely to be found on topics which avoid controversy and attract funding from the very wealthy and powerful people that would otherwise be studied. There are few topics, especially in the humanities and social sciences which are nonpolitical so self-censorship in cultural and business studies remains an ever-present problem. Self-censorship is notoriously difficult to define and research; it may take place for legitimate reasons (protecting sources) as well as illegitimate ones (not

Table 10.2 Self-censorship reported by UK social scientists (2020)

Have you ever self-censored when teaching students from autocratic states in the UK?	Yes	No	Don't Know / Prefer Not to Answer
All social scientists	20	73	7
Scholars specializing in European states	33	62	5
Scholars specializing in African states	39	58	3
Scholars specializing in China	41	55	4

Have you ever self-censored when reporting fieldwork findings?	Yes	No	Don't Know / Prefer Not to Answer
All social scientists	14	75	11
Scholars specializing in European states	19	68	13
Scholars specializing in African states	26	60	14
Scholars specializing in China	22	64	14

criticizing powerful researchers or research funders). Our 2020 survey of social scientists suggest that self-censorship is more common among specialists of regions of authoritarian states. For example, 41% of those who work on China reporting that they self-censor when, teaching compared to 20% of all social scientists.

An academic centre that focuses on a region of highly authoritarian states and is funded by an anonymous donor naturally faces questions about partiality and self-censorship. The ONGC has a research agenda which spans the whole of the Caucasus and Central Asia but with a large number of its activities focused on Azerbaijan's history and culture and the Azeri language.[69] Predictably, Armenian activists raised questions about how the Centre would cover the history and politics of the whole region. They point to the fact that there are no ethnic Armenians among its listed lecturers and visiting fellows, past and present.[70] One appointment which has caused controversy is that of a current visiting research fellow at ONGC whose project appears to support the Azerbaijani nationalist claim that the disputed area of Karabakh is a homeland of Caucasian Albanians who only became 'Armenianized' under the Russian empire in the nineteenth century.[71] In response to enquiries by the authors, the new ONGC director, Alexander Morrison, commented that the research fellow 'is being confronted and challenged by Armenian specialists in a way that rarely happens for scholars in her position. As such, the Visiting Fellowship is fulfilling the purpose we set out for it'.[72] This is a strong argument, but it raises questions which are less scholarly and pertain to risks outside the seminar room. If an ONGC researcher used their fellowship and the standing it affords them to advance Azerbaijani nationalist claims outside of the university, how would the board respond?

To this hypothetical question we may add an actual one about Gubad Ibadoghlu, the London School Economics (LSE) scholar arrested, detained, and maltreated by the Azerbaijani authorities in 2023. In the case of such imprisonments of well-known local scholars, it is common for major academic institutions studying the region to join and even lead calls for the release of the person. The London School of Economics professor of international relations Tomila Lankina commented on social media about the ONGC's 'silence' following her colleague's arrest.[73] Would the ONGC as an institution publicly join calls for Ibadoghlu's release? And does it matter if it does not? Some academics would argue that public statements on political issues by academic institutions are worthless and can put their partners at threat; others, including ourselves, call for more critical engagement, especially when governments in their field arbitrarily detain their academic colleagues.

A Question of Reputation

Beyond academic freedom concerns, there is the more general worry about reputation laundering by states and the instrumental use of academic relationships to pursue personal or political agendas. In another example that concerns both US and UK institutions, Harvard, Georgetown, Edinburgh, and Cambridge all accepted donations from Saudi Prince Alwaleed bin Talal bin Abdulaziz Alsaud to support Islamic Studies at their institutions, in spite of vehement criticism.[74] Elite networks engaging in philanthropic giving do not necessarily aim to exercise 'undue influence' and in most cases academic freedom is likely to be protected. However, it may be that the primary interest is less the advancement of certain research findings than the indirect reputational benefits of association with a prestigious funding.

We identify three potential functions of university donations for such elites. First, donors may engage in status seeking for themselves or a national or corporate brand. These donations take the form of individual donations to establish a school or centre; naming rights for buildings, libraries, and chairs; and honorary degrees and seats on the board of the university or one of its parts.[75] As discussed above, the ONGC represents all of these aspects in the founding of the centre in the name of the 'Nizami Ganjavi' national brand and role of Nargiz Pashayeva as a member of the ruling family of the country being studied.

Second, donors may go on the offensive by actively establishing or managing their reputation or that of a company or country in the UK or overseas. A clear example of this is Kremlin-connected Ukrainian oligarch Dmitro Firtash, who donated $230 million to events and programmes in Western Europe between 2010 and 2013.[76] Having established a programme in Ukrainian studies at the University of Cambridge, he used this donation strategically to plead for his standing in a UK court, in order to pursue legal action against the *Kyiv Post*.[77] He tried to argue that he suffered reputational damage in the UK, for an article published in Ukraine. While the lawsuit was unsuccessful, it shows how connected different reputation laundering pursuits are: in this case, through both philanthropic donations and SLAPP suits or 'libel tourism'.[78]

A case which appears to relate to the first two functions of reputation laundering also took place at Cambridge. In the period from 2018 to 2022, the university received close to £900,000 in research funding from LetterOne,[79] a Luxembourg-registered investment company cofounded by Russian oligarchs Petr Aven and Mikhail Fridman which manages assets worth £27 billion.[80] Aven, in particular, featured extensively in the March 2019 'Mueller report' that investigated Donald Trump's links with Russia.[81] The controversial report documented these individuals' collusion with the Russian ruling elite, asserting that Aven had made contact with Trump's team in December 2016 to establish communication between the president-elect and the Kremlin. On the back of this and other information, the EU called Aven 'one of Vladimir Putin's closest oligarchs' and Fridman a 'top Russian financier and an enabler of Putin's inner circle', adding that the two had been engaged in the effort to lift sanctions against Russia after the invasion of Crimea.[82]

That is not, however, the way in which university fund-raisers presented LetterOne to senior academics and in the university's own donation approval process. In a September 2019 email asking senior academics to support a donation and further—potentially much larger—future donations from LetterOne, Cambridge University Development and Alumni Relations (CUDAR) presented the company as a purely British concern.

They wrote: '[LetterOne] are headquartered in the UK and managed by leading UK businesspeople, many of whom are known to the University.'[83] LetterOne is headquartered in the UK and is still chaired by Labour peer and former government minister Mervyn Davies. But the Cambridge fundraisers' communication contained no mention of any Russia connection, nor any reputational risk, despite the fact that this information was readily available via Google and Wikipedia, and in the Mueller Report. Even after having these omissions pointed out to them by the head of the relevant department, and the associated serious reputational risks,[84] the university decided to accept the money anyway.

Despite internal requests, no explanation was ever offered on why the initial due diligence had omitted all mention of the obvious connection to Russian oligarchs. Immediately after the invasion of Ukraine, Cambridge released a press release asserting that 'Over the past five years, the University of Cambridge has received no research funding from organisations within the Russian Federation or from any individual or organisation currently facing sanctions by the United States, European Union or United Kingdom.'[85] The university had in fact accepted money from Russian oligarchs in 2019 even though they were under US sanctions at the time as well as when the press release was issued, but maintained that LetterOne was unconnected to its Russian cofounders. After the Russian invasion of Ukraine in 2022, Fridman and Aven had their 49% shareholding in LetterOne frozen.[86]

A third function of donations may be the instrumental use of a connection to advance the political or economic agenda of themselves or company they support. For example, the representatives of Serbian-British businessman Vuk Hamović were in discussion with the UK's Foreign Office (then called FCO) about donations to UK higher education and funding the FCO's Chevening scholarship programme. Around the same time, his UK-registered company, EFT, was under investigation by Britain's Serious Fraud Office for the embezzlement of US development funds. The wording of the emails explicitly mentions that the intent of the donations was 'the idea of raising the EFT profile in Serbia.'[87] The SFO discontinued the investigation in 2008 alongside a raft of other cases which were abandoned that year. There is no suggestion that Hamović's relationship with the FCO contributed to this outcome.

In the case of the Nizami Ganjavi centre, its status was used by one of its British board members to influence the Foreign Office directly. BFSAC—the entity through which the £10 million donation was made—held its grand debut in London in 2016 with a gala event attended by members of the House of Lords including Baroness Emma Nicholson (UK Trade Envoy for Azerbaijan) and Lord Malcolm Bruce (the foundation's British cofounder) among them.[88] Four years later, and two years after the founding of Oxford Centre, Azerbaijan had launched the military action in the disputed territory of Karabakh which would decisively turn the armed conflict in its favour. Bruce, a BFSAC trustee, wrote to Foreign Secretary Dominic Raab and referred to the Oxford Centre as 'an important symbol of inclusiveness promoted by Azerbaijan today' and went on to argue for the UK to take a position more favourable to the government in its conflict against Armenia. Bruce had been one of the most outspoken European politicians in 2004 during a Council of Europe inquiry into human rights abuses in Azerbaijan.[89]

However, in his 2020 letter, Bruce makes several claims about the origins and conduct of the conflict in Karabakh which are consistent with the official position of Azerbaijan and portrays Azerbaijan as a 'secular state with a very peaceful and tolerant people'. The letter concludes,

> I urge the government to use its influence to secure a permanent cease fire and a peace process to restore the integrity of Azerbaijan in accordance with the expressed UN resolutions and to urge a dialogue which can move Azerbaijan towards a more democratic future.[90]

But in the autumn 2023, Azerbaijani forces attacked Karabakh, brutally removed its ruling regime, and set off a mass exodus of Karabakhis that raised fears of ethnic cleansing.[91] Far from becoming 'more democratic', Azerbaijan remained a kleptocracy dominated by the Aliyev-Pashayev family.[92]

So What?

Donations and endowments have been central to the very formation and development of universities. They have never been neutral or entirely impartial. Certain fields, neglected by public funders, may not exist without it. For those, including ourselves, that criticize universities for their selling of status, funding from kleptocratic elites to the study of the region in which they hold power and have wealth potentially jeopardizes the fostering of critical thinking and the independent shaping of minds that should be at the core of higher education's mission. But worries about foreign donations and influence are but one of a series of troubles afflicting universities ranging from culture wars to industrial disputes, from the decline of university democracy to the emphasis on external funding, which lead to disquiet across academia. According to data we collected in late 2020, for one reason or another, almost 70% of UK-based social scientists think that academic freedom is under threat.[93]

This chapter has shown that a certain increase in awareness of the problem—in the wake of the Ghaddafi scandal that hit the London School of Economics and Political Science (LSE) in 2011—has not brought to an overhaul in these practices, due to the opacity and almost complete lack of regulation on the issue. The result is a distinct lack of accountability and the heightened risk that universities are selling status to the highest bidders. Moreover, there is some evidence that they may be encouraging self-censorship by their academics who worry that speaking or writing critically about the interests of their funders may adversely affect their own career or their colleagues.[94]

In the case of the ONGC, have the Pashayev-Aliyev family and their close associates been indulged by the University of Oxford? The case is complex and the evidence mixed. The evidence of direct damage to academic freedom is, thus far, absent. But the evidence of reputation laundering is more substantial. The anonymity of the donor precludes the possibility of reputation laundering in the eyes of the Information Commissioner, but this position is naïve and unsustainable. The donor would be able to cite the donation in a private setting (for example, when applying for a bank account or in residency or visa applications) to establish good standing. But outside of the personal, the reputation laundering in this case concerns a third party—the Azerbaijani elite and state—not the donor themselves. Anonymous donations can be a mechanism for reputation laundering: you conceal the kleptocratic networks and thereby accentuate the national brand.

There is little doubt that such reputation laundering has been enabled by Oxford. Nargiz Pashayeva is routinely introduced as 'a member of the Board of Directors of the Nizami Ganjavi Scientific Centre of Oxford University' when she appears at Azeri state events. For example, she was a featured guest at the Embassy of Azerbaijan in the UK's national independence celebrations in June 2023 alongside Conservative MP Bob Blackman (see Chapter 11) and Labour peer Lord David Evans (see Chapter 12). The event was reported by the embassy as celebrating 'the first democratic parliamentary republic in the Muslim East' and featured an 'exclusive photo exhibition commemorating the 100th anniversary of National Leader Heydar Aliyev [that] captivated guests by showcasing his remarkable life and outstanding achievements'.[95] As 'Nizami Ganjavi' is a brand which is widely used by a regime highly engaged in authoritarian image management, it is fair to say that the university sold its status to Azerbaijan's kleptocratic regime (see Figure 10.1).

This raises the subsequent question of how to explain this indulgence. Was it the UK's partnership with Azerbaijan, the incumbency of the Azerbaijani parties, or the work of University of Oxford's gifts committee to conceal the origins of the gift? The evidence here is even less certain given we do not know the donor's identity. With regard to the alliance effect, it is hard to imagine Oxford accepting a gift to establish a centre on Russia, China, or Iran which had a member of the ruling family on its board. But we have seen that both Cambridge and Oxford have taken gifts from those who are sanctioned oligarchs or businessmen with close ties to the Kremlin.[96] With respect to the enabler effect, Oxford has said little about the process it went through to decide to accept the anonymous donation and board membership of Pashayeva. There may also have been third party enablers unknown to the university who suggested the donation to the donor. The strongest inference we might draw from the limited available evidence is that incumbency, alliance, and enabling were all weak effects but may have interacted to cause the indulgence of the Azerbaijani elite in this case.

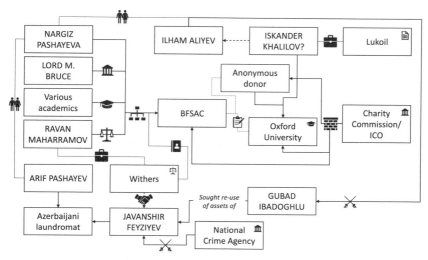

Figure 10.1 Buying Azerbaijan status

In sum, it is the lack of transparency and accountability—under conditions of self-regulation—which has allowed status seekers and reputation launderers to be indulged. The fact that we still do not know who gave the money to ONGC shows that the self-regulation of philanthropic donations at British universities is crucial to the indulgence of selling status. Status seekers typically desire publicity for something, but it is the exact form and the content of public information that counts. The pattern of concealing the sources of wealth while projecting the national brand has been characteristic of Aliyev-Pashayev reputation laundering in Europe for more than two decades.

In 2022, an amendment by Jesse Norman MP to the Higher Education Bill to add a duty for universities to disclose their donors was initially accepted by the government but then, after university lobbying, watered down to become an almost-worthless 'duty to consider'.[97] At present, moments of accountability happen in the rare cases when the student body or alumni unearths details relating to these cases. The most veritable cases of 'reputational backlash'—such as the London School of Economics Ghaddafi scandal and the Jesus College Huawei partnership—have come to the surface this way. As we were finishing this book, Oxford's student newspaper the *Cherwell* published its first article on the 'mystery £10M donor and family links to autocratic ruler'.[98] But however valuable, student activism and journalism cannot be substitutes for transparency and accountability in donations to Britain's universities.

11

Making Friends

Some of us laughed. There was a feeling at the time that we can buy anything.

—a senior Azerbaijani diplomat's reaction to
the 'caviar diplomacy' scandal[1]

In 2002, $20 million stolen from Turkmenistan was laundered through a Russian bank. The chairman of the bank, Turkmenistan-born Dmitry Leus, was found guilty of money laundering in relation to this transaction and served over three years in a Russian prison. He claims that he was scapegoated, and that the conviction was politically motivated and legally unsound.

Fast-forward to 2020, and Leus, now a permanent resident of the United Kingdom, began donating to British political parties and charitable foundations. Leus has presented himself as a man motivated by good causes, helping sick children in hospitals and promoting youth sports. He successfully gave donations to the Conservative Party, including to the political campaign of Dominic Raab, the then UK foreign secretary.[2]

Some donations were refused—including an attempted £500,000 donation to the foundation of Prince Charles, then the heir to the throne—after recipients conducted due diligence.[3] In 2022, Liam Byrne MP, a member of the UK parliament, aired allegations under cover of parliamentary privilege—again strongly denied by Leus—that Leus had ties to the FSB, Russia's successor organization to the KGB.[4] Despite this claim, in 2023, Leus—having acquired settle status and been resident in the UK for over five years—acquired British citizenship.[5] In a complex and often contradictory story, Leus appear to be a 'fence-sitter' and a man whose ambitions for status and influence have been indulged by some and indicted by others.

But Leus is not alone in this dance between money and influence. The second case we will treat in this chapter is that of Liubov Chernukhin, a US-educated investment banker of Russian origin, who found herself crossing paths with the highest echelons of British politics—from tennis matches with a prime minister to dinners with government officials. Chernukhin's lavish donations to the Conservative Party have not gone unnoticed. While she made these donations after becoming a British citizen, her personal background—as the wife of a former deputy finance minister in Vladimir Putin's government—has raised some uncomfortable questions.

These two stories underscore a much wider debate on the money flowing into esteemed institutions and political parties in the United Kingdom. As with universities, questions arise as to whether donors are exercising personal or corporate agendas. This chapter explores the world of political donations and the indulgence of making friends. It delves into the web of financial contributions originating from kleptocratic states and their potential impact on the democratic process. Such donations highlight the political ramification of the risks of the reputation-enhancing and narrative-shaping dynamics explored in previous chapters. When rights and assets are bought, wealth is explained, and status sold, it is easier to make friends and influence people.

The Only Honest Banker in Russia?

In September 2002, a Vietnamese man walked into a bank in Moscow and requested a $20 million transfer—in cash—to a foreign currency account he held at another bank in the Russian capital. The cash had originally been sent from Turkmenistan and received into an account held by a South Dakotan company controlled by a different Vietnamese man a few days before. The money was dutifully packed into a series of sports bags and transported in two journeys by car to the second bank. No banking documents were signed indicating that a transfer of such funds had taken place. The money was transferred several days later to another vehicle and driven to an unknown location.[6] After this the money disappeared, alleged to be invested in the hotel industry in the Czech Republic.[7]

It subsequently transpired that a group of individuals had stolen money from a state account held at the Central Bank of Turkmenistan and had laundered it through the two Russian banks. The main perpetrators were never identified or captured, though one suspected thief was found stabbed to death in St Petersburg.[8] However, two individuals were charged in

Moscow with being part of the group that stole the funds and were put on trial in Moscow.

One of these men was Dmitry Leus—the chairman of Russian Depository Bank, the bank that cashed out the $20 million. As a wealthy businessman in Putin's Russia, Leus may be described as a 'minigarch' in popular parlance, a successful businessman in a kleptocratic state, though one who lacks clear links to the Kremlin. He was found not guilty of being part of the group behind the theft. However, Leus was found guilty of a lesser charge, the 'legalization' of laundered funds, that he in effect had knowingly transferred money he knew to be stolen. Leus was sentenced to four years' imprisonment[9] and served three years. He maintains that he was innocent and had no knowledge the funds were stolen. However, he does not deny that his bank permitted the $20 million to be taken away in sports bags to a second bank, and that no documentation was exchanged.[10]

The case of Dmitry Leus is complex and underlines the difficulty of trying to disentangle the truth when assessing accusations of wrongdoing from a country where there are significant flaws in the legal system. These facts— that his bank received and then cashed out without documentation nearly $20 million—are not disputed by Leus; what is at stake is their interpretation. To Leus's defenders and indulgers, they indicate that he is a victim: an honest banker in a corrupt system. Leus himself claims that his conviction for money laundering in Russia was politically motivated. 'I have never been a kleptocrat', he told the *Guardian* newspaper.[11] He vehemently denies knowing that the money was stolen and said that all Russian banking laws were followed.

In order to establish himself in the UK, Leus has contracted a variety of professionals—many of them independent experts rather than enablers—to establish that his conviction was faulty and what he believes is his right to have his conviction forgotten. These include a commissioned opinion from Sergei Pashin, a former Russian judge, who cites numerous violations in the state's case against Leus and argues that the prosecution did not prove his guilt beyond a reasonable doubt.[12]

In 2008, Leus successfully applied to a Russian court to have his criminal conviction struck out—a feature of Russian law at the time which has no equivalent in the English legal system. Leus's spokesperson in the UK, Jennifer Morgan, claims that 'his conviction is no longer recognised as valid, and he is therefore permitted to be treated as though it did not exist.'[13] However, a conviction being struck out is neither the same as having it overturned—a process which recognizes that the original conviction was faulty—nor does it amount to a pardon, where a conviction is later acknowledged to have been wrong. Indeed, no court—either Russian or foreign—has ever acknowledged that Leus's conviction was unsound. Rather, it appears to equate to the English law right of rehabilitation which applies to some offences, permitting the offender to not have to disclose them in some circumstances. However, it does not prevent journalists from referring to historic convictions, nor from examining the circumstances surrounding the conviction.

Lawyers acting for Leus also commissioned a corporate intelligence company, Quintel Intelligence, to complete a due diligence report on the background to his conviction. It suggests that his conviction was orchestrated by the Russian and Turkmen authorities, with Leus a pawn in a geopolitical game in which Russia was doing a favour for Saparmurat Niyazov, the eccentric despotic president of Turkmenistan.[14] However, this report appeared to indulge Leus to a certain degree, giving no information about how documents were not exchanged when Leus's bank transferred the money, and nothing about the prosecution's case, which included allegations (denied by Leus) that Leus controlled the South Dakotan company through which the money passed.

Twenty years on, it is impossible to relitigate and recreate the complete evidence that related to the offence. As researchers, we neither trust Leus's original conviction nor its striking out. But we are left with two competing narratives. The first is that of what Leus calls 'fixers',[15] his lawyers, spokespersons, writers of paid content in the media, and even a biographer. This is that Leus is an innocent man whose conviction was political and whose innocence is established. His donations since coming to the UK are entirely altruistic; it is unjust to characterize them as reputation laundering. As Leus reported to his biographer, Simon Lee, 'I am being criticised as if I have done something wrong when I am the victim of a crime'.[16] To the extent that Leus was subject to a corrupt legal system in Russia and imprisoned in terrible conditions for three years, it is indeed fair to characterize him as a victim.

The second narrative is that although Leus is now apparently in exile, the background of his case raises the possibility that he retains fealty to Russian state actors. This is the narrative advanced by Liam Byrne in parliament under privilege and explored by a small number of journalists and researchers, including ourselves. If political considerations played a role in

Leus's conviction, they seemed to be gone by January 2006, when Leus was released on parole, over a year before the end of his sentence. Niyazov was still president of Turkmenistan and made no public statement on Leus's release. For someone who was apparently targeted by the authorities of his adopted country (Leus had Russian citizenship), Leus made a remarkable comeback in the banking industry, making millions of dollars. How did this happen?

In order to explain Leus's story, we need to go beyond the minutiae of legal detail and explore the political economy within which Leus was rehabilitated and became wealthy once more. Following his release and despite his conviction, Leus was allowed to retain his shareholding in one Russian bank and buy shares in another.[17] The report commissioned by Leus says that this was a clear sign that Leus was not guilty of the crime he went to prison for, and that 'the charges were in order to effect another (political) agenda'.[18] Yet it is a rather odd logic to put his conviction down to politics, but then to assert his early release and subsequent reintegration into the Russian banking sector was free from such influence, at a time when the Russian authorities' control over the business sector was growing. Furthermore, Leus branched out into other areas, making millions of dollars by investing in land in Sochi just after it was announced Russia was to hold the Winter Olympics there.

Research on post-Soviet Russia suggests that to succeed in business you have to be part of what academic Alena Ledeneva dubbed *sistema*—a network-based system of governance, orientated around wealth, which draws on the informal influence of clans, cliques, and political connections,[19] where having a *krysha* (literally 'roof' or protection) is vital for survival. It is via this *sistema* that business deals are done and serious money is made in Russia's kleptocracy.[20] Leus claims that he was trying to operate outside of the corrupt *sistema*, and his imprisonment is evidence that he was not a part of that system; yet it is inconceivable that anyone making tens of millions of dollars in Russia—as Leus did between 2006 and 2015 following his release— would be able to do so without a *krysha* and some kind of connections within the *sistema*.

Given this context, there are public interest questions as to how Leus has made his money, and whether he is an appropriate donor to political figures and charities. Leus and his indulgers claim he is a self-made man—a fence-sitter or perhaps an opponent of Vladimir Putin, although there are no statements on record where Leus criticizes the Russian leadership. The counterclaim is that he became a loyalist to secure his release from prison and existed for at least nine years within this system. It is not our objective here to adjudicate on that debate, but to explore how and to what extent he has been indulged.[21] Since moving to the UK in 2015, Leus has used a range of British professional enablers to push forward his version of events and stifle public interest reporting of any differing accounts. Sometimes they have succeeded. Sometimes they have not.

Entering UK High Society

The road to British citizenship for Leus was not straightforward. Following the sale of shares in his second bank for $12.5 million, Leus acquired Cypriot citizenship through their investor scheme. Thanks to his newly acquired EU citizenship, Leus was allowed to reside in the United Kingdom. He moved to London in September 2015. Leus's wife, Zhanna Leus, had originally applied for residency under a Tier 1 investor visa with Dmitry as a dependent in 2014—the year before the rules were tightened after the period of 'blind faith'—but the application was a rare instance of refusal (see Chapter 7), as Leus had apparently not disclosed his criminal conviction.

Leus says he was not seeking to conceal his criminal conviction but had simply misunderstood the requirement to disclose it on the application form, given that the conviction had been struck from the record in Russia. Indeed, little of Leus's past accompanied him to the UK. His LinkedIn profile from around the time made no mention of his positions at either Russian Deposit Bank or his second bank, Zapadny, giving only his ownership of Imperium Investments, a company he started in the UK in 2017.[22] In September 2020, Leus applied for indefinite leave to remain in the UK, using Mishcon de Reya to help process the application.

It is around this time that the making of friends in high places apparently begins. The year leading up to his 2020 application to remain in the UK saw Leus embark on a series of charitable and political donations. In November 2019, *The Daily Mirror* featured an article, with accompanying video, labelled 'ad feature' with the header 'Big-hearted businessman comes to aid of young girl fighting blood cancer'.[23] Some months later, in May 2020, *Surrey Live* ran another piece about Leus entitled 'Kind-hearted CEO donates to Runnymede Foodbank during pandemic', again labelled as an 'ad feature'.[24] In other words, the 'upstream' activities pursued by Leus, burnishing his reputation, allowed Mischon de Reya to take up the client by playing—seemingly—a 'downstream' role.

In the same month, Leus donated £500,000 to the Prince's Foundation. The heir to the throne and future King Charles III wrote to Leus,[25] saying he was 'incredibly grateful' for his 'immense generosity', writing, 'I very much look forward to seeing you' after the COVID lockdown had ended. Leus has claimed that he wanted to donate to the Prince's Foundation because it shared his values of supporting young people through sport,[26] though according to *The Times*, he made his donations only after he was promised a private meeting with the future king,[27] writing to a fixer when such a meeting did not transpire: 'If it is not possible for you to arrange this meeting, I would prefer to get my family money back, and resume the conversation when the situation will improve'.[28] Some months later the foundation attempted to return the donation when it learnt of Leus's conviction for a money-laundering offence.[29] Leus said that he has yet to receive all the money back, claiming that a £35,000 donation was accepted while some of it disappeared into the hands of the 'fixers'.[30]

Notwithstanding this setback, Leus continued his quest to enter UK high society supported by a variety of professionals. In June 2020, he repurposed one of his UK companies, Imperium Trust, originally registered in May 2018, as a charity, changing its name to the Leus Family Foundation,[31] again with Mishcon de Reya assisting.[32] *The Times* reported that this was on the suggestion of Michael Fawcett, the then chief executive of the Prince's Foundation and a former aide to Charles, who said it may make Leus's donations seem more palatable.[33]

Around this time, Leus began his political donations to the governing Conservative Party. As a British resident and crucially a Cypriot citizen (Russian citizens cannot vote or donate in the UK), Leus appeared on the electoral register, allowing him to make donations. In total, between October 2020 and July 2021, the Electoral Commission records donations of £54,500.[34] In July 2021, Leus donated a total of £25,000 in three separate payments for 'campaigning costs' for the Conservative Association in a constituency, Esher and Walton,[35] where Dominic Raab, the then Foreign Secretary, was the member of parliament. From June 2021 to February 2022, Leus also acted as the president of his own constituency's association.[36]

Leus's application for indefinite leave to remain in the UK was accompanied by a letter from Mishcon de Reya to the Home Office. It details the alleged 'miscarriage of justice' against Leus (his conviction in 2004 for money laundering) and how he was 'significantly prejudiced by the wrongful conviction'. It also mentions the humanitarian work that Leus has performed since arriving in the UK, and his donation to the Prince's Foundation.[37] Leus's application for settled status was accepted, as was his ultimate quest— British citizenship—which was granted at some point in 2023. Given the disadvantages faced by Leus, his case—despite several examples of nonindulgence—presents a clear example of the enabler effect working to secure residency (and, later, citizenship), and make political friends.

The first test of these new relationships came quickly. The end of Leus's donations to the Conservatives coincides with the beginnings of the public controversy regarding his background. In July 2021, UK media reported on Leus's donation to Dominic Raab's office, and then in September 2021 the thwarted £500,000 donation to the Prince's Foundation. When Raab's office was asked about the donation, it said: 'Mr Leus had a wrongful conviction overturned on appeal. Professional due diligence was conducted before accepting. Like all donations, it was properly and transparently declared and complies fully with the law'.[38] It was ironic that Raab's office was pointing to 'professional due diligence' in the same sentence it made an error in describing Leus's conviction—which was not overturned on appeal, but as highlighted above, struck out.[39] Many questions remained but Leus's new friends stood by him.

A Generous Spouse

A single case can only ever tell us so much. In order to make more sense, we consider a second case of a person who is more extreme in that they are a much larger donor and whose ties to the Kremlin are well-documented: Liubov Chernukhin. While their origin stories differ dramatically, both are Russian nationals who donated to the Conservative Party around the same time. Furthermore, Chernukhin's case provides clear evidence that post-communist elite donors may propose policies that benefit their personal interests and other high-net-worth individuals, as opposed to those of the kleptocracy in which their money was made.

Liubov Golubeva was born in the Soviet Union but emigrated to the United States in the 1980s, where she gained a master's degree from the NYU Stern School of Business. In 1999 she moved to the UK, embarking on a career in investment banking. She married Vladimir Chernukhin in 2007—becoming

Liubov Chernukhin—and acquired a British passport in 2011. Between 2012 and 2022, she gave the Conservative Party almost £2.3 million, making her a top 10 donor and granting her access to at least three prime ministers. Her donations won her two tennis matches with Boris Johnson and dinner with then Prime Minister Theresa May and future Prime Minister Liz Truss.[40]

Chernukhin is also a member of the Conservative Party's advisory board for significant donors, a group made up of ultra-rich donors formed by Ben Elliot, who meet monthly with the prime minister and chancellor. According to *The Times*, Chernukhin also has pragmatic concerns. She has repeatedly lobbied government ministers 'against raising the tax burden on high net-worth individuals' and has sent them research from accountancy group Ernst & Young 'on the importance of the ultra-rich for the overall economy' while a member of the donors' advisory board.[41]

But where had her money come from? Liubov may have her own source of funds through her business ties, yet an investigation by the *Guardian* indicated that substantial funds were transferred to Liubov from her husband, Vladimir.[42] One of Vladimir's companies was shown to have loaned her UK company as much as £9.4 million, with the loans later written off as 'bad debt'. There is no suggestion these loans were unlawful.[43] Documents from the Pandora Papers reveal that most of the Chernukhins' wealth is held offshore, in a network of 32 companies and three trusts holding more than £100 million in assets.[44]

In the 1990s and early 2000s, Vladimir Chernukhin was a considerable player in Russia. In September 1999, Russian Prime Minister Vladimir Putin made him deputy chairman of Vnesheconombank, a powerful state bank, making Chernukhin a government official. After Putin became president of Russia, Chernukhin served as a deputy minister of finance between 2000 and 2002. Chernukhin left the government and moved to the UK in 2004. There is much debate about why he left Russia: Chernukhin's supporters say that he had fallen out with Putin due to the fact Chernukhin was close to Mikhail Kasyanov, a former Russian finance minister who joined the opposition after leaving the government in 2004. However, Chernukhin maintained business ties in Russia, including with figures close to the Kremlin. Such 'fence-sitting' is not uncommon among Russian exiles in the UK who look to downplay their loyalist credentials, most famously the former owner of Chelsea FC Roman Abramovich who was later sanctioned by the UK.

According to the *Guardian*, Vladimir 'used his position in the Russian elite to cultivate influential business contacts while investing in private ventures, according to court documents'.[45] This is a reference to a lucrative Moscow property transaction that dated back to when Chernukhin was a senior official at Vnesheconombank.[46] In 2018, Chernukhin testified in a London court hearing that he had an arrangement with the former mayor of Moscow, Yuri Luzhkov, to secure planning permission for a development in which Chernukhin had a secret personal interest.[47]

Yet investigations have also shone light on how Chernukhin continued to fence-sit and make money from Russian deals, including with figures who remain close to the Kremlin, after he moved to the UK. Reports highlighted that in 2016, some 12 years after leaving Russia, Vladimir Chernukhin received $8 million from Suleiman Kerimov, a Russian billionaire sanctioned in 2018 by the US Treasury. In 2013, Chernukhin was a board member of Polyus Gold, Russia's largest gold producer, whose largest shareholder at the time was Kerimov.[48] Lawyers for Vladimir Chernukhin declined to confirm whether he received $8 million from Kerimov.[49] Liubov Chernukhin also appears to have a link with Kerimov, despite having apparently never lived for a significant period of time in Russia since the collapse of the Soviet Union. A year prior to her marriage to Vladimir, Liubov was appointed a director of an offshore company connected to Kerimov that had acquired a large property in north London.[50] Kerimov has denied any connection with Liubov.[51]

Liubov Chernukhin's lawyers said her political donations were not tainted by Kremlin influence and that she had never received cash from Kerimov or 'any company related to him'.[52] Furthermore, her lawyers said it was not accepted that any of Chernukhin's political donations had been funded by improper means or affected by the influence of anyone else.[53] The Conservative Party said that Lubov Chernukhin was a British citizen 'which gives her the democratic and legal right to donate to a political party', adding that donors did not influence government policy.[54]

Not Just a Continental Problem

These examples and others have elicited a wider debate about the money flowing not just into universities (see Chapter 10) and political parties, but to charities, think tanks, and the royal family. There are clear reasons why we should ensure that this money is clean. On a purely moral level, it is common and reasonable to set a high standard. It is often argued that our political leaders should not be taking money from persons or entities where there is some risk that the money is tainted, regardless of whether any strings are attached. As we have seen in the Oxford case, high-net-worth individuals might donate to universities without the aim to influence the institutions themselves or the figures that work in them, but because of the status it confers to their allies and friends. Such donations may be cited while applying for residency or citizenship, to gain kudos back home, and to accrue influence in the country of residency.

But the 'worst case scenario'—where payments, donations, and gifts have an actual effect on political decisions—occur with alarming frequency even in countries whose democracy is supposed to be strong. For example, several years before the 'academic contract of the century' with the University of Oxford, 'caviar diplomacy' was arguably the political lobbying scandal of the century with almost $3 billion laundered through a network of UK shell companies known as the Azerbaijani Laundromat. These companies were the vehicles for payments to several former members of the Council of Europe's parliamentary assembly, PACE. One of these individuals, Luca Volontè, the former chair of PACE's centre-right group, received in total more than €2 million through an Italian foundation in order to improve Azerbaijan's reputation abroad.[55] In 2021, Volontè was sentenced to four years in prison in Italy for taking bribes to help mute criticism of Azerbaijan's human rights record.[56]

Across Europe there are many examples of how European political parties are being financed with potentially illicit or tainted capital originating in post-communist kleptocracies. In 2014, France's far right National Front (since renamed National Rally) took Russian loans totalling €11 million, the largest of which came from a small bank, First Czech Russian Bank, with apparent links to the Kremlin.[57] *Buzzfeed* reported on a proposed scheme from October 2018—which ultimately failed—to funnel millions to the Lega party, headed then by Italian Deputy Prime Minister Matteo Salvini, through a Russian oil deal. Such a scheme, had it gone ahead, would have been a breach of Italian electoral law.[58] These schemes often arise through third parties which appear to be independent of the post-communist elite.

UK politicians routinely present Britain as free from this kind of corruption due to its high level of transparency—the public register of donations. However, the UK lags behind others in the West when it comes to lobbying transparency,[59] and even legal, disclosed payments and gifts may have an effect on what our politicians say. For example, between 2011 and 2020, British

MP Bob Blackman made seven trips to Azerbaijan with the three most recent trips paid for by either the Azerbaijani parliament or the Azerbaijan Embassy in London. Blackman is chair of the Azerbaijan All-Party Parliamentary Group (APPG), and freely admits being 'fed' information from the Azerbaijan embassy which he then used to lobby the UK government.[60] His position and interests are known and declared in the parliamentary register. Regarding Azerbaijan's February 2020 parliamentary elections—which, according to the OSCE, featured 'restrictive legislation and political environment [which] prevented genuine competition'[61]—Blackman is reported to have said, 'There was nothing untoward that I could see during the voting process'.[62]

This kind of work is based on relationships between elites. Secretarial support to the APPG on Azerbaijan was provided by a group called the European Azerbaijan Society, one of whose directors was the son of a powerful minister in the Azerbaijani government.[63] The APPG framed 'the discussions they have and ensuring human rights and democracy are not on their list of considerations', according to one human rights group.[64] Before dissolving in 2020, the European Azerbaijan Society took MPs, MEPs, and foreign government officials on luxury trips to Azerbaijan.[65] Research by Transparency International indicates that the group was the second biggest spending foreign lobby group in the House of Commons up to 2017.[66] Azerbaijani influence operations appear to be winding down in recent years with the closure of the BFSAC—the charity behind the anonymous donation to Oxford on whose board sat Lord Bruce (see Chapter 10)—and the Anglo-Azerbaijani Society, a body chaired by another member of the House of Lords. But these organizations were never ends in themselves but vehicles to make friends and influence others.

Moreover, procedurally, the UK system is not watertight. While shadow parliamentary groups like the Azerbaijan APPG are notoriously underregulated, even the oversight system for donations has loopholes. Any individual on the UK's electoral register can donate. As well as British and Irish nationals who are resident in the UK, citizens from any member of the Commonwealth and EU who are resident in the UK are also eligible to vote. As discussed in Chapter 7, thousands of individuals from Russia, China, and other corruption hotspots acquired passports from Commonwealth countries such as Malta, Cyprus, and St Kitts and Nevis through citizenship by investment schemes. The UK government clearly will have no oversight over the granting of Cypriot passports, for example, whose scheme was mired in corruption that allegedly reached even the country's parliament. Furthermore, a UK-registered company or limited liability partnership that conducts business in the UK can also donate to political parties, leaving the door wide open for an ostensibly British company to use loans from overseas as potential donations. One such example, highlighted by Tortoise Media's investigations, is IX Wireless, a major political donor and UK-registered company which has little to no presence in Britain and the source of whose funds is unclear.[67]

In this relatively open environment, there has been a disproportionately high rate of donations from post-communist exiles. For example, between 2010 and 2019, the Conservative Party received £3.5 million from donors born in Russia and with a Russian business background. The volume should not be exaggerated as the overall amount donated to the Conservatives in this time was £286 million. However, this means that Russian Britons, a group which constitute about 0.1% of the UK population, contributed 1.2% of the Conservatives' donations.[68] These figures may merely reflect the fact that some in the community are extremely wealthy but this in turn highlights that this wealth has been earned within the *sistema* by persons often with close ties to the state. These include former arms dealer Alexander Temerko and the financier Lev Mikheev.[69]

Since 2019, the volume of donations appears to have increased, with Leus one of the new donors to the party, albeit to date not on the same scale as others. Leus states that he has never been 'in any way whatsoever' an agent of President Putin, worked for the Russian state, or taken state assets, and, as stated above, views himself as a victim of the regime.[70] Among other major donors are individuals who, while not themselves of Russian or Eurasian background, have made their money doing business in the region. These include Mohamed Amersi, who has given around £500,000 to the Conservative Party since 2018 (see Chapter 1).[71]

Why Do Post-Communist Exiles Give to the Ruling Party?

The above analysis establishes that the UK is a fertile lobbying environment for some post-communist regimes and for the exiles and fence-sitters or others whose wealth has been earned in the region. But it is the exile donors like Leus and Chernukhin which perhaps raise the most difficult questions and require the most enabling. How have so many of those with post-Soviet connections come to give to the Conservatives? Part of the answer may concern the role of professional enablers who provide 'concierge' services to wealthy new arrivals to the UK who lack—or simply wish to improve—their pre-existing social and business networks.

One such company is Quintessentially, run by Ben Elliot, Conservative Party fundraiser and close friend of Boris Johnson. Amersi became a 'global elite' member of Quintessentially. He reports that it was Elliot who arranged for him and his Russian-born wife, Nadezhda [Nadia] Rodicheva, to have dinner with the then Prince Charles in 2013 (Elliot is the nephew of Charles's wife, Camilla). Rodicheva donated in 2017, two years before Elliot was appointed co-chair of the party when Boris Johnson became prime minister in July 2019. Amersi told the *Financial Times* that Elliot 'started seeking donations from me and Nadia for the Conservative party even before he became chair'.[72]

Enabling and networking are apparent in the phenomenon of political donations from elites whose wealth originates from post-Soviet kleptocratic states. However, it is hard to tell what difference they make. Do figures like Ben Elliot create opportunity among naturalized elites for political connections and donations that would otherwise not exist? Or are they merely responding to a pre-existing demand? The academic literature on political donors distinguishes between investors (those that seek a return), ideologues (those which have a cause), and intimates (those which seek status).[73] While corporate donors are typically investors, personal donors are commonly intimates. Both may be ideologues.[74] Meanwhile, British voters worry about political corruption, but they neither favour a taxpayer-funded party system nor make small donations at a level to support parties.[75] As the Conservative Party became more economically nationalist under Boris Johnson, it deterred some of its business supporters and increasingly needed wealthy individuals as its chief donors.[76] At first glance, naturalized post-Soviet elites look like a category of donor ready to step into the breach.

This rapid overview of political donations by post-Soviet elites allows us to draw three conclusions—each of which raises their own questions. First, donors originating from kleptocratic states are 'fence-sitters' with transnational agendas. Donors who are explicitly loyal to home governments which are hostile to Britain are likely to be turned down on reputational grounds. The donation of the fence-sitter is perhaps so difficult to assess precisely because it does not fit easily into binary categories of friend/enemy. The fence-sitter, by definition, is neither for nor against the home government but part of transnational networks of power. Chernukhin's key concern voiced to the UK government was not sanctions against Russia but the 'importance of the ultra-rich'. This agenda may be to varying degrees intimate (about themselves and their friends), invested (for their benefit), and ideological (according with their values). It may not be dissimilar to other wealthy political donors.

Second, donors originating from kleptocratic states especially understand that the primary indulgence of friendship is intimacy; it is in intimacy that common interests and ideas are found. We may assume that Conservative fundraisers like Elliot have a strong sense of their clients' demands and those wealthy and sophisticated donors like Chernukhin and Leus recognize that investment opportunities and ideological affinities are often secondary to relationships. Given his origins in late-Soviet Turkmenistan and Russia's *sistema* of networks and clans, Leus would likely have believed that donations to the foreign secretary and the charity of the heir to the British throne would only help his cause. Leus's donations to the Prince's Foundation were made in the spring/summer of 2020, a few months before he applied for permanent residency in September 2020. Indeed, his donations to the Prince's Foundation was detailed in Mishcon de Reya's letter in support of his claim for UK permanent residency, along with Charles's effusive response.[77] The following month Leus made his first donation to the Conservative Party. Leus likely gained his permanent residency status in late 2020/early 2021, and citizenship in 2023.[78]

Third, making friends is about more than political donations. Most political donors from kleptocratic states have broader reputation laundering agendas which have been indulged by professionals in other sectors including philanthropy and defamation law. This is particularly true of Dmitry Leus. His reputation laundering is evident not merely in those whom he contracted but also in the identities of the venerable institutions he targeted: the Conservative Party, the Prince's Foundation, and the Royal Institution of International Affairs (Chatham House). Leus did find indulgence more difficult due to his Russian backstory; Chernukhin's donations—despite clear connections to the Russian political elite—have raised significantly less controversy, perhaps due to her citizenship and longer history in the UK (see Figure 11.1).

	Dmitry Leus	Liubov Chernukhin
Source of Wealth	Banker, convicted of money laundering in Russia (conviction "struck off")	Banker, career outside Russia but connections to Russia through her husband, a former Russian deputy minister
Enabler effect	£500,000 donations to Prince Charles' foundation via "fixer"; Over £50,000 donations to Conservative Party	£2.3m donations to Conservative Party; Membership of donors' advisory board via Ben Elliot
Outcome	PARTIAL SUCCESS: Chairs Dominic Raab's constituency association; Donations returned by the Prince's Foundation	FULL SUCCESS: Tennis with Boris Johnson; Dinner with Theresa May and Liz Truss

Figure 11.1 Making political friends

Political Donations and the Provision of Intimacy

What can we learn from these two cases of donors to the Conservative Party whose origins and original sources of wealth lie in Russia? In both cases, enablers appear at the margins and are not central to whether a donation was accepted (although arguably, in the Leus case, enablers were central to him obtaining citizenship in Cyprus, and residency and citizenship in the UK, which is connected to the elite's ability to give donations). In both cases, we can see that association was sought and gained with the political elite—friendships were made, and an indulgence was granted. Naturally, we can say nothing for certain about whether any specific ends were attained as such details are routinely hidden from view. But nor can we say if medieval Christians really had their sins remitted. It is the process of indulgence and the intimate moments achieved along the way, not the final outcome, that matters.

With respect to our contending explanations, we can say with confidence that neither the evidence for the incumbency advantage nor for the alliance effect is strong in these Russian cases. But both appear to have played some role in others such as the Azerbaijani funding in parliament. As such, enabling appears to have made the difference but—just as with the University of Oxford in Chapter 10—that enabling is internal to the recipients of the donation and thus is 'weak' by the definitions we have used. Even on the occasions where Ben Elliot's Quintessentially was involved, Elliot was also a party member and later became its chair responsible for fundraising. Perhaps the lesson of political donations is the priority placed on intimacy by post-communist elites and exiles in the UK. This intimacy is also apparent in our final two chapters, which concern the tracking of enemies by corporate intelligence professionals and the silencing of critics by libel lawyers.

12

Tracking Enemies

We have to use anti-surveillance techniques in London now that I
learnt in Nigeria, Somalia, and Kazakhstan.
                    —Tom Burgis, journalist with *The Guardian*[1]

Arcanum Global is a private intelligence agency based in Knightsbridge,
London, and founded in 2006 by Ron Wahid. Wahid is an American and
donor to the Republican Party who claims to have considerable connections
to the US intelligence services. Arcanum includes multiple ex-spies and former
national security officials among its staff and on its board.[2] Companies like
Arcanum seek to generate for themselves some of the mystique surrounding
the intelligence agencies of Western states and claim to work within the
interests of these states and their allies. These allies include, according to the
estimation of Wahid and his colleagues, the government of Kazakhstan. In fact,
the regime of Nursultan Nazarbayev has long practiced a multivector foreign
policy in which it cooperates with Russia, China, Western states, and pretty
much anyone else willing to do business in the country on terms favourable to
its ruling elite. Arcanum, it turns out, adopts a similar philosophy.

In 2009, the fugitive Kazakh banker Mukhtar Abylazov met with Wahid
with a view to contracting the services of Arcanum to protect his interests
against the efforts of his home government to track him down. Ablyazov
had been the country's minister of energy and was then imprisoned by the
Nazarbayev government from 2002 to 2003, but returned to favour to make
billions from a bank he chaired, BTA. According to the Kazakh and UK
authorities, this money was stolen. Ablyazov was found in contempt of court
in the UK in 2012 and later lost his right to remain in Britain. But whether
Ablyazov's money was thieved is not of interest to us here—and this story has
been told countless times.[3] What interests us are the UK enablers who apparently worked both for and against Ablyazov and even tracked those covering
the case, including the FT journalist and author of *Kleptopia* Tom Burgis.

At the time they approached Ablyazov, Arcanum was already working for the other side. 'We never gave them a proposal for fighting Nazarbayev but, yes, we were working for Kazakhstan at this time', Wahid told Burgis with respect to his overtures to Ablyazov.[4] Between 2009 and 2012, the Kazakh government paid Arcanum US$3.7 million for its work in 'asset tracing' where Wahid's staff reported directly to 'some of Nazarbayev's most senior officials while being formally commissioned, at various times, by Kazakhstan's foreign lawyers'.[5] According to Ablyazov and associates targeted, the work goes beyond the forensic, financial, and legal aspects of asset tracing to a corner of the industry which skirts the line between legality and illegality. Lawyers for the family of Ilyas Khrapunov, Ablyazov's son-in-law, describe 'a surveillance campaign that amounted to illegal espionage, including bugging and a barrage of booby-trapped emails' conducted by firms including, they allege, Arcanum.[6] The firm did not respond to our opportunity to comment.

Having shown how UK professionals assist the exiled elites of kleptocracies to make political friends, in this chapter we explore the other side of this indulgence: tracking enemies. Kleptocratic regimes and their oligarchic allies also use British enablers to go after exiles and critics, subjecting them to surveillance and in some cases intimidating and otherwise harassing them. We focus on the professional sector of corporate intelligence in which London has become a world centre while noting that nonstate intelligence activities by elites are ancient and precede those of states.[7] We begin by unpacking the work of Arcanum for Kazakhstan before going on to consider how we should make sense of the shadowy world of corporate intelligence. Are such firms, agents of their host states, abusers on behalf of kleptocratic states, or asset tracers for companies and elites? We then return to the Arcanum case to assess these three options and consider what happens when the politics changes—as it did in Kazakhstan following the protests of January 2022, which spiralled into violence, leaving over 220 dead when Kazakh forces opened fire.

Tracking Kazakhstan's Enemies

Arcanum was only one of many agencies deployed by Kazakhstan in its campaign against its exiled enemies. There is no doubt the campaign was far-reaching and involved a panoply of Western professional services which sat alongside some of the more extreme tactics used by the government itself. The latter included the use of INTERPOL arrest notices, a system widely abused by authoritarian states, and the illicit rendering of Ablyazov's wife and young daughter from Italy to Kazakhstan, apparently with the cooperation of the Italian authorities.[8] Some of the (lawful) tactics which were used against Ablyazov and associates by private sector actors included extensive surveillance across Europe carried out by Diligence, a London private security firm which popped up in Chapter 7, as well as expletive-laden threats directed at one of Ablyazov's lawyers, Peter Sahlas, by Patrick Robertson of World PR, a London-based and Panama-registered company.[9] There is no suggestion that Arcanum was involved in any of these acts.

The Ablyazov story itself is apparently never-ending. In 2017, Ablyazov won his appeal against extradition at the highest level of the French courts before being reported as having lost it in December 2022.[10] Yet several lawsuits and countersuits related to the activities of Western enablers remain active including at least two arising—in the summary of a US judge hearing one of these cases in 2019—from 'threatened or asserted claims against the individuals identified by Arcanum'.[11] The Kazakh government has sought to disassociate itself from these. 'Frankly, there were many people approaching us with such proposals', Marat Beketayev, the then justice minister and former director of ENRC (see Chapter 6), commented: 'The techniques on offer were disturbing, arranging some kind of scandals, hacking emails, things like that. This is simply stupid. This works maybe for a short period of time but, in the long run, if you engage in such things, you will never be taken seriously by other countries'.[12]

However, the government of Kazakhstan continued its intimate professional relationship with Arcanum and its fight in foreign courts against its enemies and former allies. One of these is Felix Sater, a Russian-American property developer, convicted fraudster, and former Trump Organization business partner with the company Bayrock. Sater gained public notoriety for his role in as a go-between who proposed to presidential candidate Donald Trump in 2016 that sanctions against Putin regime cronies be removed. He was subsequently a subject of Robert Mueller's investigation into Russian interference in the US presidential election of 2016 (known as 'Russiagate'). The Kazakh state and its private partners face ongoing court cases related to their use of Sater as an intelligence asset against Ablyazov. While they charge Sater for breach of contract from the 'cooperation agreement' whereby he switched sides and became a witness against Ablyazov and his associates, Sater charges them with defamation.[13] It is telling that the Kazakh entities named in these suits—and in the original case against

Ablyazov—are the City of Almaty and BTA Bank, one public and one private institution (hereafter Almaty/BTA). In a kleptocracy, all partnerships are public-private as the boundary between the two is necessarily porous.

The corporate intelligence industry as a whole and Ron Wahid's London-based Arcanum in particular also trade at the intersection of public and private. According to documents from court cases from 2019 onwards, Sater was paid for his cooperation via a front company called Litco: a $100,000 monthly fee and a 16% return on all assets recovered due by Almaty and BTA. He sued his Kazakh patrons for reneging on this agreement.[14] Had the lawyers for Almaty/BTA, Boies Schiller, known that Litco was Sater's they would have been in violation of American laws against paying witnesses. However, Almaty/BTA's agreement with Sater was managed by Arcanum, who kept knowledge of the recipient of $100,000 per month on a need-to-know basis. Judge Katharine H. Parker of the Southern District of New York commented Boies Schiller 'showed an incredible lack of curiosity' about whether Sater was the owner of Litco.[15] Arcanum provided the crucial service where members of its staff provided payment to a person whom they knew to be a witness for his services rendered.[16]

Arcanum is also linked to intelligence consultant Christopher Steele and indirectly to the Mueller investigation. In addition to paying witnesses and incentivizing side-switching, Arcanum identifies and contracts specialist expertise, often from former members of the intelligence services. It was reported by the FBI that Christopher Steele, the former MI6 agent and head of their work on Russia who had produced the dossier on Trump's Russia links which had caused so much controversy after the latter's election, had also been investigating Ablyazov, Sater, and the Trump Soho development, in which the Ablyazov family invested in Trump-branded properties through Sater's Bayrock company.[17] The FBI report further revealed that Steele had provided a PowerPoint presentation on the deal which itself originated with Arcanum.[18]

Sater was apparently enraged by these claims and in his own submissions to the court sought to link Russiagate to the Ablyazov affair. Fighting back against allegations that he worked with Russia and for Trump's victory, in documents published in 2022, Sater alleged a 'nefarious plot by the Kazakhstan National Security Committee (the Kazakh KGB) and their long-time agents Arcanum to interfere in the 2016 US Presidential Election in favor of Hillary Clinton'.[19] These incredible claims have not received support from the courts. In May 2022, upholding an earlier judgement, the

192 INDULGING KLEPTOCRACY

New York court again denied Sater the right to enjoin this claim to his legal action relating to the charges of money laundering in the Ablyazov case.[20] In October 2022, it ruled against Sater again in his attempt to have key Nazarbayev regime figure Kenes Rakishev (who became the largest shareholder of BTA after it merged with Kazkommertsbank[21]) deposed regarding his relationship with persons including Hunter Biden and Vladimir Putin and the relationship between Almaty/BTA and Arcanum.[22] Part of Almaty/BTA's objection was specifically regarding details of their confidential relationship with Arcanum being disclosed.[23] It is important in the corporate intelligence sector for the exact relationships between state and private entities to remain secret.

Such back-and-forth outrageous allegations and counter-allegations are impossible to unravel. However truthful these claims, the wide-ranging activities of Arcanum on behalf of the Nazarbayev regime tell us a great deal about the centrality of private intelligence agencies to the function and dysfunction of transnational kleptocracy. This dysfunction points to a critical aspect of both Russiagate and the Ablyazov affair. The side payments and side-switching are in themselves significant. The question to ask is not whether Trump was to be Putin's man in the White House or Ablyazov a crusader for democracy; these are questions based on naïve views of statecraft, geopolitics, and autocracy. The more interesting puzzle relates to the growth of the corporate intelligence industry as both the agent of transnational kleptocracy and a for-hire auxiliary service for the courts and regulatory agencies of democracies.

Agent, Abuser, or Asset Tracer?

Arcanum is one of a myriad of firms working on private or corporate intelligence which tracks both persons and assets, sometimes to silence or intimidate the former and often with the purpose of tracking, freezing, and seizing assets. 'Corporate intelligence' includes everything from private intelligence work by Arcanum, Diligence, and similar firms on behalf of states to open-source due diligence and political risk analysis, of varying quality, by desk-bound researchers working in business intelligence. Our focus here is on 'private intelligence'—those organizations which provide the kind of indulgences mentioned in the Arcanum example—the ability to track your enemies by circumventing the law and reaching the parts that well-regulated professionals cannot reach. But in practice, the line between private intelligence and other areas of corporate intelligence is hard to ascertain.

We spoke to several industry professionals during the research for this chapter. Over the years we have also had contact with dozens of analysts who we have met at events or have approached us for opinions. As so little is in public domain, these anonymous interviewees were extremely helpful to our research. One such interviewee referred to a similar situation as above, in which they had been working for a foreign government interested in identifying individuals who may have fled the country and taken assets beyond their means. This senior expert explained that 'as the regime changed, and the elite in power changed, too, authorities decided to stop investigating one set of people and start investigating another set of people'[24] and recounted his firm's struggle with obtaining data:

> People think that we are always able to get to information—because we have backchannels, or we are willing to break banking secrecy, or, such as in this case, pierce the corporate veil. But, other than the usual databases (we mostly go through the UK courts, as high-net-worth individuals and foreign governments suing each other like to bring litigation here), we have no legal ability to find this information out.[25]

No surprise, then, that bending the law becomes a sought-after activity by clients. Another practitioner suggested that corporate intelligence firms and individual professionals differ along three spectrums: the physical-remote, intrusive-unobtrusive, and ethical-unethical. 'Given that there is little-to-no oversight', they argued, 'and the perception amongst clients that the most useful information is generally the most well-hidden, there is demand for firms and people who are willing to break the law to get to that information'.[26] Remote activities like hacking may be more intrusive and effective than physically following a target. Breaking or skirting up against data protection laws appears to be routine in the private intelligence sector.

London is a leader in providing these grey services. However, there may be specific reasons in the private intelligence domain. Patrick Grayson, the founder of GPW, one of the largest firms, links London's pre-eminence in the private intelligence market to its history as an imperial power. 'Britain has been a very fertile place for information, intelligence gathering, and that has to do with our position in the globe, the British tradition of exploring foreign parts and relying on accurate information to expand its interests', he remarked to journalists.[27] London leads globally for corporate intelligence on Europe, the Middle East, and Africa (known in the industry as EMEA)—a region which includes the former Soviet states. The field is so lucrative that anecdotal evidence suggests that the British and US intelligence agencies are losing many staff to the private sector and increasingly relying on outsourcing themselves for services they no longer provide in-house.[28]

How should we understand the purpose and significance of this wide-ranging industry? What does it tell us about the nature of today's transnational kleptocracy? There are perhaps three frames through which the corporate intelligence industry is viewed. Each may shed light on certain parts of the sector. The first of these is state centric: that private intelligence is an adjunct to or agent of national intelligence organizations in the host country. The argument that their activities are in lock step with Western foreign policy agendas is the implicit claim of Wahid and the one made by James Giffen, the American oil broker who in the 1990s facilitated millions of dollars in bribe payments to Kazakhstan's President Nazarbayev, as discussed in Chapter 14.[29] Some research on private intelligence takes this approach.[30]

Of course, there is nothing new to states using private companies and individuals as agents of their foreign and security policy.[31] However, in the post–Cold War era there was a dramatic expansion of outsourcing to private intelligence companies.[32] After the September 11 attacks, the expansion continued as the US intelligence community grew dramatically. In 2007, one former CIA senior staff member estimated that more than half of CIA staff were contractors.[33] A 2010 investigation by the *Washington Post* found that there are nearly 2,000 private intelligence companies working as subcontractors with over 850,000 persons with top secret security clearance.[34] By 2017, this had grown to around 1.2 million persons with top secret clearance in the United States.[35] One estimate suggested that there are 2.5 times as many with top secret clearance in the private intelligence sector than in the national intelligence agencies.[36]

The UK has outsourced less than the US. The British state rarely clears private professionals to the highest level of security despite having, in London, the largest global centre of for-hire private intelligence. While official secrecy limits disclosure to a greater extent in the UK, in 2017, a report of parliament's Intelligence and Security Committee (ISC) found that the annual spend on contractors was now over £1.2 billion, around one third of the agencies' budget and a threefold increase on the £400 million spent in 2011.[37] Since 2017, the ISC has not published figures and has redacted its subsequent annual reports of these data. This appears to be due to sensitivity of the agencies to public criticism of outsourcing as well as official secrecy; under pressure from the ISC, MI5 committed to a 'decontractorisation' project in 2016.[38] Outsourcing appears now to be confined to certain sectors in the UK and we know of no court cases where a UK equivalent of the Giffen defence (see Chapter 14)—'MI6 made me do it'—has been used.[39] However, UK companies, BAE Systems and AEGIS, were two of the nine leading private intelligence companies identified in a 2018 study,[40] thus there must be at least some outsourcing to the private sector.

This outsourcing is also suggested by the migration of senior British foreign policy and intelligence officials to the private sector. The industry-monitoring service Intelligence Online[41] charts these developments including the very large numbers of former senior intelligence officials and His Majesty's Ambassadors to Gulf monarchies and other hydrocarbon-rich states attracted to the private sector. Many of their specific claims are difficult to verify; however, a pattern seems to emerge. While former intelligence officers and security specialists typically start private security and corporate intelligence consultancies, former ambassadors may find their way into working in private offices, sovereign wealth funds, and other investment arms of sovereign elites in countries where they served. A recent academic study found that the Ministry of Defence, Cabinet Office, and FCDO are the three British government departments, 'particularly prone to revolving door activity amongst senior civil servants'.[42]

A second frame is more pejorative and suggests the role of private intelligence is more abusive than merely supplementary to the system. According to this perspective, private intelligence agents engage in *transnational repression*. This too is a state-centric frame which assumes that private intelligence serves a state interest. But instead of private intelligence being in the service of the host state, this perspective focuses on service to authoritarian state clients. Transnational repression occurs where a state targets its exiles and wider diaspora abroad via mechanisms ranging from surveillance and intimidation to extradition requests and assassination attempts.[43]

The UK government's role in the US renditions program and its use of torture suggests that democratic governments do use such extreme measures as a consequence of an heightened assessment of threat.[44] However, while reliable data are extremely hard to come by, the vast majority of cases have been documented by states from the Middle East, the former Soviet Union, and China.[45] For democracies, the question is much more regarding the extent to which they are complicit or even supportive of the transnational repression of their authoritarian and kleptocratic allies. The UK's foreign policy responses, for example, were judged by the US research and campaigning organization Freedom House in a 2022 report to be 'hampered by political relationships with perpetrator states'—including allies such as Azerbaijan, Bahrain, and Rwanda.[46]

Research on transnational repression suggests that it is both widespread and entails significant involvement by private intelligence and security companies.[47] However, the role of private intelligence companies in the Western world is limited to the provision of particular services, especially with regard to post-communist states who are not Western allies. The University of Exeter's Central Asian Political Exiles project documented 278 exiles from the five former Soviet Central Asian republics, most of whom had been subject to multiple incidents of transnational repression from 1998 to 2020. These incidents were categorized from stage 1 (on notice, involving arrest notices, intimidation, and surveillance), stage 2 (arrests, short-term detentions, and imprisonment in the country of exile), and stage 3 (physical attacks and assassinations in the country of exile and refoulement to the country of origin).

These data suggest that incidents, and especially extreme incidents, take place in authoritarian states which are allies of the home government of the exile, largely since asylum in democracies is difficult to attain and transnational repression is more difficult to prosecute.[48] There are exceptional cases such as the killings of post-Soviet exiles across Europe and the assassination, attempted assassination and suspicious deaths of, respectively, Alexander Litvinenko, Sergei Skripal, Boris Berezovsky, and Alexander Perepilichniy in the UK, all of whom were Russian exiles. In most of these cases, state actors or their agents in organized crime appear to be instrumental and there is no evidence suggesting that British private actors were involved. The role of Western private intelligence companies appears to be limited to surveillance and hacking[49]—stage 1 level transnational repression of the kind directed at Ablyazov. However, such surveillance may be the precursor to more serious measures—such as the rendering of Ablyazov's wife and daughter to Italy and Kazakhstan.

Arcanum denies that they are engaged in transnational repression. It is 'absurd', Wahid told Burgis. 'To assert that our work supports "repression" would mean you claim that the UK, French, Swiss and US governments and laws are complicit with Kazakhstan's "repression machine".'[50] And yet there is no doubt that private intelligence companies have a track record of using hacking, surveillance, and the softer techniques of reputation management for authoritarian state clients. Examples include the activities of Cambridge Analytica until its demise in 2018 and the London private intelligence industry's use of hackers and consultants who were former employees of the Indian company Appin.[51] Arcanum's Ablyazov-related contracts may be seen as part of the insatiable demand for an authoritarian regime to extend its control of public discourse beyond borders. For Kazakhstan, these include the contracting of PR consultants in the campaign 'Kazakhstan—open for business' and in the hiring of Tony Blair Associates to handle the fall-out after the local police killed at least 14 unarmed protestors in the Western city of Zhanaozen in 2011. But such indulgences are qualitatively different to transnational repression carried out by state agents and allies in organized crime.

A third approach to private intelligence is quite different in that it is not state-centric but assumes a world which is decentred and market based. This is the work of the *asset tracing*. Asset tracing may support the public sector activity of asset recovery but the two should not be equated. According to this approach, the focus of the industry is neither espionage nor repression, but that of the tracing of persons, companies, and disputed assets for private companies and individuals. The lion's share of corporate intelligence firms exists in this space of asset tracing, asset protection, and political risk analysis. They rarely work directly for elites and upstream businesses but market themselves towards law firms, litigants, insolvency practitioners, and investment banks whose work with kleptocrats is typically downstream from the sources of wealth. Such a business model is consistent with the phenomenon of transnational kleptocracy as its premise is that the primary interests at stake are necessarily both private *and* public. Private intelligence, as the shadier end of the corporate intelligence sector, according to one analyst, is 'driven by business needs rather than national security requirements'.[52]

From an asset tracer perspective, the ultimate objective of relationships such as that between Almaty/BTA and Arcanum is not the national interests of Kazakhstan and all its citizens but the private interests of kleptocrats such as Nazarbayev and his key partners which use the state to advance their ends. The biggest actors in this world include *both* governments *and* private businesses whose market value can grow from naught to exceed that of small states in a matter of years. Most of this business has little to do with states. For example, Arcanum Global was one of a string of major intelligence and PR companies and law firms involved in the fightback against the *Financial*

Times' reporting of fraud by the now-collapsed German financial services company Wirecard, which was once worth US$46 billion.[53]

While the precise scope of the industry is unclear, that London is considered its global capital is not. In 2017, the corporate intelligence sector in the UK was estimated to be worth around £19 billion per annum.[54] Figures from the different but somewhat comparable industry of private security may be instructive. Research by academic Sebastian Booth showed that the regulated private security industry doubled in size from 2008 to 2016—at the same time as UK police numbers and budgets were being cut under government cost-cutting measures—to around £4 billion.[55] As of January 2023, the Security Industry Authority has registered 800 companies with around 403,000 license-holding private security professionals, 36% of whom were non-UK nationals.[56]

There are several apparent similarities and some overlap between private security and private intelligence. The academic literature has long identified internationalization as the predominant contemporary trend in security and intelligence.[57] The decentralized nature of the industry, the prevalence of subcontracting and outsourcing, and the high degree of internationalization are all parallels. While the industry's scope is truly worldwide, there's no doubt that post-Soviet cases and clients are a big part of the business. 'Russian work' is a common euphemism in corporate intelligence for some of the dirtier tasks they do. Including in this category, and partly due to the enormous resources the Kazakh regime devoted to tracking Ablyazov and anyone in contact with him, Kazakhstan is close to the top of the list. 'At one point, literally everyone I know in London was working on Kazakhstan', claimed one private investigator who spoke to Burgis.[58] A lawyer made a similar statement to one of the authors regarding London's legal sector.

Asset Tracing in Post-Nazarbayev Kazakhstan

The three frames introduced above roughly map onto the three effects which we summarized in Chapter 4: the alliance effect (the agent), the incumbency advantage (the abuser), and the enabler effect (the asset tracer). Just as with the three effects, the three frames are not mutually exclusive. A company like Arcanum may play its implied role of acting in keeping with the interests of Western governments, its explicit role of protecting the assets of its patronal elites, and a more hidden role repressing those that challenge or expose these assets.

It is worth considering all three of these frames and effects as we assess private intelligence as a professional indulgence in the new context of post-Nazarbayev Kazakhstan. Did the alliance effect mean a safe home was provided for Nazarbayev regime money? Did the incumbency advantage provide these elites with a free pass while their enemies were tracked across the world by UK private intelligence companies? With respect to this indulgence, there is substantial evidence to answer both these questions affirmatively especially in combination with the enabler effect. However, there is also increasing evidence—presented below—that professionals who once hid assets for the Nazarbayev regime are now switching sides and tracing them for the new government.

We began our story by looking at professional indulgences of the capture of assets to serve kleptocracy in Kazakhstan. We end this story by considering the role of professionals in their recapture when power changes hands, as it did in a Kazakhstan after Nursultan Nazarbayev stepped down as president in 2019 and then as chair of the national security council in 2021. An ageing leader who had been in charge for 30 years, Nazarbayev had apparently made various attempts at dynastic succession to family members. However, blessed with daughters in a region of patriarchies where dynastic succession has only ever been achieved with respect to sons,[59] power transition within the family did not materialize. Instead, a complicated transition process to Nazarbayev's chosen successor, Kassym-Joomart Tokayev, took place over several years with family members retaining key positions, such as Nazarbayev's daughter Dariga returning to parliament in January 2021 and her brother-in-law Timur Kulibayev retaining his prominent position in the oil and gas industry.

In January 2022, however, everything appeared to change. Peaceful protests spread across the country and turned violent with the authorities losing control and organized criminal groups linked to members of the old Nazarbayev regime getting involved. The disorder left 227 dead and over 10,000 arrested. It also caused an internal split between those loyal to President Tokayev and the associates of Nazarbayev: the former president's longest serving prime minister and former head of the security service, Karim Massimov, was jailed for 18 years for his role in what was judged to be an attempted coup.[60] (Massimov's supporters claim the conviction is politically motivated.) Order was eventually restored. Russia sent 'peacekeepers' under the auspices of the Collective Security Treaty Organization (CSTO).

While much attention focused on geopolitics, the evidence that the protests, which began over price hikes for liquid petroleum gas, were shaped by kleptocracy was abundant.[61] Local protest groups complained of corruption in the state and its private sector partners in the mineral sectors.[62] They shouted *Shal Ket* ('Old Man Out!') against Nazarbayev, his family, and allies.[63] They demanded rises in child benefit and pensions for the poor in a country where the ruling elite have become millionaires and billionaires at the expense of the middle class.[64] In the aftermath, many were arrested on corruption charges including Nazarbayev's nephew Kairat Satybaldy in March 2022, and former justice minister Marat Beketayev in October 2023.[65]

Alongside developments in Kazakhstan was a parallel process in the UK. A few weeks after the violence, in February 2022, Margaret Hodge MP raised these issues in a special debate on Kazakhstan in the Westminster parliament. She named 29 persons (kleptocrats, oligarchs, and alleged enablers) of the Nazarbayev era elite, including several of those mentioned in previous chapters of this report including the two surviving members of the trio of oligarchs (Chapter 5) and Dariga Nazarbayeva and Nurali Aliyev (Chapter 9).[66] Hodge began:

I want to shine a light on foreign corruption in another state, not simply because that is important in itself, but because I want to highlight the UK's role in facilitating shameful wrongdoing. Put simply, Britain enables kleptocracy.[67]

James Cleverly—who later became the first British foreign secretary to visit Kazakhstan for 20 years—was the minister responding to Hodge, promising her that 'my officials, and indeed the House, will have taken note of the individuals she highlighted in her speech'.[68] Following his re-election and during his inauguration speech on 26 November 2022, President Tokayev explicitly prioritized, 'returning all the assets illegally withdrawn from the country'[69] and stated his government would be preparing a law to that end, a law that was passed in July 2023.[70] Given the UK's role as an enabler of that capital flight, this topic was surely on the agenda when Cleverly met with Tokayev on his visit to Kazakhstan in March 2023. However, thus far, the UK has not issued sanctions, nor announced any account freezing orders, UWOs, or other public civil recovery procedures against any of these individuals since the speech was made, or indeed against any other Kazakh citizen.[71]

As we have found throughout this book, the principal actors in matters of enabling and disabling kleptocracy are nonstate. Elites occupying official positions may deploy government effectively for their private interests, but this does not make the state or the national interest the driving force. British connections to Kazakhstan extend beyond capital markets (Chapter 5), real estate (Chapter 9), and corporate intelligence to an array of financial and legal services such as those of the Astana International Financial Centre and court, the consulting services of former Prime Minister Tony Blair, and the relationship with the now disgraced Prince Andrew. This is as much true for asset recovery as it is for capital flight. The Asset Recovery Fund of Kazakhstan (in Kazakh *Yelge Qaitaru*), led by financier Orazaly Yerzhanov, and the Kazakhstani Initiative on Asset Recovery (KIAR) of another oppositionist Akezhan Kazhegeldin (whose representative issued legal papers to the chairman of Kazakhmys back in Chapter 6), visited the UK several times to meet British MPs and civil society. Widely reported meetings indicate that UK investigators and firms were gearing up to trace the assets of Nazarbayev family and associated oligarchs which had been hidden by professionals from other firms.[72]

But UK companies and actors were also mobilizing to protect Nazarbayev family assets. Jusan Technologies Limited (JTL) is a British company registered to an address in St James Square just across the road from Chatham House.[73] JTL is a holding company for an alleged US$7.8 billion in assets including a number of banks and financial services companies acquired in the name of the Nazarbayev Fund.[74] It ostensibly acts as a sort of sovereign wealth fund for education projects.

In 2021, JTL was transferred to a further holding company in Nevada, a US secrecy jurisdiction. It was there that legal action was launched by JTL and the Nevada company, Jysan Holding, against, in their words, 'the effort [of the new government of Kazakhstan] to steal more than USD $1.5 billion of [their] assets'. Their complaint continued:

This corrupt and lawless campaign demonstrates the brazen thuggery of a nation—a satellite of the former Soviet Union—that has weaponized the Government's vast powers and senior-most officials to reach far outside

Kazakhstan to steal from, intimidate, and otherwise harm persons and entities.[75]

The former kleptocrats were effectively accusing their successors of following in their footsteps.

The use of this UK company to hold Nazarbayev Fund assets was reported by British journalists in February 2022, shortly after violence in Kazakhstan in which leading Nazarbayev-era figures were instrumental.[76] The reporting may have put these assets at risk of recovery by the Tokayev government, not least because it would make it harder for JTL to contract professional services to move and protect its capital. Arcanum therefore played a leading role in pushing back. Arcanum's advisor and member of the second chamber of the British parliament, the Labour Party peer Lord David Evans, also joined the JTL board in June 2022. Its CEO, Ron Wahid, took a position in August 2022.[77] Alongside the protection of its assets, JTL acted to protect its reputation—two processes that are always entwined in the enabling of kleptocracy—and it was here that the Arcanum advisor and JTL director Evans took the leading role.

In the summer of 2022, the UK arm of US law firm Boies Schiller Flexner—the firm that had almost got into trouble over Arcanum paying their witness, Felix Sater—took legal action on behalf of JTL and the Nazarbayev fund against the four UK media outlets that published a story about its assets.[78] The claim submitted by JTL to Mr Justice Nicklin in April 2023 against *The Daily Telegraph* and The Bureau of Investigative Journalists (TBIJ) is signed by Lord Evans.[79] Not only does it allege defamation in the reporting of the holding structures used for Nazarbayev Fund assets, but it extends this allegation to TBIJ's reporting of the legal action it faced from JTL and the content of its GoFundMe page which it used to raises funds for its legal defence.[80] The harm that JTL claims include 'difficulty in appointing directors based in the United Kingdom', its inability to open UK bank accounts, and that its 'plans to conduct an Initial Public Offering on the London Stock Exchange have been interrupted'.[81] In order to manage the fallout of the exposure of its assets, JTL contracted other enablers but with familiar owners. Among the costs which JTL hopes to pass on to the journalists are £480,000 in fees for 'media response and ongoing reputation and risk management services' which were provided by RJI Capital,[82] a company controlled by Ron Wahid.[83]

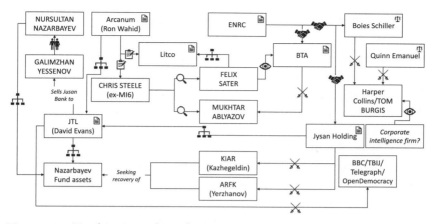

Figure 12.1 Tracking Nazarbayev's enemies

Once again, the fight over kleptocratic control took place not in the country of origin but via persons and entities located overseas, in this case in the UK and US (see Figure 12.1). No assets have thus far been recovered and the case of the Tokayev regime against the Nazarbayev Fund were reported as being settled in July 2023 after JTL sold their controlling stake to an oligarch who is related to Nazarbayev by marriage.[84] These battles in the UK and US, and the services of Arcanum among others, have had reverberations back home for old elites who have lost assets and those who have been able to retain their position in the kleptocratic system. But they also have clear implications for the freedom of speech and the press in Britain. If journalists can neither report on suspicious holding structures, nor report on legal action taken against them for reporting on those structures, nor even raise funds in public to defend themselves against that action, then freedom of speech is conspicuous by its absence.

An Undeclared War

In a November 2022 conference on SLAPPs against journalists, Tom Burgis framed his remarks in martial terms. 'We should remember what we're talking about here which is part of a war', he noted, 'It's an undeclared asymmetrical war between kleptocracy and democracy'.[85] Such bald rhetoric is fitting for the brutal facts which investigative journalists like Burgis and those at TBIJ expose. In the research for his book, *Kleptopia*, Burgis looked into the suspicious deaths in South Africa and the United States of three potential witnesses in the UK Serious Fraud Office case against Eurasian National Resources Company (ENRC), the Kazakh conglomerate. This was the SFO's longest criminal investigation which was discontinued after 10 years in August 2023. ENRC had spent around US$400 million defending the case—an amount many times that of the SFO's annual budget of around US$70 million.[86]

In the UK, the trio of oligarchs behind ENRC (reduced to a duo when Alijan Ibragimov died in 2021) retained the lawyers Taylor Wessing in their action against Burgis. In the US, they naturally retained Boies Schiller to seek to force Burgis to reveal his sources. These deceased persons were witnesses to the sometimes-violent struggle to control natural resources in Africa in which ENRC had been engaged. As Burgis described in his evidence to the Foreign Affairs Committee of the UK parliament, they were 'sources in a book about the survivors of massacres and torture, and so on'.[87] Boies Schiller were unsuccessful in litigating a claim that Burgis's book implied the business had murdered the witnesses.

However, private intelligence was also deployed against Burgis with greater effect. Fearing he may be under surveillance, and trying to protect his sources, he took precautionary measures in meeting in London with former SFO staff to discuss the ENRC case. Shortly after one meeting a letter came to light from the London arm of global law firm Quinn Emmanuel to the former SFO employee John Gibson. Burgis revealed the contents of the letter under parliamentary privilege in his evidence to the FAC:

> 'ENRC believes that on 29 September 2020, you'—that is John Gibson— 'met with Mr Burgis at an underground car park near the National Theatre, London'—five minutes' walk from here—'in a clandestine manner, and that the meeting was deliberately set up in this way to avoid detection. You attended this meeting with notebooks and folders, one of which appeared to be an orange/red notebook'.[88]

The letter was written by Justin Michaelsen, a partner at Quinn Emmanuel, with a track record of representing state-linked clients in the former Soviet Union, including Russia's Sberbank which was put under sanctions by the US in 2014 and by the UK in 2022 (after Quinn Emmanuel's work for the bank).[89] Burgis does not know which intelligence company was contracted, whether they were following him or Gibson, and whether their methods were electronic or physical. But he knew the law firm's clients intended to send a message: 'In other words, "You were being watched". What is the purpose of that if not intimidation?'[90]

Professional services in the private intelligence sector are not purely targeted against those with skin in the game—kleptocrats, oligarchs, and exiles—they also act against the journalists and researchers who investigate kleptocracy. Burgis is right that there is a war both for and against kleptocracy. Its protagonists include those that track enemies as well as those that silence critics. In our final case, we consider how we ourselves became a target in this war and lost a battle or two in the process.

13

Silencing Critics

Prof Heathershaw of King's again makes it up! The academic's . . . erroneous research was so poor and false that it needed correction, leading the institution to act to save its reputation! No litigation pressure was put. The academic needs to go back to school!
—Mohamed Amersi, X/Twitter, 30 June 2023[1]

In January 2023, Heathershaw received an email from a public relations firm, CTD Advisors, offering 'a small piece of paid work where you might be able to add your professional value.'[2] The firm is based in Mayfair, London, and Washington, DC, and counts former UK ambassador to UN and former National Security Advisor Sir Mark Lyall Grant as an advisor. It claims to operate in 'opaque business and political environments' and offer 'strategic advice to political leaders, family offices, businesses, and governments on complex matters which are at the intersection of politics, regulations, media, society, and economics to achieve the desired results.'[3] Intrigued, Heathershaw took a call with one of its directors. He asked Heathershaw to write a paid-for piece for the Government of Uzbekistan on the improvements in the country since the death of its dictator Islam Karimov. 'It's a great country, I've been there several times', the PR agent observed, 'You can have a beer there. . . . . It is a wonderful blend of East and West'.

The discussion soon turned from banalities to the task and the fee. The PR agent said he was looking for 800 words for *The Conversation*—a website which publicizes academic research and syndicates with mainstream media—at first with the ultimate aspiration of moving on to the *New York Times*, where he said he 'knew people'. He explained that they were looking for a piece which spoke about the openness of the country to business and tourism. 'Obviously', he noted, 'we expect you to write independently but to focus on the good things rather than make very critical points'. The agent asked for a fee quote from Heathershaw who told him truthfully that he hadn't worked for a PR agency before and had no idea. He said, 'I can offer you £3,000 straight away' while intimating that he was open to negotiation for a higher amount. He went on to suggest a longer-term relationship with multiple articles over a year or two with fees increasing if higher-profile publication were achieved.

After Heathershaw had declined this offer, he approached *The Conversation* to describe the approach from CTD Advisors and ask them for comment on whether they may take such an article. They replied:

> Sometimes a PR firm or other organisation such as a charity might suggest an article written by a specific academic. We make decisions about these pitches on the basis of their editorial merit and would deal directly with the author. The vast majority of our pieces don't come in this way. We never accept money in exchange for publishing specific articles, from universities, PR firms or anyone else. To preserve our role as an independent journalistic organisation, *we wouldn't accept pitches from anyone working on behalf of a government.* We are also very careful not to commission any articles that give undue promotion to a specific product or organisation. We also ask all our authors to disclose any financial or other interests they may have in the topic they want to write about (this is recorded on each article). This would include them being paid to write the article. Sometimes we decline to commission them if we feel there is a conflict of interest.[4]

According to this explanation, the only way to have such a piece accepted by *The Conversation* would be to write an 'independent' article and conceal the PR's agency's client.

Our second experience with the reputation management industry was rather different but also concerned Uzbekistan and also took place in January 2023. The three authors sat in a meeting with coauthors and senior staff from the Royal Institute of International Affairs (Chatham House) to discuss a legal challenge made against our report, *The UK's Kleptocracy Problem*, by Mohamed Amersi (see Chapter 1), and his lawyers Carter-Ruck, one of the UK's leading defamation specialists. Amersi, we may recall, had been an agent or intermediary in TeliaSonera's deals in Uzbekistan that were established by the US Department of Justice to be bribes to Gulnara Karimova, the daughter of the former president of Uzbekistan. (Amersi has always said he did not know of Karimova's relevant beneficial interest).

This and other legal challenges[5] caused harm to the dissemination work we were doing with government and parliament at a time of heightened public interest in illicit finance from the post-Soviet states. Insofar as our work informs parliament, government, and is published by high-profile institutions such as Chatham House, reasonable scrutiny is welcome, and any errors of fact will be corrected when found. But 'lawfare' by wealthy individuals and their legal enablers against 'substantially true'[6] research which is specifically written in the public interest is an entirely different matter.

Such legal actions are SLAPPs: strategic lawsuits against public participation. Contrary to Mohamed Amersi's claims, his lawyers Carter-Ruck sent at least four letters to Chatham House from December 2021 to November 2022 where they cumulatively increased the pressure on the institution, directly and indirectly threatening legal action. Far from being the subject of 'erroneous research', as Amersi later alleged on social media, the original report did not claim to offer original findings about him as his was a minor subplot in a much larger piece of research on the UK's role in post-communist kleptocracy. The 56-page report mentioned him in two sentences, paraphrasing the findings of the BBC and the *Guardian*.[7] However, the purpose here is not to rebut Amersi's public and private attacks on our research, but to shine a light on the aggressive tactics of reputation management used in 'pre-action letters' by lawyers like Carter-Ruck to manage the reputation of Amersi and others. The enormous costs facing publishers who defend themselves against such actions means that it is easier for them to concede to demands even though they are extremely unlikely to succeed in court.

In this final substantive chapter, we rather self-consciously insert ourselves into the narrative to show how we indirectly became an object of enablers. The two January 2023 examples given above—of PR and 'lawfare'—both involve British professional enablers, albeit from different sectors of the reputation management business. One offers a carrot; the other offers a stick. Having refused the carrot but been subject to the stick, it is the latter we focus on here, as it provided us with a rare data source and insight into the shadowy world of SLAPPs. However, it is important to say that the legal sector and the PR industry are more closely related than may at first be imagined. Parts of these two professional sectors indulge the same clients in complementary ways. Some professionals hold roles with multiple organizations, both those which criticize and those which indulge post-communist elites. For example, former UK Ambassador to the United Nations Mark Lyall Grant is both an advisor to CTD *and* senior advisor to Chatham House. He is also on the board of Schillings, another major player in defamation law known for its actions against public interest reporting by journalists. (There is no suggestion here that he held a conflict of interest with respect to Amersi or any other case.)

It is such personal and professional connections that link independent institutions like Chatham House to private sector firms acting on behalf of post-communist elites. Firms specializing in reputation management offer not only defensive but offensive services to their clients. On the one hand, PR agents go on the front foot to put new images of an elite or state with a poor reputation into the public domain; on the other, defamation lawyers defend these images by threatening those that conduct impartial research. The two cases illustrate the potential financial benefits and risks for researchers who come to the attention of the reputation managers. In this chapter we explore how British legal enablers *silence critics* for their clients whose wealth originates in kleptocratic environments.

From Reputation Management to Lawfare

Achieving influence extends beyond the mere establishing and laundering of reputation, the making of friends, and the tracking of enemies, to the management and protection of reputation. The professional sector of 'reputation management' is dominated by the PR industry, a business in which the UK leads the world. London has no shortage of PR professionals and fixers aiding those well-off to channel their wealth into reputation-enhancing activities designed to transform their public image into philanthropists and engaged global citizens, as will be treated in the next chapter. No qualification is needed to become a PR practitioner and the PR industry is not regulated. There are two membership bodies—the Charted Institute of Public Relations (CIPR) and Public Relations and Communications Association (PRCA)—which offer training and qualifications. They both have codes of conduct that members are asked to abide by. However, only around one in three firms are currently members of either membership body.

Occasionally, the veil is lifted on the nefarious tactics that certain PR professionals in the dark reaches of the industry employ. In 2017, Bell Pottinger was expelled from the PRCA because of the work the firm had done on behalf of the Guptas, a controversial high-net-worth family with political ties in South Africa. The firm's work attempted to influence public opinion by using racially charged language, portraying the Gupta family as victims of a conspiracy,[8] with the PRCA commenting that the campaign was 'likely to inflame racial discord in South Africa.'[9] Bell Pottinger was not a small start-up on the fringes of the industry, it was one of the largest PR firms in the UK, yet the ensuing scandal led to many of its other clients to jump ship, causing it to go into administration—the irony of a reputation management firm closing because of a bad reputation. Two of the Bell Pottinger PR agents involved in the Gupta campaign faced no personal sanction[10] and simply moved to another firm, Thoburns Communications.[11]

The 'downstream' foundation of reputation management revolves around putting positive images of the individual in the public domain to 'build' their reputation. Examples in British media are easy to find: articles extolling the virtues or deeds of the high-net-worth individual in question, accomplishments somewhat undermined by the tag 'advertisement feature' if that is noticed by the reader. Thus, we read in the *Evening Standard* about Dmitro Firtash and his wife's 'Days of Ukraine' festival in London featuring 'rousing music and dancing, and the ambiance of a Ukrainian country village fair'[12] and, as mentioned in Chapter 11, 'big-hearted' Dmitry Leus helping a young girl fighting cancer.[13]

But reputations not only need enhancing; often, they need defending too. Journalists, researchers, and activists often cast their prying eyes on wrongful acts that might have accompanied kleptocratic enrichment. Such sins can be mitigated, too. In dispensing these indulgences, no category is more adept than that of defamation lawyers. The opportunities offered by British common law in this area are so enticing that they have attracted even those without a residence in the UK to bring their lawsuits there—creating its own niche industry of 'libel tourism'.

Central to the way British common law thinks about defamation is, indeed, the very notion of reputation. Despite it being an elusive concept, English law has long been concerned with protecting it as a thing of value, to the extent that unlike in other jurisdictions, claims are only heard in the highest-level national court. The claimant does not have to prove a statement is false but merely that it has been published, is defamatory (i.e. suggests wrongdoing) and may cause serious harm to reputation.

This is a lower threshold than in other jurisdictions, where the burden on the claimant is much higher. Public figures are not treated differently, unlike, for example, in the United States. It then falls on the defendant to put together a defence, 'truth'—proving conclusively that the written or spoken words correspond to facts—being one of them. As put by British journalist Carole Cadwalladr, 'it is probably the only law on the planet in which the defendant is considered guilty until proven innocent'.[14] Even the most conscientious investigative journalists who carefully source their stories can be hugely impacted by lawsuits moved against them. The reason is the deep power asymmetry that often exists between claimant and defendant in libel cases. Frequently, the claimants' aim is not to win the case as much as to intimidate their critics, slow down their reporting, burden them financially, and thus deter others from reporting.

In what follows, we will outline the developments in British law in this area, address a few seminal and problematic cases, and explore how legal innovation has opened new avenues for abuse. There are encouraging developments: thanks to media attention and tireless campaigning, libel tourism and SLAPP suits have finally come to be recognized as a problem by UK authorities. And yet—scratch the surface, and you'll see how thorny and intractable this issue still is for those who work to expose wrongdoing. Legal reform is on its way, but in this sphere, too, indulgences and their dispensers are getting creative.

UK Defamation Law and Its Global Reach

Defamation can take the form of libel—recorded (written or spoken) assertions—or slander—orally conveyed defamatory allegations of which there is no written record. The former is more serious than the latter, and the multiplicity of ways in which recording and publishing is available in the modern world has made it the preponderant crime of the two. Defamation law is the mechanism by which UK law balances freedom of expression and the right to a reputation: Are the claimant's concerns justified or should the publisher have the right to free expression? These two notions often sit in tension.

A large part of the problem arises when information and expression run up against the much less codified concept of 'reputation'. Although England's defamation law has long been concerned with protecting it, this ephemeral and slippery concept can take various forms. Robert Post's taxonomy of reputation divides among three types: reputation can be viewed as a social construct (i.e. as honour and dignity), an economic construct (as property), and a media construct (as fame).[15] Where the claimant is a well-known individual, a celebrity, the complexities of reputational interests are amplified.[16] In trying to balance the two, UK common law has relied on both case law and statutory legislation. However, the latter has often been inconclusive and always controversial. It has thus created what has been referred to by legal scholar Matthew Collins as 'Frankenstein's monster: countless complications and piecemeal reforms riveted to the rusting hulk of a centuries' old cause of action.'[17]

The overwhelming focus on protecting reputations gave a spur to the creation of a cottage industry of professionals bent on servicing wealthy clients wishing to defend and restore what Shakespeare's Cassio described as the 'immortal part' of themselves. Elites throughout the world took note, giving rise to the phenomenon of 'libel tourism': foreigners coming to London and suing publishers—themselves frequently not from England—by taking advantage of the UK's claimant-friendly defamation laws, especially in cases where only a tenuous link with the jurisdiction exists. The incidence of such cases increased sharply in the 2000s. According to 2009 data, the number of defamation cases that reached the high court grew by 11% in 2008, with a total of 259 high court writs issued that year—the most since 2004.[18] The internet has been a publication medium which lent itself perfectly to forum shopping.

Defamation cases in England and Wales also cost far more on average than the rest of Europe, notwithstanding the emergence of some cost capping in recent years. According to David Hirst, a barrister who specializes in media law, this is 'because the cases go to the High Court and are treated as the equivalent of grand opera. In France and Germany, they go to district/local courts and cost a fraction. No one ever suggests that reputation is not properly protected in Europe.'[19] The gulf between the way the problem was dealt in the United Kingdom and the United States—another major common law jurisdiction, whose First Amendment gives increased protection to defendants—was becoming ever harder to ignore. In the mid-2000s, American actor Cameron Diaz (represented by Simon Smith of law firm Schillings[20]) brought a £33 million lawsuit in London against the US-based *National Enquirer*, which led it to block British readers access online;[21] while in another instance the *Wall Street Journal* temporarily ceased publishing its US edition in the UK.[22]

Defamation actions are not just the purview of celebrities and not just targeted at 'muck-raking journalists' but also relate to academic research, especially books on kleptocracy like this one. Having been rejected by Cambridge University Press for fear of a defamation claim, Karen Dawisha's groundbreaking book *Putin's Kleptocracy* was eventually published by Simon & Schuster in the US in 2014.[23] Most consequentially, author Rachel Ehrenfeld was sued in England over her book *Funding Evil, How Terrorism Is Financed—And How to Stop It*, on Saudi financing of al-Qaeda, which mentioned the alleged involvement of Saudi billionaire Khalid bin Mahfouz. Sued by Mahfouz, Ehrenfeld who was not domiciled in England decided not to show up in court, receiving hefty damages and an injunction (effectively, an order to destroy the book) in 2005.[24] Of the effect the libel case and the threats that preceded it had on her, Ehrenfeld wrote:

> I spent many sleepless nights worried Mahfouz would try to enforce the English judgment against me in New York. His deliberate non-enforcement left it hanging over my head like a sword of Damocles. Further aggravating the chilling effects is Mahfouz's dedicated website advertising my judgment, with more than 40 others he sued in London. The actions he took against me and others chilled American publishers from publishing books containing information on terror financiers.[25]

Ehrenfeld was ready for the worst. And yet something extraordinary happened: instead of enforcing the English court's ruling, US authorities made use of the incident as a reckoning and a call for action. In 2008, the New York legislature passed the Libel Terrorism Protection Act (also known as 'Rachel's law') and in 2010 Congress passed the Securing the Protection of our Enduring and Established Constitutional Heritage (SPEECH) Act, with discussions explicitly revolving around 'libel tourism'.[26] The act prohibits enforcement in the United States of a foreign defamation judgement that would not withstand First Amendment scrutiny if it were decided in the US. Democrat congressman Steve Cohen stated then: 'While we generally share a proud common law legal tradition with the United Kingdom, it is also true that the United Kingdom has laws that disfavour speech critical of public officials, contrary to our own constitutional tradition'. The *New York Times* poked further: 'You're an investment bank in Iceland with a complaint about a tabloid newspaper in Denmark that published critical articles in Danish. Whom do you call? A pricey London libel lawyer'.[27]

The English legal system was put to shame. In response to increasing concern over the problem, the UK government passed the Defamation Act 2013.

The new statute introduced a series of innovations aimed at raising the bar for bringing defamation claims. The threshold was heightened, specifying that the defamatory statements need to cause 'serious reputational harm' or 'serious economic loss', thus trying to deter claims of marginal merit. Peer review became a defence against libel: scholars, therefore, can no longer be sued for writings that appear in scientific journals or other peer reviewed publications, absent bad faith. (In our experience and that of other academics we know this is yet to be established in practice—see next section) Most importantly, the Act codified the defence of 'honest opinion' which replaced the old common law defence of 'fair comment'. The new concept is much more liberal, protecting honestly held opinions without the requirements that had previously narrowed the protection available.

After the reckoning of the early 2010s and the 2013 reform, it seemed, for a while, that the tide was turning against wannabe libel tourists in the UK. Although the Act only came into force in 2014, two judgements given still under the old law in 2013—*Karpov v Browder* and *Subotic v Knezevic*[28]—dealt a blow to plaintiffs who had come to the UK with the plain purpose of taking advantage of its lenient libel laws. In both cases, the Court found that there was a so-called Jameel abuse of process, relying on a 2005 case that laid the test for defamation proceedings which serve no legitimate purpose.[29] The considerations related to whether a 'real and substantial tort' has been committed in the jurisdiction: in both cases, judges held that such a tort had not been committed in the UK, because the claimants 'lacked a reputation within the jurisdiction that was capable of being prejudiced by the allegedly libelous material'.[30]

SLAPP Tactics

The legal grounds on which these cases were dismissed is an indication that the judgements were ones of minor evolution rather than revolution—as is typically the case in common law. In recent years, and despite the 2013 reforms, some UK defamation lawyers have demonstrated that the law remains open to be used against public interest research. Cases such as these fit the definition of SLAPPs—cases taken not necessarily or exclusively for their legal merit, but for the effect of silencing a critic by locking them into a long legal struggle. A similar definition by the UK Anti-SLAPP Coalition, a group of free speech organizations in July 2021, specifies academics as one group targeted by SLAPPs.

SLAPPs are abusive lawsuits pursued with the purpose of shutting down acts of public participation. These legal actions are directed against individuals and organisations—including journalists, media outlets, whistleblowers, activists, academics and NGOs—that speak out on matters of public interest.[31]

Legal action in defence of kleptocrats is not itself the indulgence of kleptocracy as it is legitimate to provide the accused with a legal defence. However, those lawyers engaging in SLAPPs on behalf of post-communist elites are wilfully offering offensive services, some of which make them noncompliant with their professional ethics guidelines.

One of the most egregious examples of this happened in 2021 when a London firm headed by Roger Gherson—whom we first met in Chapter 7 representing Maxim Bakiyev—asked for, and received, approval from the UK government to engage with Yevgeny Prigozhin. Permission was needed, as Prigozhin had been sanctioned back in 2020.[32] Prigozhin sued Eliot Higgins, the founder of the investigative group Bellingcat, in a personal capacity for merely tweeting links to the group's articles that alleged that Prigozhin led the Wagner Group, a mercenary group, the very thing that Prigozhin had been sanctioned for by the UK government. Furthermore, Prigozhin himself admitted he was the Wagner Group's leader in 2022. Lawyers from Gherson's firm, Discreet, only stopped representing Prigozhin a month after Russia launched its full-scale invasion of Ukraine. The libel case was struck out in May 2022, but left Higgins with estimated costs of £70,000.[33]

The concept of SLAPPs is unsurprisingly controversial among legal professionals. By definition, SLAPPs violate or come close to violating some of the seven principles of the Solicitors Regulation Authority (SRA) in the UK that apply to conduct of solicitors in all their dealings. Some lawyers struggle with the very concept. How can legal services be abusive in a context largely governed by the rule of law? And how do we know a SLAPP when we see one? We approach this question from the perspective of our experience of being the recipients of pre-action and responses to opportunity-to-comment letters from three law firms in each case on behalf of clients that are case-studied in this book. These are Carter-Ruck (on behalf of Mohamed Amersi, see Chapter 1), Mishcon de Reya (Dariga Nazarbayeva and Nurali Aliyev, Chapter 9), and Vardags (Dmitry Leus, Chapter 11). Lawyers' letters such as these are rarely subject to debate and analysis as they are often marked 'private and confidential'. This is true of some of the letters received by us and our publishers. Although we do not disclose privileged legal advice or personal data, Chatham House refused to give permission for our use of the letters.[34] However, on both academic and public interest grounds, we disclose contents from them all for the purpose of exploring the indulgence of silencing critics.

In each of the three cases, the factual claims made were and are substantially true, the standard required in the 2013 Defamation Act. But in each case, the law firms took issue with a handful of words to try to force the excision of their client from the report or the insertion of text to present their client in the most favourable light. Carter-Ruck disputed our paraphrasing of BBC reporting of Amersi's role in the bribe paid to Gulnara Karimova in the Chatham House report *The UK's Kleptocracy Problem* and was successful in having these sentences amended; however, it remains true that Amersi was an intermediary who approved a transaction later found to be a bribe (see Chapter 1). Mishcon de Reya contested our claims concerning the sources of wealth of Dariga Nazarbayeva and Nurali Aliyev (see Chapter 9); however, in a case of nonindulgence, we left our claims in the *Criminality Notwithstanding* report and were not subject to legal action. Vardags was successful in having Leus removed from *The UK's Kleptocracy Problem* on the grounds that he has no connection to kleptocracy; however, it remains true that he both made considerable wealth in Putin's kleptocracy (Russia's banking sector) and used this to donate to politicians and public institutions in the UK. As discussed in Chapter 11, some months after the report was published, a British MP claimed under parliamentary privilege that Leus was 'absolutely dependant on the FSB', Russia's security services.[35]

However, SLAPPs are immune to the facts of the case. They are abusive because they deploy certain tactics in violation of the SRA principles. Specifically, these tactics violated principles relating to public trust (number 2), honesty (4), and integrity (5). These violations were visible in five tactics used in the eight letters either sent to us or provided to us from which we can quote. The UK Anti-SLAPP Coalition notes that such letters are where SLAPPs begin and sometimes where they end. 'All SLAPP cases start with letters sent to journalists and/or their media outlets threatening legal action', they note in their landmark February 2023 report, 'however they may not progress beyond this point into a claim'.[36] The eight letters from Carter-Ruck, Mishcon de Reya, and Vardags demonstrate how SLAPPs work in five specific ways.

First, the law firms contacting us engaged in excessive, meritless, and aggressive claims. Carter-Ruck made the allegation on behalf of their client, Mohamed Amersi (see Chapter 1), that we and the publisher of the report, Chatham House, were part of a plot against him and his organization: 'an orchestrated and politically motivated media campaign against our client in order to sabotage the formation of the Conservative Friends of Middle East of North Africa (COMENA).'[37] Mishcon de Reya, acting for Dariga Nazarbayeva and Nurali Aliyev (see Chapter 9), alleged that our research findings 'are based on reductive and derogatory stereotypes of central Asian countries and are categorically rejected.'[38] They made it clear that they would pursue the highest level of damages if we proceeded with publication and concluded that 'we trust that, in light of the above information, you will reconsider your proposed publication.'[39]

A second set of tactics is to use new data protection rules to protect the privacy and public image of their clients. These tactics have increased since the advent of the Data Protection Act of 2018 (DPA) and the General Data Protection Rule (GDPR). A recent trend to emerge after UK libel laws were made less punitive for defendants in 2013 has been for high-net-worth individuals to try to use data protection and privacy laws to bring 'quasi-defamation' cases. Vardags's first letter to Chatham House threatened legal action if they or we made public their threats of legal action.[40] We know of no legal basis for this claim. Its second letter, less than two weeks later, was to 'provide formal notification of Mr Leus' intention to issue a claim against Chatham House for defamation and breach of the UK GDPR.'[41] While any claim on the report had no merit, Chatham House decided to concede, possibly to avoid the escalating costs and staff time that would be required to fight back. Observers noted that the claim would have been both expensive and 'meritless.'[42]

A related tactic in this area is to use the DPA's rights to enforce disclosure. Carter-Ruck threatened to use Data Subject Access Request against Chatham House, noting they would be, 'if warranted, seeking rectification and erasure of aspects of your publication.'[43] In another case, Petr Aven's claim against Orbis and later HarperCollins regarding a book, *Putin's People*, by journalist Catherine Belton (about which there is more in the next section), was based on using data protection to force changes to publications.[44] These innovative new tactics constitute strong evidence of the enabler effect in action—witting and compliant enabler behaviour on behalf of their clients.

One example which demonstrates these first two tactics of aggression and innovation in combination concerns the Organised Crime and Corruption Reporting Project (OCCRP). In September 2017, they published a wide-ranging investigation,[45] revealing a complex money-laundering scheme and exposing an Azerbaijani slush fund that handled at least $2.9 billion over a two-year period, operated through four shell companies registered in the UK. Azerbaijani authorities had tried to mitigate the reputational damage by bribing politicians through 'sweeteners' such as the Council of Europe bribery scandal (see Chapter 11).[46] One of the subjects of the investigation, Javanshir Feyziyev, decided to sue OCCRP in London despite being a member of Azerbaijan's parliament at the time (and still now, at the time of writing in September 2023).

Paul Radu—OCCRP's cofounder and a Romanian national and resident who had suddenly found himself implicated in a court battle in London—explained:

> Everything we publish is carefully fact checked, and we had plenty of legal advice ahead of publication so I was pretty sure that the case would be soon dismissed. But, to my surprise, this was not the case. The main point for me was how powerful can these figures be in using the British court system to muzzle the press. . . . SLAPPs in London are one tool in the arsenal of these autocrats. It is when you expose their infrastructure that they really get mad.[47]

Although OCCRP was eventually successful in settling the claim on favourable terms, the psychological, emotional, and practical toll their team had to endure was very high—and that was on top of a lengthy prison sentence that their journalist Khadija Ismayilova served in Azerbaijan on meritless claims (despite ECtHR judgements in her favour).

Third, defamation lawyers employ the tactic of refusing to accept contrary professional judgements and meanings. A great deal of the dispute with Carter-Ruck concerning Mohamed Amersi was about the use of the terms 'intermediary' and 'authorised' which the authors had used to paraphrase his involvement in a transaction that the US authorities later said was a bribe to Gulnara Karimova. We had used these terms as matters of academic judgement and consistent with usage in the field of academic political economy. They were, in our professional opinion, substantially true and accurate statements by any reasonable definition. But the fact that it is the court that is required to decide on a single meaning of the words creates substantial risk for the journalist or academic. Despite making concessions to avoid further time-consuming disputes, Chatham House was told in a second letter of January 2022 that 'your amendments remain inaccurate and gravely damaging to our client and to your esteemed organisation'.[48] Such tactics appear to run contrary to section 6 of the Defamation Act of 2013 which provides a defence on professional privilege grounds for academic publications which are edited and peer reviewed. While the report was not published in a scientific journal, it was subject to a rigorous editorial process and four double-blind peer reviewers.

A fourth tactic is that of asserting editorial privilege to the extent of attempting to rewrite the offending sections of text in legal style which makes them unintelligible to the average reader. In its third letter of 28 February 2022, Carter-Ruck argued that 'our client feels it is his duty (and indeed only fair considering the damaging allegations made of our client of recent) that he draws your attention to the points that remain factually inaccurate to ensure that the true position is conveyed to your readership'.[49] Indeed, Carter-Ruck on behalf of Amersi sought to rewrite the relevant section of the paper themselves. Chatham House was told: 'Our client requires the following wording . . .'. This form of wording was given to exonerate the client of all responsibility in the case. It was eight lines long and constituted an incredibly convoluted sentence. Such a sentence would never be written by an author seeking to summarize a complex issue for a wider audience.[50] When Carter-Ruck continued with the case in November 2022 after a lapse of many months, they told Chatham House that Amersi's requirements of them 'have been superseded' and demanded his complete removal from our report.[51] Chatham House did not cede to this demand, but further changes watering down the original language were made—against the wishes of the authors and without consultation with them until after the text had been agreed.[52]

A fifth tactic is to deliberately mislead. This was a tactic deployed by Vardags in its second and much-longer letter to Chatham House on behalf of Dmitry Leus. The letter falsely claimed that the report had labelled Leus a kleptocrat by including him in a report entitled *The UK's Kleptocracy Problem*.[53] In fact, the original report denoted Leus and his wife Zhanna Leus as 'exiles' and included examples of such exiles as well as other nonkleptocrats.[54] Mr Leus appears to be concerned with guilt by association, but this is not a fair legal basis on which to make an accusation of libel. Unlike in the case of Amersi, where we briefly summarize the research of others, we had conducted considerable research on Leus prior to publication and therefore knew that this claim was misleading. It nevertheless apparently succeeded in applying pressure on Chatham House, which led to the complete excision of all mentions of Leus from the report in October 2022. Chatham House stated that 'following consideration of all of the facts [and following further legal advice], concluded that the references to Mr Leus ought to be removed'.[55]

Another example of legal sleight of hand is found in Carter-Ruck's indulgence of Amersi. Less than three weeks after the public reporting of Leus's 'meritless' but successful claim, Carter-Ruck were back in touch with Chatham House and making a similarly misleading claim. The premise of the enlarged demands of Carter-Ruck in November 2022 was their claim that the authors had repeated a factual inaccuracy by repeating the BBC and *Guardian*'s claims that Amersi appeared in the Pandora Papers. At the time of the publication of *The UK's Kleptocracy Problem*, none of the papers had been published by the International Consortium of Investigative Journalists (ICIJ). In between Carter-Ruck's letter of February and its letter of November 2022 part of the papers were published in an online database. Their lawyers wrote:

> We confirm that the ICIJ's 'Pandora Papers' database reveals no positive results for the search terms that this firm has searched for. At the time of writing, neither we nor our client are alive to any evidence that our client did indeed feature in the Pandora Papers.[56]

The first of these sentences is correct. The second is not and does not follow from the first.

The 'Pandora Papers' is an ICIJ project with at least three constituent parts: 1) the original large data leak; 2) the investigations of specific persons and companies named therein; and 3) the publicly searchable online database which constitutes a tiny fraction of the original data. Amersi featured in the Pandora Papers in the second and therefore presumably the first sense. However, when the publicly searchable database was released in spring 2022—several months after our paper had been published—his name was not included. To check whether Amersi was indeed in the initial data leak, as reported by the BBC and the *Guardian*, we contacted a staff member of ICIJ who looked in the whole database and confirmed that there were no fewer than 643 mentions of Amersi.[57] Moreover, BBC and *Guardian* journalists

have confirmed to us that Carter-Ruck had been informed of Amersi's inclusion in the papers and the attendant journalistic investigation prior to
November 2022 when they made their claim in the letter to Chatham House.[58]

SLAPP Outcomes

All five of these tactics are visible in cases involving journalists which have
gone to court. To the best of our knowledge, they are characteristic of SLAPPs
and therefore the indulgence of managing reputation. The two best-known
recent examples of lawfare by UK firms on behalf of post-communist elites
show many of the same tactics and point to the fact that even victories in
these cases are rarely comprehensive success stories for free speech.

In 2021, two works of investigative journalism threw the issue of SLAPP
suits in the UK under the limelight, just before Russia's attack on Ukraine
made this problem no longer possible to ignore. Tom Burgis's *Kleptopia* and
Catherine Belton's *Putin's People*, published by HarperCollins in 2020, were
both targeted by Russian and former Soviet Union oligarchs, resulting in
legal suits costing millions. In February 2021 Anglo-Kazakh mining group
ENRC issued libel proceedings in the UK High Court against Burgis and
his publisher (see Chapter 12); a month later, several Russian oligarchs, including Roman Abramovich, and state oil company Rosneft also launched
proceedings, this time targeting Catherine Belton's book. The fact that the
claims were all received at the same time led Belton to believe that the move
had been orchestrated by the Kremlin (the claimants stated that there was
no collusion, and the timing was a coincidence).[59] Abramovich went so far
as to file a claim in Australia, despite having no business there, where there
is no 'public interest' defence. Rosneft were represented by Carter-Ruck,
Abramovich by Harbottle & Lewis, and Mikhail Fridman and Petr Aven
by CMS.

Ultimately, HarperCollins decided to settle, even though there was a good
chance it would have won the case on public interest grounds. The reason for
settling was financial: it had spent £1.5 million in the preliminary hearings
and would have had to have spent a further £2.5 million had the case continued. The Australian claim, had HarperCollins not settled, would have
cost an additional £2 million.[60] Although the settlement HarperCollins
reached with Abramovich gave him some minor text amendments, much

of the public was under the impression that Abramovich had, in fact, won contested litigation,[61] due to misreporting and use of press releases. Again, an example in which upstream enabling activities—the early PR wins, including the huge exposure through the purchase of Chelsea FC—led to easier to justify, but not less bold, downstream enabling.

Yet even though HarperCollins was wholly successful in Burgis's case and claimed a moral victory in Belton's case, editor Arabella Pike said the cost had 'spooked the market' when it came to selling translation rights to the titles: 'We went through our legal process, and in both books settled the cases. And then there were still very, very great anxieties coming from a variety of the translation publishers. It was an obstruction to some translation markets'.[62] Aside from HarperCollins's tireless support of its authors, the other element that made the difference for Burgis and Belton was the vast amount of support both of their cases have attracted from swathes of civil society and across the political spectrum.

However, 'cases like this are, when journalists are lucky enough to have spectacular four-square support, very rare'—warns Burgis—'while the vast majority of cases are those where journalists are too scared to write and their editors too scared to publish'.[63] For academics too, although we know far less about the sector, publishers too will fully or partially concede in the face of legal threats. One recent study authored by editors at Cambridge University Press details a wide variety of incidences 'of repression' against academic publishing and notes that 'smaller journals, publishers, and academic societies may simply not be equipped or inclined to handle these threats to the publishing record'.[64] This chilling effect is most visible in the threat of action rather than action itself: for every case that reaches the courts and receives some media attention, there are countless intimidatory letters sent to journalists, activists, and researchers that go unreported. Authors and publishers which successfully fight are the exception—and they rarely recover their costs in full.

Slapping Back?

The cases covered above focused on the aggressive and legal side of reputation management—SLAPPs and the phenomenon of lawfare—as opposed to the softer and productive image making which is also part of the offer of enablers. This softer side has cropped up in several of our cases, especially that of Dmitry Leus in Chapter 11. Logic suggests that reputation manage-ment for a person with questionable origins of wealth is most effective where both combine. However, the PR industry is ironically and typically secretive with little critical academic research conducted. Having become objects of it, we have begun to work with some of its more critically minded practitioners to probe the possibilities for reform. But it is the campaign against SLAPPs, supported by reform-minded lawyers, that has gained most momentum.

The purpose of SLAPPs is, by definition, to silence critics. Almost all the cases of legal letters and court cases discussed above were SLAPPs, but not all were successful. Mishcon de Reya's letters on behalf of Dariga Nazarbayeva and Nurali Aliyev in response to an opportunity to comment sent to them by Mayne and Heathershaw made baseless threats and unsub-stantiated allegations, and thereby contained some features of a SLAPP. But after Mayne and Heathershaw published their report as planned, with comments included, Mishcon de Reya did not take action.[65] In Belton's and Burgis's cases, HarperCollins, a publishing giant, had the resource to achieve moral and absolute victories. Even in the cases of Amersi and Leus, where the enablers achieved success, there has arguably been a 'Barbara Streisand effect' where the actions of Carter-Ruck and Vardags, respec-tively, on their behalf, have arguably drawn more attention to the allegations against them.

Unfortunately, these unintended outcomes do not mean that lawfare fails to silence critics. In the Chatham House cases, pre-publication legal review ascertained that no opportunity-to-comment process was necessary for any of the more than 40 named individuals. But still a lengthy process of multiple pre-action letters ensued leading to concessions for the only two—both Conservative Party donors with a history of allegations of enabling corrupt practices in post-communist states—who complained. Over 2022 and 2023 there were multiple debates in parliament on lawfare, drawing at-tention to lawyers acting on behalf of Amersi against several entities and the 'meritless' claim made by Dmitry Leus to Chatham House.[66] And even when claims are lost, the claimants may remain defiant. Having resound-ingly lost his case against Charlotte Leslie in the summer of 2023, Amersi fought on against the BBC and made threats against the authors of this book. Rebutting the criticism of him in parliament, Amersi denoted it as 'an abuse of the power of parliamentary privilege'. He went on, confusingly, to add: 'I call it a SLAPP (Strategic Limitation Against Parliamentary Privilege) or a reverse SLAPP'.

The enabler effect is clearly crucial in silencing critics—but it faces limits in both parliament and the courts. Although Carter-Ruck succeeded in making Chatham House concede, for which Amersi praised the institution, their client lost in court with respect to his four-year struggle against Charlotte Leslie and faces ongoing battles with other journalists and researchers as he seeks to protect his reputation. In Belton's case, the subsequent Russian invasion of Ukraine, the sanctions against Abramovich by the UK and other governments, and Abramovich's own role informally negotiating on behalf of Russia with Ukraine exonerated her, but still left HarperCollins and its insurer with a hefty legal bill and the book with minor revisions. If they had conceded, as Chatham House did, they may have avoided this bill. This contrast implies that the success of a SLAPP is not merely about the enabler effect but about the capability and readiness of the publisher to take the risk involved in standing up for their research.

The structural problem lingering in the background here is the failure of the state to establish the legal environment where fewer publishers concede in the face of 'meritless' claims. On 24 November 2021, 19 free-speech organizations issued a statement calling out Abramovich's lawsuits against Catherine Belton and HarperCollins as SLAPPs. In the year that followed, progress was made in the UK with the government making an explicit commitment to act on the issue of SLAPPs. Drafted by a coalition of campaigners and likeminded politicians, a model anti-SLAPP law rests on two main principles. First, that courts should be able to dismiss egregious SLAPP cases early on, and that second, the cost of bringing about a SLAPP case should be minimized for the defendant. By late 2022, it was beginning to make progress as the SRA issued a warning notice to solicitors against engaging in SLAPPs.[67]

At the anti-SLAPP conference organized by the Foreign Policy Centre in London in November 2022, the closing remarks given by Mike Freer MP, the sitting Minister for Courts and Legal Services, were nothing short of promising. 'Freedom of speech is truly the backbone of every democracy', he stated, promising action on the anti-SLAPP law, which he called 'a stellar example of how civil society and government can align their interests'.[68] During 2023, amendments were proposed in parliament to offer greater protection to public interest research on economic crime. They survived to become a section of the Economic Crime Act of November 2023. In early 2024, the government indicated that it would support a private member's bill designed to prevent SLAPPs. And yet it is too early to claim victory. Aside from the uncertainty that surrounds the effectiveness of any new law, there is also the problem that legal enablers are finding new ways to use and abuse the law to shape narratives and reputations.

14

How to Indulge No More

I'm going to give the first-class professional service to President
Nazarbayev and Kazakhstan that they need. That doesn't mean that
I didn't know that there were things going on every which way . . .
when it got into the billion numbers, that sort of bothered me when
I found out a billion dollars was missing [*laughs*].

—James Giffen, counsellor to the president of
Kazakhstan, 1991–2003[1]

James Giffen, an American who advised on trade with Russia and Eurasia
since the 1960s, is one of the original indulgers of the post-communist kleptocracy. Now deceased, Giffen did not quite frame his activity that way in
his interview with the Harriman Institute's oral history project, which was
released just after his passing. By Giffen's account, he was working for an incumbent and key American ally in the new post-Soviet region. In his own
words, he was the key advisor on the Kazakhstan side of 'probably the largest
private sector industrial project in the history of mankind'[2]—the exploration
and development of the Caspian oil and gas fields. Following several years of
negotiation and interim agreements which began during the Soviet Union, a
40-year contract to exploit the Tengiz field was signed in April 1993. Further
deals followed in the Caspian basin including what the government of
Azerbaijan called its own 'contract of the century' (as mentioned in Chapter
10). But within 10 years Giffen was indicted under the US Foreign Corrupt
Practices Act (FCPA) for his involvement in payments made in what became known as the 'Kazakhgate' corruption scandal, which established that
President Nazarbayev held a secret Swiss bank account holding millions of
dollars related to the oil deals that Giffen was helping to strike, and that a further billion dollar account holding state money was held in his name.[3]

Although he knew 'that there were things going on', Giffen claims to be
unwitting of the details of the grand corruption that was long-suspected

and later uncovered. Giffen's account of Nazarbayev's kleptocratic rule is noncommittal.

> President Nazarbayev has tried to keep everybody in line and keep them moving forward. He also kept control over money (even funds that most people didn't know about). Where did the incoming funds go? Nobody ever knew. Every which way. And, if you were arguing his case, he was using it to the benefit of Kazakhstan as needed. Others might argue that he was keeping it for his own personal account.[4]

But Giffen is clear that kleptocracy is only a problem over there. When he was tried and convicted under the FCPA in 2010, he pleaded that he was merely acting with the full consent of the CIA and according to the post-Soviet rules of the game. In short, for Giffen, kleptocracy on a transnational scale was all about incumbents and allies. Ultimately, Giffen's argument won out and the businessman escaped with minimal censure for his noncompliance: his company was just fined $32,000 for gifting 'his and her' snowmobiles to Nazarbayev and his wife. The judge even thanked Giffen for his service.[5]

Giffen's case is consistent with what we call the alliance effect: the indulging of kleptocrats and oligarchs from countries with whom the host state has good relations. According to this realpolitik perspective, corruption is derivative of power politics and enablers who serve the geopolitical interests of their countries of origin are encouraged. The United States does occasionally deal with kleptocracy in a manner consistent with the alliance effect. But as the book has shown in the British case, the vast majority of enabling is not consistent with the contours of relations between states at all. Moreover, even in Giffen's case it seems like 'first-class professional service' came first and his work for the CIA was something of a sideline for activities which were indulgent of Kazakhstan's new kleptocracy.

In this book we have sought to present a fuller explanation of transnational kleptocracy, particularly in the forms it has taken between the UK and the post-Soviet states in the three decades since Giffen's work. In our account, two other things matter more. First, there is the incumbency advantage where it is those with close relations with sitting political elite, such as Nazarbayev, whether or not that country is an ally, that are indulged by their hosts. Second, there is the enabler effect where professional service provision is shown to make the difference regardless of whether the client is an incumbent, an ally, or neither. It is this enabler effect that has come through most strongly in the preceding chapters.

Enablers like Giffen and the many we have analysed here are crucial not just to these economic relations but also to the new global politics. These enablers take many different forms. Giffen worked upstream in a manner which was certainly wilful and apparently noncompliant. Many of those we have surveyed in this book work much further downstream; some are unwitting and compliant with the law, others not. Some enablers are service providers working on behalf of kleptocrats or associates of kleptocrats who are hiding their money (Chapter 5), making a company public (Chapter 6), investing for residency (Chapter 7), buying properties (Chapter 8), and explaining their wealth (Chapter 9). Others are not third parties but internal enablers: direct sellers of indulgences such as donations to universities and political parties (Chapters 10 and 11). Perhaps the most wilful, yet technically compliant, are those that work upstream to track enemies and silence critics (Chapters 12 and 13). Like Johann Tetzel, with whom we began this book, these enablers and their indulgences are harbingers of a political transformation.

In this chapter we draw our argument together by making three conclusions about the enabling of kleptocracy based on the cases presented in this book. We then go on to consider one major objection to our analysis concerning how we treat the state: Isn't this all a failure of the British political system? Finally, and vaguely imitating Luther, we hammer home five theses about professional indulgences and how they might stop.

Three Conclusions About the Enabling of Kleptocracy

How did the three hypotheses we laid out in Chapter 4 fare with respect to our nine indulgences? Is there evidence for the presence and significance of the enabler effect? Table 14.1 summarizes our findings. It compares the strength and weakness of the three mechanisms—the alliance effect, the incumbency advantage, and the enabler effect—against the extent of the indulgence offered. The medieval church offered 'plenary' (full) and partial indulgences to those who made payments to clerics, to the church, and to charities. A full indulgence remitted all sins while a partial one remitted just some of them.

Table 14.1 What explains professional indulgence?

Indulgence	Success	Alliance Effect	Incumbency Advantage	Enabler Effect
Hiding Money	**Full**	Weak	Weak	**Strong**
Listing Companies	Partial	Weak	**Strong**	**Strong**
Selling Rights	**Full**	Weak	Weak	**Strong**
Purchasing Properties	**Full**	Weak	Weak	**Strong**
Explaining Wealth	**Full**	Weak	**Strong**	**Strong**
Selling Status	**Full**	Weak	Weak	Weak
Making Friends	Partial	Weak	Weak	Weak
Tracking Enemies	Partial	**Strong**	Weak	**Strong**
Silencing Critics	Partial	Weak	Weak	**Strong**

We adopt this language to show variation between cases and indulgences. While none of them are absolute failures the different sectors vary in terms of the extent to which kleptocratic sources of wealth were indulged. A full indulgence is denoted where our case and any comparable examples known to us illustrate a pattern of success across the case where one or more of the mechanisms is apparent. A partial indulgence occurs when success is mixed even where a mechanism or two are there. We assess that in five cases a full indulgence occurred while in four the indulgence was partial. These findings allow us to draw three conclusions about the conditions of the kleptocracy problem in the UK. This we do by assessing whether the effect was strong or weak of each of the enabler effect, the incumbency advantage, and the alliance effect. A strong effect is denoted where the mechanism appears to be necessary for the indulgence; a weak effect is denoted where it appears to have little or no effect on the process and is therefore unnecessary.

First, the enabler effect is significant across all indulgences. We evaluate the enabler effect to be strong (necessary) where there is evidence of wilful and/or noncompliant enabling at a critical juncture in the case; it is weak (unnecessary) when enabling is largely unwitting and/or compliant or is not a significant presence in the indulgence. The enabler effect is strong and apparently necessary in seven of the nine indulgences. In three cases—hiding money, selling rights, and purchasing property—where enablers successfully offered services to all-comers regardless of alliances or incumbency, its effect is strong and it is the only necessary condition for full indulgence. In terms of 'hiding money', the work of APCO Worldwide and Kroll helped a Bakiyev-linked bank clean up its reputation, when it was in fact a money-laundering vehicle. In 'selling rights', Henley & Partners, based in Jersey, has run CBI schemes for Malta and St Kitts and Nevis, providing golden passports to a range of persons including exiles and loyalists of states which are pariahs in the West. In one other case where the indulgence was partial, the enabler effect was necessary to achieve mixed success. In 'silencing critics', the enabler effect was the only condition present to achieve a partial victory. Persons like Dmitry Leus and Roman Abramovich—a fence-sitter and a loyalist exile from Russia, respectively—would not have been able to have publications amended in their favour without legal enablers Vardags and Harbottle & Lewis. In short, almost all indulgences require the enabler effect.

Second, the incumbency advantage is present across some but not all indulgences; in most cases its effect is weak. We assess the incumbency advantage to be strong (necessary) if incumbency and/or loyalism to patrons at home—regardless of whether home is an ally or not of the UK—appears to make a difference at critical junctures of the indulgence; it is weak (unnecessary) where opponents and fence-sitters appear to be indulged just as much as incumbents. Listing companies and explaining wealth are the two indulgences where incumbency advantage is strong, but in these cases, it works in combination with the enabler effect. The London Stock Exchange has welcomed companies whose wealth has been built via their favoured status in kleptocracies. But Russian and Kazakh companies with oligarchic management would not have achieved their initial listing without enablers in financial services, even if some of these companies later returned to private ownership or were investigated by the authorities—a partial indulgence. Regarding explaining wealth, the contrast between the Hajiyeva and Nazarbayeva-Aliyev cases suggests that both incumbency and enabling work together: the court accepted dubious but well-presented evidence from kleptocracies on behalf of kleptocrats—a full indulgence. However, in most other sectors exiles are indulged too, and incumbency doesn't seem to be an advantage. The Bakiyev and Karimova cases in the indulgences of hiding money and buying properties provide good evidence of professionals supporting exiles and the UK government taking little action. The UK government was willing to sell residencies to all-comers including exiles. The

Conservative Party will take money from fence-sitting exiles. Corporate intelligence will work for both sides. Libel lawyers will silence critics for clients regardless of their political affiliation.

Third, the alliance effect is weak and least significant in the UK's kleptocracy problem. We evaluate the alliance effect to be strong (necessary) if incumbents and loyalists from allies appear to be favoured in an indulgence at key moments; it is weak (unnecessary) if comparison to cases of nonallies shows they too are favoured. We discovered no clear evidence of preferential treatment for allies across the cases of indulgences with one quite telling exception. We have covered countless examples of nonpartners—including Russians who are loyalists of the Kremlin—being serviced in other sectors especially selling rights, purchasing properties, and silencing critics. The one partial exception to this is in the indulgence of tracking enemies where we see some evidence that UK-based corporate intelligence typically favours key UK partners such as Kazakhstan and, beyond our scope, the Gulf monarchies. Furthermore, in Chapter 10 we speculated that universities might be more reluctant to accept money for centres whose funding may be linked to current geopolitical adversaries of the UK rather than those countries whose partnership is not in question—keeping in line with the need to protect their institution's reputation.

However, our confidence in making this conclusion is relatively low. And the public statements of figures like Wahid and Giffen suggest that it may be the United States' geopolitical preferences which matter here, not those of the UK. A book such as this one written on the United States would likely present much more evidence of the alliance effect. The UK, unlike the US, has taken few enforcement actions against the opponents of allied countries such as Maxim Bakiyev (asylum granted and no known investigative action taken), Gulnara Karimova (houses frozen, but five years after other countries had launched investigations and begun to recover her assets), and even Mukhtar Ablyazov (granted asylum until he fled the UK in 2012). The alliance effect only becomes visible in extreme circumstances and with crude measures such as the UK's sanctioning of Russian kleptocrats and oligarchs following the 2022 invasion of Ukraine—where it was often following EU and US designations. The alliance effect is a secondary factor not merely because it works in combination with the enabler effect but in that it probably would not work outside of the US' and the dollar's hegemony.

One Caveat About the State

We conclude that the enabler effect is the predominant reason why the UK has a kleptocracy problem. It is the supply side of transnational kleptocracy—the overseas enablers working downstream from the source of wealth—that is crucial in generating demand for services and explaining the rise of kleptocracy in the UK since the 1990s. The post-communist kleptocracies are the exemplary case of this phenomenon because of their histories but they are not the only ones—as examples outside of our scope from the Gulf, Africa, and Asia illustrate. However, there is one caveat we may place on this top-line conclusion. This arises from the two cases of indulgence which are not explained by any of our three mechanisms. In terms of selling status, top UK universities take donations regardless of whether they are either loyalists or opponents of either allies or adversaries. With respect to making friends, the governing Conservative Party includes all-comers in its inner circles of donors—although it claims that none of them are loyalists to an adversary such as Russia. In both cases, 'enablers' exist largely inside the recipient organizations rather than as a third party. The concierge service Quintessentially is a nonexception to this rule in that it is run by a person, Ben Elliot, who is also a Conservative Party insider. The absence of a professional enabler class in both cases appears to be linked to the fact that in both sectors there is only minimal regulation. While political donations over £500 must be disclosed to the electoral commission, there is no such requirement for gifts to universities. In both sectors, scandals occur but typically blow over with little or no accountability.

The proviso on our overall conclusion about the enabler effect is that it is a product of a shift in power from the public to private sector. As we showed in the Chapter 2, since the mid-twentieth century, British financial and legal services have grown exponentially while the UK state has been in a period of general decline despite the steady tax burden. The Royal Navy no longer rules the waves and British diplomats no longer shape global agendas in most areas of policy. But British bankers and lawyers, UK corporate intelligence, and PR firms are hugely influential globally. Universities, civil society, and cultural industries also lead the world. Insofar as Britain is 'great'—in the terms set by the state-funded national branding campaign that has been a mainstay of UK airports over the last decade—it is in terms of these services offered by nonstate actors. As Mohamed Amersi has repeatedly said in defending his actions, 'every deal undertaken had magic circle advisors and blue chip banks'.[6] In almost all cases of enabling in this book, we've seen both big and small firms involved. We should take this seriously. It is neither a matter of 'bad apples' nor of the regulator stepping in to end their business. They're too powerful for that.

Indulgences of secrecy, protection, legitimacy, and influence cannot just be uninvented or stopped. Powerful enablers innovate beyond the reach of the regulator. Institutions which are largely self-regulating like universities and political parties are happy to oblige their donors directly without an intermediary. This caveat is not a point about the British state's reduction in size or its absence. The size of the UK economy consumed by taxes increased dramatically over the twentieth century and remained largely in the 30%–35% range, despite multiple Conservative chancellors who have tried and failed to reduce the state spend. It is only slightly below the average of advanced industrialized countries.[7] The state is present at least by its absence in every indulgence we have explored. These cases reveal that it is the character of its relationship with society and economy that has changed. It no longer appears to effectively regulate the market. Therefore, it is the rationale of the market—competition for private goods—which triumphs over collective national action and the public good.

This truth is seen most clearly in the episodes in this book where private sector indulgers and state regulators are in conflict. ENRC spent many times the Serious Fraud Office annual budget and threatened to sue the SFO to make sure, after 10 years, they closed their investigation. The UK Tier 1 Investor scheme was essentially outsourced to the private sector who processed the paperwork for thousands of new ultra-wealthy residents from kleptocracies, including at least 10 who were subsequently sanctioned. English lawyers were able to defeat one of the first investigations of the government's flagship unexplained wealth order legislation. Professionals across the real estate sector ensure that the UK's anti-money-laundering system simply doesn't apply to almost all of those with kleptocratic sources of wealth. In cases like university donations where the state is almost entirely absent, when a proposal is made in parliament for disclosure—merely a basic transparency requirement which the United States has had since the 1980s—it is effectively resisted by professional bodies and becomes a fig leaf 'duty to consider' (see Chapter 10). State weakness is most evident in the face of the private sector's success.

British state incapacity is also evident in the contrast with the United States. The UK's National Crime Agency is a pale shadow of the FBI, which apparently served as an inspiration for its creation. The UK's Anti-Bribery Act has few successes relative to the settlements enforced under the US Foreign Corrupt Practices Act and the convictions of individuals under the Racketeer Influenced and Corrupt Organizations (RICO) Act. The NCA has seen embarrassing defeats such as that of the UWO against Nazarbayeva and her son which we covered in Chapter 9. The SFO again dumped a bunch of cases, not just the ENRC investigation, not long before this book went to press.[8] Building up the capacity of these agencies is partly about finances. The UK often loses poorly paid and little-valued civil servants to the private sector early in their career. In the US, regulators have an incentive to stay longer to win big cases before cashing in on their fame. Similarly, the UK followed the US in introducing anti-corruption sanctions but with a fraction of the capacity to introduce and defend them against legal challenges; when it suddenly decided to introduce sanctions on Russian oligarchs and state-linked individuals in March 2022 it was forced to triple the size of its Office for Sanctions Implementation within a year of the invasion.[9]

It appears from this analysis that the state—or the 'British political system'—allows this to happen. As states are sovereign, in principle they can step in to stop these indulgences. If the UK funded the SFO and NCA better, closed the Tier 1 visa scheme much earlier than they did, and had used the overall civil recovery powers of the Proceeds of Crime Act (2002) more effectively, the state may have drastically curtailed the markets of enablers by now. This is an intuitive suggestion which is instinctively persuasive for those who think of global politics largely in terms of governments. But it misses two important points. The first is that private actors hold most of the expertise and the capital to the point that the public sector is always playing catch-up. The second is that service providers and regulators are deeply intertwined and cannot simply be separated from one another for the purpose of finding a solution.

This more complex story of regulators and enablers intertwined is a crucial part of the underlying story about professional indulgences. It is more a story of a change in the character of the British state in the late twentieth century to serve the needs of transnational capital and industry than the long-term decline in state capacity since the late nineteenth century which is sometimes portrayed.[10] It is reflected in common worries such as the 'revolving door' and the 'conflict of interest'. It is seen vividly in the ability of the private sector to shape legal reform processes—such as that of the Defamation Act of 2013, the Economic Crime Act of 2022, or the Higher Education Act of

2023—so they continue to provide business opportunities to make money from indulgences. Those that wish to solve this problem with the simple exercise of command-and-control state power over the enablers will find themselves disappointed. It will take many years to build back state capacity and it is unlikely to ever look anything like that of the postwar social democratic governments. The solution must instead be found in the problem. It must expose and redirect the power of the enablers.

Five Theses Against British Professional Indulgences

What would it take for professional indulgences to cease and what difference would it make? What kind of reform of the British professional services is required to close down Londongrad? And is it worth it or will the kleptocrats just be indulged elsewhere? It took 50 years from when Martin Luther launched his public campaign against indulgences for Pope Pius V to abolish their sale in 1567. The professional indulgences we have discussed in this book have only just been identified and cannot simply be banned. But it seems that their value may decline due to the continuing global transformation just as the indulgences offered by the church and the political model which sustained them were fatally undermined by the Reformation. Just as the struggle between sixteenth-century reformers and conservatives brought down indulgences, it is possible that the struggle between activists and professionals will transform the UK's kleptocracy problem. Contrary to the logic of beggar-thy-neighbour fatalism, the demise of Londongrad would set global kleptocracy back several steps. London's offer to corrupt elites is hard to replace; the offer made by Asian financial centres such as Dubai and Hong Kong is different, and hitherto less attractive for indulgence seekers. There are political obstacles and, more importantly, professional resistance to some of the more radical measures, but the political reckoning which followed the invasion of Ukraine showed that there is some space for radical reform.

Any ideas we have for how the UK might come to indulge no more are not unique but have been discussed with colleagues in the UK Anti-Corruption Coalition and beyond in civil society and parliament. Some of these proposals were placed before parliament at the time of writing in the form of amendments to the Economic Crime and Corporate Transparency Bill (ECB),[11] including as mentioned above a measure to tackle SLAPPs that feature economic crimes. However, although some progress has been made (the bill had just received Royal Assent as of time of writing) it looks as if this is an opportunity lost. But just as the state surrendered its power to the private sector over decades, it may take a long time for more effective enforcement, accountability, and transparency to be re-established within the private sector. Our five theses below need constant work for us to be rid of the problem of indulgences.

A first thesis is this: kleptocracy is serious and organized crime (SOC). Several experts (ourselves included)[12] have argued the importance of defining kleptocracy clearly in law to allow UWOs and other already existing measures a chance of success against wealth originating in kleptocratic environments. For example, Maria Nizzero draws a parallel with Italy. Italian anti-mafia laws have long broken new ground in this area in establishing that proven membership of a SOC group reduces the burden of proof required to prosecute a similar offence. Their anti-racketeering laws also allow a group to be prosecuted and impose accountabilities on all its members for their membership. Without such measures, and their recognition of the societal harm caused by serious organized crime, it is unlikely that rule of law would have been expanded in Italy. The UK may not appear to be in equivalent peril, but the relative weakness of regulators is alarming. 'A similar model in the UK', Nizzero argues, 'would assume that individuals linked with listed kleptocratic regimes benefited from this association, thus presuming that some of their assets were the proceeds of crime'.[13] Proving the relationship between an oligarch and a kleptocratic government is much easier than proving that the specific wealth used in the UK has kleptocratic origins. The Swiss prosecutor took this approach in their indictment of Gulnara Karimova which charges that she 'led a criminal organisation known as "The Office"'.[14] This is not a guilty-until-proven-innocent principle, but the finding of guilt according to evidence of actual participation in a criminal enterprise.

Second, corporate officers of professional services firms which enable kleptocracy must be held criminally liable. Specifically, the partners and responsible managers in firms that fail to prevent fraud, false accounting, and money laundering with corruptly acquired wealth may be considered criminally liable, as proposed in an amendment to the ECB in March 2023.[15] It is often hard to tell whether those that list companies, hide money, and buy properties for kleptocrats and oligarchs do so wilfully or unwittingly. But sins of omission are still sins. And negligence may still be a matter of criminal responsibility. Corporate officers whose staff don't do the proper checks—whether wilfully or unwittingly—should be legally noncompliant with economic crime legislation. At present, this is only the case for bribery and tax evasion. It should be extended to fraud and money laundering, as proposed by expert parliamentary groups.[16] Unfortunately, the Economic Crime Act of 2023 was a missed opportunity, as it only applied corporate officer criminal liability to large companies and only in the case of fraud. But, as we have seen, wilfully unwitting facilitators of money laundering are often small and medium enterprises as well as large companies.

Third, investigators and whistleblowers must be protected. In this book, we have detailed our personal experiences of being the subject of aggressive pre-action letters. However, two other categories of person are far more likely to be silenced by SLAPPS. The first group is investigative journalists who break some of the top corruption stories. ICIJ and OCCRP are regularly and simultaneously fighting dozens of legal actions; in the UK, The Bureau of Investigative Journalists (TBIJ), OpenDemocracy, and other investigative outlets are in a similar position. The second and most vulnerable group of all are whistleblowers, who lack the protections of both academics and journalists. For example, when the British whistleblower and UN Human Rights Council staff member Emma Reilly spoke out about corruption, the UN sent Swiss police to have her committed to a mental hospital; she received little support from the British government.[17] Many more cases abound of whistleblowers imprisoned for breaking data protection or nondisclosure rules. Another amendment to the ECB proposes the establishment of an office for whistleblower protection in the UK.[18] The UK government could go further and honour whistleblowers with awards. At present it appears to bestow knighthoods and peerages on political donors and those that have run companies which have been involved in kleptocratic states while leaving whistleblowers to face the costs of speaking out.

Fourth, transparency measures must be enforced and expanded into other service sectors. In recent years, company and property ownership transparency has finally been introduced in the UK with the persons of significant control (PSC) register (2016) and the register of overseas entities, which came into force in 2023 and records the owners of property-owning offshore companies. On the face of it, this makes the UK one of the most transparent countries in the world with respect to companies and real estate. However, without the reform and increased capacity of Companies House to check its data, the full level of transparency will not be achieved. Moreover, lots of secrecy remains in the system. Trusts remain nontransparent and are likely to be used more frequently. As donations to think tanks and charities remain undisclosed, donors to some of the UK's leading advocacy groups remain hidden. In the higher education sector, there remains no public reporting of donations to universities: when the authors worked with MPs to propose a duty to disclose for foreign donations over £100,000, the government, after lobbying from the industry body Universities UK, watered it down to be a duty to consider.

Fifth, incentivize the private sector and civil society to work together against kleptocracy.[19] Our first four theses have been focused on changing the relationship between regulators and enablers to tip the balance back towards the former. But for real change to occur the market incentives, not just constraints, must change. Almost all the expertise on financial and legal services is found among the professionals and in their firms. Executive fiats and bureaucratic measures often misfire or have inadvertent consequences. In the private sector, the recovery of assets which are found to be the proceeds of crime is an increasingly lucrative business albeit one hitherto dominated by low-hanging fruit. It is civil society which has tended to push for the more difficult cases. In France and Spain, assets have been recovered from Teodorin Obiang (vice president of Equatorial Guinea) and Rifat al-Assad (uncle of Bashir al-Assad of Syria). These NGO-led court cases have recovered far more assets than recent British government efforts even though many more looted assets appear to be stored in the UK. Britain also hosts NGOs with exceptional investigative capacity such as Transparency International, Global Witness, The Sentry, RAID, and Spotlight on Corruption. These organizations have shown far more determination to undertake investigations than the government itself and it is their investigations that often stimulate state actions. London is also a world-leading centre for the private sector legal and accounting expertise necessary to run successful asset recovery cases. These professionals can either continue to indulge the kleptocrats, or they can switch sides.

To stimulate the market for asset recovery from kleptocrats and oligarchs in the UK, two things need to happen. First, British law should give NGOs, as third parties, specific legal standing to bring civil recovery cases even when there is no criminal conviction in the country of the origin of the wealth. As civil cases, they must simply convince a judge that on the balance of probabilities that the sources of wealth are criminal. The second change is already beginning to occur in the private sector. Private investors now fund asset recovery cases in return for a share of the winnings at the conclusion of a successful case; insurance is also beginning to be offered to offset the risk. The size of the cut that these investors take is often large and like that taken by no-win-no-fee personal injury lawyers. Some politicians and campaigners are squeamish about the optics of allowing some of the same companies that made money out of kleptocracy from making more from countering it. Hypothetically, this is money that might be repatriated to the poor countries from which it was stolen. But the reality is that successful asset repatriation is rare and almost nonexistent from the UK. The immediate need is to stimulate the market to vastly increase the amount of kleptocratic assets being recovered. More important than the possibility of repatriation is the likely deterrent effect. The lack of accountability which has been visible throughout this book must be ended for transnational kleptocracy to be weakened.

In its 2023 'refresh' of its main foreign policy document, the British government recognized that kleptocracy is a threat to British society. It declared that an upcoming anti-corruption strategy will 'close down London as a centre for corrupt elites to launder money and enhance their reputations'.[20] We are familiar with such pronouncements from ministers unwilling to recognize that they have presided over the relative decline of their own power vis-a-vis kleptocrats and their enablers. But is there something different this time? Will the flow of indulgences finally be stopped? A shift in the normative environment against kleptocracy does seem to be occurring. As this book went to press, a weakened governing party, exposed for receiving a great deal of suspicious wealth in donation, had just been voted out of power. But to indulge no more may be too big an ask. Just to indulge a little less would be a victory.

As we have seen, in such a victory, the state is unlikely to be the primary actor. Government and the bureaucracy are secondary players in a broader global political economy which ensures capital is concentrated in the hands of the few. Without whistleblowers and dissenters, government would never have been moved to take the modest measures it is now taking. Otherwise, British professionals—as Margaret Hodge MP wrote in a report which was taken down by King's College London after a threat from Carter-Ruck on behalf of Mohamed Amersi[21]—appear to be losing their moral compass. They do so when they no longer serve the public interest but think first of the private elite networks of which they are part. These networks cannot be reformed from the outside. Much like in the sixteenth century, a rebellion from within is required. The consequence of any such revolt is uncertain but it will not succeed without powerful allies on the inside of the professions who accept there is a problem and seek change. We have seen many financial and legal professionals whose conscience or circumstances have led them to rebel against Londongrad, especially since the invasion of Ukraine. It is time for those that have indulged kleptocracy to turn against it.

Key to Figures

📋	Contracts with	👫	Familial relationship	▦	Blocking effect
🔀	Controls	🏛	Parliament/government	🏢	Apartment
🔍	Investigates	🎓	Academia	🏠	House
👁	Witness for	⚖	Legal services	🏰	Very large property
🤝	Acts for	🪪	Same address as	📄	Company
✕	(Acts) against	💼	Employment relationship		

Notes

Foreword By Oliver Bullough

1. Christopher Mele, 'Self-Service Checkouts Can Turn Customers Into Shoplifters, Study Says', *New York Times*, 10 August 2016, https://www.nytimes.com/2016/08/11/business/self-service-checkouts-can-turn-customers-into-shoplifters-study-says.html.

Preface

1. Robert N. Swanson, 'Praying for Pardon: Devotional Indulgences in Late Medieval England', in *Promissory Notes on the Treasury of Merits*, ed. Robert N. Swanson (Leiden: Brill, 2006), 215.
2. Robert B. Ekelund Jr, Robert F. Hébert, and Robert D. Tollison, 'An Economic Analysis of the Protestant Reformation', *Journal of Political Economy* 110, no. 3 (2002): 646–671.
3. Mark Greengrass, *Christendom Destroyed: Europe 1517–1648* (New York: Penguin, 2014).
4. Martin Luther, 'Martin Luther's 95 Theses', Luther.de, 2019: 28, https://www.luther.de/en/95thesen.html.
5. Luther, 'The 95 Theses', Thesis 21.
6. Luther, 'The 95 Theses', Thesis 24.
7. Luther, 'The 95 Theses', Thesis 37.
8. Luther, 'The 95 Theses', Thesis 95.
9. Ekelund et al., 'An Economic Analysis'.
10. Swanson, 'Praying for Pardon', 1.
11. Kristin Surak, *The Golden Passport: Global Mobility for Millionaires* (Cambridge, MA: Harvard University Press, 2023), 266.

Chapter 1

1. Interview by SVT's 'Uppdrag Granskning' ('Mission: Investigation') in Daisy Sindelar and Farruh Yusupov, 'New Documents Suggest Fresh Evidence of TeliaSonera Ties to Karimova', Radio Liberty, 22 May 2013, https://www.rferl.org/a/sweden-teliasonera-uzbekistan-karimova/24993135.html.
2. CWEIC, 'CWEIC: About', https://www.cweic.org/our-board/mohamed-amersi/ (accessed 15 January 2023).
3. The only countries ranked below Uzbekistan in Transparency International's Corruption Perceptions Index in 2007 were Haiti, Iraq, Somalia, and Myanmar (see https://www.transparency.org/en/cpi/2007, accessed 10 May 2024). Iraq and Somalia were unstable at the time, both subject to American military interventions. Myanmar faced a series of economic and political protests in 2007, and its telecoms sector was underdeveloped and lacked European investment. Haiti in 2007 had several telecoms providers, some domestic and others from elsewhere in the Caribbean, but attracted little European investment. TI's index analyzes perceived levels of public sector corruption, which is relevant to telecoms deals, which needed approval from the Uzbek state for the granting of licences, frequencies, and so on.
4. Gulnoza Saidazimova, 'Uzbekistan: President's Daughter Takes Another Step Toward "Throne"', Radio Liberty, 5 February 2008, https://www.rferl.org/a/1079436.html. For example, the English-language *Moscow Times* reported in 2004 that a Russian telecoms company paid almost $160 million for Uzdonrobita, a company co-owned by Karimova, 33 times what the company valued itself two years prior. In the same article, Karimova's former financial adviser accused her of forcing one of Uzdonrobita's former owners to give her 20% of the company for free, and alleged that she had enriched herself through the company via fraudulent invoices. See Simon Ostrovsky, 'MTS Pays Premium to Uzbek "Princess"', *Moscow Times*, 19 July 2004, https://www.themoscowtimes.com/archive/mts-pays-premium-to-uzbek-princess.

5. United States District Court, Southern District of New York, 'United States of America V Gulnara Karimova, Bekhzod Akhmedov, Indictment', https://www.justice.gov/opa/press-rele ase/file/1141641/download (accessed 10 May 2024), para 45.
6. Telia's statement of fact agreed with Dutch authorities. The senior manager is unnamed but is denoted 'X1'.
7. USA V Karimova, Akhmedov, para 48.
8. Joanna Lillis, 'Uzbekistan: Swedish Telekom Graft Probe Makes Twist Toward Karimova', Eurasianet, 9 January 2013, https://eurasianet.org/uzbekistan-swedish-telekom-graft-probe-makes-twist-toward-karimova. Telia itself admitted Elden's knowledge of Karimova's involvement in a press release from 2013, but obfuscated about the knowledge that executives who came after Elden had, which has since been proven by the US investigation and other documentation. See 'Comment From TeliaSonera Related to Information in the Media', Telia Company, 8 January 2013, https://news.cision.com/telia-company/r/comment-from-teliasonera-related-to-information-in-the-media,c9354764.
9. Andreas Cervenka, 'Diktator gör miljardklipp på Telia', SvD Näringsliv, 11 February 2008, https://www.svd.se/a/842f02f3-0ea5-3df2-a66c-359a8b81e677/diktator-gor-miljardkl ipp-pa-telia.
10. Tom Burgis, 'The Donor, the Russian Deals and the Conservative Money Machine', Financial Times, 7 July 2021, https://www.ft.com/content/5dab0a3e-687a-446f-8e55-58c999d4321f.
11. UK Parliament, 'Lawfare and UK Court System: col 569', UK Parliament, 2022, https://hansard. parliament.uk/commons/2022-01-20/debates/4F7649B7-2085-4B51-9E8C-32992CFF7726/ LawfareAndUKCourtSystem. In response to the authors, Amersi commented: 'Detailed UBO KYC and due diligence was conducted by an army of lawyers on ownership questions and source of funds. At that point in time, despite wide but unsubstantiated media reporting, no evidence was found of any wrongdoing, given this the transaction went ahead. At no time did [my company] have any responsibility for doing KYC or UBO checks'.
12. Part of the 2007 agreement stated that Takilant Ltd had the option of buying back its shares in Ucell, which it was enacting in late 2009, with Amersi now enlisted to advise. Up until late 2009, Amersi had not been involved with the Uzbek deal, and he was not copied in on any of the messages mentioned.
13. Harry Davies, 'Major Tory Donor Advised on Uzbekistan Deal Later Found to Be $220m Bribe', Guardian, 4 October 2021, https://www.theguardian.com/news/2021/oct/04/major-tory-donor-advised-on-uzbekistan-deal-later-found-to-be-bribe-mohamed-amersi.
14. The Dictionary of Corruption states that 'agents and intermediaries often play legitimate roles in normal business transactions; the terms may encompass sales agents, business consultants, introducers, facilitators, distributors, shipping agents, lawyers and other professional advisors and other third parties providing business services'. Tom Shipley, 'Agents and Intermediaries', in Dictionary of Corruption, ed. Robert Barrington, Elizabeth David-Barrett, and Rebecca Dobson Phillips (Newcastle upon Tyne: Agenda, 2024), 11. For the avoidance of doubt, we are not claiming that Amersi paid a bribe or even that there are serious grounds to believe that he paid a bribe or committed any other corrupt act. We are saying that he was an intermediary—an important and well-paid advisor—with respect to a payment that was ultimately determined to be a bribe. There are therefore probable grounds for investigating whether he was a witting party to that bribe.
15. The original deal was £30 million for 26%, whereas TeliaSonera sold 20% for $220 million.
16. USA V Karimova, Akhmedov.
17. Jamey Keaton, 'Swiss Indict Daughter of Former Uzbek President in Bribery, Money Laundering Case Involving Millions', AP News, 29 September 2023, https://apnews.com/article/karimov-daughter-uzbekistan-switzerland-money-laundering-13bab394922b35fa9fa937161b5db843. The man is described as the 'former general director of the Uzbek subsidiary of a Russian telecommunications company' in the original press release issued by the Swiss authorities. Le Conseil federal: Communiqués, 'Ouzbékistan: Gulnara Karimova et l'ex-directeur d'une société de télécommunication déférés devant le Tribunal pénal fédéral', 28 September 2023, https:// www.admin.ch/gov/fr/accueil/documentation/communiques.msg-id-97944.html. Akhmedov was the general director of Uzdonrobita from 2002 to 2012. Uzdonribita was headquartered in Uzbekistan, but, from 2004, was an indirect subsidiary of Russian company MTS. See USA V Gulnara Karimova, 2–3. The authors spoke to a noted expert on the case who said that the unnamed man could only be Akhmedov, based on this material.
18. Davies, 'Major Tory Donor'.

19. Amersi claimed in an email to one of the authors that a 'proper fee' for this work should have been in excess of $3 million, citing research from Thomson Reuters. Mohamed Amersi, Letter to John Heathershaw, 18 August 2023.

20. Davies, 'Major Tory Donor'.

21. 'TeliaSonera Says Some Eurasia Deals May Have Broken Law', Reuters, 2 April 2014, https://www.reuters.com/article/teliasonera-eurasia-idUKL5N0MU3SN20140402. Excerpts of the Norton Rose report seen by *The Guardian* state the findings 'should be subject to further testing' (See Davies, 'Major Tory Donor').

22. Davies, 'Major Tory Donor'.

23. Amersi backed up this statement by saying that Uzbekistan received a sovereign risk rating of BB from Global Insight. Amersi, Letter to John Heathershaw.

24. Amersi further stated that he voluntarily gave evidence to law enforcement agencies in Switzerland, Sweden, and the US, and that no wrongdoing on his part was found. He added that the Swiss authorities did a forensic review of all of his financial statements and those of his company and found no wrongdoing. He claimed that the $220 million payment for Ucell's shares represented 'fair market value' and that Takilant Ltd was 'a well-established partner of Telia by the time I came to be involved'. Amersi added that TeliaSonera's lawyers K&L Gates and Houtoff Buruma performed KYC and UBO checks on Takilant Ltd and that this was carefully reviewed by a Swedish law firm, Mannheimer Swartling. Amersi, Letter to John Heathershaw.

25. For example, when interviewed by the Russian authorities in 2012, having fled Uzbekistan, Akhmedov said: 'Later Serkan Elden quit Fintur [a company operating in Kazakhstan part-owned by TeliaSonera] and starting in July 2007, Tero Kivisaari—the president of TeliaSonera Eurasia—Esco Rytkonen—vice president of TeliaSonera—and Tolga Imishmen, who agreed to the presentation of Karimova's conditions, led continuing talks with me'. *Protokol doprosa svidetlya* / Record of interrogation of the Witness [Akhmedov interview with Russian authorities], 10 September 2012.

26. Davies, 'Major Tory Donor'.

27. Bhavin Kothari, 'The Opening of the Amersi Foundation Lecture Room, Brasenose College, Oxford University', The Amersi Foundation, 15 December 2019, https://amersifoundation.org/the-opening-of-the-amersi-foundation-lecture-room-brasenose-college-oxford-university/.

28. One Young World, 'Making Sense of Corruption | Mohamed Amersi', www.youtube.com, 2018, https://www.youtube.com/watch?v=UzGfdHFy24A.

29. Burgis, 'The Donor, The Russian Deals'.

30. Times Radio, 'Reform the Party or I'll Stop Donations, Says Major Tory Donor | Mohamed Amersi', www.youtube.com, 2022, https://www.youtube.com/watch?v=bqnR3EqkLzA.

31. Davies, 'Major Tory Donors'.

32. Davies, 'Major Tory Donors'. In an all-caps reply to an opportunity to comment letter, Amersi stated: 'SOMEONE WHO IS GENUINELY TRYING TO DEFEND HIS REPUTATION IS NOT A SLAPPER, BUT INSTEAD IS SOMEONE WHO IS SEEKING VINDICATION ON ACCOUNT OF A MALICIOUS, BIASED, MISINFORMED AND ILL-CONCEIVED CAMPAIGN AGAINST HIM'. Amersi, Letter to John Heathershaw.

33. Nick Cohen, 'No One Is Safe From the Rich Elite's Abuse of British Law. Just Ask Charlotte Leslie', *The Observer*, January 22, 2022, https://www.theguardian.com/commentisfree/2022/jan/22/no-one-is-safe-from-rich-elite-abuse-british-law-ask-charlotte-leslie.

34. Amersi denies that he was aware of what his friend was saying or that this individual was operating on his instructions. Cohen, 'No One Is Safe'.

35. The Honorable Mr Justice Nicklin, Approved Judgment, Mohamed Amersi Claimant- and (1) Charlotte Leslie, (2) CMEC UK & MENA Limited, Royal Courts of Justice, Case No: QB-2021-004630, para 240.

36. Hansard, Lawfare, Volume 735: debated on Thursday 29 June 2023, col 528, https://hansard.parliament.uk/commons/2023-06-29/debates/AB9B8F81-7AE0-446A-81E8-6F50DFE7BCC2/Lawfare.

37. Amersi, Letter to John Heathershaw.

38. Amersi, Letter to John Heathershaw.

39. In rebutting those that accuse him of enabling kleptocracy, Amersi also pointed to the legal analysis of Joshua Ray, legal counsel for Bekhzod Akhmedov. This article argues that the $220 million share buyback agreement was not a bribe because it was at a market rate, and that even if Karimova was behind Takilant Ltd, it was not relevant as she was not a foreign official in charge of telecoms at the time the payment was made. Ray's article pushes back at anti-corruption more

broadly and the settlements which the accused are forced to make under pressure from the US government. He compares the US government's 'near-perfect record' in its corruption cases to North Korean elections and argues its settlement agreements 'are unsupported' by the evidence (550). But as counsel for the defence, Ray is hardly an impartial source. His article demonstrates little knowledge (or perhaps disregard) of political economy in Uzbekistan and its kleptocratic form. Moreover, he fails to spend any time considering the alternative explanation for why most FCPA cases are settled: they are so complex and their defendants so well-resourced that the government only picks cases that it knows it can win. Joshua L. Ray, 'The Continuing Façade of FCPA Enforcement: A Critical Look at the Telia DPA', *New York University Journal of Law & Business* 17 (2020): 547.

40. Mohamed Amersi, Letter to John Heathershaw, emphasis added.
41. In the analysis of Joshua Ray, Bekzod Akhmedov's lawyer, they aren't bribes anyway, and the individual can probably avoid a guilty verdict if they stand up to the US government. See note 51.
42. FPRI, 'FPRI Welcomes Mohamed Amersi to its Board of Trustees', 29 June 2023, https://mailchi. mp/fpri/bt-news-23-06-24?e=c264ffbd99.
43. Conservative Foreign and Commonwealth Council, 'Key People', 10 May 2024, https://www.cfc conline.org.uk/key-people.
44. Tom Burgis, *Cuckooland: Where the Rich Own the Truth* (London: William Collins, 2024).
45. It is a separate question as to whether there is evidence of misconduct which may make him legally liable for his enabling.
46. Chatham House, 'Foreign Secretary Liz Truss', event transcript, 8 December 2021, https://chath amhouse.soutron.net/Portal/DownloadImageFile.ashx?fieldValueId=6400, 16.
47. Rupert Neate and Rupert Neate Wealth correspondent, 'UK Failure to Tackle "Dirty Money" Led to It Laundering Russia's War Funds', *The Guardian*, 30 June 2022, https://www.theguard ian.com/business/2022/jun/30/uk-failure-to-tackle-dirty-money-led-to-it-laundering-russ ias-war-funds.
48. National Crime Agency, 'National Economic Crime Centre Leads Push to Identify Money Laundering Activity', 17 May 2019, https://www.nationalcrimeagency.gov.uk/news/national-economic-crime-centre-leads-push-to-identify-money-laundering-activity.
49. Oliver Bullough, *Moneyland: Why Thieves and Crooks Now Rule the World and How to Take It Back* (London: Profile Books, 2018).
50. Tom Burgis, *Kleptopia: How Dirty Money Is Conquering the World* (Glasgow: William Collins, 2020).
51. Sarah S. Chayes, *Thieves of State: Why Corruption Threatens Global Security* (New York: Norton, 2015).
52. Nate Sibley and Ben Judah, *Countering Global Kleptocracy: A New US Strategy for Fighting Authoritarian Corruption*, Kleptocracy Initiative (Washington, DC: Hudson Institute, 2021); Transparency International, 'Who Is Opening the Gates for Kleptocrats?', https://www.trans parency.org/en/news/who-is-opening-the-gates-for-kleptocrats (accessed 4 August 2021); Global Witness, 'The Cycle of Kleptocracy: A Congolese State Affair Part III', https://www. globalwitness.org/en/campaigns/oil-gas-and-mining/congolese-kleptocracy/ (accessed 4 August 2021).
53. HM Government, *Integrated Review Refresh: Responding to a More Contested and Volatile World Presented to Parliament by the Prime Minister by Command of His Majesty* https://www.gov.uk/ government/publications/integrated-review-refresh-2023-responding-to-a-more-contested-and-volatile-world/integrated-review-refresh-2023-responding-to-a-more-contested-and-volat ile-world (March 2023), 49.
54. Financial Conduct Authority (FCA), *Finalised Guidance: FG 17/6 The Treatment of Politically Exposed Persons for Anti-Money Laundering Purposes*, https://www.fca.org.uk/publication/ finalised-guidance/fg17-06.pdf (accessed 19 October 2021), 10.
55. Transparency International, 'What Is Grand Corruption and How Can We Stop It?', https:// www.transparency.org/en/news/what-is-grand-corruption-and-how-can-we-stop-it (accessed 4 August 2021).
56. Chris Walker and Melissa Aten, 'The Rise of Kleptocracy: A Challenge for Democracy', *Journal of Democracy* 29 (2018): 20–24.
57. Catherine Owen, Tena Prelec, and Tom Mayne, *The Illicit Financialisation of Russian Foreign Policy Mapping the Practices That Facilitate Russia's Illicit Financial Flows*, University of Birmingham, SOC-ACE, May 2022, https://www.birmingham.ac.uk/documents/college-soc ial-sciences/government-society/publications/illicit-financialisation-of-russian-foreign-pol

icy-report.pdf; David Lewis and Tena Prelec, *New Dynamics in Illicit Finance and Russian Foreign Policy*, University of Birmingham, SOC-ACE, August 2023, https://static1.squarespace.com/static/63e4aef3ae07ad445eed03b5/t/64d9c7660051ed7fd7e34902/1691993959995/SOCACE-RP17-NewDynamics-Aug23.pdf.

58. Tuesday Reitano, *Political Won't? Understanding the Challenges of Countering IFFs*, University of Birmingham, SOC-ACE, June 2022, https://www.birmingham.ac.uk/documents/college-social-sciences/government-society/publications/political-wont-paper.pdf.

59. Jody LaPorte, 'Foreign Versus Domestic Bribery: Explaining Repression in Kleptocratic Regimes', *Comparative Politics* 50, no. 1 (2017): 87.

60. Walker and Aten, 'The Rise of Kleptocracy'; Stephen E. Hanson and Jeffrey S. Kopstein, 'Understanding the Global Patrimonial Wave', *Perspectives on Politics* 20, no. 1 (2022): 237–249.

61. V-Dem Institute, 'Autocratization Changing Nature?', 6, 2022, https://v-dem.net/media/publications/dr_2022.pdf.

62. For example, Nigeria, Mexico, Brazil, South Africa during the presidency of Jacob Zuma, or some Balkan countries characterized by high levels of state capture, such as Serbia, Montenegro, or Bosnia-Herzegovina.

63. Karen Dawisha, *Putin's Kleptocracy: Who Owns Russia?* (New York: Simon & Schuster, 2015); Catherine Belton, *Putin's People: How the KGB Took Back Russia and Then Took on the West* (London: HarperCollins, 2020).

64. Freedom House, 'From Democratic Decline to Authoritarian Aggression: 5/5', 2022, https://freedomhouse.org/sites/default/files/2022-04/NIT_2022_final_digital.pdf.

65. Matthew Page and Jody Vittori, 'Kleptocratic Adaptation: Anticipating the Next Stage in the Battle Against Transnational Kleptocracy', National Endowment for Democracy, January 2023, https://www.ned.org/wp-content/uploads/2023/01/NED_FORUM-Kleptocratic-Adaptation.pdf.

66. Daron Acemoglu, Thierry Verdier, and James A. Robinson, 'Kleptocracy and Divide-and-Rule: A Model of Personal Rule', *Journal of the European Economic Association* 2, no. 2–3 (2004): 163.

67. LaPorte, 'Foreign Versus Domestic Corruption'.

68. John Heathershaw, M. Anne Pitcher, and Ricardo Soares de Oliveira, 'Transnational Kleptocracy and the International Political Economy of Authoritarianism', *Journal of International Relations and Development* 26, no. 2 (2023): 215–223.

69. We specifically exclude intellectual and cultural elites from our analysis.

70. A minigarch is an individual from a former Soviet country who has been successful in business but on a significantly smaller scale than an oligarch. Their net worth is likely to run to the tens of millions of dollars, rather than hundreds of millions, or billions. Unlike the vast majority of oligarchs, minigarchs can exist, and even thrive, without close links to the ruling elite by simply playing the rules of the game set by the ruling elite.

71. Mark Galeotti, 'Boris Johnson's Russian Oligarch Problem', *Foreign Policy*, 24 July 2019, https://foreignpolicy.com/2019/07/24/boris-johnsons-russian-oligarch-problem/.

72. The judgements and terms of anti-money-laundering law practitioners differ slightly. By definition, kleptocrats form part of a group deemed 'politically exposed persons' (people who hold senior positions in any government, parliament, or state company), who, along with their close relatives, are subject in certain sectors in the UK and EU to enhanced checks regarding their sources of wealth. Oligarchs and exiles would be deemed 'high-risk individuals' as their sources of wealth emanates from high-risk countries and will also be subject to additional checks.

73. When we say 'kleptocratic origins' we refer to wealth built from high-level networks and businesses in kleptocratic countries, rather than simply state theft.

74. Jennifer Bussell, 'When Do Middlemen Matter? Evidence From Variation in Corruption in India', *Governance* 31, no. 3 (2018): 465–480. For definition of 'illicit' see discussion on page 10 of this volume.

75. HM Government, Economic Crime Plan, 2023–2026, https://assets.publishing.service.gov.uk/media/642561b02fa8480013ec0f97/6.8300_HO_Economic_Crime_Plan_2_v6_Web.pdf, 42. Emphasis added.

76. Kimberly Kay Hoang, *Spiderweb Capitalism: How Global Elites Exploit Frontier Markets* (Princeton, NJ: Princeton University Press, 2022), xiii–xiv.

77. Hoang, *Spiderweb Capitalism*, 2. Emphasis added.

78. The UK's 2020 National Risk Assessment says: 'Professional services remain attractive to criminals as a means to create and operate corporate structures, invest and transfer funds to disguise their origin, and lend layers of legitimacy to their operations. . . . While there have been

improvements in the supervision of accountancy and legal service providers, in part due to the work of OPBAS, these services remain prevalent in law enforcement cases' and 'The property sector faces a high risk from money laundering, due to the large amounts that can be moved through or invested in the sector, and the low levels of transparency'. HM Treasury/Home Office, *National Risk Assessment of Money Laundering and Terrorist Financing 2020* (London: HM Treasury), https://assets.publishing.service.gov.uk/government/uploads/system/uploads/atta chment_data/file/945411/NRA_2020_v1.2_FOR_PUBLICATION.pdf, 5, 107.

79. Janine Wedel, *Unaccountable: How the Establishment Corrupted Our Finances, Freedom and Politics and Created an Outsider Class* (New York: Simon & Schuster, 2014); Casey Michel, *American Kleptocracy: How the US Created the World's Greatest Money Laundering Scheme in History* (New York: St. Martin's, 2021); Hal Weitzman, *What's the Matter With Delaware? How the First State Has Favored the Rich, Powerful, and Criminal—and How It Costs Us All* (Princeton, NJ: Princeton University Press, 2022).

80. Oliver Bullough, *Butler to the World: How Britain Helps the World's Worst People Launder Money, Commit Crimes, and Get Away With Anything* (New York: Macmillan, 2022); Tom Burgis, *Cuckooland: Where the Rich Own the Truth* (Glasgow: William Collins, 2024).

81. Mark Hollingsworth and Stewart Lansley, *Londongrad: The Inside Story of the Oligarchs* (London: Fourth Estate, 2010).

82. Kevin Morgan and Nadir Kinossian, 'Dismantling Londongrad: The Dark Geography of Dirty Money', *European Planning Studies* (2023): 1–17; Matthew Collin, Florian M. Hollenbach, and David Szakonyi, *The End of Londongrad? The Impact of Beneficial Ownership Transparency on Offshore Investment in UK Property*, Working Paper No. wp-2023-11, World Institute for Development Economic Research (UNU-WIDER), 2023.

83. HM Government, *Global Britain*.

84. HM Government, *Integrated Review Refresh*.

85. John J. Mearsheimer, 'Why the Ukraine Crisis Is the West's Fault: The Liberal Delusions That Provoked Putin', *Foreign Affairs* 93, no. 5 (2014): 77–89.

86. Christopher Walker, 'What Is "Sharp Power"?', *Journal of Democracy* 29, no. 3 (2018): 9–23.

87. Ricardo Soares De Oliveira, *Magnificent and Beggar Land: Angola Since the Civil War* (Oxford: Oxford University Press, 2015).

88. Michael G. Findley, Daniel L. Nielson, Jason C. Sharman, *Global Shell Games: Experiments in Transnational Relations, Crime, and Terrorism* (Cambridge: Cambridge University Press, 2014). Michael G. Findley, Daniel L. Nielson, and Jason C. Sharman, *A Global Field Experiment on Regulatory Compliance in the Finance Industry*, December 2021, https://cdn.centralbankbaha mas.com/download/003202700.pdf.

89. Alexander A. Cooley and Jason C. Sharman, 'Transnational Corruption and the Globalized Individual', *Perspectives on Politics* 15, no. 3 (2017): 732–753.

90. As discussed, much of the wealth accumulated by elites will be illicit rather than illegal, we define this broadly to include the movement of money of suspect or dubious or unclear origin to facilitate high value purchases or further investments. See Alexander Cooley, John Heathershaw, and Jason C. Sharman, 'Laundering Cash, Whitewashing Reputations', *Journal of Democracy* 29 (2018): 39–53; Alexander Cooley, John Heathershaw, and Ricard Soares de Oliveira, 'Transnational Uncivil Society Networks: Kleptocracy's Global Fightback Against Liberal Activism', *European Journal of International Relations* 30, no. 2 (2024): 382–407.

91. John Heathershaw, Alexander Cooley, Tom Mayne, Casey Michel, Tena Prelec, Jason Sharman and Ricardo Soares de Oliveira, *The UK's Kleptocracy Problem*, December 2021, 50–54, https:// ore.exeter.ac.uk/repository/bitstream/handle/10871/131303/Final_CH_Kleptocracy%20Rep ort%20tweaked%20not%20excised.pdf. The one case not in our property database is within our scope conditions.

Chapter 2

1. As quoted by Betty Dodson. See Melissa Gira Grant, 'Betty Dodson's Feminist Sex Wars', Truthout, 16 December 2023, https://truthout.org/articles/betty-dodsons-feminist-sex-wars/ ?tmpl=component&print=1.

2. Will Dunn, 'How Global Britain Props Up Putin's Gangster State', *The New Statesman*, 12 March 2022, https://www.newstatesman.com/culture/books/2022/03/how-global-britain-props-up-putins-gangster-state.

3. Vanessa Ogle, 'Funk Money: The End of Empires, The Expansion of Tax Havens, and Decolonization as an Economic and Financial Event', *Past & Present* 249, no. 1 (November 2020): 213–249.
4. Bullough, *Butler to the World*.
5. Jason C. Sharman, *The Money Laundry: Regulating Criminal Finance in the Global Economy* (Ithaca, NY: Cornell University Press, 2011); Jason C. Sharman, *The Despot's Guide to Wealth Management* (Ithaca, NY: Cornell University Press, 2017).
6. Nicholas Shaxson, *Treasure Islands: Tax Havens and the Men Who Stole the World* (London: Macmillan, 2011); Nicholas Shaxson, *The Finance Curse: How Global Finance Is Making Us All Poorer* (New York: Grove Press, 2019).
7. Ronen Palan, Richard Murphy, and Christian Chavagneux, *Tax Havens: How Globalisation Really Works* (Ithaca, NY: Cornell University Press, 2011).
8. David Harvey, *A Brief History of Neoliberalism* (Oxford: Oxford University Press, 2005).
9. Daniel Haberly and Darius Wójcik, *Sticky Power: Global Financial Networks in the World Economy* (Oxford: Oxford University Press, 2022).
10. Ron Harris, 'The Private Origins of the Private Company: Britain 1862–1907', *Oxford Journal of Legal Studies*, 33, Issue 2 (Summer 2013): 339–378.
11. Giovanni Arrighi, *The Long Twentieth Century: Money, Power, and the Origins of Our Times* (London: Verso, 1994).
12. David Edgerton, *The Rise and Fall of the British Nation: A Twentieth-Century History* (London: Penguin, 2018).
13. Karl Polanyi, *The Great Transformation: The Political and Economic Origins of Our Time* (Boston: Beacon Press by arrangement with Rinehart & Company, Inc. 1944), 35.
14. Kenneth Pomeranz, *The Great Divergence: China, Europe, and the Making of the Modern World Economy* (Princeton, NJ: Princeton University Press, 2000).
15. The facts of this increase of inequality are well established, most recently in the work of Thomas Piketty and Gabriel Zucman. Their interpretation has become a matter of controversy apparently due to the challenge they make to the neoclassical models which dominate the profession of economics. See Piketty, *Capital in the Twenty-First Century* (Cambridge: Harvard University Press, 2014) and Zucman, *The Hidden Wealth of Nations: The Scourge of Tax Havens* (Chicago: University of Chicago Press, 2015).
16. Daniel Domeher, Emmanuel Konadu-Yiadom, and Godfred Aawaar, 'Financial Innovations and Economic Growth: Does Financial Inclusion Play a Mediating Role?', *Cogent Business & Management* 9, no. 1 (2022), doi.org/10.1080/23311975.2022.2049670.
17. Ian M. Kerr, *A History of the Eurobond Market: The First 21 Years* (London: Euromoney Publications Limited, 1984).
18. Shaxson, *Treasure Islands*; Bullough, *Moneyland*.
19. Sheldon T. Rabin, 'Soviet-Owned Banks in Europe: Their Development and Contribution to Trade with the West', PhD Thesis (1977), The Johns Hopkins University, Baltimore, USA.
20. Bullough, *Butler to the World*, 39.
21. Rabin, 'Soviet-Owned Banks'.
22. Bullough, *Butler to the World*, 41.
23. Bullough, *Butler to the World*, 45.
24. Bullough, *Butler to the World*, 46.
25. Edgerton, *The Rise and Fall of the British Nation*, 225.
26. Palan et al., *Tax Havens*, 125.
27. Bullough, *Butler to the World*, 69.
28. Bullough, *Butler to the World*, 70.
29. Carl Pacini and Nate Wadlinger, 'How Shell Entities and Lack of Ownership Transparency Facilitate Tax Evasion and Modern Policy Responses to These Problems, *Marquette Law Review* 102 (2018): 115.
30. Palan et al., *Tax Havens*, 149.
31. Shaxson, *Treasure Islands*, 20–24.
32. Phillip Loft, 'The UK Overseas Territories and Their Governors', House of Commons Library, 30 June 2022, https://researchbriefings.files.parliament.uk/documents/CBP-9583/CBP-9583.pdf.
33. Shaxson, *Tax Havens*, 22.
34. Christina Freeland, *Sale of the Century: The Inside Story of the Second Russian Revolution* (London: Abacus, 2005), 13–14.
35. Freeland, *Sale of the Century*, 16.

36. Freeland, *Sale of the Century*, 16.
37. Mark Galeotti, 'Controlling Chaos: How Russia Manages Its Political War in Europe', European Council on Foreign Relations, September 2017, https://ecfr.eu/publication/controlling_chaos_how_russia_manages_its_political_war_in_europe/.
38. Dawisha, *Putin's Kleptocracy*.
39. Mikhail Zygar, *All the Kremlin's Men: Inside the Court of Vladimir Putin* (New York: PublicAffairs, 2016).
40. Kiryl Haiduk, 'The Political Economy of Post-Soviet Offshore', in *After Deregulation: Global Finance in the New Century*, ed. Libby Assassi, Anastasia Nesvetailova, and Duncan Wigan (Basingstoke: Palgrave Macmillan, 2007), 250–267.
41. Palan et al., *Tax Havens*, 148–149.
42. Oxford Analytica, 'Russian Outflows to Continue With or Without Sanctions', *Oxford Analytica Daily Brief*, 15 May 2019, https://dailybrief.oxan.com/Analysis/DB243875/Russian-outflows-to-continue-with-or-without-sanctions.
43. Claus Offe and Piere Adler, 'Capitalism by Democratic Design? Democratic Theory Facing the Triple Transition in East Central Europe', *Social Research* 58, no. 4 (Winter 1991): 865–892.
44. Francis Fukuyama, *The End of History and the Last Man* (Los Angeles: Free Press, 1992).
45. Alexander Cooley and John Heathershaw, *Dictators Without Borders: Power and Money in Central Asia* (New Haven, CT: Yale University Press, 2017), 30.
46. Cooley and Heathershaw, *Dictators Without Borders*, 32.
47. Tena Prelec, 'The Transition Game: The Persistence of Elites and Extractive Practices in the Energy Sector in Successor Yugoslav States', PhD diss., School of Law, Politics and Sociology, University of Sussex, October 2020.
48. Gil Eyal, Eleanor R. Townsley, and Ivan Szelenyi, *Making Capitalism Without Capitalists* (London: Verso Books, 2001).
49. As in other post-communist countries including Bulgaria, see Venelin I. Ganev, *Preying on the State: The Transformation of Bulgaria After 1989* (Ithaca, NY: Cornell University Press, 2007).
50. Will Bartlett, *Europe's Troubled Region: Economic Development, Institutional Reform, and Social Welfare in the Western Balkans* (London: Routledge, 2008).
51. Branko Milanovic, 'Explaining the Increase in Inequality During the Transition', World Bank, June 1998, https://www.imf.org/external/np/eu2/kyrgyz/pdf/milanovi.pdf.
52. Zsoka Koczan, 'Being Poor, Feeling Poorer: Inequality, Poverty and Poverty Perceptions in the Western Balkans', International Monetary Fund, February 2016, https://www.imf.org/external/pubs/ft/wp/2016/wp1631.pdf.
53. Dusna Pavlović, 'Is European Enlargement Policy a Form of Non-Democracy Promotion?', *Journal of International Relations and Development* 26 (2023): 324–346.
54. Kristin Surak, *The Golden Passport: Global Mobility for Millionaires* (Cambridge, MA: Harvard University Press, 2023), 263.
55. Acts 22:28.
56. Kristin Surak, 'Millionaire Mobility and the Sale of Citizenship', Taylor & Francis, May 24, 2020, www.tandfonline.com/doi/abs/10.1080/1369183X.2020.1758554; Jelena Dzankic, *The Global Market for Investor Citizenship* (New York: Springer International Publishing, 2019).
57. Surak, *The Golden Passport*, 262.
58. Henley & Partners, 'About Us', 2023, https://www.henleyglobal.com/about.
59. Henley, 'About Us'.
60. David Segal, 'Rogue Despots and the Collapse of a P.R. Firm', *New York Times*, 5 February 2018, https://uoelibrary.idm.oclc.org/login?url=https://www.proquest.com/historical-newspapers/rogues-despots-collapse-p-r-firm/docview/2611737858/se-2.
61. Haroon Siddique, 'Tony Blair Advises Kazakh President on Publicity After Killing of Protesters', *The Guardian*, 24 August 2014, https://www.theguardian.com/politics/2014/aug/24/tony-blair-advice-kazakh-president-protesters.
62. Public Relations and Communications Association, 'PR and Communications Census 2019', 2019, https://www.prca.org.uk/sites/default/files/PRCA_PR_Census_2019_v9-8-pdf%20%285%29.pdf.
63. Francis Ingham, '"PR Industry Roars Back"—2021 PRCA UK Census', Public Relations and Communications Association, 2021, https://www.prca.org.uk/PR-industry-roars-back-2021-PRCA-UK-Census.

64. Louis Goss, 'UK's Professional Services Sector Weathers Economic Headwinds', *City AM*, 13 August 2022, https://www.cityam.com/uks-professional-services-sector-weathers-economic-headwinds/
65. Dunn, 'How Global Britain Props Up Putin's Gangster State'.
66. Jerry Harris, 'Statist Globalization in China, Russia and the Gulf States', in *The Nation in the Global Era* (Leiden: Brill, 2009), 29–53.
67. *Financial Times*, 'How London Became the Dirty Money Capital of the World', 22 April 2022, https://www.ft.com/video/d3bafb94-9dbd-4c1e-8016-8cd8331960f1.
68. Tax Justice Network, 'The State of Tax Justice 2020: Tax Justice in the Time of Covid-19', November 2020. https://taxjustice.net/wp-content/uploads/2020/11/The_State_of_Tax_Justice_2020_ENGLISH.pdf.

Chapter 3

1. Catherine Nixey, 'Boris Brags About London's Exotic Army of Billionaires', *The Times*, 28 November 2014, https://www.thetimes.co.uk/article/boris-brags-about-londons-exotic-army-of-billionaires-7jf7grc3z2q. You can listen to Johnson's immediate backtracking as someone preserved the soundbite—see https://www.reddit.com/r/london/comments/2n9br2/boris_johnson_expressing_his_feelings_about_why/.
2. James Boswell, *The Life of Samuel Johnson LLD*, First volume (London: Cadell and Davies, 1791), 404.
3. Hilary Osborne and Kevin Rawlinson, 'Empty Homes: Normal Rules Do Not Apply to Super-Rich in London', *The Guardian*, 1 August 2017, https://www.theguardian.com/society/2017/aug/01/empty-homes-normal-rules-do-not-apply-to-super-rich-in-london.
4. Gohil, R. V [2018] EWCA Crim 140 (15 February 2018) (2018);
     Gohil v Gohil [2015] UKSC 61 (14 October 2015) (2015).
5. UNODC, 'DIGEST OF ASSET RECOVERY CASES COSP/2013/CRP.10', 2013.
6. Author interview with Benton, 2021.
7. Preko, R V [2015] EWCA Crim 42 (3 February 2015) (2015).
8. Author interview with Hollingsworth, 2022.
9. Hollingsworth and Lansley, *Londongrad*.
10. Alexander Halban, 'Former Soviet Oligarchs March on London Courts', Littleton Chambers, 4 October 2019, https://littletonchambers.com/former-soviet-oligarchs-march-on-london-courts/.
11. Maria Pevchikh, Twitter post, 2022, https://twitter.com/pevchikh/status/1501878768423653380.
12. UK Government, 'Press Release: Foreign Secretary Announces 65 New Russian Sanctions to Cut Off Vital Industries Fuelling Putin's War Machine', 24 March 2022, https://www.gov.uk/government/news/foreign-secretary-announces-65-new-russian-sanctions-to-cut-off-vital-industries-fuelling-putins-war-machine.
13. Jane Croft, 'London Lawfare: How Lawyers Helped Russia's Super-Rich', *Financial Times*, 22 May 2022. https://www.ft.com/content/6eb485df-90cc-428a-b4f3-7f2c5de42c84.
14. Croft, 'London Lawfare'.
15. Jonathan Ames, 'Former Soviet Oligarchs March on London to Fight Legal Battles', *The Times*, 9 May 2019. https://www.thetimes.co.uk/article/5f6fce00-71a6-11e9-a116-49ac88679a93.
16. Elisabeth Schimpfössl, *Rich Russians: From Oligarchs to Bourgeoisie* (Oxford: Oxford University Press, 2018).
17. David Beetham, *The Legitimation of Power* (London: Bloomsbury, 2013).
18. Jason Lewis, 'Duke's Southyork Deal Investigated', *The Sunday Telegraph*, 27 May 2012. https://www.pressreader.com/uk/the-sunday-telegraph/20120527/281595237580233.
19. Guy Adams, 'Was Southyork Bought to Launder for a Kazakh Tycoon?', *Mail Online*, 11 February 2022, https://www.dailymail.co.uk/news/article-10503949/GUY-ADAMS-Andrew-Fergies-Southyork-bought-launder-millions-Kazakh-tycoon.html.
20. Adam Lusher, 'Prince Andrew Facing Questions Over the Sale of His Mansion to Kazakh Oligarch', *The Independent*, 23 May 2016, https://www.independent.co.uk/news/uk/prince-andrew-facing-questions-over-the-sale-of-his-mansion-to-kazakh-oligarch-a7043101.html.
21. David Leigh and Stephen Bates, 'Prince Andrew and the Kazakh Billionaire', *The Guardian*, 29 November 2010, https://www.theguardian.com/uk/2010/nov/29/prince-andrew-kazakh-billionaire.

22. FCG, 'Financial Crime Guide: A Firm's Guide to Countering Financial Crime Risks (FCG)', 2023, https://www.handbook.fca.org.uk/handbook/FCG.pdf.3.2.7: 'Situations that present a higher money laundering risk might include, but are not restricted to: customers linked to higher risk countries or business sectors; or who have unnecessarily complex or opaque beneficial ownership structures; and transactions which are unusual, lack an obvious economic or lawful purpose, are complex or large or might lend themselves to anonymity'.

23. As it has since emerged, the prince had shown similar disregard to the exploitation of underage girls happening under his eyes in the Epstein case.

24. Guy Adams, 'The Truth About Andrew's £15m House Sale: As Furore Grows Over Prince's Links to Corrupt Kazakh Regime, We Expose New Details Surrounding the Mysterious Sale of Prince's Marital Home to Oligarch', *The Daily Mail*, 23 May 2016, https://www.dailymail.co.uk/news/article-3603746/The-truth-Andrew-s-15m-house-sale-furore-grows-Prince-s-links-corrupt-Kazakh-regime-expose-new-details-surrounding-mysterious-sale-Prince-s-marital-home-oligarch.htm.l.

25. Sudip Kar-Gupta, 'Coutts Fined 8.75 Million Pounds for Money Laundering Failures', Reuters, 26 March 2012. https://www.reuters.com/article/uk-coutts-fine-idUKBRE82P0BL20120326.

26. Adam Lusher, 'Prince Andrew Facing Questions Over the Sale of His Mansion to Kazakh Oligarch. Allegations Come Days After Palace Strongly Denied He Was a Fixer in an Attempted £385 Million Kazakhstan Business Deal', *Independent*, 23 May 2016, https://www.independent.co.uk/news/uk/prince-andrew-facing-questions-over-the-sale-of-his-mansion-to-kazakh-oligarch-a7043101.html.

27. Adam Lusher, 'Buckingham Palace Denies Claims Prince Andrew Was a "Fixer" in Kazakhstan Deal', *Independent*, 21 May 2016, https://www.independent.co.uk/news/uk/buckingham-palace-prince-andrew-fixer-kazakhstan-a7041186.html.

28. Guy Adams, 'Andrew and "a £4m Kickback": Duke Brokered £385m Deal for Greek Firm and Corrupt Regime While Acting as British Trade Envoy . . . So Is That How He Paid for His £13m Ski Chalet?', *The Daily Mail*, 20 May 2016, https://www.dailymail.co.uk/news/article-3601690/Andrew-4-million-kickback-Duke-brokered-385m-deal-Greek-firm-corrupt-regime-acting-British-trade-envoy.html.

29. Lusher, 'Buckingham Palace Denies Claims'.

30. Matthew T. Page, '"West African Elites" Spending on UK Schools and Universities: A Closer Look', Carnegie Endowment for International Peace, January 2021, https://carnegieendowment.org/files/Page_AfricaUK_Corruption_1.pdf

31. Page, 'West African Elites'.

32. Michael Ani and Segun Adams, 'Nigeria's Political Elite Stuck With Country's Neglected Healthcare System', 30 March 2020, https://businessday.ng/exclusives/article/nigerias-political-elite-stuck-with-countrys-neglected-healthcare-system/.

33. Ibrahim Abubakar, Sarah L. Dalglish, Blake Angell, Olutobi Sanuade, Seye Abimbola, Aishatu Lawal Amanu, et al., 'The Lancet Nigeria Commission: Investing in Health and the Future of the Nation', *The Lancet* 399, no. 10330 (March 19, 2022): 1155–1200.

34. As discussed in Chapter 12, one Kremlin-linked figure, Yevgeny Prigozhin, did manage to pursue a libel lawsuit while sanctioned, by getting his UK law firm to apply to the government for dispensation, although this loophole was closed after Russia's full-scale invasion of Ukraine.

35. Usually, family members are loyalists. Karimova's primary motivation was accruing capital to the extent that it actually caused a rift with her father—she was arrested in Uzbekistan while her father was still president. Loyalist figures, like Timur Kulibayev, may become 'agnostic' once a change in power has occurred, as it did in Kazakhstan formally in 2019 and in reality through violence in 2022. Some may even switch sides, maintaining loyalist credentials.

36. Catherine Belton, 'In British PM Race, a Former Russian Tycoon Quietly Wields Influence', Reuters, 19 July 2019, https://www.reuters.com/investigates/special-report/britain-eu-johnson-russian/.

37. Quintel Intelligence Report, July 2018.

38. Henry Dyer, 'Former Russian Banker Dmitry Leus Who Donated £25,000 to Dominic Raab Is "Absolutely Dependent on the FSB", MP Claims', *Insider*, 7 July 2022, https://www.businessinsider.com/dominic-raab-donor-absolutely-dependent-on-the-fsb-mp-claims-2022-7?r=US&IR=T.

39. The authors wrote to Leus on 6 December 2023 to provide him with an opportunity to comment on the matters discussed in this book. He did not reply.

40. United Nations High Commissioner for Refugees, 'Refworld | Amnesty International Report 2003—Kazakstan', Refworld, 2003, https://www.refworld.org/docid/3edb47d81c.html.

41. Kirstin Ridley, 'English Judge Says Fugitive Oligarch Defrauded Kazakh Bank BTA', Reuters, 19 March 2013, https://www.reuters.com/article/uk-ablyazov-ruling-idUKBRE92I11J20130319; Rupert Neate, 'Arrest Warrant for Kazakh Billionaire Accused of One of World's Biggest Frauds', *Guardian*, 16 February 2012, https://www.theguardian.com/business/2012/feb/16/arrest-warrant-kazakh-billionaire-mukhtar-ablyazov/.

42. Thomas Rowley, 'As Kazakhstan Burns Over Inequality, the Elite's Wealth Is Safe and Sound in London', OpenDemocracy, 6 January 2022, https://www.opendemocracy.net/en/odr/-kazakhstan-burns-elites-wealth-safe-in-london/ .

43. Ridley, 'English Judge'.

44. Masha Gessen, 'Comrade in Arms', *Vanity Fair*, 13 November 2012, https://www.vanityfair.com/news/politics/2012/11/roman-abramovich-boris-berezovsky-feud-russia.

45. Ian Cobain, 'Boris Berezovsky Inquest Returns Open Verdict on Death', *Guardian*, 27 March 2014, https://www.theguardian.com/world/2014/mar/27/boris-berezovsky-inquest-open-verdict-death.

46. Edward Lucas, *Deception: Spies, Lies and How Russia Dupes the West* (London: Bloomsbury, 2012, 176.

47. Heidi Blake, Tom Warren, Richard Holmes, Jason Leopold, Jane Bradley, and Alex Campbell, 'From Russia With Blood: 14 Suspected Hits on British Soil That the Government Ignored', 15 June 2017, *Buzzfeed News*, https://www.buzzfeednews.com/article/heidiblake/from-russia-with-blood-14-suspected-hits-on-british-soil.

48. The presentation was made on a live stream hosted on YouTube in March 2021 by the PCD Group ('the business networking club for international private wealth professionals') about unexplained wealth orders. The video was originally available (at https://www.youtube.com/channel/UC4A2mBYqFcs3LRovD-Mqclw) but was later changed to 'private' and then removed. The comments were made at 59"10.

49. PCD Club, 'Unexplained Wealth Orders', 59"54.

50. PCD Club, 'Unexplained Wealth Orders', 1"07"30.

51. PCD Club, 'Unexplained Wealth Orders', 1"05"00.

Chapter 4

1. Miles Johnson, 'Wagner Inc: A Russian Warlord and His Lawyers', *Financial Times*, 24 January 2023, https://www.ft.com/content/8c8b0568-cdd1-4529-a4fd-82e57983ddc5.

2. Page and Vittori, 'Kleptocratic Adaptation'.

3. 'Russian Tycoon Pugachev Loses UK Asset Freeze Appeal', Reuters, 19 December 2014, https://www.reuters.com/article/us-britain-russia-pugachev-idINKBN0JX1J620141219.

4. National Crime Agency, 'UKFIU Suspicious Activity Reports (SARs) Annual Report', 2022, https://nationalcrimeagency.gov.uk/who-we-are/publications/632-2022-sars-annual-report-1/file, 6.

5. National Crime Agency, 'UKFIU', 6.

6. National Crime Agency, 'UKFIU', 8.

7. Helen Taylor and Daniel Beizsley, 'A Privileged Profession?" Spotlight on Corruption, 19 October 2022, https://www.spotlightcorruption.org/wp-content/uploads/2022/10/Privileged_Profession.Exec_.Summary.pdf.

8. Taylor and Beizsley, 'A Privileged Profession?'

9. Daniel Kaufmann and Pedro C. Vicente. 'Legal Corruption', *Economics & Politics* 23, no. 2 (2011): 195–219.

10. Tena Prelec and Ricardo Soares de Oliveira, 'Enabling African Loots: Tracking the Laundering of Nigerian Kleptocrats' Ill-Gotten Gains in Western Financial Centres', *Journal of International Relations and Development* 26 (2023): 272–300.

11. It should be noted, however, that business executives who used to work for such firms have told the authors that the problem is even starker, as large firms' involvement in handling highly dubious capital starts often in the early stages, too. This should be probed by further research.

12. Brooke Harrington, *Capital Without Borders: Wealth Managers and the One Percent* (Cambridge, MA: Harvard University Press, 2016).

13. Transparency International, 'At Your Service: Investigating How UK Businesses and Institutions Help Corrupt Individuals and Regimes Launder Their Money and Reputation', October 2019,

https://www.transparency.org.uk/sites/default/files/pdf/publications/TIUK_AtYourServ
ice_WEB.pdf, 14.

14. Karin Svedberg Helgesson and Ulrika Mörth. 'Client Privilege, Compliance and the Rule of
Law: Swedish Lawyers and Money Laundering Prevention', *Crime, Law and Social Change* 69
(2018): 227–248.

15. Cooley et al., 'Transnational Uncivil Society'.

16. Cooley et al., 'Transnational Uncivil Society'.

17. Herbert Kitschelt and Steven I. Wilkinson, eds., *Patrons, Clients and Policies: Patterns of
Democratic Accountability and Political Competition* (Cambridge: Cambridge University Press,
2007), 7.

18. Jana Hönke, 'Transnational Clientelism, Global (Resource) Governance, and the Disciplining
of Dissent', *International Political Sociology* 12, no. 2 (2018): 110.

19. Hönke, 'Transnational Clientelism'. See also Gerasimos Tsourapas, 'Global
Autocracies: Strategies of Transnational Repression, Legitimation, and Co-optation in World
Politics', *International Studies Review* 23, no. 3 (2021): 616–644.

20. Henry Farrell and Abraham L. Newman, 'Domestic Institutions Beyond the Nation-
State: Charting the New Interdependence Approach', *World Politics* 66, no. 2 (2014): 350.

21. Lukas Hakelberg, *The Hypocritical Hegemon: How the United States Shapes Global Rules Against
Tax Evasion and Avoidance* (Ithaca, NY: Cornell University Press, 2020).

22. In short, the traditional belief is that anti-corruption work by international civil society will
have an effect on the country in question, with corrupt actors outed, and the relevant polit-
ical/business sector cleansed—efforts from the 'outside' causing change 'inside' the country
(hence, 'outside-in', a positive effect). Yet the theory behind uncivil society suggests that corrupt networks inside the country form linkages outside in democratic countries to help protect
and sustain them (hence, 'inside-out', a negative effect). See Cooley and Heathershaw, *Dictators
Without Borders*.

23. Henry E. Hale, *Patronal Politics: Eurasian Regime Dynamics in Comparative Perspective*
(Cambridge: Cambridge University Press, 2014); Dawisha, *Putin's Kleptocracy*; Cooley and
Heathershaw, *Dictators Without Borders*.

24. Loriana Crasnic, 'Resistance in Tax and Transparency Standards: Small States' Heterogenous
Responses to New Regulations', *Review of International Political Economy* 29, no. 1
(2022): 255–280.

25. Loriana Crasnic, Nikhil Kalyanpur, and Abraham Newman, 'Networked
Liabilities: Transnational Authority in a World of Transnational Business', *European Journal of
International Relations* 23, no. 4 (2017): 906–929.

26. Cooley et al., 'Transnational Uncivil Society'.

27. Hoang, *Spiderweb Capitalism*.

28. Al-Suwaidi, Noura Ahmed, and Haitham Nobanee, 'Anti-Money Laundering and Anti-
Terrorism Financing: A Survey of the Existing Literature and a Future Research Agenda', *Journal
of Money Laundering Control* 24, no. 2 (2021): 398; Jack A. Blum, Michael Levi, R. Thomas
Naylor, and Phil Williams, 'Financial Havens, Banking Secrecy and Money Laundering', *Trends
in Organized Crime* 4 (1998): 69.

29. Anthony Amicelle, 'Towards a "New" Political Anatomy of Financial Surveillance', *Security
Dialogue* 42, no. 2 (2011): 161–178; Helgesson and Mörth, 'Client Privilege'.

30. Tim Büthe and Walter Mattli, *The New Global Rulers* (Princeton, NJ: Princeton University Press,
2011); Eleni Tsingou, 'Club Governance and the Making of Global Financial Rules', *Review of
International Political Economy* 22, no. 2 (2015): 225–256.

31. Harrington, *Capital Without Borders*, 1.

32. Brooke Harrington and Leonard Seabrooke, 'Transnational Professionals', *Annual Review of
Sociology* 46 (2020): 400.

33. Karin Svedberg Helgesson and Ulrika Mörth, 'Involuntary Public Policy-Making by For-Profit
Professionals: European Lawyers on Anti-Money Laundering and Terrorism Financing',
JCMS: Journal of Common Market Studies 54, no. 5 (2016): 1226.

34. Helgesson and Mörth, 'Involuntary Public Policy-Making', 1227–1228.

Chapter 5

1. Maxton Walker, 'Kyrgyz President Attacks UK for "Hosting a Guy Who Robbed Us"', *The
Guardian*, 14 July 2013, https://www.theguardian.com/world/2013/jul/14/kyrgyzstan-presid
ent-atambayev-maxim-bakiyev.

2. 'Case Studies', APCO Worldwide, 2023, https://apcoworldwide.com/work/case-studies/.
3. Global Witness, *Grave Secrecy: How a Dead Man Can Own a UK Company and Other Hair-Raising Stories About Hidden Company Ownership* (2012), https://cdn.globalwitness.org/arch ive/files/gravesecrecy.pdf, 12.
4. Author interview (Mayne) with individual from international financial institution, 2010.
5. Kubat Kasymbekov, 'Гуревич: Семья Бакиева вывела из страны $200–300 миллионов (видео)', Radio Liberty (Kyrgyz service), 30 August 2018, https://rus.azattyk.org/a/kyrgyzstan _evgeniy_gurevitch_intervju/29461999.html.
6. Global Witness, *Grave Secrecy*, 52.
7. Global Witness, *Grave Secrecy*, 49.
8. Global Witness, *Grave Secrecy*, 12. The general director of the company behind the bank IT system told Global Witness that it was 'just impossible to use' the system 'for any falsification or fraud', adding that it had been subject to IT security audit numerous times with no accusations of impropriety levelled against it. He added that the system was developed in a way that did not allow any operations which were not within officially approved bank procedures, in line with National Bank of Kyrgyzstan requirements, and added that the allegations made against his company were part of the 'political attack' against AUB (Global Witness, *Grave Secrecy*, 13.)
9. Global Witness, *Grave Secrecy*, 9.
10. Global Witness, *Grave Secrecy*, 8.
11. Kasymbekov, 'Гуревич'.
12. 'Banks' Management of High Money-Laundering Risk Situations How Banks Deal With High-Risk Customers (Including Politically Exposed Persons), Correspondent Banking Relationships and Wire Transfers', Financial Services Authority, 2011, https://www.fca.org.uk/publication/ corporate/fsa-aml-final-report.pdf.
13. Findley et al., *Global Shell Games*.
14. Tom Mayne and John Heathershaw, *Criminality Notwithstanding. The Use of Unexplained Wealth Orders in Anti-Corruption Cases*, ACE Global Integrity (March 2022), https://ace.glob alintegrity.org/wp-content/uploads/2022/03/CriminalityNotwithstanding.pdf, 9.
15. Global Witness, *Undue Diligence: How Banks Do Business With Corrupt Regimes* (March 2009), https://cdn2.globalwitness.org/archive/files/import/undue_diligence_lowres.pdf, 26.
16. Global Witness, *Grave Secrecy*, 37.
17. One of the researchers on this report was one of this book's authors (Mayne) when a campaigner at the anti-corruption NGO Global Witness.
18. 'Company Register Statistics', 2014, https://webarchive.nationalarchives.gov.uk/ukgwa/201 41104110620/http://www.companieshouse.gov.uk/about/businessRegisterStat.shtml.
19. Global Witness, *Grave Secrecy*, 31.
20. UK Government, 'UK's "First Ever" Successful Prosecution for False Company Information', Companies House, 23 March 2018, https://www.gov.uk/government/news/uks-first-ever-suc cessful-prosecution-for-false-company-information.
21. UK Government, 'Companies Register Activities: 2020 to 2021', Companies House, 24 June 2021, https://www.gov.uk/government/statistics/companies-register-activities-statistical-rele ase-2020-to-2021/companies-register-activities-2020-to-2021.
22. UK Government, 'Companies Register Activities: 2021 to 2022', Companies House, 30 June 2022. https://www.gov.uk/government/statistics/companies-register-activities-statistical-rele ase-2021-to-2022/companies-register-activities-2021-to-2022.
23. UK Government, 'Incorporated Companies in the UK July to September 2022', Companies House, 27 October 2022, https://www.gov.uk/government/statistics/incorporated-companies-in-the-uk-july-to-september-2022/incorporated-companies-in-the-uk-april-to-june-2022.
24. Global Witness, *Grave Secrecy*, 9.
25. Casey Michel, 'We Finally Know Why a Former GOP Presidential Nominee Joined the Most Crooked Bank in Central Asia', *Think Progress*, 28 August 2018. https://archive.thinkprogress. org/paul-manafort-bob-dole-board-of-crooked-bank-central-asia-413f55b4ce82/.
26. Global Witness, *Grave Secrecy*, 59.
27. Global Witness, *Grave Secrecy*, 61–62.
28. Michel, 'We Finally Know'.
29. APCO also told Global Witness that it informed AUB that APCO's services would only continue so long as all recommendations made by the independent board members were accepted by AUB management and the bank hired an independent due diligence firm to conduct a review

of and improve its anti-money-laundering procedures. APCO also said it saw no evidence of money laundering. Global Witness, *Grave Secrecy*, 61–62.

30. Michel, 'We Finally Know'.
31. Walker, 'Kyrgyz President Attacks UK'.
32. Christie Smythe and Jeremy Hodges, 'US Case Ends Against Ex-Kyrgyz Leader Bakiyev's Son', *Bloomberg*, 10 May 2013, https://www.bloomberg.com/news/articles/2013-05-09/u-s-case-ends-against-ex-kyrgyz-leader-bakiyev-s-son.
33. Kasymbekov, 'Гуревич'.
34. US Department of Justice, 'Justice Department Repatriates Forfeited Funds to the Government of the Kyrgyz Republic', US Department of Justice, 26 February 2019, https://www.justice.gov/opa/pr/justice-department-repatriates-forfeited-funds-government-kyrgyz-republic.
35. Scoop News, 'Cablegate: Lunch With Max: Soup to Nuts', 22 September 2009, https://www.scoop.co.nz/stories/WL0909/S00023.htm.
36. Kasymbekov, 'Гуревич'.
37. John F. Tierney, 'Mystery at Manas. Strategic Blind Spots in the Department of Defense's Fuel Contracts in Kyrgyzstan Report of the Majority Staff', Subcommittee on National Security and Foreign Affairs, Committee on Oversight and Government Reform, US House of Representatives, December 2010, https://www.washingtonpost.com/wp-srv/politics/documents/subcommittee_report_12222010.pdf.
38. Akipress, 'Kyrgyz General Prosecutor, UK Minister of State for Justice Discuss Mutual Legal Assistance in Connection With Court Sentences Taken Effect for Maksim Bakiyev', 9 October 2014, https://akipress.com/news:549245:Kyrgyz_General_Prosecutor,_UK_Minister_of_State_for_Justice_discuss_mutual_legal_assistance_in_connection_with_court_sentences_taken_effect_for_Maksim_Bakiyev/.

Chapter 6

1. The Times, 'Sykes in Retreat as Oligarchs Strike Fear Into Copper Giant', 8 June 2011, https://www.thetimes.co.uk/article/sykes-in-retreat-as-oligarchs-strike-fear-into-copper-giant-fpffhnwwp0v.
2. This chapter is based on research work completed by one of the authors (Mayne) when a senior campaigner at the anti-corruption NGO Global Witness.
3. Simon Goodley and Mark Hollingsworth, 'Vladimir Kim Accused of Giving False Evidence in Kazakh Court', *The Guardian*, 24 October 2012, https://www.theguardian.com/business/2012/oct/24/vladimir-kim-accused-false-evidence.
4. From notes of author (Mayne), who was in attendance.
5. Global Witness, *Risky Business: Kazakhstan, Kazakhmys Plc and the London Stock Exchange* (2010), https://www.globalwitness.org/en/reports/risky-business, 25.
6. Kazhegeldin later dropped the case and pursued Kim via other legal methods.
7. Global Witness, *Risky Business*, 33.
8. Forbes, 'Vladimir Kim', https://www.forbes.com/profile/vladimir-kim/ (accessed 20 February 2023). The website gives real-time net worth, but Kim was Kazakhstan's richest man in 2005 and beyond, according to *Forbes* at least.
9. Eurasian Natural Resources Corporation PLC, 'Transforming Resources. ENRC. Admission to the Official List and to Trading on the London Stock Exchange', 2007, https://kase.kz/files/emitters/GB_ENRC/gbenrcf9_2008e.pdf, 190; Christopher Thomas and Jonathon Guthrie, 'Chairman Quits Besmirched Miner', *Financial Times*, 24 April 2013, https://www.ft.com/content/15e61abe-ac31-11e2-a063-00144feabdc0.
10. Global Witness, *Risky Business*, 7.
11. Clara Denina and Dasha Afanasieva, 'Exclusive: Kazakh Mining Company Erg Looks to Spin Off and List Assets—Sources', Reuters, 22 February 2018, https://www.reuters.com/article/us-mining-erg-assetsales-exclusive-idUSKCN1G6268.
12. Kim's words were featured in a documentary in 2014 by *Al Jazeera* ("Kazakhstan: Poisoned Legacy", *Al Jazeera*, 19 February 2014, https://www.aljazeera.com/program/people-power/2014/2/19/kazakhstan-poisoned-legacy). Kim announced at an AGM that Kazakhmys had supplied lead dust to the smelter in Shymkent, Kazakhstan, but it would be closed down. At the following AGM, company chair, Simon Heale, announced that no recording of the meeting was allowed.
13. Global Witness, 'Shell Knew', 10 April 2017, https://www.globalwitness.org/en/campaigns/oil-gas-and-mining/shell-knew/.

14. Kate Burgess, Joanna Chung, Arkady Ostrovsky, and Helen Thomas, 'Dicey Russian Flotations Challenge London Investors' Appetite for Risk', *Financial Times*, 6 December 2005.
15. Global Witness, *Risky Business*, 12.
16. Global Witness, *Risky Business*, 12.
17. Jonathan Aitken, *Nazarbayev and the Making of Kazakhstan* (London: Continuum, 2009), 72.
18. Global Witness, *Risky Business*, 6.
19. Global Witness, *Risky Business*, 20.
20. Global Witness, *Risky Business*, 10, 20–21. The report documented statements from at least three sources that said that Nazarbayev was the true controller of Kazakhmys plc. Years later, in 2021, OCCRP reported that the unofficial third wife of Nazarbayev, now Kazakhstan's former president, received $30 million apparently for almost nothing, in a transaction featuring a BVI company that had links to both Kim and Ni. The woman in question, Assel Kurmanbayeva, received the money two months after Vladimir Ni's death in 2010 from a company taken over by Ni's daughter, it was alleged. See Miranda Patrucic and Ilya Lozovsky, 'Secretive Offshore Maneuvers Enriched Unofficial Third Wife of Kazakhstani Leader Nursultan Nazarbayev', OCCRP, 3 October 2021, https://www.occrp.org/en/the-pandora-papers/secretive-offshore-maneuvers-enriched-unofficial-third-wife-of-kazakhstani-leader-nursultan-nazarbayev.
21. 'Different From You and Me', *Mining Journal*, 19 November 2014, https://www.mining-journal.com/mj-comment/news/1148419/different-from-you-and-me. This gift was, Kazakhmys plc said, a reward for Ni's 'longstanding business relationship with Mr Kim'. Yet at that point Kim and Ni had only been working officially together for seven years at Kazakhmys. Prior to this Ni was working for the president.
22. Global Witness, *Risky Business*, 21. Samsung's sale of its shares was not reported until the time of the Kazakhmys IPO.
23. Global Witness, *Risky Business*, 14.
24. Global Witness, 'Lanesborough Hotel Bill', 13 July 2010, https://cdn.globalwitness.org/archive/files/lanesborough_hotel_bill.pdf.
25. Tom Burgis, 'Mining Group Arranged Paris Trip for Kazakh Prime Minister's Family', *Financial Times*, 8 September 2020, https://www.ft.com/content/7a14a6cf-067e-4f27-b8b2-82bf00c2477e.
26. In response to the *Financial Times*, KAZ Minerals (formerly Kazakhmys) said it 'found no evidence of payment by the company (or by any of its employees) for these travel arrangements, and no evidence of a request for, or expectation of, payment by the company or by any of its employees for these travel arrangements'. Burgis, 'Mining Group Arranged Paris Trip'.
27. Global Witness, *Risky Business*.
28. Author comments (Mayne) based on correspondence and telephone calls with the FCA circa 2010.
29. The article by the *Financial Times* was published one month before KAZ Minerals plc (a restructured Kazakhmys) delisted from the LSE.
30. 'Kazakhmys' Kim Makes Way for Independent Chairman', Reuters, 11 May 2012, https://www.reuters.com/article/kazakhmys-idUKWLA792120120511.
31. 'Kaz Minerals Promotes Chief Financial Officer to CEO', Reuters, 27 April 2017, https://www.reuters.com/article/kaz-moves-idUSL4N1HZ4UQ.
32. Investigace, 'A Real-Life Game of Monopoly in Mariánské Lázně', 10 January 2019, https://web.archive.org/web/20220626012611/https://www.investigace.eu/a-real-life-game-of-monopoly-in-marianske-lazne/.
33. April C. Murelio, 'Tractebel Among Companies Under Investigation', Power Online, 28 December 1999, https://www.poweronline.com/doc/tractebel-among-companies-under-investigation-0001; Elisabeth Debourse, 'Kazakhgate: Une pièce en huit actes pour comprendre l'affaire', *Paris Match*, 31 January 2017, https://parismatch.be/actualites/societe/6269/kazakhgate-une-piece-en-huit-actes-pour-comprendre-laffaire.
34. 'Chodiev, Le Businessman Belgo-Kazakh Toujours Discret, Souvent Suspect', RTBF, 26 February 2015, https://www.rtbf.be/info/belgique/detail_patokh-chodiev-le-businessman-belgo-kazakh-aussi-discret-que-suspect?id=8917187. In contrast to the lack of detail in the prospectus of Kazakhmys plc, the money-laundering allegations were mentioned by ENRC in its UK listing prospectus, but in typical 'enabler' language: 'The Company has been advised by the Founders that the investigation relates to allegations of tax evasion in respect of the 1996 tax year. Any use by the Founders of the monies that should, allegedly have been paid in tax could constitute money laundering under Belgian law, and as a result, although it is derived from tax

issues, the investigation has been categorised as a money-laundering investigation. The investigation, which commenced in 1996 and could ultimately lead to criminal sanctions, has attracted widespread publicity. To date no charges have been brought against the Founders [the trio].' See Eurasian Natural Resources Corporation PLC, Admission to the Official List and to Trading on the London Stock Exchange, Prospectus, 2008, https://kase.kz/files/emitters/GB_ENRC/gbe nrcf9_2008e.pdf, 24.

35. RTBF, 'Chodiev'.
36. Yann Philippin, Alain Lallemand, Thierry Denoël, and Mark Eeckhaut, 'Judicial Probe Widens to French Secret Services' Role in "Kazakhgate" Deal', Mediapart, 8 November 2017, https://www.mediapart.fr/en/journal/international/181117/judicial-probe-widens-french-secret-services-role-kazakhgate-deal.
37. 'Chamber Approves Conclusions of Kazakhgate Commission', Brussels Times, 26 April 2018, https://www.brusselstimes.com/48031/chamber-approves-conclusions-of-kazakhgate-com mission; 'Ex-President of Belgian Senate Charged With Corruption', News.am, 7 May 2018, https://news.am/eng/news/450085.html.
38. 'Update 2-Enrc Settles Deal to Buy CAMEC for $955 Mln', Reuters, 18 September 2009, https://www.reuters.com/article/enrc-camec-idUSL021190020090918.
39. Antony Sguazzin and Brett Foley, 'Rautenbach to Pay S. African Fine to End 10-Year Legal Battle', Bloomberg, 21 September 2009, https://www.bloomberg.com/news/articles/2009-09-21/rautenbach-to-pay-s-african-fine-to-end-10-year-legal-battle?leadSource=uverify%20wall; 'SANCTIONED: Muller Conrad "Billy" Rautenbach', OCCRP, https://cdn.occrp.org/proje cts/suisse-secrets-interactive/en/person/26/muller-conrad-billy-rautenbach/ (accessed 13 May 2024).
40. Burgis, Kleptopia.
41. 'Submission to the Working Group on the Issue of Human Rights and Transnational Corporations and Other Business Enterprises', OHCHR, 27 February 2020, https://www.ohchr.org/Documents/Issues/Business/2020Survey/Civil_society/RAID.pdf, 10.
42. 'Credit Suisse Banked and Financed Zimbabwean Fraudster in Deal That Saved Mugabe', OCCRP, 20 February 2022, https://www.occrp.org/en/suisse-secrets/credit-suisse-banked-and-financed-zimbabwean-fraudster-in-deal-that-saved-mugabe.
43. Neil Hume, 'ENRC—"More Soviet than City" [Updated]', Financial Times, 8 June 2011, https://www.ft.com/content/9a614911-6e4c-366e-acae-254cc2c4ae84.
44. OCCRP, 'Sykes in Retreat'.
45. Serious Fraud Office, 'ENRC Ltd', 17 May 2021, https://www.sfo.gov.uk/cases/enrc/.
46. Franz Wild and William Clowes, 'ENRC Sues UK Fraud Cops as Corruption Charges Loom', Bloomberg, 26 March 2019, https://www.bloomberg.com/news/articles/2019-03-26/enrc-sues-u-k-fraud-cops-before-decision-on-corruption-charges. The article notes: 'The names in the Swiss ruling were replaced with letters, but people familiar with the decision confirmed the references were to Gertler and Dezita'.
47. Financial Times, 'Mining Group ENRC Sues SFO for £70m Over Corruption Probe', 26 March 2019, https://www.ft.com/content/8e9cc1f4-4fe3-11e9-b401-8d9ef1626294.
48. Serious Fraud Office, 'ENRC Ltd', 24 August 2023.
49. Jasper Jolly, 'Which London-Listed Russian Firms Could Be Hit by Sanctions?' The Guardian, 18 February 2022, https://www.theguardian.com/world/2022/feb/18/which-london-listed-russian-firms-could-be-hit-by-sanctions.
50. Joshua Chaffin, 'Expat Russians Fear Cold Front in "Londongrad"', Financial Times, 24 March 2018, https://www.ft.com/content/f4764c5e-2e9f-11e8-a34a-7e7563b0b0f4.
51. Chaffin, 'Expat Russians'.
52. Intelligence and Security Committee of Parliament, 'Russia', 21 July 2020, https://isc.independ ent.gov.uk/wp-content/uploads/2021/03/CCS207_CCS0221966010-001_Russia-Report-v02-Web_Accessible.pdf, 54.
53. Hume, 'ENRC'.
54. Oliver Morgan, 'A Gun at the Mod's Head', 18 March 2001, The Observer, https://www.theguard ian.com/business/2001/mar/18/theobserver.observerbusiness17.
55. 'US Embassy Cables: A Stormy Meeting in Kazakhstan', The Guardian, November 29, 2010, https://www.theguardian.com/world/us-embassy-cables-documents/141608.
56. Daniel Boffey, 'Mandelson's Speeches for Multi-Billion Fund Run by Andrew's Kazakh Friend', Daily Mail Online, December 5, 2010, https://www.dailymail.co.uk/news/article-1335809/Man delsons-speeches-multi-billion-fund-run-Andrews-Kazakh-friend.html.

57. Stella Roque, 'Ex-UK PM Tony Blair Advised Kazakh President for Estimated $29.1 Mil', OCCRP, 20 November 2001, https://www.occrp.org/en/daily/5169-ex-uk-pm-tony-blair-advises-kazakh-president-for-estimated-20-mil.

58. Simon Walters and Jason Lewis, 'Blair Aide Reopens Bitter Feud With Axed "Mad Cow" Mandarin—in Speech to Kazakh Dictator's Cronies', *Daily Mail*, 20 April 2013, https://www.dailymail.co.uk/news/article-2312216/Blair-aide-reopens-bitter-feud-axed-mad-cow-mandarin—speech-Kazakh-dictators-cronies.html.

59. Glen Owen, 'Alastair Campbell's Job With Dictator Was "Set Up by Tony Blair"', *Mail on Sunday*, 26 October 2013, https://www.dailymail.co.uk/news/article-2477665/Alastair-Campbells-job-dictator-set-Tony-Blair.html .

60. Forbes, 'Profile: Vladimir Kim', https://www.forbes.com/profile/vladimir-kim/. The net worth updates in real time, so may be different from the $4.6 billion that was given when the page was last accessed by the authors on 4 December 2023. Kim's net worth had hit $5 billion earlier in 2023.

61. Global Witness, *Risky Business*, 22.

62. 'Victims of Corruption', Rights and Accountability for Development (RAID), 28 January 2020, https://www.raid-uk.org/victimsofcorruption.

Chapter 7

1. Al Jazeera, 'The Cyprus Papers Undercover', 12 October 2020, https://www.youtube.com/watch?v=Oj18cya_gvw. A slightly edited version of the same remark is given at the start of the programme at 00:19; the line is transcribed here as 'They all have their reasons'.

2. Global Witness, *Blood Red Carpet: How Does the Son of the Former President of Kyrgyzstan Live in a £3.5m Surrey Mansion, Despite Convictions in His Homeland for Grand Corruption and the Attempted Murder of a UK Citizen*, March 2015, https://www.globalwitness.org/documents/17790/global_witness_blood_red_carpet_march_2015.pdf.

3. UK High Court, 'Daley V Bakiyev, England and Wales (Queen's bench Division)', 29 July 2016, https://www.casemine.com/judgement/uk/5a8ff76460d03e7f57eac0f7.

4. US Department of Justice, 'Justice Department Repatriates Forfeited Funds to the Government of the Kyrgyz Republic', 26 February 2019, https://www.justice.gov/opa/pr/justice-department-repatriates-forfeited-funds-government-kyrgyz-republic.

5. The White House, 'United States Strategy on Countering Corruption', December 2021, https://www.whitehouse.gov/wp-content/uploads/2021/12/United-States-Strategy-on-Countering-Corruption.pdf.

6. Henley & Partners, 'Residence and Citizenship by Investment', 2023, https://www.henleyglobal.com/.

7. Tristin Hopper, '"Greed" Blamed After Canada Punishes St. Kitts and Nevis', *National Post*, 28 December 2015, https://nationalpost.com/news/world/greed-blamed-as-buy-a-passport-program-lands-st-kitts-and-nevis-off-canadas-visa-waiver-list.

8. 'Conflicts of Interest and Controversial Clients: Henley & Partners' Caribbean Business', OCCRP, 18 March 2022, https://www.occrp.org/en/investigations/conflicts-of-interest-and-controversial-clients-henley-and-partners-caribbean-business.

9. OCCRP, 'Conflicts of Interest'.

10. Hannes Grassegger, 'Der Mann der keine Grenzen kennt [The man who knows no borders]', *Das Magazin*, 10 December 2022, https://www.hannesgrassegger.com/reporting/der-mann-der-keine-grenzen-kennt.

11. In response, Henley said that the company and its chairman had always 'adhered to all laws and regulations applicable in all the jurisdictions they have ever operated in and currently operate'. See OCCRP, 'Caribbean Business'.

12. FinCen, 'FinCEN Advisory—FIN-2014-A004', 20 May 2014, https://www.fincen.gov/resources/advisories/fincen-advisory-fin-2014-a004.

13. Henley said the 'full due diligence and governance responsibility' on passport applicants lay with St. Kitts and Nevis. Government of Canada, 'St. Kitts and Nevis Citizens Now Need a Visa to Travel to Canada', 22 November 2014, https://www.canada.ca/en/immigration-refugees-citizenship/news/notices/notice-kitts-nevis-citizens-need-visa-travel-canada.html.

14. OCCRP, 'Caribbean Business'.

15. OCCRP, 'Caribbean Business'.

16. Global Witness / Transparency International, 'European Getaway: Inside the Murky World of Golden Visas', 10 October 2018, https://www.globalwitness.org/en/campaigns/corruption-and-money-laundering/european-getaway/.
17. Transparency International / Global Witness, 'European Getaway', 29.
18. Luke Harding and David Pegg, 'How "Golden Passports" Firm Lays on VIP Service to Colourful List of Clients', The Guardian, 22 April 2021, https://www.theguardian.com/world/2021/apr/22/how-golden-passports-firm-lays-on-vip-service-to-colourful-list-of-clients.
19. Malta Immigration, 'Citizenship by Investment Malta', 2022, https://www.maltaimmigration.com/.
20. Nick Theodoulou, 'Malaysian Fugitive Battles Passport Revocation', Cyprus Mail, 1 September 2022, https://cyprus-mail.com/2022/09/01/malaysian-fugitive-battles-passport-revocation/.
21. The St Kitts & Nevis passport was later deactivated and was apparently never used. See Tan Xue Ying, 'Jho Low's St Kitts and Nevis Passport Deactivated—Report', The Edge-Malaysia, 8 November 2018, https://theedgemalaysia.com/article/jho-lows-st-kitts-and-nevis-passport-deactivated-%E2%80%94-report.
22. 'The Undesirables Who Tried and Failed to Buy a Maltese Passport', Times of Malta, 24 April 2021, https://timesofmalta.com/articles/view/the-undesirables-who-tried-and-failed-to-buy-a-maltese-passport.867055.
23. Lucinda Pearson, 'The Golden Visa Industry Needs Regulating Now', Transparency International EU, 29 March 2021, https://transparency.eu/the-golden-visa-industry-needs-regulating-now/.
24. Antony Barnett, '£2 Million Passport—Welcome to Britain: Dispatches', Channel 4 UK, 22 July 2019, https://www.channel4.com/press/news/ps2-million-passport-welcome-britain-dispatches.
25. These fast-track options only accelerated permanent residency, not citizenship, and only for the main applicant not their dependents. 'UK Scraps Rich Foreign Investor Visa Scheme', BBC News, 17 February 2022, https://www.bbc.co.uk/news/uk-politics-60410844.
26. Tier 1 (General) and Tier 1 (Graduate entrepreneur) were also offered.
27. Migration Advisory Committee, 'Migration Advisory Committee Annual Report 2015/16', October 2016, https://assets.publishing.service.gov.uk/government/uploads/system/uploads/attachment_data/file/562454/MAC_Annual_Report_2015-16.pdf.
28. David Pegg, 'The "Golden Visa" Deal: "We Have in Effect Been Selling Off British Citizenship to the Rich"', The Guardian, 4 July 2017, https://www.theguardian.com/uk-news/2017/jul/04/golden-visa-immigration-deal-british-citizenship-home-office.
29. Sarah Kunz, 'The UK Investor Visa: History, Aims and Controversies', University of Bristol, Policy Report 64, May 2021, https://www.bristol.ac.uk/media-library/sites/policybristol/briefings-and-reports-pdfs/2021/PolicyBristol%20State%20of%20Play%20Kunz%20T1%20investor%20visa.pdf.
30. Kunz, 'The UK Investor Visa', plus unpublished research provided by Dr Sarah Kunz, University of Bristol.
31. Susan Hawley, George Havenhand, and Tom Robinson, 'Red Carpet for Dirty Money', Spotlight on Corruption, July 2021, https://www.spotlightcorruption.org/wp-content/uploads/2021/07/Golden-Visa-Briefing.-Final1.pdf.
32. See Table 7.1.
33. KPMG, 'Private Equity Market in Kazakhstan', May 2019, https://assets.kpmg.com/content/dam/kpmg/kz/pdf/2019/09/KPMG-Private-Equity-Market-in-Kazakhstan-ENG-2019.pdf.
34. TI / Global Witness, 'European Getaway'.
35. Barnett, '£2 Million Passport'. The initial investment threshold also increased from £1 million to £2 million.
36. 'Tier 1 (Investor) Entry Clearance Visa Applications by Country of Nationality, Main Applicants', https://www.whatdotheyknow.com/request/details_of_tier_1_investor_visa#incoming-753828 (accessed 9 July 2024).
37. David Metcalf, 'The "Investor Route" to UK Citizenship Should Be Reformed', LSE British Politics and Policy, 3 November 2014, https://blogs.lse.ac.uk/politicsandpolicy/the-investor-route-to-uk-citizenship/.
38. 'Migration Advisory Committee Examines the Tier 1 (Investor) Route and Is Sceptical of the Benefits', EIN, 25 February 2014, https://www.ein.org.uk/news/migration-advisory-committee-examines-tier-1-investor-route-and-sceptical-benefits.
39. Metcalf, 'The "Investor Route"'.

40. Hawley et al., 'Red Carpet for Dirty Money'.
41. Hawley et al., 'Red Carpet for Dirty Money'.
42. Spotlight on Corruption, 'Press Release: Supreme Court Decision Highlights Abuse of the UK's Golden Visa Regime', 21 June 2023, https://www.spotlightcorruption.org/supreme-court-gol den-visa-regime/.
43. Cristina Gallardo, 'UK Scraps Golden Visas for Foreign InvestorsAmid Russian Money Crackdown', *Politico*, 17 February 2022, https://www.politico.eu/article/uk-scraps-golden-visas-for-foreign-investors-amid-dirty-money-crackdown/.
44. Hawley et al., 'Red Carpet for Dirty Money'.
45. Gallardo, 'UK Scraps Golden Visas'.
46. Hawley et al., 'Red Carpet for Dirty Money"
47. UK Parliament, 'The Tier 1 (Investor) Route: Review of Operation Between 30 June 2008 and 6 April 2015', 12 January 2023, https://questions-statements.parliament.uk/written-statements/detail/2023-01-12/hcws492.
48. Kunz, 'The UK Investor Visa'.
49. Sara Farolfi, David Pegg, and Stelios Orphanides, 'The Billionaires Investing in Cyprus in Exchange for EU Passports', *The Guardian*, 17 September 2017, https://www.theguardian.com/world/2017/sep/17/the-billionaires-investing-in-cyprus-in-exchange-for-eu-passports.
50. Maarten Vink, Luuk van der Baaren, Rainer Bauböck, Iseult Honohan and Bronwen Manby, 'GLOBALCIT Citizenship Law Dataset, v1.0, Country-Year-Mode Data (Acquisition)" Global Citizenship Observatory, 2021, https://hdl.handle.net/1814/73190.
51. Prabhu Balakrishnan, 'Antigua Citizenship for $1.5m Investment in Film Production', 21 August 2018, https://citizenshipbyinvestment.ch/index.php/2018/08/21/film-production-company-funded-by-cbi-program-in-antigua/.
52. Kunz, 'The UK Investor Visa'.
53. David Pegg, Sara Farolfi, Craig Shaw, and Michael Pereria, 'Corrupt Brazilian Tycoon Among Applicants for Portugal's Golden Visas', *The Guardian*, 18 September 2017, https://www.theg uardian.com/world/2017/sep/18/portugal-golden-visas-corrupt-brazilian-tycoon-among-app licants.
54. Axel Bugge, 'Portugal Interior Minister Resigns Over "Golden Visa Probe"', Reuters, 16 November 2014, https://www.reuters.com/article/uk-portugal-minister-idUKKCN0J00Z12 0141116.
55. Sara Farolfi, David Pegg, and Stelios Orphanides, 'Cyprus 'Selling' EU Citizenship to Super Rich of Russia and Ukraine', *The Guardian*, 17 September 2017, https://www.theguardian.com/world/2017/sep/17/cyprus-selling-eu-citizenship-to-super-rich-of-russia-and-ukraine.
56. Mark Scott, 'Europe's Having a Distress Sale on Visas', *New York Times*, 9 February 2015, http://www.nytimes.com/2015/02/10/business/europes-having-a-distress-sale-on-visas.html?_r=0+%5B
57. 'Passport Dealers of Europe: Navigating the Golden Visa Market—News', Transparency International, 6 March 2018, https://www.transparency.org/en/news/navigating-european-gol den-visas.
58. 'Cyprus's Dirty Secrets', Al Jazeera, 26 August 2020, https://www.ajiunit.com/article/cypruss-dirty-secrets/.
59. Al Jazeera, 'The Cyprus Papers Undercover', 43:30.
60. 'Malta Tightens Passport Sale Terms Under EU Pressure', BBC News, 30 January 2014, https://www.bbc.co.uk/news/world-europe-25959458.
61. Wilhelmine Preussen, 'EU Takes Malta to Court Over "Golden Passport" Program', *Politico*, 29 September 2022, https://www.politico.eu/article/eu-malta-values-not-for-sale-eu-to-court-over-golden-passports/.
62. Republic of Cyprus, ΕΚΘΕΣΗ ΤΗΣ ΕΡΕΥΝΗΤΙΚΗΣ ΕΠΙΤΡΟΠΗΣ ΤΩΝ ΚΑΤ" ΕΞΑΙΡΕΣΗ ΠΟΛΙΤΟΓΡΑΦΗΣΕΩΝ ΑΛΛΟΔΑΠΩΝ ΕΠΕΝΔΥΤΩΝ ΚΑΙ ΕΠΙΧΕΙΡΗΜΑΤΙΩΝ [Report of the Investigation Committee on the Exception of Citizenship of Foreign Investors and Businessmen]. Presided by Judge Miron Nicolatos, Lefkosia', 7 June 2021, 716, https://www.pio.gov.cy/assets/pdf/newsroom/2021/06/REPORT-NICOLATOU%20COMMITTEE_220 621.pdf
63. 'Cyprus Wrongly Issued Passports Despite Warnings, Probe Concludes', Euronews, 8 June 2021, https://www.euronews.com/2021/06/08/cyprus-wrongly-issued-passports-despite-warnings-probe-concludes.

64. 'Cyprus Accused of Selling Golden Visas to the Corrupt and Criminals', 26 August 2020, Schengen Visa Info, https://www.schengenvisainfo.com/news/cyprus-accused-of-selling-gol den-visas-to-the-corrupt-and-criminals/

65. Theodoulou, 'Malaysian Fugitive'.

66. OCCRP, 'Caribbean Business'.

67. OCCRP, 'Caribbean Business'.

68. Al-Jazeera, 'Cyprus Papers', 11:00.

69. According to lawyer Andreas Pittadjis, who was secretly filmed in the documentary. Al-Jazeera, 'Cyprus Papers', 43:30.

70. Al-Jazeera, 'Cyprus Papers', 46:45.

71. Al-Jazeera, 'Cyprus Papers', 50:40.

72. Al Jazeera, 'Cyprus Papers', 17:55.

73. Al-Jazeera, 'Cyprus Papers', 16:00.

74. Al-Jazeera, 'Cyprus Papers', 42:00.

75. Al-Jazeera, 'Cyprus Papers', 26:45.

76. In response to the documentary, Pittadjis said that he 'understood from the outset that what was proposed involved money laundering and criminal activities and that everything he did there- after amount to "fishing for more details" '. He said that when the fixers did not provide a copy of the Chinese client's passport, he made a report to Cyprus' anti-money-laundering unit.

77. Al Jazeera, 'Cyprus Papers', 16:10.

78. 'Fresh Trial for Al Jazeera Passport Sting', *Cyprus Property News*, 11 October 2023, https:// www.news.cyprus-property-buyers.com/2023/10/11/fresh-trial-for-al-jazeera-passport-sting/ id=00167845. Pittadjis will represent the other three men in the upcoming trial. Syllouris and Giovanis have pled not guilty. The third man was about to plead as we went to press.

79. Barnett, '£2 Million Passport'.

80. Barnett, '£2 Million Passport'.

81. Jack Freeland, 'Five Top Tips on UK Investor Visas', FreeMovement.org, 24 January 2021, https://freemovement.org.uk/five-top-tips-on-uk-investor-visas/.

82. Barnett, '£2 Million Passport'.

83. Barnett, '£2 Million Passport'.

84. Barnett, '£2 Million Passport'.

85. Barnett, '£2 Million Passport'.

86. TI / Global Witness, 'European Getaway'.

87. TI / Global Witness, 'European Getaway'.

88. TI / Global Witness, 'European Getaway', 41.

89. Kristin Surak, 'Who Wants to Buy a Visa? Comparing the Uptake of Residence by Investment Programs in the European Union', *Journal of Contemporary European Studies*, 30(1), 151-169. October 2020 https://doi.org/10.1080/14782804.2020.1839742; . M. Grell-Brisk, 'Eluding National Boundaries: A Case Study of Commodified Citizenship and the Transnational Capitalist Class', *Societies* 8, no. 2 (2018): 35; R. Ramtohul, '"High Net Worth" Migration in Mauritius: A Critical Analysis', *Migration Letters; Luton*, 13, no. 1 (2016): 16–32.

Chapter 8

1. 'From Russia with Cash', Channel 4, 2015, https://www.dailymotion.com/video/x3ho0n1. The real estate agent was approached by what he thought was a Russian government official who told him that the money for the property purchase had been stolen from the Russian state budget. The estate agent was referring to the fact that at that time real estate agents did not have to perform due diligence on prospective buyers, yet they still had to report suspicions of money laundering.

2. 'OE-IRM Amira Air Bombardier BD-700-1A10 Global Express (Gilles Brion)', Planespotters. net, 1 October 2010, https://www.planespotters.net/photo/150666/oe-irm-amira-air-bombard ier-bd-700-1a10-global-express.

3. Freedom For Eurasia (FFE), *Who Enabled the Uzbek Princess? Gulnara Karimova's $240 mil- lion Property Empire*, March 2023, https://freedomeurasia.org/wp-content/uploads/2023/03/ Who-Enabled-the-Uzbek-Princess-web-2.pdf, 54.

4. Mary Dejevsky, 'She Is the Jet-Setting Daughter of Uzbekistan's Notorious Dictator, and Married Into One of the Nation's Wealthiest Families. But Her Bitter Divorce Could Derail America's War on Terror. Now She Tells Her Story for the First Time', *Independent*, 7 January 2004, https://www. independent.co.uk/news/world/asia/she-is-the-jetsetting-daughter-of-uzbekistan-s-notori

ous-dictator-and-married-into-one-of-the-nation-s-wealthiest-families-but-her-bitter-divorce-could-derail-america-s-war-on-terror-now-she-tells-her-story-for-the-84765.html.

5. Ostrovksy, 'MTS Pays Premium'.

6. 'Swedish Telecom Took Shortcut in Central Asia', OCCRP, 29 December 2012, https://www.occrp.org/en/investigations/1765-swedish-telecom-took-shortcut-in-central-asia.

7. OCCRP, 'Swedish Telecom'.

8. Strictly speaking, PEPs are only people in senior positions of state power. However, for anti-money-laundering purposes, regulated sectors are meant to treat business associates and close family members of PEPs in the same manner, with mandatory enhanced due diligence. Thus, the term 'PEP' has come to mean these groups as well.

9. FFE, 'Who Enabled the Uzbek Princess?', 54.

10. 'Public Library of US Diplomacy', Wikileaks, September 2005, https://wikileaks.org/plusd/cab les/05TASHKENT2473_a.html.

11. US Department of Justice, 'United States of America V Gulnara Karimova and Bekzod Ahmedov', United States District Court Southern District of New York, 7 March 2019, https://www.justice.gov/opa/press-release/file/1141641/dl.

12. Christian Eriksson, 'Serious Fraud Office Targets Luxury Surrey Mansion Linked to the "Robber Baron" of Uzbekistan', *Finance Uncovered*, 27 January 2020, https://www.financeuncovered.org/stories/serious-fraud-office-targets-luxury-surrey-mansion-linked-to-the-robber-baron-of-uzbekistan. 'Telia Pays Nearly $1 Billion in Penalties, Resulting in the Largest-Ever FCPA Resolution', Kirkland & Ellis, 25 September 2017, https://www.kirkland.com/siteFiles/Publicati ons/Telia_Pays_Nearly_$1B_in_Penalties.pdf.

13. US Department of Justice, 'Vimpelcom Limited and Unitel LLC Enter Into Global Foreign Bribery Resolution of More than $795 Million', United States Seeks $850 Million Forfeiture in Corrupt Proceeds of Bribery Scheme', 18 February 2016, http://www.justice.gov/opa/pr/vimpel com-limited-and-unitel-llc-enter-global-foreign-bribery-resolution-more-795-million.

14. Radio Free Europe / Radio Liberty, 'Jailed Gulnara Karimova Offers $686 Million Frozen in Swiss Bank for Freedom', 26 February 2020, https://www.rferl.org/a/jailed-gulnara-karimova-offers-686-million-frozen-in-swiss-bank-for-freedom/30455680.html.

15. FFE, 'Who Enabled the Uzbek Princess?'

16. 'Valuable Artefacts Seized From Gulnara Karimova's Homes', Uzbek Forum for Human Rights, 14 January 2020, https://www.uzbekforum.org/valuable-artefacts-seized-from-gulnara-karimo vas-homes/; Radio Free Europe, 'Gulnara Karimova's Swiss Mansion Being Searched for Precious Art Objects', January 13, 2020. https://www.rferl.org/a/gulnara-karimova-s-swiss-mansion-being-searched-for-precious-art-objects/30374410.html.

17. FFE, 'Who Enabled the Uzbek Princess?'

18. 'Other Notices', *The Gazette*, 13 December 2019, https://www.thegazette.co.uk/notice/3449404.

19. Kirkland & Ellis, 'Telia Pays Nearly $1 Billion in Penalties, Resulting in the Largest-Ever FCPA Resolution', 25 September 2017, https://www.kirkland.com/siteFiles/Publications/Telia_P ays_Nearly_$1B_in_Penalties.pdf.

20. Casey Michel, 'US Postpones Seizing Gulnara Karimova's Assets', *The Diplomat*, 2 August 2016, https://thediplomat.com/2016/08/us-postpones-seizing-gulnara-karimovas-assets/

21. US Department of the Treasury, 'United States Sanctions Human Rights Abusers and Corrupt Actors Across the Globe', 21 December 2017, https://home.treasury.gov/news/press-releases/ sm0243.

22. 'UPDATE 1-Court Freezes Takilant Account in Telia-Linked Probe', Reuters, 15 October 2012, https://www.reuters.com/article/teliasonera-takilant-idUKL5E8LF9VH20121015. 'Banking Millions Frozen in Telia Affair', Sveriges Radio, 22 January 2013, https://sverigesradio.se/artikel/ 5417308.

23. Radio Free Europe / Radio Liberty, 'Swiss Announce Karimova Money-Laundering Probe', 12 March 2014, https://www.rferl.org/a/switzerland-karimova-investigation-uzbekistan-money-laundering/25294326.html.

24. Anna Callaghan, 'Raids Against Karimova Confirmed', OCCRP, 10 July 2013, https://www.occrp.org/en/daily/37-ccblog/ccblog/2049-raids-against-karimova-confirmed.

25. Callaghan, 'Raids Against Karimova Confirmed'; Sherpa, 'A Missed Opportunity: France's Return of Gulnara Karimova's Illegally Acquired Assets', 20 May 2020, https://www.asso-she rpa.org/a-missed-opportunity-frances-return-of-gulnara-karimovas-illegally-acquired-assets; 'France Returns $10 Million to Tashkent That Was "Illegally" Earned by Late Uzbek President's

Daughter', Radio Free Europe, 15 February 2022, https://www.rferl.org/a/uzbekistan-10-mill
ion-france-karimova/31704780.html.

26. Serious Fraud Office, 'Today at the High Court, the SFO Took Control of Three Luxury
Properties From Convicted Fraudster Gulnara Karimova', X [Twitter] account, 8 August 2023,
https://twitter.com/UKSFO/status/1688946105449381888.

27. Seventy-two of the 88 post-Soviet elite properties in London in our published dataset are held by
incumbents. Only three of the remaining 16 were purchased and retained by nonincumbents.

28. 'Uzbekistan's Gulnara Karimova Linked to Telecoms Scandal', BBC News, 27 November 2012,
https://www.bbc.com/news/world-asia-20311886.

29. Armenia, Azerbaijan, Belarus, Kazakhstan, Kyrgyzstan, Moldova, Russia, Tajikistan, and
Uzbekistan.

30. Alexi Mostrous, 'Prince and Oligarch's Mansion Deal', *The Times*, 10 June 2016, https://www.
thetimes.co.uk/article/prince-and-oligarch-s-mansion-deal-hflfbq0dg.

31. Author's own research (Mayne). The properties are 41 Upper Grosvenor St / 41 Reeves Mews;
42 Upper Grosvenor St; 42 Reeves Mews; Sunninghill Park, Ascot; and 27 Green Street. A sixth
property on Holland Park was used by Kulibayev's girlfriend and their children, but its ownership is unclear.

32. Global Witness, *Blood Red Carpet*.

33. Authors' own research.

34. Miranda Patrucic et al., 'Azerbaijan's Ruling Aliyev Family and Their Associates Acquired
Dozens of Prime London Properties Worth Nearly $700 Million', OCCRP, 3 October 2021,
https://www.occrp.org/en/the-pandora-papers/azerbaijans-ruling-aliyev-family-and-their-ass
ociates-acquired-dozens-of-prime-london-properties-worth-nearly-700-million.

35. Transparency International, 'Identities Revealed in First UWO Case', 10 October 2018, https://
www.transparency.org.uk/identities-revealed-first-uwo-case.

36. HM Treasury and Home Office, 'National Risk Assessment of Money Laundering and Terrorist
Financing', December 2020, 107, https://assets.publishing.service.gov.uk/media/5fdb34abe
90e071be47feb2c/NRA_2020_v1.2_FOR_PUBLICATION.pdf.

37. Channel 4, 'From Russia With Cash', 42:00. The UK's AML regulations at the time did not require estate agents to do due diligence on potential buyers, but they were still required to report
suspicions of money laundering.

38. Conor Shiling, 'RICS to Expel Agent Exposed in Channel 4 Documentary', *Estate Agent Today*,
14 September 2016, https://www.estateagenttoday.co.uk/breaking-news/2016/9/rics-to-expel-
agent-exposed-in-channel-4-documentary.

39. The Gazette, 'Other Notices'. Additional information from land registry records.

40. Mahamet, 'Thread: Karimov's Future Son-in-Law Serves Kazakh 'Big Men'', ThePoliticalForums,
17 April 2012, http://thepoliticalforums.com/threads/2856-Karimov%E2%80%99s-futureson-
in-law-serves-Kazakh-%E2%80%9CBig-men%E2%80%9D. In fact, Madumarov was President
Karimov's former son-in-law at this point, as he had been briefly married to Gulnara in 2008.

41. OCCRP, 'Swedish Telecom'.

42. FFE, 'Who Enabled the Uzbek Princess?'

43. Andy Verity, 'Gulnara Karimova: How Uzbek President's Daughter Built a £200m Property
Empire', BBC News, 13 March 2023, https://www.bbc.co.uk/news/world-64915348.

44. FFE, 'Who Enabled the Uzbek Princess?'

45. Solicitors Regulation Authority, 'Confidentiality of Client Information—Guidance', 30 June 2022,
https://www.sra.org.uk/solicitors/guidance/confidentiality-client-information/. Similarly, legal
professional privilege no longer applies 'where a lawyer's assistance has been sought to further
a crime or fraud', something referred to as the crime/fraud exemption. See 'Legal Professional
Privilege: The Law Society Guidance on Its Usage', the Fraud Lawyers Association, 9 April 2013,
https://www.thefraudlawyersassociation.org.uk/publications/Legal-Professional-Privilege-
The-Law-Society-Guidance-on-its-usage.pdf; 'Legal Professional Privilege-the Crime-Fraud
Exception', LexisNexis, 9 October 2022, https://www.lexisnexis.co.uk/legal/guidance/legal-
professional-privilege-the-crime-fraud-exception.

46. FFE, 'Who Enabled the Uzbek Princess?'

47. Certain transactions, such as property purchases, can only continue once consent has been given
by the National Crime Agency, although the transaction can continue if the legal professional
has not heard from the NCA within seven working days, with consent to continue assumed.

48. 'At Your Service', Transparency International, 24 October 2019, https://www.transparency.org.
uk/sites/default/files/pdf/publications/TIUK_AtYourService_WEB.pdf, 26.

49. Transparency International, 'At Your Service', 26.
50. Luke Harding, 'UK Law Firm Accused of Failings Over Azerbaijan Leader's Daughters' Offshore Assets', *The Guardian*, 16 May 2018, https://www.theguardian.com/world/2018/may/16/uk-law-firm-accused-of-failings-over-azerbaijan-leaders-daughters-offshore-assets.
51. Neil Rose, 'Solicitor Receives Hefty Fine in Case With Link to Panama Papers', Legal Futures, 14 January 2019, https://www.legalfutures.co.uk/latest-news/solicitor-receives-hefty-fine-in-case-with-link-to-panama-papers; Luke Harding, 'Azerbaijan Leader's Daughters Tried to Buy £60m London Home With Offshore Funds', *The Guardian*, 21 December 2018, https://www.theguardian.com/uk-news/2018/dec/21/azerbaijan-leaders-daughters-tried-to-buy-60m-lon don-home-with-offshore-funds.
52. Max Walters, 'Panama Papers Solicitor Fined £45,000', *Law Gazette*, 15 January 2019, https://www.lawgazette.co.uk/law/panama-papers-solicitor-fined-45000-/5068873.article.
53. 'Landes Limited', Companies House, 2023, https://find-and-update.company-information.serv ice.gov.uk/company/03289621/officers.
54. 'Beatrice Alliance Ltd', Companies House, 2023, https://find-and-update.company-information. service.gov.uk/.
55. 'Sherlock Holmes and the Mystery of the Kazakh Millions', SourceMaterial, 10 November 2020, https://www.source-material.org/sherlock-holmes-and-the-mystery-of-the-kazakh-millions/; Mayne and Heathershaw, *Criminality Notwithstanding*, 47.
56. 'Companies Act 2006', The National Archives, 2006, http://www.legislation.gov.uk/ukpga/2006/46/section/1112.
57. FFE, 'Who Enabled the Uzbek Princess?'
58. 'Russia & CIS', Quastels, 25 June 2021, https://web.archive.org/web/20210625012133/https://www.quastels.com/services-for-individuals/russia-cis/.
59. 'Tanya Laidlaw', Quastels, 13 September 2022, https://www.quastels.com/team/tanya-laidlaw/.
60. 'Our Team', Quastels, 3 March 2022, https://www.quastels.com/our-team/#member-1707-info.
61. Tanya Laidlaw, 'LinkedIn', https://www.linkedin.com/posts/tanya-laidlaw-1032a0191_chorno byl-europeanunion-standwithukraine-activity-6903604164472233984-FI-Y (accessed 13 May 2024). Laidlaw left Quastels in November 2023.
62. Kristian Lasslett, Fatima Kanji, and Daire Mcgill, *A Dance With the Cobra—Confronting Grand Corruption in Uzbekistan*, International State Crime Initiative, 2017, http://statecrime.org/data/2017/08/Full-Report-with-Executive-Summary.pdf, 42.
63. Natalia Antelava, 'Gulnara Karimova: How Do You Solve a Problem Like Googoosha?" BBC News, 16 January 2014, http://www.bbc.co.uk/news/magazine-25742130.
64. Eli Moskowitz, 'Switzerland to Return to Uzbekistan $131M From Karimova Accounts', OCCRP, 15 September 2020, https://www.occrp.org/en/daily/13114-switzerland-to-return-to-uzbekistan-131m-from-karimova-accounts.
65. 'Uzbekistan Seeks Buyer for Luxury Villa of Ex-Leader's Daughter', Reuters, 16 April 2021, https://www.reuters.com/world/asia-pacific/uzbekistan-seeks-buyer-luxury-villa-ex-leaders-daughter-2021-04-16/.
66. 'Part of Gulnara Karimova's Frozen Funds May Be Returned to Takilant, Justice Ministry of Uzbekistan Comments on the Case', Kun.uz, 24 December 2021, https://kun.uz/en/news/2021/12/24/part-of-gulnara-karimovas-frozen-funds-may-be-returned-to-takilant-justice-ministry-of-uzbekistan-comments-on-the-case.
67. Jamey Keaton, 'Swiss Indict Daughter of Former Uzbek President in Bribery, Money Laundering Case Involving Millions', AP News, 29 September 2023, https://apnews.com/article/karimov-daughter-uzbekistan-switzerland-money-laundering-13bab394922b35fa9fa937161b5db843.
68. 'Swedish Court Finds Former Telia CEO Not Guilty of Bribery in Uzbekistan Probe', Reuters, 15 February 2019, https://www.reuters.com/article/telia-verdict-idUSL5N20A2OP.
69. 'Registration Search For 9H-IRA', PlaneLogger.com, https://www.planelogger.com/Aircr aft/Registration/9H-IRA/819844; 'OE-IRM, Photo Date Oct 26, 2014 (Jonathan Mifsud)', JetPhotos.com, https://www.jetphotos.com/photo/8341977 (both accessed 13 May 2024).
70. 'Aircraft 9H-IRA Data', Airport-data.com, https://www.airport-data.com/aircraft/9H-IRA.html (accessed 13 May 2024).
71. 'Uzbek Authorities Seek to Freeze 50 Million Malta-Based Jet of Former Dictator's Daughter', *The Malta Independent*, 30 July 2017, https://www.independent.com.mt/articles/2017-07-29/local-news/Uzbek-authorities-seek-to-freeze-50-million-Malta-based-jet-of-former-dictator-s-daughter-6736177195.

Chapter 9

1. Dominic Casciani, 'Unexplained Wealth Order Focuses on London Mansion', BBC News, 10 March 2020, https://www.bbc.co.uk/news/uk-51809718.
2. Casciani, 'Unexplained Wealth Order'.
3. Joshua Rozenberg, 'Time to Rethink the Serious Fraud Office?', Rozenbergsubstack.com, 3 January 2023, https://rozenberg.substack.com/p/time-to-rethink-the-serious-fraud/.
4. In this chapter we will refer to the made protagonists by their first names to distinguish them from each other and from the ruling Aliyevs of Azerbaijan, who are not related.
5. *Moskovskiy komsomolets*, 16 July 2008. Translated from the Russian by the authors.
6. These were Nurbank's deputy chairman, Zholdas Timraliyev and another bank official, Aybar Khasenov. See Mayne and Heathershaw, *Criminality Notwithstanding*.
7. The mayor was Imangali Tasmagambetov. See 'Trial on Nurbank Attack Case Under Threat of Failure', *Kazakhstan Today*, 15 May 2007, https://www.kt.kz/eng/society/trial_on_nurbank_attack_case_under_threat_of_failure_1153415787.html.
8. Joanna Lillis, 'Kazakhstan: The Domestic Implications of Rakhat Aliyev's Precipitous Fall', Eurasianet, 2007, https://eurasianet.org/kazakhstan-the-domestic-implications-of-rakhat-aliyevs-precipitous-fall-0.
9. Refworld, 'Kazakhstan: Trouble Within the First Family', 29 May 2007, https://www.refworld.org/docid/46c58ee928.html.
10. Matthew Vella, 'Investigators Told of Rakhat Aliyev's Alleged Money Laundering Network', *Malta Today*, 30 July 2013, https://www.maltatoday.com.mt/news/national/28709/investigators-told-of-rakhat-aliyev-s-alleged-money-laundering-network-20130729#.Y_NX-HbP1D8.
11. Michael Nikbakhsh, 'Justizminister Brandstetter: "Da Werde Ich Zornig"', www.profil.at, 9 April 2016, https://www.profil.at/wirtschaft/justizminister-brandstetter-rakhat-aliyev-panama-6308168.
12. Tagdyr, 'The "Nurbank" Murder Case—Verein Tagdyr', 19 May 2014, https://web.archive.org/web/20140519112016/http://en.tagdyr.net/the-nurbank-murder-case/.
13. Ewen MacAskill and Luke Harding, 'Ex-Kazakhstan Official Was Not Murdered in Austrian Jail, Judge Rules', *The Guardian*, 17 December 2015, https://www.theguardian.com/world/2015/dec/17/ex-kazakhstan-was-not-murdered-in-austrian-jail-judge-rules.
14. 'Epic Murder Trial Tests Austrian Justice', BBC News, 10 July 2015, https://www.bbc.co.uk/news/world-asia-32922277.
15. BBC News, 'Epic Murder Trial'.
16. International Centre for the Settlement of Investment Disputes, 'Written Submission of a Non-Disputing Party, Submitted by Serik Medetbekov, Caratube International Oil Company LLP V The Republic of Kazakhstan', ICSID Case No. ARB/08.12, 2010, paras 8, 11 and 1.
17. Global Witness, *Mystery on Baker Street. Brutal Kazakh Official Linked to £147m London Property Empire*, https://www.globalwitness.org/documents/18036/Mystery_on_baker_street_for_digital_use_FINAL.pdf (accessed 15 May 2024). Mayne was one of the researchers on this report.
18. Global Witness, *Mystery on Baker Street.*
19. HM Treasury / Home Office, 'Action Plan for Anti-Money Laundering and Counter-Terrorist Finance', April 2016, https://assets.publishing.service.gov.uk/government/uploads/system/uploads/attachment_data/file/517993/6-2118-Action_Plan_for_Anti-Money_Laundering__print_.pdf, para 2.32.
20. 'Unexplained Wealth Orders: Guilty Until Proven Innocent?', *Lawyer Monthly*, https://www.lawyer-monthly.com/2019/10/unexplained-wealth-orders-guilty-until-proven-innocent/ (accessed 13 May 2024).
21. Benjamin Kentish, 'Oligarchs Face Being Forced to Explain Source of Their Wealth', *The Independent*, 3 February 2018, https://www.independent.co.uk/news/uk/politics/oligarchs-corruption-unexplained-wealth-order-money-laundering-russia-ben-wallace-london-a8192401.html.
22. 'The Russian Laundromat Exposed—OCCRP', OCCRP, 2017, https://www.occrp.org/en/laundromat/the-russian-laundromat-exposed/; Benjamin Kentish, "Oligarchs Suspected of Corruption Faced Being Forced to Explain Source of Their Wealth', *The Independent*, 3 February 2018, https://www.independent.co.uk/news/uk/politics/oligarchs-corruption-unexplained-wealth-order-money-laundering-russia-ben-wallace-london-a8192401.html.
23. Annie-Marie Ottaway, 'Not So Fast . . . UK Court of Appeal Denies NCA a Shot at Redemption Following First UWO Defeat', *National Law Review*, 25 June 2020, https://www.natlawreview.

com/article/not-so-fast-uk-court-appeal-denies-nca-shot-redemption-following-first-uwo-defeat.

24. Henry Foy, 'Are Unexplained Wealth Orders the Cure for Britain's Reputation as a Haven for Dirty Money?', *Financial Times*, 30 April 2018, https://www.ft.com/content/8eaf63e4-43e2-11e8-93cf-67ac3a6482fd.

25. National Crime Agency, 'Supreme Court Refuses Appeal Against Unexplained Wealth Order—National Crime Agency', 21 June 2021, https://web.archive.org/web/20210621080719/https://www.nationalcrimeagency.gov.uk/news/supreme-court-refuses-appeal-against-unexplained-wealth-order.

26. UK High Court 'NCA v AAG Trusteeship Ltd and Natura Ltd, Fifth Witness Statement of Nicola Bartlett', 2018, para 3.12(2).

27. Patrick Sawyer, 'Wife of Azeri Banker Spent £30k on Chocolates at Harrods in One Day as Part of £16m Spree', *The Telegraph*, 28 May 2019, https://www.telegraph.co.uk/news/2019/05/28/wife-azerbaijani-banker-spent-16m-harrods-bought-30k-chocolate/.

28. UK High Court, 'NCA v Zamira Hajiyeva, Witness statement of Zamira Hajiyeva', 18 May 2018; BBC News, 'Woman in £16m Harrods Spend Fights Wealth Seizure', BBC News, 12 December 2019, https://www.bbc.co.uk/news/uk-50763204.

29. Mayne and Heathershaw, *Criminality Notwithstanding*, 13.

30. Mayne and Heathershaw, *Criminality Notwithstanding*, 28.

31. Mayne and Heathershaw, *Criminality Notwithstanding*, 29.

32. Mayne and Heathershaw, *Criminality Notwithstanding*, 29.

33. Jane Croft, 'Extradition of Azeri Banker's Wife Blocked by UK Court', *Financial Times*, 26 September 2019, https://www.ft.com/content/d7fb00d8-e078-11e9-9743-db5a370481bc .

34. Mayne and Heathershaw, *Criminality Notwithstanding*, 59–60.

35. Mayne and Heathershaw, *Criminality Notwithstanding*, 57.

36. UK High Court, 'NCA v Baker et al. Approved Judgment', 8 April 2020, paras 58 and 100.

37. Mayne and Heathershaw, *Criminality Notwithstanding*.

38. Ed Smyth, 'Blog: Unexplained Wealth Orders Discharged—'Tenacious' NCA to Appeal', Kingsley Napley, 2020, https://www.kingsleynapley.co.uk/insights/blogs/criminal-law-blog/unexplained-wealth-orders-discharged-tenacious-nca-to-appeal.

39. 'NCA V Baker Judgment', para 72. He is referred to as 'President Nazarbayeva', the feminine form of the name Nazarbayev.

40. 'NCA V Baker Judgment', para 77.

41. UK Government, 'Home Secretary's Speech to the FCA's Financial Crime Conference', 14 November 2016, https://www.gov.uk/government/speeches/home-secretarys-speech-to-the-fcas-financial-crime-conference.

42. UK Government, 'Home Secretary's Speech'.

43. Micheal Holden, 'British Police Say: We're Coming After "Dirty Money" But It Might Take Time', Reuters, 10 April 2018, https://www.reuters.com/article/britain-crime-moneylaundering/british-police-say-were-coming-after-dirty-money-but-it-might-take-time-idINKBN1HH2WT?edition-redirect=in.

44. UK Government, 'United Kingdom Anti-Corruption Strategy 2017–2022 Year 2 Update', 2018, https://assets.publishing.service.gov.uk/government/uploads/system/uploads/attachment_data/file/902020/6.6451_Anti-Corruption_Strategy_Year_2_Update.pdf, 16; House of Commons, 'Unexplained Wealth Orders', 2022, https://researchbriefings.files.parliament.uk/documents/CBP-9098/CBP-9098.pdf.

45. UK High Court, 'Hajiyeva V National Crime Agency, Court of Appeal (Civil Division)', 5 February 2020, https://www.casemine.com/judgement/uk/5e3cfe8a2c94e01eb6605d1c, para 40.

46. David Pegg and Henry Dyer, 'Tory Donor's Name Removed From Kleptocracy Report After "Meritless" Libel Threat', *The Guardian*, 18 October 2022, https://www.theguardian.com/politics/2022/oct/18/tory-donors-name-removed-from-kleptocracy-report-after-meritless-libel-threat.

47. James Bayley and Emily Taylor, 'Big-Hearted Businessman Comes to Aid of Young Girl Fighting Blood Cancer', *The Mirror*, 13 November 2019, https://www.mirror.co.uk/news/uk-news/big-hearted-businessman-comes-aid-20834331; John Stevens, 'Dominic Raab Accepted £25,000 From Ex-Russian Banker Whose Money Was Shunned by Prince Charles' Charitable Foundation', *Daily Mail*, 12 November 2021, https://www.dailymail.co.uk/news/article-10196913/Dominic-Raab-accepted-25-000-ex-Russian-banker.html; Jacob Thorburn, 'Prince

Charles "Offered to Meet" Russian Banker Seeking UK Citizenship as Thanks for £535,000 Gift to Prince's Foundation—as Regulator Probes Charity's Dealings With Controversial Donor Linked to Money-Laundering', *Mail Online*, 12 September 2021, https://www.dailymail.co.uk/news/article-9982261/Prince-Charles-Gushing-letter-says-Prince-intended-meet-controversial-Russian-donor-gift.html.

48. Jake Ryan, 'Britain's FBI Targets People-Smugglers and Threatens to Seize Property', *Mail Online*, 21 November 2020, https://www.dailymail.co.uk/news/article-8973527/Britains-FBI-targets-people-smuggling-kingpins-threatens-seize-McMafia-property-portfolios.html.
49. Correspondence between the National Crime Agency and the authors, 28 January 2022.
50. 'Sherlock Holmes and the Mystery of the Kazakh Millions', SourceMaterial, 10 November 2020, https://www.source-material.org/sherlock-holmes-and-the-mystery-of-the-kazakh-millions/.
51. SourceMaterial, 'Sherlock Holmes'.
52. 'Economic Crime (Transparency and Enforcement) Act 2022', Legislation.gov.uk, 2022, https://www.legislation.gov.uk/ukpga/2022/10/contents/enacted.
53. 'Economic Crime (Transparency and Enforcement) Act 2022'.
54. 'Economic Crime (Transparency and Enforcement) Act 2022'.

Chapter 10

1. '"The Signing Ceremony That Took Place at the University of Oxford Is Comparable to the Contract of the Century in the Field of Science, Education and Culture for Azerbaijan"—Professor Nargiz Pashayeva', AZERTAC, 28 May 2018, https://azertag.az/en/xeber/1167129.
2. 'Gubad Ibadoghlu', Human Rights Commission, https://humanrightscommission.house.gov/defending-freedom-project/prisoners-by-country/Azerbaijan/Gubad-Ibadoghlu (accessed 15 May 2024).
3. 'Accusations and Political Arrest: The Case of Gubad Ibadoglu', Meyden TV English, 30 August 2023, https://www.youtube.com/watch?v=ohxYpQjKcSQ.
4. 'The Kleptocracy Strikes Back. An Azerbaijani Economist Should Be Freed', Editorial Board, *Washington Post*, 6 August 2023, https://www.washingtonpost.com/opinions/2023/08/06/azerbaijan-arrest-gubad-ibadoghlu/.
5. Interview with Arif Mammadov, September 2023.
6. '£10 Million Gift to Endow the Study of Azerbaijan, the Caucasus and Central Asia at Oxford', University of Oxford Development Office, 24 May 2018. https://www.development.ox.ac.uk/news/the-oxford-nizami-ganjavi-centre.
7. For instance, in April 2022 the Information Compliance Team of the university stated that 'the University has also received funding from the British Foundation for the Study of Azerbaijan and the Caucasus (a British organisation), further details of which can be found at https://www.development.ox.ac.uk/news/the-oxford-nizami-ganjavi-centre' (although the reference to the BFSAC as the source of funding was later removed from this link). See Information Compliance Team, 'Reply to Request for Information Under the Freedom of Information Act', University of Oxford, 5 April 2022.
8. David Matthews, 'Concern Over Azerbaijan Ruling Family Influence at Oxford Centre', *Times Higher Education*, 22 July 2021, https://www.timeshighereducation.com/news/concern-over-azerbaijan-ruling-family-influence-oxford-centre.
9. '"The Signing Ceremony", AZERTAC.
10. By the government of Azerbaijan's own account of the original contract of the century, 'Heydar Aliyev's return to the government by the request of the people in 1993 laid the foundation for important changes in the political and economic life of Azerbaijan'. See the Ministry of Energy of The Republic of Azerbaijan, 'Contract of the Century', 31 January 2020, https://minenergy.gov.az/en/neft/esrin-muqavilesi. According to academic accounts, the former Soviet politburo member and head of the Azerbaijan KGB returned to power during a political crisis prior to nationwide elections, proceeded to establish a highly corrupt and patrimonial dictatorship with a cult of personality ('Heydarism'), and gained almost complete economic control for members and clients of the Aliyev family. See David Fletcher, 'Fanfare in a Void: The Cult of Heydər Əliyev in Contemporary Azerbaijan', *Slavonic and East European Review*, 4 January 2022, https://muse.jhu.edu/pub/427/article/815988/summary; Kopeček, Vincent, 'How to Capture a State? The Case of Azerbaijan', Politicke Vedy, Univerzita Mateja Bela, 2016, https://www.ceeol.com/search/article-detail?id=376438.

11. Elizabeth Militz, 'Public Events and Nation-Building in Azerbaijan', in *Nation-Building and Identity in the Post-Soviet Space: New Tools and Approaches*, ed. Rico Isaacs and Abel Polese (London: Taylor & Francis, 2016), 176–194.

12. 'Caviar Diplomacy: How Azerbaijan Silenced the Council of Europe', European Stability Initiative, May 2012, https://www.esiweb.org/publications/caviar-diplomacy-how-azerbaijan-silenced-council-europe.

13. Swanson, 'Introduction', 5.

14. Anand Giridharadas, *Winners Take All: The Elite Charade of Changing the World* (New York: Vintage, 2019).

15. Beth Breeze, *In Defence of Philanthropy* (Newcastle upon Tyne: Agenda Publishing, 2021).

16. 'Azerbaijan: Who Owns What? Part 1—The First Lady's Family"', Wikileaks, 27 January 2010, https://wikileaks.org/plusd/cables/10BAKU54_a.html.

17. 'PASHA Group In Brief', Pasha Holding, 2023, https://pasha-holding.az/en/about-us/pasha-holding-group-in-brief/.

18. Interview with Arif Mammadov, Brussels, October 2022.

19. See e.g. Maria Zholobova, 'The Aliyevs' Nest: The Family of Azerbaijan's President Has Found a Home Near Moscow', OCCRP, 15 March 2019, https://www.occrp.org/en/investigations/the-aliyevs-nest-the-family-of-azerbaijans-president-has-found-a-home-near-moscow.

20. This is a deal that came under fire because their company offered a much lower price than an American competitor, and the requirements of the tender were changed after it had been awarded to them, to encompass a construction area that was twice as large as initially foreseen. Companies linked to the Montenegrin president's brother and sister benefited from it. See Centre for Investigative Journalism of Montenegro, 31 October 2020, http://www.cin-cg.me/sje nke-nad-azerbejdzanskom-investicijom-u-crnoj-gori-portonovi-je-vlasnistvo-cerki-predsjedn ika-azerbejdzana/.

21. Sarah Chayes, 'The Structure of Corruption in Azerbaijan', Carnegie Endowment for International Peace, June 2016, https://carnegieendowment.org/files/8_Azerbaijan_Full_W eb1.pdf; Gubad Ibadoghlu, 'Retrospective Assessment of Corruption Risks and Perspective Assessment of Future Activities of SOCAR', July 2022, https://papers.ssrn.com/sol3/papers. cfm?abstract_id=4168843.

22. For example, Aynura Farmanova, a lecturer in the Academy of Public Administration under the president of the Republic of Azerbaijan and member of the ruling New Azerbaijan Party (Yeni Azərbaycan Partiyası), wrote an article in the Russian-based journal Science and the World. See Farmanova, 'Mrs Mehriban Aliyeva's Multifaceted Activity Serves to Expand International Reputation of Azerbaijan', Russian Scientific Index, 29 July 2019, https://elibrary.ru/item. asp?id=43914048.

23. Wikileaks, 'Azerbaijan: Who Owns What? Part 1'.

24. Interview with Arif Mammadov, Brussels, October 2022.

25. President of the Republic of Azerbaijan Ilham Aliyev, 'Structure', https://president.az/en/pages/ view/administration/structure (accessed 12 September 2023).

26. Interview with Arif Mammadov, Brussels, October 2022.

27. Shahin Abbasov, 'Azerbaijan: Foundation Finances Renovations at Versailles, Strasbourg', *Eurasianet*, 26 August 2009, http://www.eurasianet.org/departments/insightb/articles/eav0827 09a.shtml.

28. ESI, 'Caviar Diplomacy'.

29. Jody LaPorte, 'Hidden in Plain Sight: Political Opposition and Hegemonic Authoritarianism in Azerbaijan', *Post-Soviet Affairs* 31, no. 4 (2015): 339–366.

30. European Stability Initiative, 'The European Swamp (Caviar Diplomacy Part 2): Prosecutors, Corruption and the Council of Europe', December 2016, https://www.esiweb.org/publications/ european-swamp-caviar-diplomacy-part-2-prosecutors-corruption-and-council-europe.

31. 'Ilham Aliyev Received Members of the Board of Trustees of Nizami Ganjavi International Center', President.az, 15 March 2017, https://president.az/en/articles/view/23123.

32. 'Baku Forum Uses Medieval Poet to Promote Human Rights', 12 February 2019, ifact.ge, https://web.archive.org/web/20200809090102/https://ifact.ge/en/baku-medieval-poet/. The Azerbaijani president's official decisions to fund the NGIC can be found at "About Activities Related to Nizami Ganjavi International Center', 23 August 2017 https://e-qanun.az/framew ork/36432 and 15 March 2018, https://e-qanun.az/framework/38328.

33. '£10 Million Gift to Endow the Study of Azerbaijan, the Caucasus and Central Asia at Oxford', University of Oxford Development Office, 24 May 2018, https://www.development.ox.ac.uk/news/the-oxford-nizami-ganjavi-centre.

34. *CASE-Ross Support of Education: United Kingdom and Ireland 2020, Generating Philanthropic Support for Higher Education*, Council for Advancement and Support of Education, 13 May 2020, https://www.case.org/system/files/media/file/CASE-Ross_2020Report_2018-19.pdf.

35. Tena Prelec, Saipira Furstenberg, John Heathershaw, and Catarina Thomson, 'Is Academic Freedom at Risk From Internationalisation? Results From a 2020 Survey of UK Social Scientists', *International Journal of Human Rights*, 26, no. 10 (2022): 1709.

36. 'How the International Education Strategy Is Championing the UK Education Sector Overseas', The Education Hub blog, 8 October 2021, https://educationhub.blog.gov.uk/2021/10/08/how-the-international-education-strategy-is-championing-the-uk-education-sector-overseas/.

37. Email communication from the Public Affairs and Communications Directorate, University of Oxford, 21 October 2021 (available in private archive).

38. Information Compliance Team, 'Reply to Request for Information'. The authors also attempted to get information from the Charity Commission as BFSAC is a charity registered in the UK. However, the foundation's financial reports were not available on the site of the Charity Commission. We eventually received these records subsequently through direct inquiry, under the Freedom of Information Act (FOIA), to the Charity Commission; and yet the documents we received had only one figure: £0. In other words, despite the £10 million donation, the financial reports of the charity were simply blank. Despite supposed transparency, charities in the UK are not required to reveal their owners nor universities their donors.

39. Information Commissioner's Notice, Freedom of Information Act 2000 (FOIA) Decision notice, Reference: IC-217933-T3T1, 18 April 2023, https://ico.org.uk/media/action-weve-taken/decision-notices/2023/4024977/ic-217933-t3t1.pdf.

40. University of Oxford, 'Reply to Request for Information Under the Freedom of Information Act', Ref 202206/888, 16 May 2023, 2.

41. It also noted that Nargiz Pashayeva is the sister-in-law of the president of Azerbaijan and that the risk of the donation was high due to the size of the gift. 'Reply to Request for Information Under the Freedom of Information Act', 2023, 4–5.

42. Information Commissioner's Notice, 6–7.

43. Alexander Dukalskis, *Making the World Safe for Dictatorship* (Oxford: Oxford University Press, 2021).

44. The ICO also states: 'It is difficult to see how anyone could attempt to exert influence by proposing, but not actually making, a donation'. Once again, there is a certain naiveté here in that showing willing is an important marker of loyalty in all systems but especially in kleptocracies'. Information Commissioner's Notice, 10.

45. Jenna Corderoy and Billy Stockwell, 'Revealed: £281m of Secret Cash Poured Into UK Universities', OpenDemocracy, 13 December 2023, https://www.opendemocracy.net/en/dark-money-investigations/uk-russell-group-universities-secret-donations-millions-lobbying/.

46. 'Information Commissioner's Notice', 8.

47. There is a near three-fold increase in philanthropic donations over the last decade (from £0.5bn to £1.3bn), but these are not split by donor or country of origin. *CASE-Ross Support of Education: United Kingdom and Ireland 2020, Generating Philanthropic Support for Higher Education*, 13 May 2020, https://www.case.org/system/files/ media/file/CASE-Ross_2020Report_2018-19.pdf.

48. 'Aliyev Family Winds Up Its UK Cultural Diplomacy Networks', Intelligence Online, 28 December 2022, https://www.intelligenceonline.com/corporate-intelligence/2022/12/28/aliyev-family-winds-up-its-uk-cultural-diplomacy-networks,109877073-eve.

49. Orbis, 'The British Foundation for the Study of Azerbaijan and the Caucasus', company report, downloaded 5 November 2021. This information was also present on the pages of the UK's Charity Commission but it was later removed from them after the dissolution of the foundation. See 'The British Foundation for the Study of Azerbaijan and the Caucasus, Charity number 1169381', Charity Commission for England and Wales, https://register-of-charities.charitycommission.gov.uk/charity-search/-/charity-details/5080778/trustees (accessed 15 May 2024).

50. His profile page on Withers LLP, the law office he is employed at, states that 'since 2019, [he has been] working . . . to defend our client, a high-profile Azerbaijani MP and businessman, in the case of a multi-million pound Account Freezing Order against the National Crime Agency. Judgement on the largest contested Account Freezing Order case to date was delivered in January

2022 by Westminster Magistrates Court'. 'Ravan Maharram—Experience', Withers Worldwide, https://www.withersworldwide.com/en-gb/people/ravan-maharram/experience-tab#details (accessed 11 September 2023).

51. Steve Swann and Dominic Casciani, 'Court Approves £5.6m Seizure Over Money Laundering', BBC, 31 January 2022, https://www.bbc.co.uk/news/uk-60203664.

52. '£10 Million Gift to Endow the Study of Azerbaijan, the Caucasus and Central Asia at Oxford', University of Oxford Development Office, 24 May 2018, https://www.development.ox.ac.uk/news/the-oxford-nizami-ganjavi-centre. For the earlier version of the same page, stating that the gift was possible 'thanks to generous philanthropic support from the British Foundation for the Study of Azerbaijan and the Caucasus (BFSAC)', see https://web.archive.org/web/20190806171712/https://www.development.ox.ac.uk/news/the-oxford-nizami-ganjavi-centre.

53. 'British Foundation for Study of Azerbaijan and Caucasus solemnly presented in London', AZERTAC, 1 February 2017, https://www.azernews.az/nation/108208.html.

54. Khalilov's own links to Russia run deep and he is part of a council promoting Azerbaijani-Russian business links. In March 2006, President Aliyev awarded Khalilov with a 'Progress Order' that includes 'contributions in the sphere of science, culture, literature, arts, public education and health'. In 2011, Aliyev attended the opening of Khalilov's hotel in Baku, giving a speech. Khalilov's sons sit on two governmental sports boards. In June 2016, Aliyev awarded Khalilov with a 'For the Service of the Fatherland' order for 'strengthening friendship between peoples and the development of the Azerbaijani diaspora'. See President of the Republic of Azerbaijan Ilham Aliyev, 'Azərbaycan diasporunun inkişafındakı xidmətlərinə görə bir qrup şəxsin təltif edilməsi haqqında Azərbaycan Respublikası Prezidentinin Sərəncamı', 2 June 2016, https://president.az/az/articles/view/20163/print; Shahin Abbasov, 'Azerbaijan: Is the Kremlin Up to Old Tricks?" *Eurasianet,* March 12, 2013. https://eurasianet.org/azerbaijan-is-the-kremlin-up-to-old-tricks.

55. Until the end of August 2023.

56. 'The Woolf Inquiry: An Inquiry Into the LSE's links With Libya and Lessons to Be Learned', London School of Economics, October 2011, https://www.lse.ac.uk/News/News-Assets/PDFs/The-Woolf-Inquiry-Report-An-Inquiry-into-LSEs-Links-with-Libya-and-Lessons-to-Be-Learned-London-School-of-Economics-and-Political-Sciences.Pdf.

57. Alexander Cooley, Tena Prelec, John Heathershaw, and Tom Mayne, 'Reputation Laundering in the University Sector of Open Societies: An International Forum Working Paper', National Endowment for Democracy, 25 May 2021, https://www.ned.org/reputation-laundering-in-the-university-sector-of-open-societies-working-paper/;Alexander Cooley, Tena Prelec, and John Heathershaw, 'Foreign Donations in the Higher Education Sector of the United States and the United Kingdom: Pathways for Reputation Laundering', *Journal of Comparative and International Higher Education* 14, no. 5 (2022): 43–79.

58. Cooley et al., 'Reputation Laundering'; Cooley et al., 'Foreign Donations'.

59. 'Wealth-X Due Diligence and Risk Mitigation in Donor Prospect Research: Overview Guide', Altrata, 12 December 2022, 1, https://altrata.com/articles/the-new-rules-of-due-diligence-in-donor-prospect-research

60. The guide goes on to point to the burden for researchers, not just to undertake the normal PEP and sanctions checks, but to 'define what is acceptable in terms of ESG [Environment, Social and Governance], DEI [Diversity, Equality and Inclusion], and other modern, critical perspectives'. There is thus a need for help: 'Internal researchers should look for third parties that can become extensions of their own in-house teams, not replacements'. Altrata, *Wealth-X Due Diligence*, 1, 3.

61. Cooley et al., 'Foreign Donations', 63.

62. 1965, amended in 1998; section 117.

63. Kate O'Keeffe, 'Education Department Investigating Harvard, Yale Over Foreign Funding', *Wall Street Journal,* 13 February 2020, https://www.wsj.com/articles/education-department-investigating-harvard-yale-over-foreign-funding-11581539042.

64. Valero de Urquia, Beatriz, 'Huawei Accused of "Reputation Laundering" After Jesus Collaboration', *Varsity,* 28 February 2020, https://www.varsity.co.uk/news/18836.

65. Saipira Furstenberg, Tena Prelec, and John Heathershaw, 'The Internationalization of Universities and the Repression of Academic Freedom', Freedom House, Special Report 2020, https://freedomhouse.org/report/special-report/2020/internationalization-universities-and-repression-academic-freedom.

66. We have concealed details of this project to protect our interviewee. The prohibition on the use of the word 'authoritarian' and the surveillance were made independently by two other

participants in the project. Instead, they were directly instructed to use 'strong leadership' in their outputs and presentations. In this case, the programme was funded by the UK, but it was conducted in partnership with several regime-connected universities in countries that are all widely regarded as authoritarian by social scientists studying the region. Many academics shy away from the use of the word 'authoritarian' for both its pejorative connotations and limited explanatory power. However, there is a certain irony in compelling that the term is not used.

67. In 2014, Heathershaw's colleague Alexander Sodiqov was imprisoned for 36 days in Tajikistan after being detained while conducting an interview with a civil society leader. See John Heathershaw and Parviz Mullojonov. 'The Politics and Ethics of Fieldwork in Post-Conflict Environments: The Dilemmas of a Vocational Approach', in *Doing Fieldwork in Areas of International Intervention*, ed. Berit Blisemann de Guevara and Morten Bøås (Bristol: Bristol University Press, 2020), 93–112.

68. Email from Edmund Herzig to the author, used with permission. Herzig's response stated that 'The ONGC has a board of management whose composition and remit are designed to guarantee that (Oxford) academics drawn from several parts of the collegiate university retain control of the work and academic direction of the Centre. Five of the Board's seven members are nominated by Oxford faculties and divisions, two by BFSAC, one of the latter being Professor Pashayeva and the other being a UK academic. That board reports to the Faculty Board of Oriental Studies and upwards through the Humanities Division to the University level'.

69. 'Events', Oxford Nizami Ganjavi Centre, 2023, https://www.ongc.ox.ac.uk/events.

70. Email from UK-based Armenian scholar, used with permission.

71. The visiting research fellow at the ONGC and the only one directly working on Karabakh is Kamal Imranli-Lowe, a historian whose project addresses 'perceptions of the Albanian homeland, church, and identity', see Oxford Nizami Ganjavi Centre, 'Kamala Imranli-Lowe', https://www.ongc.ox.ac.uk/people/kamala-imranli-lowe (accessed 15 May 2024). The claim cited in the text is one that Imranli-Lowe has made repeatedly in published work. See Kamala Imranli-Lowe, 'Karabakh', in *The Nagorno-Karabakh Conflict: Historical and Political Perspectives*, ed. M. H. Yavuz and M. Gunter (London: Routledge, 2022), 18–19; see also Kamala Imranli-Lowe, 'The Polities of the Caucasus and the Regional Powers in the Medieval and Early Modern Period', *Caucasus Survey* 8, no. 3 (2020): 258–277.

72. Alexander Morrison, email to the authors, 13 September 2023.

73. Tomila Lankina, X/Twitter post, 26 July 2023, https://twitter.com/TomilaLankina/status/1684 262603822882816.

74. Gitika Ahuja, 'Saudi Prince Donates $40 Million to Harvard, Georgetown Universities', *ABC News*, 13 December 2005, https://abcnews.go.com/International/story?id=1402008.

75. Cooley et al., 'Foreign Donations'.

76. Taras Kuzio, 'The Ukrainian Diaspora as a Recipient of Oligarchic Cash', *New Eastern Europe*, 26 August 2016, https://neweasterneurope.eu/2016/08/26/the-ukrainian-diaspora-as-a-recipient-of-oligarchic-cash/.

77. 'UK Judge Dismisses Firtash Libel Law Suit Against Kyiv Post', *Kyiv Post*, 24 February 2011, https://archive.kyivpost.com/article/content/ukraine-politics/uk-judge-dismisses-firtash-libel-lawsuit-against-k-98219.html.

78. Andrew Griffin, Jesse Waldman, and Tristan Dunn, 'University Donations Enable Libel Tourism', *Varsity*, 27 January 2011, https://www.varsity.co.uk/news/3112.

79. 'Statement on Funding Related to Russia and Ukraine', University of Cambridge, March 2022, https://www.cam.ac.uk/notices/news/statement-on-funding-related-to-russia-and-ukraine.

80. Mark Vandevelde and Paul Murphy, 'LetterOne Chair Mervyn Davies Receives Bumper Payout After Russian Oligarchs' Exit', *Financial Times*, 9 June 2023, https://www.ft.com/content/d4641 ba3-74f9-4e48-916b-c76ad0afe846.

81. Special Counsel Robert S. Mueller, III, *Report on the Investigation Into Russian Interference in the 2016 Presidential Election*, Volume I of II, March 2019, https://www.justice.gov/archives/sco/file/1373816/download.

82. EU Council, 'Council Implementing Regulation (EU) 2022/336', 28 February 2022, https://eur-lex.europa.eu/legal-content/EN/TXT/PDF/?uri=CELEX:32022R0336#:~:text=Gen der%3A%20Male%20Petr%20Aven%20is%20one%20of%20Vladimir%20Putin"s%20clos est%20oligarchs.

83. Available in private archive, 6 September 2019.

84. Available in private archive, 6 September 2019.

85. University of Cambridge, 'Statement on Funding'.

86. In 2023 the company appointed Brandon Lewis MP, a former chair of the Conservative Party and briefly member of the cabinet of Lis Truss, as an advisor. The role was reported to earn Lewis £250,000 alongside his day job as the member of parliament for Great Yarmouth in eastern England. See Rowena Mason, 'Tory Party's Ex-Chair to Be Paid to Advise Firm With Links to Sanctions-Hit Russians', *The Guardian*, 17 November 2023, https://www.theguardian.com/politics/2023/nov/17/ex-tory-party-chair-to-be-paid-to-advise-firm-with-ties-to-sanctioned-russians.

87. Emails available at 'EFT—A Freedom of Information Request', WhatDoTheyKnow, https://www.whatdotheyknow.com/request/eft (accessed 8 September 2023).

88. AZERTAC, 'British Foundation for Study of Azerbaijan'.

89. ESI, 'Caviar Diplomacy'.

90. The Rt Hon Lord Bruce of Bennachie Kt PC, Letter to the Rt Hon Dominic Raab MP, 2020, available at https://www.facebook.com/emin.milli/posts/3419781664784310 (accessed 12 September 2023).

91. Thomas De Waal, 'A Tragic Endgame in Karabakh', Carnegie Europe, 22 September 2023, https://carnegieeurope.eu/2023/09/22/tragic-endgame-in-karabakh-pub-90620.

92. In a comment to *The Cherwell*, Oxford's student newspaper, Lord Bruce wrote that his 'only interest was and remains in securing a long-term settlement and improvement in Azerbaijan-Armenia relations', and stated that he has 'been critical of the regime in Azerbaijan and the lack of free and fair elections'. See Antelm, 'Oxford Centre'.

93. Prelec et al., 'Is Academic Freedom at Risk From Internationalisation?"

94. Prelec et al., 'Is Academic Freedom at Risk From Internationalisation?"

95. 'The Tale of Two Countries Working Toward Sustainable Development', *Whytt Magazine*, 3 June 2023, https://london.mfa.gov.az/en/news/3229/the-tale-of-two-countries-working-toward-sustainable-development?

96. However, Oxford has received greater gifts since 2000, including larger donations from those whose wealth also stems from former Soviet oil fields. For example, Leonard Blavatnik's £75 million donation to establish the Blavatnik School of Government in 2010 was described by then Oxford chancellor Chris Patten as 'a once-in-a-century opportunity for Oxford'. 'School of Government Launched at Oxford University', BBC, 20 September 2010, https://www.bbc.co.uk/news/uk-england-oxfordshire-11370396.

97. Jesse Norman X/Twitter post, 17 June 2023, https://twitter.com/Jesse_Norman/status/1670084311901523969; see also Corderoy and Stockwell, 'Revealed: £281m'.

98. Suzanne Antelme, 'Oxford Centre With Mystery £10M Donor and Family Links to Autocratic Ruler Silent on Regime's Imprisonment of LSE Academic', *Cherwell*, 16 October 2023, https://cherwell.org/2023/10/16/oxford-centre-mystery-10m-donor-family-links-to-autocratic-ruler-silent-on-imprisonment-lse-academic/.

Chapter 11

1. ESI, 'Caviar Diplomacy'.

2. Leus's total accepted donations are £54,500 according to the Electoral Commission Database. See 'Donations', Electoral Commission, 2023, https://search.electoralcommission.org.uk/Search/Donations?currentPage=1&rows=10&query=leus&sort=AcceptedDate&order=desc&tab=1&et=rd&isIrishSourceYes=true&isIrishSourceNo=true&prePoll=false&postPoll=true°ister=none&optCols=IsAggregation; 'The Register of Members' Financial Interests as at 1 November 2021', UK Parliament, 5 November 2021, https://publications.parliament.uk/pa/cm/cmregmem/211101/contents.htm.

3. Gabriel Pogrund and Dipesh Gadher, 'Prince Charles Offered to Meet Controversial Russian Donor', *The Sunday Times*, 12 September 2021, https://www.thetimes.co.uk/article/prince-charles-offered-to-meet-controversial-russian-donor-0xpc3v30k#Echobox=1631382807; Times Politics, 'Leus Made His Donations Only After Bortrick Promised He Would Get a Private Meeting With Charles at a Scottish Castle in Return the Prince's Foundation Accepted the Money From Leus via an Intermediary, a UK Foundation Belonging to a Saudi Businessman but Controlled by Bortrick', Twitter, 11 September 2021, https://twitter.com/timespolitics/status/1436750414104379399?lang=de.

4. Dyer, 'Former Russian Banker Dmitry Leus Who Donated £25,000 to Dominic Raab Is 'Absolutely Dependent on the FSB', MP Claims'. Leus vehemently denies this claim and there is no evidence in the public domain to corroborate it.

5. Crude Accountability, *Politically Motived? The Story of Dmitry Leus*, June 2024, https://crud eaccountability.org/wp-content/uploads/Politically-motivated-story-dmitry-leus-web.pdf.

6. 'Prigovor Imenem Possiiskoi Federatsii, 9 marta 2004 goda, gor. Moskva, Leusa Dmitriya Isaakovicha & Garabaeva Murada Redjepovicha' ['Sentence issued in the name of the Russian Federation of Dmitry Isaakovich Leus and Murad Redjepovich Garabaev', dated 9 March 2004, Moscow]'. The prosecution doubted the Vietnamese man was present at the bank, and that Leus had orchestrated the transfer through a shell company he controlled at his own bank. The Vietnamese man in question said he did not open an account at the bank, but had lent his passport to a friend.

7. 'Po Delu Bankira Kakayeva Privlechen Shofer Burshteyn', Kommersant, 15 December 2009, https://www.kommersant.ru/doc/1292791.

8. Kommersant, 'Po Delu Bankira'.

9. 'Prigovor Leusa Dmitriya Isaakovicha', 2004.

10. This was established during Leus's criminal trial in 2004. See 'Prigovor Imenem Possiiskoi Federatsii, 9 marta 2004 goda'. Leus maintained that it was the receiving bank's responsibility to draw up the documentation, but surely, had the transaction been above board, Leus's bank would have insisted on documentation, as without it there was no record or confirmation that the money had actually been transferred.

11. Pegg and Dyer, 'Tory Donor's Name Removed'.

12. Crude Accountability, *Politically Motived?*, 48–50.

13. Pegg and Dyer, 'Tory Donor's Name Removed'. A further report was commissioned by Leus's lawyers from Professor William Bowring, one of the UK's leading experts on Russian criminal law. Bowring cites the judge who struck out Leus's conviction, who took account of the fact that Leus had two children, had behaved well since his conviction and parole, and because his criminal record was interfering with his work as a banker. Bowring concludes that Leus was not obliged to disclose his previous conviction for any purpose in Russia following the striking out.

14. Crude Accountability, *Politically Motived?*, 44–45.

15. Kate Mansey and Mark Hollingsworth, 'New Riddle Over Missing £500,000: Russian Banker Donated Cash for Prince Charles's Foundation—Yet a Year On, £200,000 Is With One Society Fixer, £100,000 With Another and the Charity Has Nothing', *Daily Mail*, 11 September 2021, https://www.dailymail.co.uk/news/article-9981415/New-riddle-missing-500-000-Russian-ban ker-donated-cash-Prince-Charless-foundation.html.

16. This quote appears in the chapter of a biography of Leus being written which was sent to Chatham House by its author following the publication of a report coauthored by the three present authors and colleague in which Leus's case was featured. The report was excised of all mentions of Leus by Chatham House after legal threats were made by Leus and his lawyers Vardags. See Chapter 13. The biography is apparently being written by Simon Lee, former vice chancellor of Leeds Metropolitan University. Lee resigned from his post at Leeds Metropolitan in 2009 amidst allegations of bullying. Further allegations of excessive expense claims by Lee and his wife, who was not a member of staff, but acted as an informal 'ambassador' for Leeds Met, led to a statement of concern from the then universities minister, David Willets. An investigation by KPMG found that staff, including Lee, bought items on university purchase cards without supplying receipts to justify the expenditure, but found no evidence of wrongdoing by Lee or his wife. The unreceipted expenditures counted for around 10% of Lee's nonfuel expenses, totalling about £7,500. There was also lack of evidence of formal approval of Lee's wife's overseas trips, three of which were completed without her husband. Lee is currently professor at Aston University. See Chris Brooke, 'Auditors Called in Over Bill for Exotic Holidays Taken by Former University Chief's Wife', *The Daily Mail*, 23 April 2009, https://www.dailymail.co.uk/news/arti cle-1172594/Auditors-called-exotic-holidays-taken-university-chiefs-wife.html; https://bulli edacademics.blogspot.com/2009/02/ultimatum-leeds-met-put-to-its-vice.html; 'Leeds Met Expenses Probe "Exonerates" Lee', *Times Higher Education*, 11 September 2009, https://www. timeshighereducation.com/news/leeds-met-expenses-probe-exonerates-lee/408114.article.

17. He retained shares in Russian Depository Bank, which he later sold for $3.5 million. He then—in 2006, the same year as his release from prison—bought shares in another bank, Zapadny ("Western") for $3 million which he sold seven years later for £13.5 million. Crude Accountability, *Politically Motived?*, 62, 68.

18. Crude Accountability, *Politically Motived?*, 62.

19. Alena Ledeneva, *Can Russia Modernise? Sistema, Power Networks and Informal Governance* (Cambridge: Cambridge University Press, 2013).

20. Dawisha, *Putin's Kleptocracy*; Belton, *Putin's People*.

21. For the avoidance of doubt, we are not claiming that Leus was a Putin loyalist or even that there are serious grounds to believe that he was. We are saying that his business activities before and after his time are consistent with those of a relatively junior person of the *Sistema*, regardless of whether his original conviction was legitimate. There are therefore probable grounds for investigating whether he is a Putin loyalist and owes his wealth to Putin's kleptocracy. Furthermore, those that enabled Leus and/or received his donations have not investigated these sources of wealth properly.

22. Companies House, 'Imperium Investments Ltd Filing History—Find and Update Company Information', 2023, https://find-and-update.company-information.service.gov.uk/company/10827538/filing-history.

23. James and Taylor, 'Big-Hearted Businessman Comes to the Aid of Young Girl Fighting Blood Cancer'.

24. Charlotte Gosling, 'Kind-Hearted CEO Donates to Runnymede Foodbank During Pandemic', *SurreyLive*, 26 May 2020, https://www.getsurrey.co.uk/special-features/kind-hearted-ceo-donates-runnymede-18276703.

25. Jacob Thoburn, 'Prince Charles "Offered to Meet" Russian Banker Seeking UK Citizenship as Thanks for £535,000 Gift to Prince's Foundation—as Regulator Probes Charity's Dealings With Controversial Donor Linked to Money-Laundering', *Daily Mail*, 13 September 2021, https://www.dailymail.co.uk/news/article-9982261/Prince-Charles-Gushing-letter-says-Prince-intended-meet-controversial-Russian-donor-gift.html

26. Thoburn, 'Prince Charles "Offered to Meet" Russian Banker', 2021.

27. Pogrund and Gadher, 'Prince Charles Offered'; Times Politics, 'Leus Made His Donations Only After Bortrick Promised He Would Get a Private Meeting With Charles'.

28. Times Politics, 'Leus Made His Donations'.

29. Kate Mansey and Mark Hollingsworth, '"£200k of My Donation to Charles's Charity Has Been Effectively STOLEN": Pressure on Prince and His Aides Grows as Furious Banker Claims "Gift" to Royal's Scottish Project Was Declined After Ethics Committee Branded Him Unsuitable—But NOT Fully Returned', *Daily Mail*, 27 August 2022, https://www.dailymail.co.uk/news/article-11152835/Middlemen-stole-200-000-ex-bankers-donation-Prince-Charles-charity-money-rejected.html.

30. Mansey and Hollingsworth, 'New Riddle Over Missing £500,000'.

31. Companies House, 'Leus Family Foundation', 2023, https://find-and-update.company-information.service.gov.uk/company/11348643/filing-history. See filing dated 23 November 2020.

32. Companies House, 'Leus Family Foundation'.

33. Gabriel Pogrund, Dipesh Gadher, and Roya Nikkhah, 'The Russian Banker, the Royal Fixers and a £500,000 Riddle', *The Times*, 11 September 2021, https://www.thetimes.co.uk/article/the-russian-banker-the-royal-fixers-and-a-500-000-riddle-vvgc55b2s.

34. Electoral Commission, 'Register of Political Party Donations and Loans in Great Britain', 2023, https://www.electoralcommission.org.uk/political-party-donations-and-loans-great-britain.

35. UK Parliament, 'House of Commons Session 2021–22'; Jim Fitzpatrick, 'Tory Donor "Reliant on Russia's FSB" Has Name Removed From Kleptocracy Report', *openDemocracy*, 19 October 2022, https://www.opendemocracy.net/en/dmitry-leus-chatham-house-conservative-donor-dominic-raab-russia-fsb-intellience/.

36. Henry Dyer, 'Former Russian Banker and Tory Donor Dmitry Leus Was President of a Conservative Party Association', *Business Insider*, 3 May 2022, https://www.businessinsider.com/ex-russian-banker-and-donor-made-president-of-tory-association-2022-3?r=US&IR=T.

37. Dmitry Leus, 'Application for Settled Status Under the EU Settlement Scheme', Mishcon de Reya, September 2020. A copy of the letter was seen by the authors.

38. John Stevens, 'Dominic Raab Accepted £25,000 From Ex-Russian Banker Whose Money Was Shunned by Prince Charles's Charitable Foundation', *Daily Mail*, 12 November 2021, https://www.dailymail.co.uk/news/article-10196913/Dominic-Raab-accepted-25-000-ex-Russian-banker.html.

39. Mikey Smith, 'Exclusive: Foreign Secretary Dominic Raab Takes £25,000 in Donations From Former Russian Bank Chief', *Mirror*, 30 July 2021, https://www.mirror.co.uk/news/politics/foreign-secretary-dominic-raab-takes-24655257.

40. John Stevens, Jason Groves, and Jake Hurfurt, 'Revealed: Russian Oligarch's Wife Paid £135,000 for Dinner With Theresa May and SIX Female Cabinet Ministers to Be Pictured With Them at a Hotel That Is the Favourite of Royals', *Daily Mail*, 1 May 2019, https://www.dailymail.co.uk/

news/article-6976843/Its-Ladies-night-Theresa-Cabinet-rivals-Brexit-feud-one-London-hotel.html.

41. Gabriel Pogrund and Henry Zeffman, 'The Tory Donors With Access to Boris Johnson's Top Team', *The Sunday Times*, 20 February 2022, https://www.thetimes.co.uk/article/the-ultra-rich-tory-donors-with-access-to-boris-johnsons-top-team-96bvcwcxl.

42. Harry Davies and Luke Harding, 'Revealed: Top Female Tory Donor's Vast Offshore Empire With Husband', *The Guardian*, 4 October 2021, https://www.theguardian.com/news/2021/oct/04/tory-party-top-female-donor-lubov-chernukhin-vast-offshore-empire-husband.

43. Davies and Harding, 'Revealed: Top Female Tory Donor's'.

44. Pandora Papers, 'Questions Over Tory Donations by Ex-Russian Minister's Wife', *BBC*, 4 October 2021, https://www.bbc.co.uk/news/uk-politics-58711151.

45. Jon Ungeod-Thomas, 'Russian-Born Husband of Tory Donor "Earned Millions via Oligarch Connections"', *The Guardian*, 26 March 2022, https://www.theguardian.com/world/2022/mar/26/russian-born-husband-of-tory-donor-earned-millions-via-oligarch-connections.

46. Ungeod-Thomas, 'Russian-Born Husband'.

47. Pandora Papers, 'Questions Over Tory Donations', 2021. As Vnesheconombank was funding the project, this was arguably a conflict of interest on behalf of Chernukhin. In response to a BBC documentary that reported on these allegations, lawyers for the Chernukhins disputed the characterization of Chernukhin's testimony and said, 'the suggestion that he acted improperly whilst an official of the state is wholly untrue' and he 'has not accumulated his wealth. . . . in a corrupt manner'.

48. Luke Harding, 'Tory Donor's Husband 'Given $8m by Kremlin-Linked Oligarch', *The Guardian*, 21 September 2020. https://www.theguardian.com/politics/2020/sep/21/tory-donors-husband-given-8m-by-kremlin-linked-oligarch.

49. Harding, 'Tory Donor's Husband', 2020.

50. The company was connected to Kerimov through its directors, and the website of one of the designers involved in renovating the property identified the clients (in other words, the owners of the property) as 'Mr and Mrs K'. Liubov Chernukhin told reports that she 'does not recall consenting in writing' to being a director of this firm. Jack Wright, 'Ukraine War: Major Tory Donor 'Listed as Director of Firm Secretly Owned by Oligarch Close to Putin'', *Daily Mail*, 21 April 2022, https://www.dailymail.co.uk/news/article-10738175/Ukraine-war-Major-Tory-donor-listed-director-firm-secretly-owned-oligarch-close-Putin.html.

51. Harding, 'Tory Donor's Husband'.

52. Harding, 'Tory Donor's Husband'.

53. Davies and Harding, 'Revealed: Top Female Tory Donor's'.

54. Davies and Harding, 'Revealed: Top Female Tory Donor's'.

55. This is a documented instance of upstream enabling in this field. Volontè worked with his PACE colleague, Elkhan Suleymanov, an Azerbaijani politician and the man charged with the task of improving the country's image in Europe by Azerbaijan's President Aliyev. Volontè subsequently persuaded his party to vote against a 2013 report by the council that highlighted Azerbaijan's political prisoners. See Luke Harding, Caelain Barr, and Dina Nagapetyants, 'UK at Centre of Secret $3bn Azerbaijani Money Laundering and Lobbying Scheme', *The Guardian*, 4 September 2017, https://www.theguardian.com/world/2017/sep/04/uk-at-centre-of-secret-3bn-azerbaijani-money-laundering-and-lobbying-scheme.

56. Zdravko Ljubas, 'Italian Court Sentences Former Council of Europe MP for Bribery', OCCRP, 14 January 2021.
    https://www.occrp.org/en/daily/13628-italian-court-sentences-former-council-of-europe-mp-for-bribery.

57. Gabriel Gatehouse, 'Marine Le Pen: Who's Funding France's Far Right?', *BBC*, 3 April 2017, https://www.bbc.co.uk/news/world-europe-39478066.

58. Alberto Nardelli, 'Revealed: The Explosive Secret Recording That Shows How Russia Tried to Funnel Millions to the "European Trump"', *BuzzFeed News*, 10 July 2019. https://www.buzzfeednews.com/article/albertonardelli/salvini-russia-oil-deal-secret-recording. Italian investigators started investigating these claims in 2019. In January 2023, however, the Public Prosecutor's Office in Milan announced that they were filing a motion to dismiss, because the inquiry did not bring enough evidence about the exact way in which the oil deal would have financed Salvini's party. See Lorenzo Tondo, 'Italian Prosecutors Investigate League Over Alleged Russian Oil Deal Claims', *The Guardian*, 11 July 2019. https://www.theguardian.com/world/2019/jul/11/matteo-salvinis-party-under-investigation-for-alleged-russian-oil-deal;

'La Procura di Milano ha chiesto l'archiviazione della presunta trattativa per far arrivare fondi illegali dalla Russia alla Lega' ('Milan's Public Prosecutor has brought a motion to dismiss the inquiry into alleged illegal donations from Russia to the League'), *Il Post*, 17 January 2023, https://www.ilpost.it/2023/01/17/lega-russia-archiviazione/.

59. For example, see 'Lifting the Lid on Lobbying', Transparency International, 2015 https://www.transparency.org.uk/sites/default/files/pdf/publications/TI-UK_Lifting_the_Lid_on_Lobbying.pdf; 'In Whose Interest', Transparency International, 2018, https://www.transparency.org.uk/sites/default/files/pdf/publications/In_Whose_Interest_WEB3.pdf.

60. James Dowsett and Thomas Rowley, 'Revealed: Tory MP Was "Fed" Propaganda by Azerbaijani Embassy for Parliamentary Debates', *Open Democracy*, 4 February 2022, https://www.opendemocracy.net/en/opendemocracyuk/bob-blackman-azerbaijan-lobbying-javanshir-feyziyev/.

61. Office for Democratic Institutions and Human Rights, 'DIHR Election Observation Mission Final Report', 9 February 2020, https://www.osce.org/files/f/documents/7/e/457585_0.pdf.

62. Dowsett and Rowley, 'Revealed: Tory MP', 2022.

63. 'US Embassy Cables: Azerbaijan Minister Trying to Ape Abramovich, Says US', *The Guardian*, 6 December 2020, https://www.theguardian.com/world/us-embassy-cables-documents/250614.

64. 'Tweet Action! Exposing MP's Links With the Aliyev Regime', Platform London, https://platformlondon.org/teas/ (accessed 15 May 2024).

65. Jamie Doward and Charlotte Latimer, 'Plush Hotels and Caviar Diplomacy: How Azerbaijan's Elite Wooed MPs', *The Guardian*, 24 November 2013, https://www.theguardian.com/world/2013/nov/24/azerbaijan-caviar-diplomacy-for-mps.

66. Transparency International, 'In Whose Interest?', 5.

67. Catherine Neilan, 'Tory MPs Accepted Donations Worth Thousands From Mystery Donors', *Tortoise*, 19 January 2023, https://www.tortoisemedia.com/2023/01/09/tory-mps-accepted-donations-worth-thousands-from-mystery-donors.

68. The ONS (2020) estimates that Britons born in Russia number 73,000.

69. Seth Thévoz and Peter Geoghegan, 'Revealed: Russian Donors Have Stepped Up Tory Funding', *OpenDemocracy*, 5 November 2019, https://www.opendemocracy.net/en/dark-money-investigations/revealed-russian-donors-have-stepped-tory-funding.

70. Unpublished interview with Dmitry Leus conducted by Simon Lee.

71. The Electoral Commission, 'Political Party Donations and Loans in Great Britain', 2023. https://www.electoralcommission.org.uk/political-party-donations-and-loans-great-britain.

72. Tom Burgis, Sebastian Payne, Kadhim Shubber, Jim Pickard, Jasmine Cameron-Chileshe, and George Parker, 'Inside Boris Johnson's Money Network', *Financial Times*, 30 July 2021, https://www.ft.com/content/8c6041ff-a223-43e9-9e45-53c3f7cf47f7.

73. Peter L. Francia, John C. Green, Paul S. Herrnson, Lynda W. Powell, and Clyde Wilcox, *The Financiers of Congressional Elections: Investors, Ideologues, and Intimates* (New York: Columbia University Press, 2017).

74. Iain Mcmenamin, 'Introduction', in *If Money Talks, What Does It Say? Corruption and Business Financing of Political Parties* (Oxford: Oxford University Press 2013), 1–5.

75. Sam Power, 'Introduction: Party Funding and Corruption in Advanced Industrial Democracies', in *Party Funding and Corruption: Political Corruption and Governance* (London: Palgrave Macmillan, 2020), 8..

76. Iain McMenamin, 'Party Identification, the Policy Space and Business Donations to Political Parties', *Political Studies* 68, no. 2 (2019): 293–310.

77. Mark Hollingsworth, 'The Russian Banker Who Used Donations to Prince Charles's Charity in His Bid for UK Residency', *Daily Mail*, 18 August 2021, https://www.dailymail.co.uk/news/article-9936469/Russian-banker-used-donations-Prince-Charless-charity-bid-UK-residency.html. Mishcon's letter was written before the foundation attempted to return the donation to Leus.

78. Crude Accountability, *Politically Motivated?*, 3.

Chapter 12

1. Foreign Policy Centre, 'Anti-SLAPP conference, DAY 1: Anti-SLAPP Conference "Spotlighting Solutions"', YouTube, https://www.youtube.com/watch?v=yLBysMRrtRQ&t=2950s (accessed 15 May 2024).

2. 'Our Executive Team', Arcanum Global, 2023, https://arcanumglobal.com/arcanum-team/our-leadership-team/.

3. For example, Cooley and Heathershaw, *Dictators Without Borders*, 54–79.

4. Tom Burgis, 'Spies, Lies and the Oligarch: Inside London's Booming Secrets Industry', *Financial Times*, 28 September 2017, https://www.ft.com/content/1411b1a0-a310-11e7-9e4f-7f5e6 a7c98a2.

5. Burgis, 'Spies, Lies and the Oligarch'.

6. Arcanum deny these allegations. They said to the FT: 'Swiss prosecutors did not lodge any complaints against Arcanum as their examination found the accusations baseless'. Burgis, 'Spies, Lies and the Oligarch'.

7. In the US, for example, George Washington was using agents before the founding of the republic.

8. Cooley and Heathershaw, *Dictators Without Borders*, 69–71.

9. Burgis, *Kleptopia*.

10. 'Mukhtar Ablyazov Loses Refugee Status by Decision of French Court', 12 December 2022, Kaztag.kz, https://kaztag.kz/en/news/mukhtar-ablyazov-loses-refugee-status-by-decision-of-french-court.

11. Katherine H. Parker, 'Opinion and Order', *City of Almaty V. Ablyazov*, 15-CV-05345 (AJN) (KHP) (S.D.N.Y. July 3, 2019), https://casetext.com/case/city-of-kaz-v-ablyazov-9?resultsNav= false, 3.

12. Burgis, 'Spies, Lies and the Oligarch'. Beketayev was director of ENRC from 2008 to 2014. In October 2023, he was arrested in Kazakhstan on corruption charges.

13. Parker, 'Opinion and Order'.

14. *City of Almaty V. Ablyazov*, 15-CV-05345 (AJN) (KHP) (S.D.N.Y. Jul. 3, 2019), 4, 5, and 7.

15. *City of Almaty V. Ablyazov*, 2020 WL 13558984 (S.D.N.Y. May 19, 2020).

16. For a discussion see Burgis, *Kleptopia*, 44, n.395.

17. City of Almaty, Kazakhstan, and BTA Bank JSC, Plaintiffs, V. Felix Sater, United States District Court, S.D. New York, 6 May 2022, https://casetext.com/case/city-of-almaty-v-sater-19.

18. City of Almaty, Kazakhstan, and BTA Bank JSC.

19. City of Almaty, Kazakhstan, and BTA Bank JSC.

20. City of Almaty, Kazakhstan, and BTA Bank JSC.

21. Kazkommertsbank was itself later merged with Halyk, Kazakhstan's largest bank, which is owned by Timur Kulibayev and Dinara Nazarbayeva. As noted in Chapter 3, Rakishev helped broker Kulibayev's purchase of Prince Andrew's house.

22. United States District Court Southern District of New York. 'City of Almaty, Kazakhstan and BTA BANK JSC, Plaintiffs, -against- Felix Sater, et al., Defendants', Courthouse News, 18 October 2022, 4, https://www.courthousenews.com/wp-content/uploads/2022/10/almaty-sater-sdny-deposition-strike.pdf.

23. United States District Court Southern District of New York, 8.

24. Interview with corporate intelligence professional based in London, March 2020.

25. Interview with corporate intelligence professional based in London, March 2020.

26. Interview with corporate intelligence professional based in London, January 2023.

27. Luis Ramirez, 'London's Spy Industry Thrives in Private Sector', *Voice Of America*, 10 February 2017. https://www.voanews.com/a/london-spy-industry-private-sector/3718445.html.

28. Ramirez, 'London's Spy Industry'.

29. Matthew G. Yeager, 'The CIA Made Me Do It: Understanding the Political Economy of Corruption in Kazakhstan', *Crime, Law and Social Change* 57 (2012): 441–457 (2012).

30. Tim Shorrock, *Spies for Hire: The Secret World of Intelligence Outsourcing* (New York: Simon & Schuster, 2008); Frederic Lemieux, *Intelligence and State Surveillance in Modern Societies: An International Perspective* (Leeds: Emerald Group Publishing, 2018).

31. Ruth Delaforce, 'Public and Private Intelligence: Historical and Contemporary Perspectives', *Salus Journal*, 1, no. 2 (2013): 21–39.

32. Armin Krishnan, 'The Future of US Intelligence Outsourcing', *Brown Journal of World Affairs*, 18, no. 1 (2011): 195–211.

33. Robert Baer, 'Just Who Does the CIA's Work?', *Time*, 20 April 2007, https://content.time.com/time/nation/article/0,8599,1613011,00.html.

34. Dana Priest and William M. Arkin, 'A Hidden World, Growing Beyond Control', *Washington Post*, 19 July 2010, https://www.washingtonpost.com/investigations/top-secret-america/2010/07/19/hidden-world-growing-beyond-control-2/.

35. Zachary B. Wolf, 'The Number of People with Top Secret Clearance Will Shock You', *CNN*, 16 August 2022, https://edition.cnn.com/2022/08/15/politics/classified-information-what-matters/index.html.

36. Armin Krishnan, 'The Future of US Intelligence Outsourcing', *The Brown Journal of World Affairs*, 18, no. 1 (2011): 196.
37. Intelligence and Security Committee of Parliament, *Annual Report 2016–2017*, 20 December 2017, https://isc.independent.gov.uk/wp-content/uploads/2021/01/2016-2017_ISC_AR.pdf, 70.
38. ISC, *Annual Report 2016–2017*, 71.
39. This may, of course, simply be because of the effectiveness of the British culture and bureaucratic system of official secrets. While former government minister Jonathan Aitken spent time in prison when he perjured himself after facilitating bribes to Saudi Arabian officials over the al-Yammah arms deal of the 1980s, by the 2000s Prime Minister Tony Blair shut down a Serious Fraud Office investigation into the Saudi deals.
40. Lemieux, *Intelligence and State Surveillance in Modern Societies*, 197–198.
41. See https://www.intelligenceonline.com/ (accessed 15 May 2024).
42. Rhys Andrews and Malcolm J. Beynon., 'The Revolving Door in UK Government Departments: A Configurational Analysis'. *Regulation & Governance* (2023), https://doi.org/10.1111/rego.12544.
43. Dana Moss, 'Transnational Repression, Diaspora Mobilization, and the Case of the Arab Spring', *Social Problems* 63, no. 4 (2016): 480–498.
44. Ruth Blakeley and Sam Raphael, 'British Torture in the "War on Terror"', *European Journal of International Relations* 23, no. 2 (2017): 243–266.
45. Freedom House's transnational repression database counts 608 incidents with the five most active perpetrator states as China (214 incidents), Turkey (111), Egypt (42), Tajikistan (38), and Russia (32). The most extensive and global academic database, Alex Dukalskis's Authoritarian Actions Abroad (AAAD), has 1,177 incidents with a top 5 of Uzbekistan (195 events), China (167), North Korea (156), Turkey (111), and Russia (74). See Alexander Dukalskis, Saipira Furstenberg, Yana Gorokhovskaia, John Heathershaw, Edward Lemon, and Nate Schenkkan, 'Transnational Repression: Data Advances, Comparisons, and Challenges', *Political Research Exchange* 4, no. 1 (2022), https://doi.org/10.1080/2474736X.2022.2104651.
46. Yana Gorokhovskaia and Isabel Linzer, 'Case Study: United Kingdom', in *Defending Democracy in Exile: Policy Responses to Transnational Repression* (Washington, DC: Freedom House, June 2022), 1.
47. For a summary see Alexander Dukalskis, *Making the World Safe for Dictatorship* (Oxford: Oxford University Press, 2021), 67–79.
48. See, Saipira Furstenberg, Edward Lemon, and John Heathershaw. "Spatialising State Practices Through Transnational Repression." *European Journal of International Security* 6, no. 3 (2021): 358–78. https://doi.org/10.1017/eis.2021.10.
49. John Scott-Railton, Adam Hulcoop, Bahr Abdul Razzak, Bill Marczak, Siena Anstis, and Ron Deibert, 'Dark Basin: Uncovering a Massive Hack-for-Hire Operation', Citizen Lab Research Report No. 128, University of Toronto, June 2020, https://citizenlab.ca/2020/06/dark-basin-uncovering-a-massive-hack-for-hire-operation/.
50. Burgis, 'Spies, Lies and the Oligarch'.
51. Franz Wild, Ed Siddons, Simon Lock, Jonathan Calvert, and George Arbuthnott, 'Inside the Global Hack-for-Hire Industry', Bureau of Investigative Journalism, 5 November 2022, https://www.thebureauinvestigates.com/stories/2022-11-05/inside-the-global-hack-for-hire-industry.
52. Maria A. Robson, 'Risk Analysis Beyond Government Agencies: Conceptualizing Private Sector Intelligence', *Journal of European and American Intelligence Studies* 1, no. 2 (2018): 31–48, at 45.
53. Dan McCrum, 'Billion-Dollar Fraud: Inside the Five-Year Wirecard Investigation', *Australian Financial Review*, 2 October 2020. https://www.afr.com/companies/financial-services/billion-dollar-fraud-inside-the-five-year-wirecard-investigation-20200923-p55yfa.
54. Ramirez, 'London's Spy Industry'.
55. Sebastian Booth, 'The Post-Crisis Regulation of the UK Private Security Industry', PhD diss., University of York, April 2019, 144.
56. Security Industry Authority, 'Sia Licence Holders', Gov.UK, 18 December 2020, https://www.gov.uk/government/statistical-data-sets/sia-licence-holders.
57. Jaap De Waard, 'The Private Security Industry in International Perspective', *European Journal on Criminal Policy and Research* 7, no. 2 (1999): 143–174; Rita Abrahamsen and Michael C. Williams. *Security Beyond the State: Private Security in International Politics* (Cambridge: Cambridge University Press, 2010).
58. Burgis, 'Spies, Lies and the Oligarch'.

59. Twice. In Azerbaijan, from Heydar to Ilham Aliyev in 2003, and in Turkmenistan from Gurbanguly to Serdar Berdimuhamedow in 2022. Nazarbayev has long been rumoured to have fathered two sons with his third 'wife', yet the eldest son—who is believed to be around 18 years old—has yet to appear in any significant public or private role in Kazakhstan.

60. Olzhas Auyezov, 'Former Kazakh Security Boss Jailed for 18 Yrs Over Role in Attempted Coup', Reuters, 24 April 2023, https://www.reuters.com/world/asia-pacific/former-kazakh-security-boss-jailed-18-yrs-over-role-attempted-coup-2023-04-24/.

61. Tom Burgis, 'Nazarbayev and the Power Struggle Over Kazakhstan's Future', 13 January 2022, Financial Times, https://www.ft.com/content/a1633129-2dc4-428e-96fa-5d52fd714a00?shareType=nongift.

62. Äsem Zhapisheva, List of Requirements of the People's Committee of Kazakhstan, 5 January 2022, Twitter, https://twitter.com/zhapisheva/status/1478601976279711745.

63. Thomas Rowley, 'As Kazakhstan Burns Over Inequality, the Elite's Wealth Is Safe and Sound in London', openDemocracy, 6 January 2022, https://www.opendemocracy.net/en/odr/-kazakhstan-burns-elites-wealth-safe-in-london/?utm_source=tw

64. Edward Schatz, 'Kazakhstan's Leaders Promised Middle-Class Comfort. Then They Raised Prices', Washington Post, 7 January 2022, https://www.washingtonpost.com/politics/2022/01/07/kazakhstans-leaders-promised-middle-class-comfort-then-they-raised-prices/?tid=ss_tw.

65. 'Ex-Minister of Justice Marat Beketayev Arrested for Two Months', 24 October 2023, KazTag, https://kaztag.info/en/news/ex-minister-of-justice-marat-beketayev-arrested-for-two-months. Beketayev's case is ongoing as of press time. Satybaldy was subsequently jailed (see 'Kazakh Ex-Leader's Nephew Sentenced to 6 Years for Embezzlement', Reuters, 26 September 2022, https://www.reuters.com/world/asia-pacific/kazakh-ex-leaders-nephew-sentenced-6-years-embezzlement-2022-09-26).

66. Heathershaw and Mayne provided some of the evidence to support some of Hodge's speech.

67. UK Parliament, 'Kazakhstan: Anti-Corruption Sanctions', Hansard, 3 February 2022, https://hansard.parliament.uk/commons/2022-02-03/debates/41000B02-86AB-499E-8547-0F5AA84611B0/KazakhstanAnti-CorruptionSanctions.

68. UK Parliament, 'Kazakhstan'.

69. Kassym-Jomart Tokayev, 'Inauguration Speech, Kazakhstan', Official Website of the President of the Republic of Kazakhstan, 26 November 2022, https://www.akorda.kz/en/speech-by-the-president-of-kazakhstan-kassym-jomart-tokayev-at-the-inauguration-ceremony-26102635.

70. 'The Head of State Signed the Law "On the Return of Illegally Acquired Assets to the State"', Official Website of the President of the Republic of Kazakhstan, 12 July 2023, https://akorda.kz/en/the-head-of-state-signed-the-law-on-the-return-of-illegally-acquired-assets-to-the-state-1262957.

71. The previous two sentences were written for the Foreign Policy Centre, 'Britain as a "Force for Good" in Central Asia Working Group: Kazakhstan Paper', December 2022, https://fpc.org.uk/wp-content/uploads/2022/02/Reset-Required-Evaluation-Report-2022.pdf.

72. 'Kazakh Government and Opposition Reorganise Their London Support to Asset Recovery Efforts', Intelligence Online, 20 March 2023, https://www-intelligenceonline-com.uoelibrary.idm.oclc.org/corporate-intelligence/2023/03/20/kazakh-government-and-opposition-reorganise-their-london-support-to-asset-recovery-efforts,109925035-art.

73. Companies House, 'Jusan Technologies Ltd—Overview', Gov.UK, 2023, https://find-and-update.company-information.service.gov.uk/company/12538192.

74. Ed Siddons, Simon Lock, Franz Wild, and Matt Oliver, 'Kazakh Ex-Dictator Used UK Company to Help Protect His $8 Billion Business Empire', Bureau of Investigative Journalism, 17 February 2022, https://www.thebureauinvestigates.com/stories/2022-02-17/kazakh-ex-dictator-used-uk-company-to-help-protect-8-billion-business-empire.

75. United States District Court, District of Nevada, 'Jysan Holding vs Government of Kazakhstan', Case 2:23-cv-00247-JAD-VCF Document 1 Filed 06/02/23', 1., https://casetext.com/case/jysan-holding-llc-v-republic-of-kaz-4.

76. 'Kazakh Ex-Dictator Used UK Company to Help Protect His $8 Billion Business Empire', Bureau of Investigative Journalism, 17 February 22, https://www.thebureauinvestigates.com/stories/2022-02-17/kazakh-ex-dictatorused-uk-company-to-help-protect-8-billion-business-empire.

77. Companies House, 'Jusan Technologies Ltd—Officers', Gov.UK, 2023, https://find-and-update.company-information.service.gov.uk/company/12538192/officers.

78. Rupert Neate, 'Four Media Outlets Facing Libel Claims Over Nursultan Nazarbayev Reports', *The Guardian*, 21 September 2022, https://www.theguardian.com/world/2022/sep/21/four-media-outlets-facing-libel-claims-over-reporting-nursultan-nazarbayev-fund.
79. High Court of Justice King's Bench Division, 'JTL vs The Bureau of Investigative Journalism and Telegraph Media Group Limited, Re-Amended Particulars of Claim by Order of Mr Justice Nicklin Dated 5 April 2023, Claim No.: QB-2022-002660'. https://pressgazette.co.uk/media_law/labour-peer-confidentiality-court-fight-telegraph-tbij-and-open-democracy/.
80. High Court of Justice, 'JTL vs The Bureau', 16–17.
81. High Court of Justice, 'JTL vs The Bureau', 14–15.
82. High Court of Justice, 'JTL vs The Bureau', 14.
83. 'RJI Capital (UK) Limited. People: Persons of Significant Control', Companies House, https://find-and-update.company-information.service.gov.uk/company/05561688/persons-with-significant-control (accessed 15 May 2024).
84. The new owner Galimzhan Yessenov had previously had a minority share in Jusan and is married to the daughter of Nursultan Nazarbayev's nephew. See Nariman Gizitdinov, 'Kazakh Bank Buyout to End Biggest Legal Tussle of Post-Nazarbayev Era', *Bloomberg News*, July 13, 2023, https://www.bloomberg.com/news/articles/2023-07-13/bank-buyout-to-end-biggest-legal-tussle-of-post-nazarbayev-era?leadSource=uverify%20wall.
85. Foreign Policy Centre, 'Anti-SLAPP Conference, DAY 1'.
86. 'RAID Statement Following the UK SFO Announcement to Close the Corruption Investigation Into Mining Giant ENRC', RAID, 25 August 2023, https://raid-uk.org/raid-statement-following-the-uk-sfo-announcement-to-close-the-corruption-investigation-into-mining-giant-enrc/.
87. Foreign Affairs Committee, 'Oral Evidence: Use of Strategic Lawsuits Against Public Participation, HC 1196', House of Commons, 15 March 2022, https://committees.parliament.uk/oralevidence/9907/pdf/, 5.
88. Foreign Affairs Committee, 'Oral Evidence', 7
89. Ben Ellery and Jonathan Ames, 'City Lawyers Give Oligarchs "Weapons Against Scrutiny"', *The Times*, 18 March 2022, https://www.thetimes.co.uk/article/city-lawyers-give-oligarchs-weapons-against-scrutiny-3z8f9jhm3.
90. Foreign Affairs Committee, 'Oral Evidence', 7.

Chapter 13

1. Mohamed Amersi X/Twitter post, 30 June 2023, https://twitter.com/moamersi/status/1674759292346421251. Note: John Heathershaw does not work for King's College, either at Cambridge or London universities, and had no involvement in the writing of the King's College report. For an anthology of the legal pressure used by Mr Amersi and Carter-Ruck to stifle reporting about his past business activities, see Tom Burgis, *Cuckooland* (London: William Collins, 2024).
2. Email to John Heathershaw, 20 January 2023.
3. CTD Advisors, 2023, https://ctdadvisors.com/.
4. Email correspondence with Stephen Harris, Deputy Editor, *The Conversation UK*, 31 March 2023. Emphasis is authors' own.
5. Pegg and Dyer, 'Tory Donor's Name Removed'.
6. This is the phrase used in the official commentary to the Defamation Act 2013 in regard to protected speech: 'subsection (1) provides for the new defence to apply where the defendant can show that the imputation conveyed by the statement complained of is substantially true. This subsection reflects the current law as established in the case of Chase v News Group Newspapers Ltd(4), where the Court of Appeal indicated that in order for the defence of justification to be available 'the defendant does not have to prove that every word he or she published was true. He or she has to establish the "essential" or "Substantial" truth of the sting of the libel'. See Defamation Act 2013, Chapter 26, Commentary on Sections
    Section 2: Truth, section 14, https://www.legislation.gov.uk/ukpga/2013/26/section/2/notes?view=plain. Publication on matter of public interest is also protected and dealt with in another section.
7. While Heathershaw had written about the Telia case in his 2017 book, Amersi himself only became an object of the authors' research after he acted against Chatham House; at this point we looked more extensively into the details—as he demanded—and began 18 months of research on his case. See Cooley and Heathershaw, *Dictators Without Borders*, Chapter 5.

8. 'The Guptas, Bell Pottinger and the Fake News Propaganda Machine', *TimesLive*, 4 September 2017, https://www.timeslive.co.za/news/south-africa/2017-09-04-the-guptas-bell-pottinger-and-the-fake-news-propaganda-machine.

9. Mark Sweney, 'Bell Pottinger Expelled From PR Trade Body After South Africa Racism Row', *The Guardian*, 4 September 2017, https://www.theguardian.com/business/2017/sep/04/bell-pottinger-expelled-from-pr-trade-body-after-south-africa-racism-row.

10. The government abandoned an attempt to have three former Bell Pottinger executives disqualified as company directors more than five years after the public relations agency collapsed.

11. Thoburns, 'Team', 2023, https://thoburns.com/team.

12. 'Firtash Foundation Presents Days of Ukraine in the UK' (advertisement feature), *Evening Standard*, 14 October 2013, https://www.standard.co.uk/culture/firtash-foundation-presents-days-of-ukraine-in-the-uk-8878904.html

13. Bayley and Taylor, 'Big-Hearted Businessman Comes to Aid of Young Girl Fighting Blood Cancer'.

14. 'Carol Cadwalladr, Investigative Journalist', Foreign Policy Centre, 2023, https://fpc.org.uk/carole-cadwalladr-investigative-journalist/.

15. Robert C. Post, 'The Social Foundations of Defamation Law: Reputation and the Constitution', *California Law Review* 691 (1986): 699–719.

16. David Rolph, 'Building and Rebuilding Reputations: Reflections on the Role of Defamation Law in the Life of a Celebrity', in *Law and Creativity in the Age of the Entertainment Franchise*, ed. Kathy Bowrey and Michael Handler (Cambridge: Cambridge University Press, 2014), 103–122.

17. Matthew Collins, *Collins on Defamation* (Oxford: Oxford University Press, 2014).

18. Mark Sweney, 'Surge in "Libel Tourism" Brings 11% Rise in Cases', *The Guardian*, 20 November 2009,
https://www.theguardian.com/uk/2009/nov/20/surge-libel-tourism-rise-cases.

19. Interview with David Hirst and authors, February 2023. Full disclosure: Hirst has worked with the authors in providing legal advice on libel risks and read this book in advance of publication.

20. 'Diaz Gets Damages from Enquirer', *Hollywood Reporter*, 19 February 2011, https://www.hollywoodreporter.com/business/business-news/diaz-gets-damages-enquirer-130417/.

21. 'Celebrity Settles UK Libel Suit With National Enquirer', Reporters Committee for Freedom of the Press, 5 March 2007, https://www.rcfp.org/celebrity-settles-uk-libel-suit-national-enquirer/.

22. Sweney, 'Surge in "Libel Tourism" Brings 11% Rise in Cases'.

23. Edward Lucas, 'Putin: A Man With a Past', *Politico*, 16 October 2014. https://www.politico.eu/article/putin-a-man-with-a-past/.

24. Laura Carpenter, 'England and Wales High Court (Queen's Bench Division) Decisions', *Bailii*, 3 May 2005, https://www.bailii.org/ew/cases/EWHC/QB/2005/1156.html.

25. Rachel Ehrenfield, 'How I Fight "Libel Tourism"', *The Guardian*, 27 March 2009, https://www.theguardian.com/commentisfree/libertycentral/2009/mar/27/freedom-of-speech-al-qaida.

26. 'Obama Approves US "Libel Tourist" Laws', BBC, 11 August 2010, https://www.bbc.com/news/uk-10940211

27. Doreen Carvajal, 'Britain, a Destination for "Libel Tourism"', *New York Times*, 20 January 2008, https://www.nytimes.com/2008/01/20/technology/20iht-libel21.1.9346664.html.

28. Karpov V Browder and others [2013] EWHC 3071 (QB) and Subotic V Knezevic [2013] EWHC 3011 (QB).

29. Jameel (Yousef) V Dow Jones & Co Inc [2005] EWCA Civ 75.

30. Paul Dacam (Hogan Lovells), 'UK: Judges Strike a Blow to Libel Tourism', *Lexology*, 18 October 2013, https://www.lexology.com/library/detail.aspx?g=a70d237a-588f-44ce-8231-aac0c0df909f.

31. 'On Countering Legal Intimidation and SLAPPs in the UK: A Policy Paper', UK Anti-SLAPP Coalition/Foreign Policy Centre, July 2021, https://fpc.org.uk/wpcontent/uploads/2021/07/Policy-Paper-Countering-legal-intimidation-and-SLAPPs-in-the-UK.pdf.

32. 'Press Release: UK Sanctions Alexey Navalny's Poisoners', UK.gov, 15 October 2020, https://www.gov.uk/government/news/uk-sanctions-alexey-navalnys-poisoners.

33. Prigozhin said that he had brought court cases against journalists who had made the claims as 'in any issue there should be room for sport'. Shaun Walker, 'UK Government "Let Lawyers Bypass Sanctions" to Help Putin Ally Sue Journalist', *The Guardian*, 24 January 2023, https://www.theguardian.com/politics/2023/jan/24/uk-government-let-lawyers-bypass-sanctions-to-help-putin-ally-sue-journalist.

34. Bronwen Maddox, Director of Chatham House, wrote: 'To be clear, we do not give, nor have we ever given our consent to you or the other authors to publish the content of the letters that were sent to Chatham House by Mr Amersi/Carter-Ruck or Mr Leus/Vardags or any other communication between Chatham House and the authors of the report'. Letter to John Heathershaw, 26 October 2023.

35. Leus vehemently denies this claim and there is no evidence in the public domain to corroborate it. See Dyer, 'Former Russian Banker Dmitry Leus Who Donated £25,000 to Dominic Raab Is "Absolutely Dependent on the FSB", MP Claims'.

36. 'London Calling', Foreign Policy Centre, 2002, https://fpc.org.uk/wp-content/uploads/2022/04/London-Calling-Publication-February-2023.pdf, 14.

37. Letter from Carter-Ruck to Chatham House, 23 December 2021, 3.

38. Letter from Mishcon de Reya to John Heathershaw, 29 September 2021, 4.

39. Letter from Mishcon de Reya to John Heathershaw, 29 September 2021, 5.

40. Letter from Vardags to Chatham House, 31 August 2022, paragraph 5.

41. Letter from Vardags to Chatham House, 13 September 2022, paragraph 3.

42. Pegg and Dyer, 'Tory Donor's Name Removed'. Chatham House preferred the following summary of their actions: 'Chatham House, on the basis of professional legal advice, decided to remove the reference to Mr Leus'. Letter to John Heathershaw, 26 October 2023.

43. Letter from Carter Ruck to Chatham House, 26 January 2022, 2.

44. 'Catherine Belton, Journalist and Author of "Putin's People: How the KGB Took Back Russia and Then Took on the West"', Foreign Policy Centre, 15 February 2023, https://fpc.org.uk/catherine-belton-journalist-and-author-of-putins-people-how-the-kgb-took-back-russia-and-then-took-on-the-west/.

45. 'The Azerbaijani Laundromat', OCCRP, 4 September 2017. https://www.occrp.org/en/azerbaijanilaundromat/.

46. 'Caviar Diplomacy—How Azerbaijan Silenced the Council of Europe', European Stability Initiative, 24 May 2012, https://www.esiweb.org/publications/caviar-diplomacy-how-azerbaijan-silenced-council-europe.

47. 'Day 1: Anti-SLAPP Conference "Spotlighting Solutions"'.

48. Letter from Carter-Ruck to Chatham House, 26 January 2022, 1.

49. Letter from Carter-Ruck to Chatham House, 28 February 2022, 1

50. The sentence was as follows: 'These include Mohamed Amersi, who has given more than £500,000 to the Conservative Party since 2018, and who was revealed in the Pandora Papers—which Mr Amersi believes is because of his purported use of offshore companies as part of tax planning but not due to the Uzbekistan deal which he believes was revealed through a leaked excerpt of the internal Norton Rose Fulbright report and the reliance on Michaela Ahlberg's testimony which he is currently challenging—to have advised on a payment made by Swedish telecoms company TeliaSonera to an offshore company subsequently found to be controlled by Gulnara Karimova (Annex, numbers 95–99)'. Letter from Carter-Ruck to Chatham House, 28 February 2022, 2.

51. Letter from Carter-Ruck to Chatham House, 8 November 2022, 2.

52. Chatham House would prefer this sentence to read: 'Chatham House did not cede to this demand but edited the text to correct an inaccuracy that had inadvertently been made, consulting the authors after the text had been agreed and to which they acquiesced'. Letter from Chatham House to John Heathershaw, 26 October 2023.

53. Letter from Vardags to Chatham House, 13 September 2022, paragraph 86.

54. Heathershaw et al., 'The UK's Kleptocracy Problem', 53.

55. Letter from Chatham House to John Heathershaw, 26 October 2023.

56. Letter from Carter-Ruck to Chatham House, 8 November 2022, 2.

57. This has been further confirmed to us in writing by the ICIJ in September 2023. A staff member wrote: 'There are 643 hits for Amersi in the Pandora documents and 588 for Mohamed Amersi. I can't confirm that every single one is about Mr Amersi but it is clear that very many are'. (Correspondence available in private archive).

58. On 17 August 2023, on being given opportunity to comment, Carter-Ruck replied: 'Neither we nor our client Mr Amersi are aware of being told by the Guardian and BBC that Mr Amersi "figured in some 600+ entries of the International Consortium for Investigative Journalism's (ICIJ) offshore leaks database including in the Pandora Papers themselves". Please could you confirm the correspondence in which, or occasion when, this was communicated to this firm (providing as much detail as possible)?'

59. Interview with Catherine Belton with author, April 2023.
60. A similar approach based on what was proportionate led to settlements in the Aven and Fridman cases. The Rosneft claim was thrown out at the first hearing. Interview with Catherine Belton with author, April 2023.
61. 'Anti-Slapp Conference', Foreign Policy Centre, 30 November 2022, https://anti-slappconfere nce.info/.
62. Lauren Brown, "'Terror' Stopping Great Work From Being Published in the UK, Pike Warns', *The Bookseller*, 21 October 2022, https://www.thebookseller.com/news/terror-stopping-great-work-from-being-published-in-the-uk-nibbies-winner-pike-warns.
63. 'Anti-SLAPP Conference 2022', Foreign Policy Centre, November 2022, https://anti-slappcon ference.info/.
64. Jennifer Wright, Ann Avouris, Matthew Frost, and Sally Hoffmann, 'Supporting Academic Freedom as a Human Right: Challenges and Solutions in Academic Publishing', *International Journal of Human Rights* 26, no. 10 (2022): 1741–1760.
65. The report in question was Tom Mayne and John Heathershaw, *Criminality Notwithstanding: The Use of Unexplained Wealth Orders in Anti-Corruption Cases*, Anti-Corruption Evidence Research Programme, March 2022, https://ace.globalintegrity.org/wp-content/uploads/2022/03/Cri minalityNotwithstanding.pdf.
66. Pegg and Dyer, 'Tory Donor's Name Removed'.
67. 'Strategic Lawsuits Against Public Participation', Solicitors Regulation Authority, 28 November 2022, https://www.sra.org.uk/solicitors/guidance/slapps-warning-notice/.
68. Foreign Policy Centre, 'Anti-SLAPP Conference 2022'.

Chapter 14

1. George Gavrilis, 'The Reminiscences of James H. Giffen [interview]', Harriman Institute, 6 May 2019, https://oralhistory.harriman.columbia.edu/interview/40.
2. Gavrilis, 'The Reminiscences'.
3. Eurasianet, 'Top Oil Consultant Indicted in New York in Case With Implications for Kazakhstan', 31 March 2003, https://eurasianet.org/top-oil-consultant-indicted-in-new-york-in-case-with-implications-for-kazakhstan; Global Witness, *Time for Transparency. Coming Clean on Oil, Mining and Gas Revenues*, March 2004, https://www.globalwitness.org/docume nts/17833/time_for_transparency.pdf, 15.
4. Gavrilis, 'The Reminiscences'.
5. Giffen was also found guilty of a misdemeanor charge for failing to check a box on his tax returns. and was ordered to pay a $25 fine. Clay Risen, 'James Giffen, Who Was Embroiled in "Kazakhgate," Dies at 81', *New York Times*, 4 November 2022, https://www.nytimes.com/2022/11/04/business/james-giffen-dead.html.
6. Mohamed Amersi, Twitter/X post, 28 February 2024, https://twitter.com/moamersi/status/1762926329622622694.
7. 'The UK's Tax Burden in Historical and International Context', Office of Budget Responsibility, March 2023, https://obr.uk/box/the-uks-tax-burden-in-historical-and-international-context/.
8. 'UK's SFO Drops Probes Into Kazakh Miner ENRC, Rio Tinto', Reuters, 24 August 2023, https://www.reuters.com/markets/commodities/uks-sfo-drops-probes-into-kazakh-miner-enrc-rio-tinto-2023-08-24/.
9. 'UK Anti-Corruption Sanctions: A Year in Review', Redress, April 2022, https://redress.org/wp-content/uploads/2022/05/A-Year-In-Review_Anti-corruption-Sanctions-Report_1.04.2022.pdf.
10. Edgerton, *The Rise and Fall*.
11. UK Parliament, *Economic Crime and Corporate Transparency Bill, Sixth Marshalled List of Amendments to Be Moved in Grand Committee*, 4 May 2023, https://bills.parliament.uk/publi cations/50980/documents/3365/.
12. Heathershaw et al., 'Towards a Strategy for Countering Kleptocracy: Five Steps to Address the UK's Kleptocracy Problem', written evidence submitted to the UK Parliament, 11 March 2022, https://committees.parliament.uk/writtenevidence/107077/html/.
13. Maria Nizzero, 'How to Seize a Billion: Exploring Mechanisms to Recover the Proceeds of Kleptocracy', RUSI, December 2022, https://static.rusi.org/rusi-emerging-insights-how-to-seize-a-billion-exploring-mechanisms-to-recover-the-proceeds-of-kleptocracy.pdf, 19.

14. John Revill, 'Swiss Accuse Daughter of Ex-Uzbek President of Running a Criminal Organisation', Reuters, 28 September 2023, https://www.reuters.com/world/swiss-accuse-daughter-ex-uzbek-president-running-criminal-organisation-2023-09-28/.

15. UK.gov, 'Economic Crime and Corporate Transparency Bill', 16 March 2023, https://bills.parliament.uk/publications/50357/documents/3152.

16. APPG Anti-Corruption and Responsible Tax, 'Written Evidence Submitted by the APPG on Anti-Corruption & Responsible Tax', 5 January 2024, https://committees.parliament.uk/writtenevidence/127415/pdf/.

17. Ben Steele (director), 'The Whistleblowers: Inside the UN', BBC TV, 21 June 2022, https://www.bbc.co.uk/programmes/m0018ljw.

18. UK Parliament, 'Economic Crime and Corporate Transparency Bill, Sixth Marshalled List of Amendments to Be Moved in Grand Committee', 4 May 2023, https://bills.parliament.uk/publications/50980/documents/3365/.

19. What follows was initially proposed by our colleague Professor Jason Sharman in a letter to the Foreign Commonwealth and Development Office in late 2022.

20. HM Government, *Integrated Review Refresh 2023: Responding to a More Contested and Volatile World*, March 2023, https://assets.publishing.service.gov.uk/government/uploads/system/uploads/attachment_data/file/1145586/11857435_NS_IR_Refresh_2023_Supply_AllPages_Revision_7_WEB_PDF.pdf, 49.

21. Mohamed Amersi claims that he and Carter-Ruck did not request that the report was taken down and did not embark on legal action against King's College London. He wrote to us: 'We offered to engage with them . . . and to provide underlying documentation they did not take they suffer up much to our astonishment they took down the whole report'. Letter to John Heathershaw, 18 August 2023, 6.

Index